D1552671

Imagining the Fetus

AAR
AMERICAN ACADEMY OF RELIGION
CULTURAL CRITICISM SERIES

SERIES EDITOR
Jacob N. Kinnard, Iliff School of Theology

A Publication Series of
The American Academy of Religion and Oxford University Press

ANTI-JUDAISM IN FEMINIST RELIGIOUS WRITINGS
Katharina von Kellenbach

CROSS CULTURAL CONVERSATION
(Initiation)
Edited by Anindita Niyogi Balslev

ON DECONSTRUCTING LIFE-WORLDS
Buddhism, Christianity, Culture
Robert Magliola

THE GREAT WHITE FLOOD
Racism in Australia
Anne Pattel-Gray

IMAG(IN)ING OTHERNESS
Filmic Visions of Living Together
Edited by S. Brent Plate and David Jasper

CULTURAL OTHERNESS
Correspondence with Richard Rorty, Second Edition
Anindita Niyogi Balslev

FEMINIST POETICS OF THE SACRED
Creative Suspicions
Edited by Frances Devlin-Glass and Lyn McCredden

PARABLES FOR OUR TIME
Rereading New Testament Scholarship after the Holocaust
Tania Oldenhage

MOSES IN AMERICA
The Cultural Uses of Biblical Narrative
Melanie Jane Wright

INTERSECTING PATHWAYS
Modern Jewish Theologians in Conversation with Christianity
Marc A. Krell

ASCETICISM AND ITS CRITICS
Historical Accounts and Comparative Perspectives
Edited by Oliver Freiberger

VIRTUOUS BODIES
The Physical Dimensions of Morality in Buddhist Ethics
Susanne Mrozik

IMAGINING THE FETUS
The Unborn in Myth, Religion, and Culture
Edited by Vanessa R. Sasson and Jane Marie Law

AMERICAN ACADEMY OF RELIGION

Imagining the Fetus

The Unborn in Myth, Religion, and Culture

Edited by

VANESSA R. SASSON

JANE MARIE LAW

OXFORD
UNIVERSITY PRESS
2009

OXFORD
UNIVERSITY PRESS

Oxford University Press, Inc., publishes works that further
Oxford University's objective of excellence
in research, scholarship, and education.

Oxford New York
Auckland Cape Town Dar es Salaam Hong Kong Karachi
Kuala Lumpur Madrid Melbourne Mexico City Nairobi
New Delhi Shanghai Taipei Toronto

With offices in
Argentina Austria Brazil Chile Czech Republic France Greece
Guatemala Hungary Italy Japan Poland Portugal Singapore
South Korea Switzerland Thailand Turkey Ukraine Vietnam

Copyright © 2009 by The American Academy of Religion

Published by Oxford University Press, Inc.
198 Madison Avenue, New York, New York 10016

www.oup.com

Oxford is a registered trademark of Oxford University Press.

All rights reserved. No part of this publication may be reproduced,
stored in a retrieval system, or transmitted, in any form or by any means,
electronic, mechanical, photocopying, recording, or otherwise,
without the prior permission of Oxford University Press.

Library of Congress Cataloging-in-Publication Data

Imagining the fetus : the unborn in myth, religion, and culture / edited by Vanessa R. Sasson
and Jane Marie Law.
p. cm. — (American Academy of Religion religion and culture series)
Includes bibliographical references and index.
ISBN 978-0-19-538004-0 (cloth); 978-0-19-538005-7 (pbk.)
1. Fetus—Religious aspects. 2. Theological anthropology.
I. Sasson, Vanessa R. II. Law, Jane Marie.
BL256.I43 2009
202'.2—dc22 2008026800

9 8 7 6 5 4 3 2 1
Printed in the United States of America
on acid-free paper

Contents

Contributors

ELLEN BRADSHAW AITKEN is dean of the Faculty of Religious Studies at McGill University in Montreal, where she also teaches Early Christian History and Literature. She is the author of *Jesus' Death in Early Christian Memory: The Poetics of the Passion* (2004) and *Loosening the Roots of Compassion: Meditations for Holy Week and Eastertide* (2006), in addition to numerous articles on early Christian literature. She (with Jennifer Berenson Maclean) is also the cotranslator of Flavius Philostratus's *Heroikos* (2001) and the coeditor of *Philostratus's Heroikos: Religion and Cultural Identity in the Third Century* C.E. (2004). Her current research focuses on early Christian ritual practices and the veneration of heroes in the Hellenistic and Roman world and on the Epistle to the Hebrews. She holds degrees from Harvard University and the University of the South.

ANDRÉ COUTURE is an Indologist and professor of the History of Religions at the Faculté de théologie et de sciences religieuses, Université Laval, Québec, Canada. Couture has published on a wide variety of topics. Of special interest in this context are his translations of chapters 30–78 of the *Harivamsha* (*L'enfance de Krishna,* 1991); of the Appendix I, no. 41, of the *Harivamsha* (*La vision de Mārkaṇḍeya et la manifestation du Lotus,* 2007); and of Bhāsa's *Bālacarita* (in *Théâtre de l'Inde ancienne,* ed. Lyne Bansat-Boudon, 2006).

EVA DE CLERCQ graduated from the University of Ghent (Belgium) in Oriental Languages and Cultures (Indology) in 2003. Her Ph.D. dissertation was titled "A Critical Study of Svayambhūdeva's *Paümacariu,* a Jain version in Apabhraṃśa of the *Rāmāyaṇa.*" She is currently a guest professor at Ghent, working on the narratives of Kṛṣṇa and the *Mahābhārata* in Jainism.

FRANCES GARRETT is assistant professor of Buddhist Studies at the University of Toronto. She is author of *Religion, Medicine and the Human Embryo in Tibet,* which links aspects of Tibetan medicine to expressions of culture, religion, art, and literature through a study of embryology in Tibetan literature. Her research considers the intersections among tantric practice, ritual and occult knowledge, and medical theory, and what these tell us about the processes of institutional and ideological change in Tibet.

SALLIE HAN is assistant professor of Anthropology at SUNY College at Oneonta. Her chapter on fetal ultrasound imaging in the United States derives from her dissertation, which examined the pregnancy practices of American middle-class women. She received her Ph.D. in cultural anthropology from the University of Michigan in 2006.

GWYNN KESSLER received her Ph.D. in rabbinics, with a specialization in midrash, from the Jewish Theological Seminary. She is currently an assistant professor in the Department of Religion at the University of Florida in Gainesville.

ROBERT KRITZER is a professor at Kyoto Notre Dame University. He specializes in *abhidharma* and early Yogācāra and is the author of two books: *Rebirth and Causation in the Yogācāra Abhidharma* (1999); and *Vasubandhu and the Yogācārabhūmi: Yogācāra Elements in the Abhidharmakośabhāṣya* (2005). He has written on the intermediate existence (*antarābhava*) and accounts of childbirth in Indian Buddhism, as well as on the meaning of the term Sautrāntika. Other interests include the relation between Buddhism and the Indian medical tradition and the traditional study of the *Abhidharmakośa* in Japan. He was the Numata Visiting Professor of Buddhist Studies at McGill University for the winter term of 2006.

JANE MARIE LAW is associate professor of Japanese Religions and the director of Graduate Studies in the Asian Religions Ph.D. Program at Cornell University. She has been teaching at Cornell since 1989 and was the director of Religious Studies from 1997 to 2004. She is the author of *Puppets of Nostalgia* (1997), considered the definitive study of Japanese ritual puppetry, and editor of two books, *Waiting for the Dawn: Mircea Eliade in Perspective* (coedited with David Carrasco, 1985; reprint, 1991) and *Religious Reflections on the Human Body* (1992). She is the translator of numerous plays and texts from Japanese, and the author of more than a dozen articles on Japanese religions and on issues in Religious Studies. She is currently working in the area of cultural memory in Japan and Eastern Europe.

JUSTIN THOMAS MCDANIEL is an associate professor of Buddhist and Southeast Asian Studies at the University of California (Riverside). He received his Ph.D. in the Department of Sanskrit and Indian Studies at Harvard University in 2003. He has lived and worked in Southeast Asia for several years. His research foci include Lao, Thai, Pali, Sanskrit, and Khoen literature, Southeast Asian history, Buddhist ritual and liturgy, and manuscript preservation. His first book is titled *Gathering*

Leaves and Lifting Words: Histories of Buddhist Monastic Education in Laos and Thailand (2008).

DANIEL C. PETERSON was born and raised in Southern California and has lived for extended periods in Switzerland, Israel, and Egypt. He is now a professor of Islamic Studies and Arabic at Brigham Young University, as well as a director of the Neal A. Maxwell Institute for Religious Scholarship, which, among other undertakings, has produced a computer-searchable database of the Dead Sea Scrolls, electronically published a selection of Syriac manuscripts from the Vatican Apostolic Library, and recovered writing from burned papyri in Petra and the ruins of ancient Herculaneum. Author of *Muhammad: Prophet of God* (2007), Peterson is also the founder and editor in chief of Brigham Young University's Middle Eastern Texts Initiative, which publishes dual-language translations of classical Arabic and Syriac books, and he has been extremely active in Mormon studies.

CATHERINE PLAYOUST is a lecturer in New Testament and related literature at Jesuit Theological College in Melbourne, Australia. She received her Th.D. in New Testament and Christian Origins from Harvard Divinity School in 2006, with a dissertation titled "Lifted Up from the Earth: The Ascension of Jesus and the Heavenly Ascents of Early Christians." She specializes in canonical and noncanonical Christian literature from the first three centuries of the common era, attending to how traditions are developed and refashioned as they enter new social and theological contexts.

VANESSA R. SASSON is a professor of Religious Studies in the Liberal Arts Department of Marianopolis College, where she has been teaching since 1999. She is also a research fellow in the Department of Biblical and Religious Studies at the University of the Free State and an adjunct professor of Comparative Religion at McGill University. She is the author of *The Birth of Moses and the Buddha: A Paradigm for the Comparative Study of Religions* (2007). Her interests focus on myths and religious hagiography, ordination for women in Theravāda Buddhism, and interfaith dialogue.

NIKKY-GUNINDER KAUR SINGH is the Crawford Family Professor of Religious Studies at Colby College. Her interests focus on poetics and feminist issues. Singh has published extensively in the field of Sikhism, including *The Birth of the Khalsa: A Feminist Re-Memory of Sikh Identity* (2005), *The Feminine Principle in the Sikh Vision of the Transcendent* (1993), *Sikhism* (1993), and *Metaphysics and Physics of the Guru Granth Sahib* (1981). Her translated works include *Cosmic Symphony: The Early and Later Poems of Bhai Vir Singh* (2008) and *The Name of My Beloved: Verses of the Sikh Gurus* (1995; reprint, 2001). Her views have also been aired on television and radio in America, Canada, England, Australia, and India. In the summer of 2005, she met with Dr. Manmohan Singh, the prime minister of India, to discuss the problems facing women in the Punjab, including their basic right to exist—the tragedy of female feticides.

MARTEN STOL was born in 1940 in the Netherlands. He studied Classical and Semitic languages at Leiden University. In 1983, he became a full professor of Assyriology at Vrije Universiteit in Amsterdam. He is a specialist in the field of social and economic history of the Old Babylonian period (1900–1500 B.C.) and Babylonian medicine. His books include *On Trees, Mountains, and Millstones in the Ancient Near East* (1979), *Altbabylonische Briefe* (1981, 1986), *Epilepsy in Babylonia* (1993), and *Birth in Babylonia and the Bible* (2000).

CAROLYN E. TATE, professor of Pre-Columbian Art History at Texas Tech University, focuses on gender issues, creation stories, urban genesis and planning, and the spiritual and religious bases of Mesoamerican beliefs. Her book, *Yaxchilan: The Design of a Maya Ceremonial City* (1992), explores how Maya notions of aesthetics, ancestor worship, and astronomy influenced monumental art and architecture. She has curated numerous exhibitions, including *The Olmec World: Ritual and Rulership* (with F. Kent Reilly; the Art Museum, Princeton University, 1995), *Human Body/Human Spirit: A Portrait of Ancient Mexico* (Carlos Museum, Emory University, and the Royal Ontario Museum, 1993). She has held fellowships at the Harvard Center for the Study of World Religions, Dumbarton Oaks, and the Clark Art Institute. A book in progress provides a fresh interpretation of the Olmec: *Images of Gestation, Stories of Creation: Women and the Unborn in Olmec Art.*

Imagining the Fetus

Introduction: Restoring Nuance to Imagining the Fetus

Vanessa R. Sasson and Jane Marie Law

In contemporary Western culture, the word "fetus" introduces either a political subject or a literal, medicalized entity. Neither of these frameworks gives sufficient credit to the vast array of literature and oral traditions emerging from religious cultures around the world that see within the fetus a symbol, a metaphor, an imagination. It is our argument that the fetus has been hijacked by two dominant and powerful modes—the political and the medical—and the potential of the fetus as symbol to serve as a gateway to imagination has been reduced as a result. This book grows out of the acknowledgment of the fact that, throughout much of human history and across most of the world's cultures, when the fetus was imagined, it enjoyed a much wider range of symbolic and cultural subjectivities, often contributing possibilities of inclusivity, emergence, liminality, and transformation.

The editors recognize that even within contemporary language of the fetus as political or medical subject, the fetus functions as both a symbol and a sign—a symbol of the vulnerable, the unrecognized, even the violated; as a sign, pointing toward one's ethical stand on issues of modern culture from embryonic stem cell research to abortion and the debate about when life begins. This circumscription of the fetus as literal subject has limited its symbolic potential, and our symbolic language is the poorer for it. The purpose of this book is to restore the nuance of the symbolism of the fetus, liberating it from the stultifying parameters of the abortion/embryonic stem cell debate, giving it room once again to function as a symbol of greater and more complex human emotions, dilemmas, and aspirations.

It has been well noted that the current cultural tendency to regard the fetus as both a medicalized entity and a political subject has been generated in large part by the relatively new phenomenon of widely available photographic and sonographic images. From the first in utero images of the fetus that appeared in *Life* magazine on April 30, 1965 (highly manipulated images designed, at the dawn of the abortion debate, to depict fetal personhood in visual form), to the now nearly routine procedure of pregnant women viewing sonographic images of their unborn fetuses, the fetus has moved from the realm of the largely imagined and unseen to that of the literal and visual in just one generation.[1] Such contemporary viewing of the fetus has led to an unfortunately narrow range of questions: Does the fetus have personhood and rights? Is it a boy or a girl? How many weeks of gestation is it at? Is it healthy or malformed? In other words, the questions generated by the widespread availability of the fetus as image are decidedly literal, medical, and/or political in nature. It would appear that from the vantage point of the human symbolic imagination, the nuance and texture of the questions being generated by imagining the fetus are in an inverse relationship to the availability of concrete depictions of the fetus in utero. We might query, Is it true that the more we see concretely, the less we imagine and symbolize?

Imagining the fetus and attempting concomitantly to depict it is not a new enterprise. Carolyn E. Tate's chapter in this volume demonstrates how important visualizing the fetus was to the Olmec people more than three thousand years ago. The Olmec carved sculptures of fetuses out of stone, some towering more than two meters in height, as part of a larger cosmogonic architecture engraved onto the landscape. Their images of the fetus were, moreover, strikingly accurate depictions of various stages of fetal development, illustrating a meticulous eye on the part of the carvers for their appropriated symbol.[2] Robert Kritzer's chapter here likewise highlights careful attention paid to detail in imagining the fetus. He explores Indian Buddhist embryology and notes how accurate the descriptions of fetal development were—particularly surprising given that these texts were produced in male monastic settings. Marten Stol, in his examination of ancient Near Eastern embryology, comes to the same conclusion. Jane Marie Law argues that the Japanese Leech Child derives its name from a careful observation of miscarried fetal tissue. So although our current technologies may allow us to see the fetus in utero with less (or even no) risk to the woman's body or the fetus, the impetus to view the fetus and observe it in detail is nothing new in human history. The question has to do with the demographic availability of these images and the imaginative purposes to which they are put in a given cultural context.

1. A number of excellent monographs address this cultural phenomenon and its implications in contemporary visual and political culture. See R. P. Petchesky, "Fetal Images: The Power of Visual Culture in the Politics of Reproduction," *Feminist Studies* 13, 2 (1987): 263–92 for a discussion of how a visual image can assume both a descriptive role and a vehicle for imagination and mythologizing. A thoroughgoing collection addressing how visual images in the contemporary era affect the politics of reproduction is L. M. Morgan and M. W. Michaels, eds., *Fetal Subjects, Feminist Positions* (Philadelphia: University of Philadelphia Press, 1999). See also R. Rapp, "Real-Time Fetus: The Role of the Sonogram in the Age of Monitored Reproduction," in *Cyborgs and Citadels: Anthropological Interventions in Emerging Sciences and Technologies,* ed. G. L. Downey and J. Dumit (Santa Fe, N.M.: American School of Research: 1997), 23–57.

2. Newman's work, *Fetal Positions: Individualism, Science, Visuality* (Stanford, Calif.: Stanford University Press, 1996) traces the European history of obstetrical drawings of the fetus from the ninth century CE onward, demonstrating that the desire to visually represent or "see" the fetus has been a consistent subject of interest for a very long time.

Even with such historical and religious precedents, however, we nevertheless find ourselves in a very particular situation today. In her chapter in this volume, Sallie Han explores the phenomenon of "seeing" fetuses in modern Western culture, and demonstrates how sonography has managed to radically alter our relationship—on both a public and private level—with the fetus. Songraphic images have transformed the ambiguity of the fetus into something much more fixed and, consequently, much more marketable. She notes in particular the new phenomenon of "ultrasound boutiques" that provide jubilant and expectant families with a wide range of consumer goods. The photo albums produced render the fetus a commodity to be consumed and thus translate into a sense of parental appropriation available to both parents, and not just the pregnant, experiencing body of the woman. Han argues that this phenomenon can be located in our "ocularcentrism," a term she uses to describe our cultural need for constant visual evidence and stimulation. Imaging (and subsequently imagining) the fetus in this context leads to very strong, easily manipulated emotive responses. So long as the fetus is not "seen" or visually emphasized, it remains a liminal, transient, and obscure entity. It remains part of the mother's body and is understood as a creature in the process of becoming, one that has not yet become. By visually imaging the fetus, however, be it in vivid color on the cover of *Life* magazine, in a hazy grayscale sonography printout fawned over by expectant parents, or in manipulated images produced by antiabortion activists, one easily concludes that it exists independently, as a being already become. The image freezes the fetus temporally, and its transient, transformative nature consequently slips past the viewer's consciousness.

Such occularcentrism, to use Han's term, which in this case presents us with a barrage of freeze-framed images of fetuses, limits symbolic imagination. Rather than functioning as an opportunity for mythic enchantment, the fetus is reduced to an occasion for political arguments and medical investigations. Politically, such images serve to liberate the fetus from its mother's body, creating the illusion that it exists independently, floating in space somewhere far away. It was no accident that the *Life* images showed the fetus floating in a sea of stars, providing a cosmic, as opposed to uterine, home for these almost mythical beings. Indeed, this is one of Karen Newman's principal arguments, as she notes a tendency in contemporary society to regard the fetus as somehow separate from the female body carrying it.[3] Petchesky likewise argues that sonographic images of the fetus tend to represent it as "primary and autonomous, the woman as absent or peripheral."[4]

It is tempting to regard this isolationist language of the fetus vis-à-vis the mother as solely a product of the modern age. In her chapter in this volume, however, Vanessa R. Sasson demonstrates that these same tendencies to marginalize the pregnant woman appear in the Buddha's fetal narratives, as the Buddha is described as having been encased in a palace while gestating in his mother's womb, physically separated from her body. He fed himself with the nectar of a celestial lotus flower brought to him by the god Brahmā, so as to not even use his mother's body for food.

3. This argument is strewn throughout her book, but see in particular Newman, *Fetal Positions*, 11–15.

4. Petchesky, "Fetal Images," 268.

The Buddha is therefore entirely isolated and independent, and the mother is marginalized, eventually to the point of extinction: seven days after she gives birth, she dies. Eva De Clercq likewise brings forth numerous examples of early Jain fetal narratives in which mothers are so marginalized that their sons seem to gestate without them. The Jain example of a fetal transfer furthermore suggests that if a mother is not good enough, she, and not the fetus, can be replaced with another womb. All of these arguments suggest that imagining the fetus as separate from the mother is a common tendency in how people have conceived of this inescapable period of human life. It can be argued, then, that the power of women as givers of life and their apparent singular position during these months of gestation has not been an unproblematic reality in various cultural settings and traditions.

Nikky-Guninder Kaur Singh, however, brings forth a much more positive religious expression of motherhood in her chapter on the Sikh tradition. She notes how mother-centered the Guru Granth Sahib is, with imagery of fertility remarkably recurrent throughout the Sikh textual tradition. She argues that Sikh scripture takes the female body seriously, recognizing in the pregnant woman a symbol of continuity and an ability to affirm life over death. Singh argues that the pregnant woman and her fetus are ultimately one in the pages of the Guru Granth Sahib, and Singh laments the fact that modern Sikh culture has largely forgotten the female-affirming beauty of its tradition, as evidenced by a recent surge in female feticides in the Punjab. Justin McDaniel likewise notes the ritual importance of motherhood in Southeast Asia, as he describes the fascinating ritual transformation of the dead into new fetuses during funerals, which is achieved via the incantation of various segments of a particular corpus of Buddhist philosophical literature identified as a kind of ritual mother, leading the dead into its new life. Although hagiographically, mothers in Buddhism might be largely dismissed, McDaniel's chapter demonstrates how revered the role of motherhood is as it becomes attached to these extremely sophisticated texts. Undeniably, the mother plays a pivotal role in the life of the fetus, and the social, political, or religious response to her reveals a larger underlying perspective.

The above discussion demonstrates how richly situated fetal symbolism can be within larger imaginations of the human condition. The fetus can express key cultural and religious priorities and serve as a vehicle for political propositions and religious identities. It can, moreover, symbolically reveal profound human needs and emotions, such as the universal experience of vulnerability. Indeed, what greater expression of human vulnerability than a fetus, utterly possessing a woman's body on the one hand and yet completely dependent on that body on the other? It is no surprise that in contemporary North America, where significant instability and economic fragility are emerging, an antiabortion movement has arisen with fierce determination to protect that which appears most vulnerable. Expressions such as "fetal violation" ultimately communicate an undercurrent of profound social instability, and thus it may be argued that the rise of such vehement doctrine concerning the fetus is in fact a signal for a much more serious social vulnerability brimming beneath the surface.

Daniel C. Peterson notes this relationship between fetal symbolism and political/social expression in his chapter on the Islamic Prophet Muhammad. He argues that the early legends surrounding Muhammad in the womb, which produced a series of miraculous phenomena, functioned in part to articulate the political sovereignty of Islam. He notes in particular the legends of the sudden extinction of the eternal Zoroastrian fires at the moment of the Prophet's conception—an obvious indicator of such a strategy. Catherine Playoust and Ellen Bradshaw Aitken make a similar argument about the early Christian relationship to the unborn. Focusing primarily on the Lukan narrative about John the Baptist and early apocryphal accounts of Mary and Jesus in the womb, they demonstrate how the unborn function to establish relationships between competing religious groups. With such a focus, the vulnerability of the unborn is replaced by a larger social, cultural, and religious agenda.

The vulnerability of the fetus can also indicate another symbolic nexus: that of violating the other. Jane Marie Law's chapter concludes with the problematic postwar imagination of the violated pregnant female body, with the well-documented allegation of fetuses cut from the bodies of women in the Nanjing massacre in December of 1937, and the manner in which this image of Japanese wartime military atrocity has haunted postwar Japanese cultural memory. She argues that this violation takes the common practice of demoralizing a wartime population through rape to a new level of showing disregard for the humanity of the other. This image of the violated fetus comes to operate in a symbolic landscape of postwar Japan coming to terms with its past.

All three of these modalities of imagining the fetus vis-à-vis the female body carrying it—as divorced from the fetus, as central to it and positively evaluated, and as dehumanized along with the fetus—suggests that imagining the fetus always brings us into conversation with a continuum of other stages of life: conception, motherhood, and the role of women in society in a given situation (including war).

One of the more commanding symbols associated with the fetus to emerge from this volume is creation/transformation. Many of the essays in this volume have touched on this subject, with the fetus revealing yet again social and cultural values. André Couture, in his chapter on Krishna, shows how one might read Krishna's fetal narrative as a cosmogony, with Krishna's creation functioning as a microcosmic map for the creation of the universe. His emergence is thus directly paralleled with the emergence of the macrocosm. Sasson, on the other hand, notes how the Buddha defies the laws of creation and transformation. The Buddha's fetal narratives present a being of awakening already in the womb, and thus a being already become. And Nikky Singh explores an entirely different perspective as she urges her readers of Sikh scripture to remember the creative potential represented by the fetus, with divinity lying deep within.

Other contributors in this volume emphasize the power of inscription provided by the symbolic fetus. The fetus is the ultimate blank slate, and, as Gwynn Kessler so aptly demonstrates in her contribution, religious traditions are quick to inscribe their priorities and principles onto it. The rabbinic literature she explores is laced with such inscriptions, Jacob and Esau functioning as perfect examples in this regard. Jacob was appropriated as a patriarch of the Jewish tradition, whereas Esau was relegated to its outskirts. Jacob was consequently believed to have studied Torah in the womb, was circumcised there, and jumped for joy in his mother's belly whenever they passed a synagogue. Esau, sharing the very same womb, did the opposite. Such an example demonstrates, according to Kessler, that the literature uses the image of the fetus to inscribe Jewishness as something already established in the womb.

A similar phenomenon can be found in Tibetan Buddhist embryology, as Frances Garrett points out. Karma is inscribed onto the fetus, so that it brings into the world the baggage of its past actions. And because it bears the marks of its samsaric existence, it functions as mythic evidence for Buddhist teachings. The fetus's gradual transformation, moreover, mirrors the religious path structure that must also take place in stages. Robert Kritzer joins Garrett in this regard, arguing that the extensive descriptions in the Indian embryological literature of the suffering experienced by fetuses, emphasizing as they do the horror that is *saṃsāra*, are designed to motivate the reader to embark upon the religious path of liberation. Jane Marie Law's article suggests that it is the view of a fetus as a being with agency that has prevailed in Japanese imaginings of the fetus, but with special attention paid to those fetal beings who are somehow unique (i.e., a mythical imperial fetus) or in the wrong place (miscarried or aborted).

This discussion does not exhaust the range of imagination of the fetus in human history. As diverse as the fields of inquiry are here—embryology, mythology, philosophy, ritual, cultural memory—all of the contributions share the same goal: to uncover the potential of fetal symbolism to focus attention on or problematize important dimensions of human experience in various cultures around the world. The modern Western imagining of the fetus is, as we said above, too deeply obscured by the venues and debates of reproduction politics, medicine, and obstetrics. We would not argue that the fetus does not belong in those areas, but we challenge the tendency to corral it there. A literature search for scholarship dealing with the effects of modern scientific fetal imagery on contemporary legal or ethical imagination yields a wealth of excellent monographs, only a few of which are noted here. But very little has been produced of late that surveys the vast array of imaginings of the fetus outside the current medicalized and politicized arena. Religious studies has more to contribute than to weigh in on the ethical debates about fetal personhood. Scholars of religion have much to say about the other ways of imagining the fetus, and these imaginary modes could have a great deal to say about other problems in society, such as gender, war and peace, self-cultivation, power and hegemony, and coming to terms with the past. Although neither of us lament the medical advances made possible by developments in fetal sonography, both of us wish to see the broader range of human meanings often conveyed through imagining the fetus, the fetal/mother relationship, and the processes of conception, in utero development, and birth.

An introduction seems as suitable a place as any to comment on the process of editing a volume with this scope. The editors have recognized the impossibility of covering every religious tradition featuring fetal mythologies and embryologies. In some cases, because of the continuing controversy over abortion in the United States, we found that many scholars working on material highly relevant to these discussions are reluctant to publish in this field for fear that their work would be read or quoted out of context or used for ends not in keeping with their own understandings of the traditions they represent. For this reason, some of the major religious traditions are covered either broadly or in limited historical contexts.

The reader will also notice a wide range of academic voices and rhetorical styles in the chapters of this volume. We felt that the variety of scholarly styles intrigued by this topic would itself be a point of interest to the reader.

We have intentionally not imposed an interpretative framework on the multiplicity of traditions and academic disciplines represented here. The reader is welcome to read individual chapters in comparison with others, but comparison was not the sole interpretive exercise intended by this collection of chapters. The reader might also use this collection to see the vast differences and scope of issues arising, in traditions and in the interpretations of scholars, from this one symbolic focal point.

We have attempted, as best we can, to assemble a group of scholars working on major world religious traditions. Unfortunately, while oral indigenous traditions have often produced the most fascinating mythologies of the fetus, currently there is a dearth of scholars working on fetal mythology in these traditions. It is our hope that this volume can serve as a beginning, encouraging scholars of myth, ritual, and symbol to ask some of the same questions that embarked us on this project: How is the fetus imagined in a particular tradition? What special powers does it have? What stories indicate its degree of agency to influence human life, its own destiny, and even the cosmos? What other social, religious, and cultural virtues, problems, and concerns are worked through by crafting and presenting narratives about fetal life? Our hope is that these questions will continue to be addressed by scholars of religion in the near future, and that they might use this particular volume as a jumping off point for further research and not as an end.

In many ways it is fitting that this volume should be produced through a series within the American Academy of Religion. This project is, rightly, a true child of the AAR. The editors Jane Marie Law and Vanessa R. Sasson first met at a regional meeting of the Eastern International Region of the American Academy of Religion in March of 2003. This meeting coincided exactly to the hour with the commencement of the current Iraq War. As the military strategy known as "Shock and Awe" was unleashed over Baghdad and broadcast in vague distant images on the television (labeled by CNN as "Shock and Awe Now Underway in Baghdad"), we discussed images and mythologies of hope, fecundity, transformation, and generation. In our anguish at the state of world affairs, we looked to the work of our own scholarship to see what the range of images of human creativity could be. That original impetus for this volume took us into discussions we never imagined were present in this rich material. The idea of this volume was born, if you will, in that conversation at the AAR dinner. But the AAR served as a gestational setting for this volume in other ways as well.

It was through the national meetings of the American Academy of Religion, in Atlanta in 2003 and San Antonio in 2004, and the Eastern International Regional meeting in Montreal in 2005 that we convened many of the scholars to contribute to this project. It is our hope that this volume, an incomplete beginning though it is, will serve as a conceptual alternative to the stultifyingly narrow mode of imagining the fetus that dominates our culture today.

WORKS CITED

Morgan, L. M., and M. W. Michaels, eds. *Fetal Subjects, Feminist Positions*. Philadelphia: University of Philadelphia Press, 1999.

Newman, K. *Fetal Positions: Individualism, Science, Visuality*. Stanford, Calif.: Stanford University Press, 1996.

Petchesky, R. P. "Fetal Images: The Power of Visual Culture in the Politics of Reproduction." *Feminist Studies* 13, 2 (1987): 263–92.

Rapp, R. "Real-Time Fetus: The Role of the Sonogram in the Age of Monitored Reproduction." In *Cyborgs and Citadels: Anthropological Interventions in Emerging Sciences and Technologies*, ed. G. L. Downey and J. Dumit, 23–57. Santa Fe, N.M.: American School of Research, 1997.

The Story of Saṃkarṣaṇa's and Kṛṣṇa's Births: A Drama Involving Embryos

André Couture

The *Harivaṃśa* (a long supplement to the *Mahābhārata*) contains the well-known story of Saṃkarṣaṇa's and Kṛṣṇa's births, which involves the killing of six fetuses, the miscarriage of a seventh and, finally, the exchange of the newborn Kṛṣṇa for a newborn girl. Episodes such as these have a rather odd ring to them; so much so that most modern interpreters simply recount them without hazarding any additional commentary. Though scholarly literature contains numerous mentions of these episodes, few attempts have been made to explain the underlying logic of such narratives. Examining these narratives for evidence of recurrent patterns and comparing them generally to similar stories found in other parts of the world,[1] or specifically to the myths of Heracles,[2] have contributed little to our understanding of their significance. As I believe is the case with the other episodes from Kṛṣṇa's childhood, the birth story cannot be dismissed as a mere hodgepodge of legends borrowed from the Ābhīras or similar pastoral tribes. The supposedly pastoral origin of these legends, a position that has held sway for decades, is based on questionable arguments. Reinterpreting the story on a symbolic level as if it were the fantasy of an overactive imagination does not do justice to the genre either. In what follows, rather than accept either of these positions, I will instead attempt to show how the Brahmins, those talented storytellers, carefully crafted this narrative using material drawn from their own Vedic tradition to address their audience's concerns. Such a long-standing tradition of narrative

1. See W. Ruben, *Krishṇa: Konkordanz und Kommentar der Motive seines Heldenlebens* (Istanbul, n.p., 1944).

2. See B. Preciado-Solis, *The Kṛṣṇa Cycle in the Purāṇas* (Delhi: Motilal Banarsidass, 1985).

adaptation may likely have been a routine cultural practice and, as such, deserves careful analysis.

Brian K. Smith has rightly insisted that, in the ancient Brahmanical context, worlds as well as human beings were understood to have been generated in a state of imperfection. Even as cosmic realities and human beings first appear, they are usually described as either too similar to each other and therefore redundant (*jāmi*), or too differentiated or scattered (*pṛthak*) to allow them to be productive. "That which is *jāmi* precludes production of true being because there are no sufficiently distinct components to join together; that which is *pṛthak* precludes production because no connections are possible between overly individualized components. All true being locates itself (or, rather, is made and placed) between these twin excesses of identity and isolation."[3] To create a cosmos or a perfect human being, additional labor usually carried out by specific actions called rites (*karman*) is required. Smith's research, which should be taken into account here, makes clear that, in the Indian context, a new creation often passes through a preliminary step of insufficiency or excess before its complete realization. The story of Saṃkarṣaṇa's and Kṛṣṇa's births has to be situated against the backdrop of a procreative activity that engenders incomplete beings in need of later transformations to be viable. Seen in this light, this entire story is in no way peculiar and should first be examined in its own setting. My aim here is therefore to reexamine this "fetus story" in conjunction with stories coming out of the same tradition in an effort to discover its meaning inside the new religion of devotion to Kṛṣṇa, which emerged a few centuries before the common era.[4]

The Story of Saṃkarṣaṇa's and Kṛṣṇa's Births according to the *Harivaṃśa*

A presentation, in its entirety, of the oldest and longest extant version of the episode is necessary as we begin our analysis. The story, which is found in the *Harivaṃśa* 40–48, runs as follows.

The scene takes place at the end of the era preceding the present Kaliyuga, that is, the Dvāparayuga. Viṣṇu is awakened from a long cosmic sleep by Brahmā and the gods, all of whom are eager to speak with him. On behalf of them all, Brahmā first notices that the goddess Earth is in a paradoxical situation. Carrying out their royal tasks with the greatest of care, the kings multiply and trample down her body. They build so many cities and villages that there is no more space left on her surface. Oppressed, the Earth needs to be relieved of her burden. Viṣṇu agrees to meet with her on the summit of Mount Meru. All of them listen to her complaints. She gets straight to the point and says that she is counting on Viṣṇu's help, just as she had on so many occasions in the past. All the celestials agree that it is Viṣṇu's function to relieve Earth of her burden and they are ready to collaborate. Brahmā

3. Brian K. Smith, *Reflections on Resemblance, Ritual, and Religion* (Delhi: Motilal Banarsidass, 1998), 53.

4. The *Harivaṃśa-parvan*, which dates to the second or third century CE, reflects a trend of devotion to Kṛṣṇa attested to at least two centuries before our era.

accepts and confesses he has already taken the initiative of sending some of the protagonists onto earth who will take part in the war of the Bhāratas, having himself created this well-known means of stopping the proliferation of kings. Then, Brahmā concludes that it is time for him to retire.

Wandering all around the worlds in search of new battles, the wise Brahmin Nārada goes to the assembly of the gods and notices that Viṣṇu has delayed his descent onto the earth. He points out that, in the meanwhile, the gods had to go to Mathurā on other urgent business. All of the *asuras, daityas,* and *dānavas* whom Viṣṇu had so brilliantly defeated in an earlier battle—which had been waged by the gods for the sake of Tārakā, Bṛhaspati's wife—have now come back to the city under the leadership of King Kaṃsa, the latest incarnation of the great *asura* Kālanemi. Having assumed the name of Keśin, the ancient Hayagrīva is also there; Ariṣṭa became a bull also named Ariṣṭa; Lamba, Khara, Varāha, and Kiśora, in succession, became the herder Pralamba, the ass Dhenuka, and the wrestlers Cāṇūra and Muṣṭika.

Viṣṇu smiles and simply answers that he already knows all of this and is waiting for Brahmā to prepare a terrestrial residence for him. Brahmā then quickly reveals an ancient curse to him. During a sacrifice, Kaśyapa, one of the main progenitors of all living beings, stole Varuṇa's cows with the help of his spouses, Aditi and Surabhi; he was then condemned to become a herder named Vasudeva, accompanied by both women who once again become his spouses under the names of Devakī and Rohiṇī. Leaving his celestial body, Viṣṇu will be born from Vasudeva and Devakī.

As soon as Nārada learns the news, he hurries to Mathurā and tells Kaṃsa about Viṣṇu's plans. In anger, Kaṃsa orders his servants to put the couple under arrest and to kill all of Devakī's babies (or fetuses, *garbha*) as soon as they are born. Considering the situation, Viṣṇu says to himself that after Kaṃsa kills Devakī's first seven babies, he will deposit his self (*ātman*) into the eighth embryo (47.10). He goes immediately under the earth to a region called *pātāla* and fetches a group of six embryos (*garbha*) of *dānavas* precisely called Ṣaḍgarbhāḥ ("The Six Fetuses"). In fact, these embryos are sons of the former Kālanemi (47.12). Brahmā granted them the favor that they would not be killed by any enemy, divine or human. Since they preferred Brahmā's protection, Hiraṇyakaśipu, whom Kālanemi referred to as his father (38.19), cursed them. In an attempt to thwart Brahmā's favor, Hiraṇyakaśipu condemned them to fall victim of the wrath of his own father reborn as King Kaṃsa. He told them: "Since, disregarding me, you got a favor from Brahmā, by choosing Brahmā's friendship, you forsake me and became my enemies. Therefore I abandon you. You will be made famous under the name given to you by your father, Ṣaḍgarbhāḥ. Your father himself will kill you all in the fetal state [*garbhagatān*]. You, the great *asuras* Ṣaḍgarbhāḥ, will become the six Devakī's fetuses [*garbha*], so that Kaṃsa may kill you while you are still embryos [*garbhasthān*]" (47.20–22).

Then Viṣṇu enters their body in the guise of a dream (*svapnarūpeṇa*), extracts (*niṣkṛṣya*) their vital principles (*prāṇeśvarān*), and gives them to Nidrā (or Yoganidrā), who is Sleep personified and the spouse who serves Viṣṇu-Nārāyaṇa during the cosmic night. Viṣṇu tells her to insert (*yojayasva*) the vital principles, one after the other, into Devakī's womb. He also asked her to transfer in the seventh month Devakī's seventh embryo into Rohiṇī, another of Vasudeva's wives (*saptamo devakīgarbho . . . saṃkrāmayitavyas te saptame māsi rohiṇīm*, 47.30). Viṣṇu says: "Because the embryo has been withdrawn [from Devakī's womb] to be inserted into [another womb] [*saṃkarṣaṇāt tu garbhasya*], the child will be called Saṃkarṣaṇa. He will be my elder brother, resembling the moon. Kaṃsa will think that Devakī lost this seventh child [literally, the seventh fetus fell, *patito devakīgarbhaḥ saptamaḥ*] from fright, and will make every effort to prevent me, the eighth child, from being conceived in her womb" (47.31–32). Viṣṇu also orders Nidrā to be born in Yaśodā, the spouse of Nandagopa, Vasudeva's herder, at exactly the same time as he himself will be born as Devakī's eighth child, in the eighth month (*aṣṭamasya tu māsasya*, 47.36). He also warns her that they will exchange mothers and that she will be considered to be Devakī's daughter. Moreover, Nidrā is told that she will be killed by Kaṃsa and appear in front of her killer as a great and ferocious goddess. Nidrā assures Viṣṇu that she will fully collaborate and disappears.

Everything occurs as Viṣṇu said. Devakī has seven children. Kaṃsa kills the six first as soon as each of them is born, each time dashing them against a rock. The goddess provokes the miscarriage of Rohiṇī's child, rips the fetus from Devakī's womb, and places it into Rohiṇī's womb, announcing that since the fetus was drawn (*karṣaṇa*) from Devakī's womb and deposited into her, she will give birth to a child who will be named Saṃkarṣaṇa (*karṣaṇenāsya garbhasya svagarbhe cāhitasya vai / saṃkarṣaṇo nāma śubhe tava putro bhaviṣyati //* 48.6). Devakī conceives an eighth child in which Hari (or Viṣṇu) establishes his dwelling. Obeying Viṣṇu's orders, Nidrā is conceived in Yaśodā's womb, and both of them are born in their eighth month and at exactly the same time. Most versions call this girl Ekānaṃśā (one and without any portion, probably a reference to the new moon). When Kṛṣṇa is born, all sorts of portents appear upon the earth. Conscious of the danger incurred by his son, Vasudeva brings the baby to the cow-settlement (*vraja*) where Nandagopa and Yaśodā are living and carries the little girl back to Mathurā. As soon as he is warned of the birth of a girl, Kaṃsa seizes her and smashes her head against the same rock. The girl jumps into the sky and is transformed into a threatening goddess who reveals to Kaṃsa that his killer is already born.

The *Viṣṇupurāṇa* (fourth or fifth century) and the *Brahmapurāṇa* (a later text) have a shorter version of the story.[5] A description of the marriage of Vasudeva and Devakī is added. While driving the car of the newlyweds, Kaṃsa hears a voice saying that the eighth child of this woman will kill him. But Vasudeva, trying to soothe the king, promises to deliver all the children that she may bring forth to him. To better explain the threat, the narrator returns to the cosmic setting. These texts first mention a different birth story, one already known in the *Mahābhārata* (1.189.30–31).

5. The *Bhāgavatapurāṇa* (ninth or tenth century) (*Śrīmad Bhāgavatamahāpurāṇa*, with Sanskrit text and English translation, parts 1 and 2, Gorakhpur, India: Gita Press, 1971) follows the same pattern as the *Viṣṇupurāṇa* (Sanskrit text and English translation by H. H. Wilson, Delhi: Nag Publishers, 1989) and the *Brahmapurāṇa* (Delhi: Nag Publishers, 1985).

As soon as Viṣṇu hears Brahmā describing the sufferings of Earth, he plucks two hairs, one white and one black, and says to the gods that these hairs will descend upon Earth and relieve her of the burden of her distress by killing Kaṃsa, who is Kālanemi himself (*Viṣṇu Purāṇa* 5.1.59–64). Nārada informs Kaṃsa, who decides to confine Vasudeva and Devakī so as to kill each of their babies. According to these versions, the six babies are the sons of Hiraṇyakaśipu (rather than Kālanemi's sons as in the *Harivaṃśa*), introduced by Nidrā into Devakī's womb at Viṣṇu's command. Viṣṇu told her:

> Go, Nidrā, and by my command, conduct successively [into Devaki's womb] the six embryos [*ṣaḍgarbhāḥ*] who reside at the bottom of the *pātāla*. When these have been put to death by Kaṃsa, the one called Śeṣa, a part of me, will be born in her womb through a small part [of my energy (*tejas*)] as her seventh child. Rohiṇī is Vasudeva's other wife who resides in the cow-settlement; Goddess, you shall conduct this [part of me] into her womb as if it were a [normal] birth. People will say that Devakī miscarried from this seventh child through the anxiety of imprisonment and from fear of the king of the Bhojas [i.e., Kaṃsa]. The child will be known by the name of Saṃkarṣaṇa since he was extracted [*garbhasaṃkarṣaṇāt*] [from his mother's womb and inserted into another womb]. He shall be a hero and look like the peak of the White Mountain. Then I shall be born in Devakī's womb and you must immediately go into Yaśodā's womb. In the night of the eighth lunation of the dark half of the month of Nabhas, in the season of the rains, I shall be born. You shall receive birth on the ninth. (5.1.71–77)

After more explanations to the goddess, the text quickly mentions the killing of the first six embryos, the transfer of the seventh, the births of Kṛṣṇa and the goddess, and the exchange of babies.

King Janamejaya's "Natural" Interpretation of the Story of Kṛṣṇa's Birth

Before becoming a warrior (*kṣatriya*) able to fight against enemies like Jarāsaṃdha, Viṣṇu must first pass through the stage of embryo in Devakī's womb at Mathurā. His childhood is spent as a herder in Nandagopa's cow-settlement, but he later returns to Mathurā and starts fighting with divine weapons. In the *Harivaṃśa*, King Janamejaya is so struck by the incongruity of Viṣṇu's passage through a uterus that his first exchange with the Brahmin Vaiśaṃpāyana deals with this very question. "How is it possible that Viṣṇu who is inhabited by Prosperity [*śrīgarbha*] came to be carried in the [impure] womb[6] [*garbha*] of a terrestrial woman" (cf. 30.8)? Even if Janamejaya knows full well that Viṣṇu and Sacrifice are one and the same, he nevertheless seems unable to move beyond the physical level. His question, which

6. See the texts gathered by Minoru Hara ("A Note on the Buddha's Birth Story," in *Indianisme et bouddhisme: Mélanges offerts à Mgr. Étienne Lamotte* [Louvain, Belgium: Université Catholique de Louvain, 1980], 143–57).

includes an eloquent praise of Viṣṇu, changes little by little into a short treatise on embryology that it may prove useful to quote here.

> 35 For the Veda-knowers, he [i.e., Viṣṇu] is the one to be known [*vedya*]. For those who are characterized by might [*prabhava*], he is the mightiest [*prabhu*]. For the beings [*bhūta*], he is identical with Soma. For those who shine like fire, he is identical to Agni.
>
> 36 For human beings [*manuṣya*], he is identical with mind [*manas*]. For ascetics, he is identical with ascetic power [*tapas*]. For those who behave wisely, he is discipline. For those who are full of energy [*tejasvin*], he is also energy [*tejas*].
>
> 37 For all creations, he is the creator, the ultimate cause of worlds. For those who deserve confrontation, he is confrontation [*vigraha*], as well as the issue [*gati*] for those seeking an issue [*gatimant*].
>
> 38 Wind [*vāyu*] has its origin in space [*ākāśa*]. Fire has wind for its breath. Gods have fire for their breath, and Madhusūdana [i.e., Viṣṇu] is the breath of fire.
>
> 39 Blood [*śonita*] originates from the organic fluid [*rasa*]. From blood, flesh [*māṃsa*] is said to originate. From flesh fat [*medas*] originates, and from fat, it is explained that bone [*asthi*] originates.
>
> 40 From bone, marrow [*majjā*] originates. From marrow, sperm [*śukra*] originates. From sperm, the fetus [*garbha*] originates through an action based on the organic fluid [*rasa*].
>
> 41 The first part [of the fetus], that is made of water, is said to be the *soma*-mass [*saumya rāśi*]. As is well known, the fetus produces heat, which is called the second mass [*dvitīya rāśi*].
>
> 42 It should be known that sperm is made of *soma* and menstrual blood [*ārtava*] of fire [*pāvaka* = *agni*]. Both [elements] originate in the organic fluid [*rasa*]; their power [*vīrya*] is [the action of] both Moon and Sun.
>
> 43 Sperm is classified as phlegm [*kapha*], and menstrual blood as bile [*pitta*]. Heart is the seat of phlegm, and bile is established in the navel.
>
> 44 Tradition says that the heart, being in the middle of the body, is the seat of thought, and that the brilliant fire stands inside the navel and the throat.
>
> 45 Mind should be regarded as Prajāpati, and phlegm as *soma*; tradition says that bile is fire, [so that] everything that moves is made of fire and *soma*.
>
> 46 The fetus, once set in motion, becomes a mass of flesh [*arbuda*], and wind makes its entrance, accompanied by the supreme Self [*paramātman*].
>
> 47 Then, standing in the body, it divides itself into five—*prāṇa, apāna, samāna, udāna* and *vyāna*—and increases anew.
>
> 48 While circulating, *prāṇa* increases its first seat [i.e., the middle of the body of the fetus]; *apāna*, the rear of the body; *udāna*, the top of the embodied being.
>
> 49 *Vyāna* allows complete extension of the limbs, and *samāna* stabilizes [the digested food]. Then [the Self] becomes able to apprehend beings through the senses [*indriya*].

> 50 Earth, wind, space, water, and fire form the group of five [elements]. Tradition teaches that the senses [of the fetus] come into relationship with each of these elements.
>
> 51 They say that the body is made of earth, the breath is made of wind, the cavities of the body originate from space, the liquids [of the body] originate from water,
>
> 52 and that the light in the eye is fire [*tejas*]. The regulator of the [senses] is said to be the mind, and through its power, ordinary objects are set in motion [and shown to the Self].
>
> 53 Since this is the way the Puruṣa [i.e., Viṣṇu] goes about emitting all the eternal worlds, how can he assume a human nature in this perishable world?[7]

According to King Janamejaya, the growth of the embryo depends on three great deities (Viṣṇu, Soma, and Agni), three principles (wind, water, and fire), and three humors (*vāyu* or breath, *kapha* or phlegm, *pitta* or bile). He affirms that the entire world is supported by Moon and Sun, or by Soma (the ambrosia contained in the moon, and the corresponding ritual beverage) and Agni, or simply by water and fire. Considered as the result of the union of sperm (= water) and menstrual blood (= fire), the embryo is composed of two masses, a *soma*-mass and an *agni*-mass, which explains the presence in the human being of the phlegm and bile. Nevertheless, behind or beyond these two principles exists a third principle, *vāyu* (wind) or *prāṇa* (breath), which ultimately depends on Viṣṇu himself. Janamejaya's question makes clear that Viṣṇu is the god who governs all creatures, including the growth of beings in the embryonic state. How is it therefore possible for the great Viṣṇu, asks Janamejaya, to pass through all the steps of the development of the embryo? The information alluded to in Janamejaya's question concurs with the conception of the development of the embryo found in similar Brahmanical texts. Of course, Vaiśaṃpāyana knows all this, but decides not to follow up with this sort of reasoning. Basically, the Brahmin's answer moves the discussion with the king onto another plane. Before reviewing Viṣṇu's various manifestations (*prādurbhāva*) in the human world, he immediately reminds the king that Viṣṇu is the Yajña-Puruṣa, the Sacrifice-Man, who sacrificed himself and from whom all parts of the universe are born (cf. *Harivaṃśa* 31.3–9). The great Viṣṇu will appear in Devakī's womb once again, but not the way Janamejaya imagines.

The fact that Viṣṇu the Sacrifice manifests himself as the one who sacrifices as well as the object of sacrifice opens up at least two options that might shape different interpretations of the episode of his birth on earth. First, a sacrificer cannot sacrifice without passing through a period of initiation (*dīkṣā*), and the story of Viṣṇu's manifestation could have used this line of interpretation. The specialists on the question of sacrifice know that man *is* the sacrifice and that, as sacrificer, he is

7. *Harivaṃśa* 30.35–53 (my translation); also A. Couture, *L'enfance de Krishna*. Traduction des chapitres 30 à 78 du *Harivamsha* (Paris: Cerf; Québec: Les Presses de l'Université Laval, 1991), 89–91.

the measurement of the elements used in the sacrifice.[8] The sacrificer even comes to be initiated by means of a rite in which the priests make the sacrificer an embryo such that he is born again and dons a divine body. This analogy is developed in texts describing the rites. G. U. Thite gives the following summary of the explanations found in the *Śatapathabrāhmaṇa*.

> The water is sprinkled upon him [the sacrificer] and it symbolises the seed. Thus having made him possessed of seed, the priests consecrate him. With the fresh butter, the sacrificer is anointed. For that appertains to the embryos. They conduct him to the hut of the consecrated. The hut of the consecrated is the womb (*yoni*) and they conduct him to his own womb. The cloth covering the sacrificer is the amnion (*ulba*). The black antelope's skin is the placenta (*jarāyu*). The closing of the hands of the sacrificer is similar to that of [an] embryo (cp. [compare] also ŚB [*Śatapathabrāhmaṇa*] III.1.3.28, 2.2.26–28; 3.3.12). When the sacrificer being about to build an alter undergoes the consecration he pours into the fire-pan as seed in to the womb, his own self composed of metres, stomas, vital airs and deities (ŚB X.4.2.29).[9]

Kṛṣṇa is the manifestation of Viṣṇu, the best of men (*puruṣottama*) and the personification of sacrifice.[10] As such, his passage through a uterus could be likened to a sort of initiation (*dīkṣā*). As a result of the ascetic practices he endures during his initiation, the initiated (*dīkṣita*) is said to sacrifice his own self, so that the offerings he pours into the fire in the subsequent parts of the ritual are interpreted as substitutes for his own body. One possible reading of Kṛṣṇa's life as Viṣṇu's manifestation could have been to say that his dedicated life as a warrior is likened to a sacrificial offering preceded by a period of initiation. Then, Kṛṣṇa's total life (from his conception onward) would be structured as the sacrifice itself. That said, it must be admitted that this interpretation is not explicitly formulated in this context and has to be dismissed.

A second line of interpretation could be envisaged in the Brahmanical context. Even if it is not specified in the *Harivaṃśa*, King Janamejaya is undoubtedly aware of the fact that, during the embryonic period, Brahmins practice multiple prenatal rites aimed at protecting the mother and her fetus. In the Hindu tradition, the *saṃskāras* are cleansing rites or rites intended to achieve states of perfection which accompany human beings throughout life and begin not with the ceremonies surrounding birth, but much earlier with impregnation. The human being spends up to ten lunar months in the womb. The fetus grows little by little in the obscurity and silence of its mother's womb before being born. This period of time appears to be particularly dangerous for the new life as well as for the mother. The *garbhādhāna* (or conception), *puṃsavana* (or quickening of a male child), and *sīmantonnayana* (or hair-parting of the pregnant woman) are rituals intended to keep both mother

8. *Śatapathabrāhmaṇa*, trans. J. Eggeling. 5 vols. (Delhi: Motilal Banarsidass, 1972), 3.1.4.23.
9. G. U. Thite, *Sacrifice in the Brāhmaṇa-Texts* (Poona, India: Poona University Press, 1975), 119.
10. Cf. *Harivaṃśa* 30–31.

and child safe, to prepare the womb, to purify the fetus, to remove any obstacles to its growth, and even to influence its sex. According to the various treatises of dharma, these rites can either be performed on the mother once and for all or repeated after each impregnation.[11] Even though these preparatory rites are well known and may have been mentioned in this context, neither King Janamejaya nor the Brahmin Vaiśaṃpāyana mentions any of these in the present context. Such Brahmanical rituals are touched on later in the story[12] but not for the embryonic period itself.

Nevertheless, since the Viṣṇu who manifests himself in the human world is Sacrifice personified, one cannot help but think that the significance of his coming must be interpreted at a cosmic level. This is exactly the point that Vaiśaṃpāyana emphasizes.

The Cosmic Context of the Story of Saṃkarṣaṇa's and Kṛṣṇa's Births

Before moving on to more specific issues, an examination of the setting of this birth story would seem to be in order. From the above summary and the analysis of Vaiśaṃpāyana's answer to Janamejaya's question, it must already be clear that Kṛṣṇa's birth and the whole affair of the fetuses have a cosmic significance. Kṛṣṇa's destiny is embedded in the complex story of another of Viṣṇu's descents into the world. The story is located in the end of the third *yuga*, the Dvāparayuga, the age of the world coming just before the present Kaliyuga, a period of deep suffering for Earth. One of the protagonists of the *Mahābhārata*, Kṛṣṇa sides with the Pāṇḍavas against the Kauravas, and acts as Arjuna's charioteer, becoming, as it were, Arjuna's intelligence (*buddhi*).[13] Nevertheless, to explain why a new manifestation of Viṣṇu is needed at that very time, the *Harivaṃśa* refers to another urgent matter (*kāryāntara*), the catastrophic situation of Earth in the city of Mathurā during Kaṃsa's reign. Kaṃsa is an *asura* (46.3), one of the traditional and recurring enemies of the gods. He is described as a new incarnation of Kālanemi, a great *asura* who was killed by Hari during the first age (*kṛtayuga*) (*Harivaṃśa* 32–38) and whose name means "the rim [of the wheel] of time," an evocation of the wheel of births and deaths, the flux of a world submitted to an unending transmigration. His father, Hiraṇyakaśipu (the son of Kaśyapa and Diti, *Harivaṃśa* 3.58), belongs to the same family of heroes, being also a *daitya* or *dānava* who formerly had been defeated by Viṣṇu disguised as a Man-Lion (*narasiṃha*). There would be no reason to narrate Kṛṣṇa's birth in detail if he were intended merely to follow the normal path of human life. Kṛṣṇa is one of Viṣṇu's manifestations, the personification of all sacrificial values, appearing once more on Earth to annihilate King Kaṃsa and mark the domination of dharmic forces over the forces of dissolution. This story, with its weird episodes like the massacre of fetuses, must have been narrated

11. Lakshmi Kapani, *La notion de saṃskāra*, Tome I (Paris: De Boccard, 1992), 81–100.

12. See *Harivaṃśa* 49.3; 49.30, 628*; 50.2, 629*; 79.1sq.

13. Cf. *Kaṭha Upaniṣad* 3.3, where the intellect (*buddhi*) is compared to the rider (*sārathi*) of the chariot that is the body. (See *Upaniṣads*, trans. Patrick Olivelle [Oxford: Oxford University Press, 1996, 238–39].)

precisely for its cosmic effects. It takes place inside a text claiming to be a *purāṇa*, an ancient tradition, made of paradigmatic stories having an impact on the condition of the whole world. Kṛṣṇa is not an ordinary person, and his birth story has to make this point clear to its listeners and readers.

As it takes on cosmic proportions, a mythology of the fetus becomes a cosmogony. An old hymn of the *Ṛgveda* (10.121) presents Hiraṇyagarbha, the Golden Embryo, as a sort of secret epiphany of the Creator, containing the germ of the whole universe to be created. "In the beginning the Golden Embryo arose [*hiraṇyagarbha*]. Once he was born, he was the one lord of creation. He held in place the earth and this sky. . . . When the high waters came, pregnant with the embryo that is everything, bringing forth fire, he arose from that as the one life's breath of the gods."[14] Likewise, several other old texts speak of a golden egg containing an embryo from which Prajāpati, the lord of creatures, is born. This *garbha* has a golden or yellow color (as Kṛṣṇa has a yellow garment), but no specific name. Creatures are contained in an indefinite whole, waiting for their *nāman*, their names, a sign of their passage from nonbeing (*asat*) to specific existence (*sat*). The Golden Embryo points to a sort of prehistory of the universe, a story of the creatures before they were created. The *Chāndogya Upaniṣad* contains the following account explaining why Brahman, the ultimate essence of the cosmos, is said to be the sun:

> In the beginning this world was simply what is non-existing; and what is existing was that. It then developed and formed into an egg. It lay there for a full year and then it hatched, splitting in two, one half becoming silver and the other half gold. The silver half is this earth, while the golden half is the sky. The outer membrane is the mountains; the inner membrane, the clouds and the mist; the veins, the rivers; and the amniotic fluid, the ocean. Now, the hatchling that was born was the sun up there. And as it was being born, cries of joy and loud cheers rose up in celebration, as did all beings and all desires.[15]

The Purāṇic cosmogony appears to insert some old story of this sort into a more complex narrative. For our present needs, a few lines from chapter 1 of the *Harivaṃśa* should suffice to illustrate this point:

> Desirous of creating various creatures, Lord Viṣṇu Svayaṃbhū at first emits waters in which he then ejaculates [*tāsu vīryam avāsṛjat*]. Tradition [*śruti*] says that these waters were formerly designated as *nārāḥ*; because his first sojourn [*ayana*] took place in them, he is called Nārāyaṇa. The egg, lying in the waters, has a golden color. Tradition teaches that Brahmā is born there on his own and was [therefore] called Self-existent [Svayaṃbhū]. Having lived there for a full year, Lord Hiraṇyagarbha divided the egg into two, that is into heaven and earth.[16]

14. *Ṛgveda* 10.121.1 and 7 (*The Rig Veda, An Anthology*. One Hundred and Eight Hymns, Selected, Translated, and Annotated by Wendy Doniger O'Flaherty [Delhi: Penguin Books India, 1981, 27]). See Jean Varenne, *Cosmogonies védiques* (Paris: Les Belles Lettres, 1982), 218.

15. *Chāndogya Upaniṣad* 3.19.1–3 (in *Upaniṣads*, Olivelle's translation, 127).

16. *Harivaṃśa* 1.23–26, my translation.

The text is quite clear: Hiraṇyagarbha, the Golden Embryo, is Viṣṇu himself. Having produced the waters, he hatched a golden egg from which Brahmā is born, and from Brahmā all the creatures.

At first sight, the story of the yellow-garmented Kṛṣṇa's birth has no relationship with the Hiraṇyagarbha myth. The first six fetuses are killed, the seventh fetus "falls" and is transferred to the cow-settlement (*vraja*) to continue its growth, Kṛṣṇa being the eight baby to be born. Nevertheless, when one realizes that the births of the first seven children prepare Kṛṣṇa's birth and that all of them are part of the same continuum, they must all be taken into account if we are to understand the last birth. Moreover, it is probably not by chance that Viṣṇu, having reflected (*cintayām āsa*, 47.9) about the best way to enter the human world, went to the *pātāla* where all six embryos were "lying in a water-womb-house" or "in a cell or adytum made of water" (*jalagarbhagṛheśayāḥ*, 47.23), similar to the amniotic waters in which the fetus is immersed. The *pātāla* is the lowermost region in a vast realm made of seven regions located under an earth conceived as a boat floating on the cosmic waters. According to the *Mahābhārata* and *Purāṇas*, Snake Śeṣa also lives in the same region. The Ṣaḍgarbhāḥ and Snake Śeṣa are all entities originating from regions connected to these cosmic waters and, when considered altogether, closer to the Golden Embryo than it might at first appear. Nevertheless, while linked to the Ṣaḍgarbhāḥ through a common origin in the same *pātāla*, given his close relationship with Kṛṣṇa, Śeṣa-Saṃkarṣaṇa always remains distinct from them. More analysis is therefore needed to explain the specificity of the seventh embryo.

The Story of Kṛṣṇa's Birth and Other Stories Related to Aditi's Sons

In the Purāṇic mythology, the wise progenitor Kaśyapa received thirteen spouses from the *prajāpati* Dakṣa (*Harivaṃśa* 2.47; 3.24). Aditi is one of them and, according to *Harivaṃśa* 3.50–51, she gave birth to Viṣṇu, Indra, Aryaman, Dhātṛ, Tvaṣṭṛ, Pūṣan, Vivasvant, Savitṛ, Mitra, Varuṇa, Aṃśa, and Bhaga, who are known as the *ādityas*. The present story deals with a new manifestation of Viṣṇu as Kṛṣṇa. The main versions of the story consider Vasudeva, the father of Kṛṣṇa, to be the incarnation of Kaśyapa, and his mother, Devakī, to be a new Aditi. The identification of Rohiṇī with Surabhi, the mother of the cows and another of Kaśyapa's spouses, is also mentioned.

Instead of considering Viṣṇu as Aditi's eldest son, as the *Harivaṃśa* apparently does, older texts often present Mārtāṇḍa (a form of the sun) as Aditi's youngest son. Benjamin Preciado-Solis has convincingly argued that the story of Kṛṣṇa's birth has a relationship with the myth of the birth of Mārtāṇḍa. Attested to in the hymn 10.72 of the *Ṛgveda*, Mārtāṇḍa is considered to be the last of Aditi's eight sons. "Eight sons are there of Aditi, who were born of her body. With seven she went forth among the gods, but she threw Mārtāṇḍa, the son, aside."[17] Mārtāṇḍa has been cast away by Aditi and therefore is linked to death. When commenting on those who,

17. *Ṛgveda* 10.72.8, Doniger O'Flaherty's translation, 39.

in a certain ritual, offer a rice-pap to the *ādityas*, the *Śatapathabrāhmaṇa* (an old ritual commentary) refers to this passage and adds the following explanations.

> Now Aditi had eight sons. But those who are called "the gods, sons of Aditi" were only seven, for the eighth, Mārtāṇḍa, she brought forth unformed: it was a mere lump of bodily matter as broad as it was high. Some, however, say that he was of the size of a man. The gods, sons of Aditi, then spake, "that which was born after us must not be lost: come let us fashion it." They accordingly fashioned it as this man is fashioned. The flesh which was cut off him, and thrown down in a lump, became an elephant: hence they say that one must not accept an elephant [as a gift], since the elephant has sprung from man. Now he whom they thus fashioned was Vivasvat, the Āditya [or the sun]; and of him [came] these creatures.[18]

Aditi's last son was not born like the others. He arrived unformed (*avikṛta*) as a shapeless mass of flesh that the gods fashioned as a man. The word *mārtāṇḍa* (elsewhere written *mārtaṇḍa*) can be analyzed as the *vṛddhi* (the strongest vowel gradation) of *martāṇḍa*, with the meaning of "born from a dead egg." The predicate applies to the sun who, according to these myths, was born with a monstrous body needing to be reshaped before becoming a peaceful world-enlightening deity. The myth reflects the paradoxical situation of a sun which, at one and the same time, is necessary for life but risks burning up all living beings. This condition of "excessive differentiation"[19] is still in a state of chaos that must be corrected, if creation is to become cosmos.

The *Maitrāyaṇī Saṃhitā* (another old ritual commentary), also quoted by Preciado-Solis, gives another version of Mārtāṇḍa's birth that is closer to the story under study here.

> Wishing for children Aditi cooked a pap. She ate what was left over [*ucchiṣṭa*]. Dhātṛ and Aryaman were born to her. She cooked another. She ate what was left over. Mitra and Varuṇa were born to her. She cooked another. She ate what was left over. Aṃśa and Bhaga were born to her. She cooked another. She thought: Each time I eat what is left over, two sons are born to me. Probably I shall get something still better when I eat beforehand. After she had eaten beforehand she served the pap. Her two next sons spoke even as children in the womb: "We both shall be as much as all the sons of Aditi." The sons of Aditi searched for someone to procure their abortion [*nirhantāram*]. Aṃśa and Bhaga procured the abortion of those two. Therefore no oblation is made to them at the sacrifice. Instead Aṃśa's portion is the stake in betting. Bhaga ["Fortune"] went abroad. Therefore people say: "Go abroad, you meet fortune there!" Due to his vital energy Indra rose up. The other fœtus fell down dead.

18. *Śatapatha-Brāhmaṇa* 3.1.3–4, Vol. 2, 12–13, with slight changes.
19. See Smith, *Reflections*.

> This, forsooth, was Mārtāṇḍa of whom men are the descendants. Now Aditi turned to her sons saying: "This should be mine, this ought not to perish uselessly." They said: "He should then call himself one of us, he should not look down on us." This, verily, was Aditi's son Vivasvat, the father of Manu Vaivasvata and Yama. Manu dwelled in this, Yama in yonder world.[20]

Mārtāṇḍa's birth is preceded by the birth of six sons. When Aditi decided to take the first part of the pap, her haste caused the abortion of her next babies. Aṃśa and Bhaga, who helped with the abortion, were punished. These two sons were Indra, who, in spite of the abortion, rose up because of his vital energy, and Mārtāṇḍa, who was supposed to die but was called back to life by his brothers at his mother's request and gave birth to Manu, the first human being, and Yama, the lord of the dead.

The *Taittirīya Saṃhitā* (a third old ritual commentary) relates a similar story that also deserves to be looked at in this context.

> Aditi, desirous of offspring, cooked a Brahman's mess for the Sādhya gods; to her they gave the remains [*uccheṣaṇa*], she ate it, she became pregnant [*reto 'dhatte*], of her the four Ādityas were born. A second [mess] she cooked; she reflected, "They have been born for me from the remains; if I eat first, then stronger ones will be born from me"; she ate first, she became pregnant, from her was born an egg which miscarried [*vyṛddham āṇḍam ajāyata*]. She cooked a third [mess] for the Ādityas, [saying] "Let this labour be for enjoyment to me"; they said, "Let us choose a boon; let him who shall be born hence be one of us; let him who shall be prosperous among his offspring be for our enjoyment"; then was born the Āditya Vivasvant.[21]

In this last case, the first four *ādityas* were born from the leftovers of a meal that Aditi cooked for the *sādhya* gods. Then, Aditi cooked a second mess and decided to eat first, thinking she would have a stronger son, but she miscarried. She only succeeded with the third meal and Vivasvant, the sun, was born as her last and most powerful son.

These stories tend to show that Sun, the *āditya* who has the most problematic relationship with human beings (he can burn all beings, yet he is a condition for all life), is also given an unusual birth (unformed embryo, abortion or miscarriage). It seems probable, as Preciado-Solis has rightly observed, that Kṛṣṇa's birth was modeled upon such old stories, especially since, in the *Taittirīya Saṃhitā* version, the first four sons are followed by a fifth one who aborted and a sixth one who survived (see accompanying table).

20. Wilhelm Rau's translation of *Maitrāyaṇī Saṃhitā* 1.6.12 in "Twenty Indra Legends," in *German Scholars on India*, Vol. 1 (Delhi: Cultural Department of the Embassy of FRG, 1973), 202, quoted by Preciado-Solis, *The Kṛṣṇa Cycle in the Purāṇas*, 62.

21. *Taittirīya Saṃhitā* 6.5.6 (*The Veda of the Black Yajus School entitled Taittirīya Sanhitā*, 2 vols. [Delhi: Motilal Banarsidass, 1967]), 541–42.

Narrative Parallels to the *Harivaṃśa* Version of the Story of Saṃkarṣaṇa's and Kṛṣṇa's Births: A Synoptic Table

Śatapatha-Brāhmaṇa 3.1.3-4	7 first sons;	the 8th son, unformed, reshaped into Vivasvant (the sun).
Maitrāyaṇī Saṃhitā 1.6.12	6 first sons (the 5th and 6th were punished, because they helped with the abortion of the 7th and 8th sons);	the 7th and 8th sons aborted; the 7th became Indra who rose up due to his own energy; the 8th is Mārtāṇḍa (the sun), who fell down dead before being called back to life.
Taittirīya Saṃhitā 6.5.6	4 first sons;	the 5th son aborted; the 6th son = Vivasvant (the sun).
Mahābhārata 1.91-93	7 first sons drowned;	the 8th son = Bhīṣma, who is forced to renounce all sexual activity.
Mahābhārata 1.13 sq.	1,000 first sons to be born from Kadru, and who are later condemned to perish;	the 1st son to be born half-formed from Vinatā = Aruṇa (the sun's charioteer); the 2nd son to be born from Vinatā, whose excessive fire has to be withdrawn = Garuḍa (Viṣṇu's mount).
Harivaṃśa 41-48	The 6 fetuses (Ṣaḍgarbhāḥ), transferred from the Pātāla to be born from Devakī's womb and killed by Kaṃsa;	the 7th son miscarried from Devakī and transferred into Rohiṇī's womb = Saṃkarṣaṇa; the 8th son from Devakī, whose brightness must be reduced, carried to the cow-settlement and exchanged with Yaśodā's baby = Kṛṣṇa.

Preciado-Solis quotes another story, drawn from the *Mahābhārata,* which has a structure similar to that of Kṛṣṇa's birth. The gods involved are not the *ādityas*, but the *vasus*, and the story appears in the first book (chaps. 91–93) as an explanation of the birth of Bhīṣma. Cursed by Brahmā for having looked at Gaṅgā's naked body, King Mahābhiṣa was condemned to be born upon the earth as Śāntanu and to have the same Gaṅgā for his wife. At about the same time, the *vasus* were also condemned to be reborn in a human womb. As soon as they are born, they are to be thrown into the waters. In fact, seven of them were born from Gaṅgā and drawn, while the eighth son became the famous Bhīṣma. Not only are a series of embryos killed as if in preparation for the birth of the eighth, but the embryos have to pass through the waters, in the same way as did the Ṣaḍgarbhāḥ before Kṛṣṇa's birth. In Bhīṣma's birth story, no seventh child similar to Saṃkarṣaṇa appears, but curiously enough, the eighth son renounces all sexual activity, a sort of voluntary castration that fits the pattern observed in the stories quoted earlier.

I cannot close this section without considering the version of the story of Garuḍa's birth that also occurs in the *Ādiparvan* (bk. I of the *Mahābhārata*, chaps. 13–53) and which shares a very similar structure to the story under study here. Kaśyapa granted a wish to each of his spouses, Kadru and Vinatā. Kadru chose to have a thousand snakes, whereas Vinatā preferred two vigorous sons. After a pregnancy of five hundred years, the former became the mother of a multitude of snakes. Eager to see her children, Vinatā broke the first egg and saw a half-formed son ("the upper half of his body was fully grown, the other half stunted"[22]) who, at once, cursed his mother, condemning her to become her co-wife's slave for five hundred years. One day, Kadru entered into a discussion with Vinatā, of whom she was jealous, about the color of Uccaiḥśravas, the horse of the sun. According to Vinatā, the horse was entirely white, whereas Kadru said its tail was black. They made a bet, and they stipulated that the loser would become the other's slave. All save one of the serpents refused to help their mother and were condemned to perish later in Janamejaya's sacrifice. One of Kadru's sons, however, was willing to disguise himself as jet black horse hairs and hung himself from Uccaiḥśravas's tail. The next morning, when both women saw the horse, Vinatā had to admit that the horse's tail was black and accordingly she agreed to subjugate herself to Kadru. When his time had come, the second of Vinatā's sons broke the shell of his egg, became gigantic in size and began to blaze monstrously. Garuḍa was born like a bird with the brightness of Fire (*agni*). As soon as he receives praise from the gods, he agrees to "withdraw" his burning rays (*Mahābhārata* 1.20.15). Garuḍa places Vinatā's half-formed son in front of the sun so that he can block its rays and prevent all beings from being scorched. Thus Vinatā's first son came to be known as Aruṇa, the sun's charioteer.

Even if, in this story, Kaśyapa's descent comes from two different wives, their sons, egg-hatched snakes and birds, can be placed on the following continuum: a multitude of snakes destined to be destroyed, the half-formed Aruṇa to whom an important cosmic function is given, and the over-blazing Garuḍa whose flames have to be withdrawn before becoming Viṣṇu's mount. As shown in the table, in spite of many differences, the story of Kṛṣṇa's birth shares an identical narrative device concerning the last son with all these stories. The device serves to explain the birth of an excessively powerful being (the sun, the terrible Bhīṣma, the eagle Garuḍa, or the great Kṛṣṇa), whose strength has to be curtailed so that it might be tolerated inside the world. The penultimate son often receives the opposite treatment, since he is miscarried and continues his growth in some other way. There is another difference between the epic cases and those mentioned in the ritual texts referred to. In these older texts, the first sons to be born from Aditi are gods who keep on existing after the birth of Aditi's last son. In contrast to the *Mahābhārata* and the *Harivaṃśa*, here the first sons perish, whereas the seventh son, in Garuḍa's birth story, protects living beings from the deadly sun and, in the narrative of Kṛṣṇa's birth, becomes the strange Saṃkarṣaṇa, the incarnation of Snake Śeṣa, who acts as Kṛṣṇa's elder brother.

The Place of Śeṣa-Saṃkarṣaṇa in the Story of Kṛṣṇa's Birth

The most original item inside the story of Kṛṣṇa's birth must surely be the presence of a character named Saṃkarṣaṇa, the incarnation of Snake Śeṣa or "Rest." His

22. *Mahābhārata* 1.14.16 (*Mahābhārata I. The Book of the Beginning*, trans. and ed. J. A. B. van Buitenen [Chicago: University of Chicago Press, 1973], 72).

very existence challenges the goddess Nidrā's ingenuity. Unless explicitly stated,[23] Saṃkarṣaṇa (also called Balarāma, Rāma, Bala, etc.) always accompanies Kṛṣṇa. During Kṛṣṇa's childhood, Saṃkarṣaṇa has no independent existence; he rather duplicates Kṛṣṇa, and the narrator Vaiśaṃpāyana does not hesitate to say that Saṃkarṣaṇa and Kṛṣṇa form a unique body that has been duplicated (56.26).

The summary of the story that I presented at the beginning of this chapter reflects the sort of hesitation witnessed in the way the *Harivaṃśa* speaks of Saṃkarṣaṇa. The Ṣaḍgarbhāḥ, having accepted Brahmā's favor, form a distinct group of former enemies of the gods. As they were lying together in the *pātāla*, Viṣṇu went down there to fetch them. Nevertheless, Vaiśaṃpāyana says that Devakī gave birth to seven embryos (48.1). Once liberated from her seventh fetus, Devakī is said to have conceived the child which motivated Kaṃsa to kill her first seven children (48.8). Śeṣa-Saṃkarṣaṇa is counted among the first seven, but has also a specific destiny. Thanks to the goddess, he will be extracted from Devakī's womb at the seventh month and will continue his growth one more month in Rohiṇī's womb, a spouse of Vasudeva dwelling in Nandagopa's cow-settlement. From then on, Saṃkarṣaṇa is known as Kṛṣṇa's elder brother, also called Rauhiṇeya, Rohiṇī's son (49.3,7; 54.21; 56.29; 57.10; etc.); he and Kṛṣṇa form such a close-knit unit (*atiprasaktau*, 51.12) that Nandagopa wonders about their relationship. Later, during his ablutions in the waters of the Yamunā, the sage Akrūra sees Snake Śeṣa along with Viṣṇu, and realizes that both brothers are Śeṣa's and Viṣṇu's incarnations (70.15–38).

Snake Śeṣa is said to support the earth upon his head (*Mahābhārata* 1.32.13–25). He is also the one who, at the end of a cosmic era (*kalpa*), draws all beings together (*saṃkarṣayasi bhūtāni*).[24] This cosmic explanation of Saṃkarṣaṇa's name concurs with the etymology unanimously given by the stories of the childhood. Saṃkarṣaṇa received his strange name because Devakī's seventh embryo was drawn from or ripped from (*saṃkarṣaṇa* or *karṣaṇa*) her womb before being inserted into Rohiṇī's womb, whose own baby is said to have "fallen" (*patati*). The *Viṣṇupurāṇa* is explicit: "At the end of the *kalpa*, Rudra, who is identical with Saṃkarṣaṇa, blazing with flames of venomous fire, proceeds from the mouths of this [snake] and devours the three worlds."[25] Located under the earth and supporting her, this celebrated snake completes Viṣṇu's work. At the end of the *kalpa*, he takes on a terrible form and sets the worlds ablaze, destroying them completely aside from a remnant that is also represented as Snake Śeṣa, who serves as the couch on which Viṣṇu-Nārāyaṇa sleeps during the cosmic night and symbolizes the material side of existence (*prakṛi*).

From what we have just seen, Saṃkarṣaṇa, who appears to be famous because of his physical strength (*bala*), is also related to the violence associated with final destruction. Very nearly killed by the goddess who tore him from his mother's womb, Devakī's seventh embryo is quickly picked up, transferred to another womb

23. See Kāliya's story, *Harivaṃśa* 55.1; his absence during the *Mahābhārata* war.

24. *Matsyapurāṇa* 248.46–47 (Ānandāśrama Sanskrit Series 54, Poona, India, 1909).

25. *kalpānte yasya vaktrebhyo viṣānalaśikhojjvalaḥ / saṃkarṣaṇātmako rudro niṣkramyātti jagattrayam // Viṣṇupurāṇa* 2.5.19 (my translation).

and thus saved by the goddess. One does not need an in-depth knowledge of the *Purāṇas* to understand that Saṃkarṣaṇa follows precisely the same trajectory as Snake Śeṣa, of whom he is said to be the incarnation. The sequence of episodes found in the story of Kṛṣṇa's birth—the destruction of the living beings (the Ṣaḍgarbhāḥ killed by Kaṃsa), a remnant saved (Śeṣa-Saṃkarṣaṇa) and the appearance of an all-encompassing deity (Viṣṇu-Nārāyaṇa-Kṛṣṇa)—is the typical pattern of the mythology of the cosmic dissolution (*pralaya*). There is no new creation (*pratisarga*) without a purification and its attendant destruction. The cosmic renewal is the raison d'être of the dissolution of *pralaya*, as well as the ultimate aim of the appearance of Kṛṣṇa in the human world. The likeliest conclusion to be drawn from this strange "coincidence" is that this piece of mythology involving fetuses forms a mythic prehistory to Viṣṇu's manifestation as Kṛṣṇa. The *puruṣottama* Viṣṇu comes upon the earth to inaugurate a new way of life and cannot perform such a task without a rehearsal of the *pralaya*. As the Puruṣottama's elder brother, Saṃkarṣaṇa summarizes the violence supposed by the destruction of an outdated world and its reduction to a remnant (*śeṣa*), which symbolizes the inescapable support of the *prakṛti* or the material world. Since the cosmic evolution described in the *Purāṇas* cannot be carried out without the active presence of the great goddess, accordingly Viṣṇu could not appear in the world to confuse the enemies of dharma without the unfailing collaboration of the goddess Nidrā or Yoganidrā. After having killed the *asura* Kālanemi, Viṣṇu is said to have retreated to his celestial hermitage and lay down on a couch served by Nidrā, "a goddess born from his own body, one who obeys his commands."[26] Presented as the overarching *māyā* who is able to confound the world (*mohayañ jagad, Harivaṃśa* 40.34), Nidrā also points to the cosmic significance of this entire set of episodes.

The Story of Saṃkarṣaṇa's and Kṛṣṇa's Births and the Myths of the Sun's and Moon's Births

A good test for the relevance of the analysis proposed here would be to assess its contribution, if any, to enabling a lucid interpretation of a difficult text such as the *Harivaṃśa*. Since establishing continuity between the sections of the text dealing with the solar and lunar lineages, on the one hand, and Kṛṣṇa's biography, on the other, constitutes one of the main difficulties encountered by the interpreters of this text, I would now like to suggest that the close reading we propose uncovers a link between Saṃkarṣaṇa's and Kṛṣṇa's birth and two of the most important birth stories related in the earlier section, thus confirming the unity of a large part of the book.

In fact, after a survey of the creation by Brahmā, the *Harivaṃśa* describes the solar lineage in which the story of Vivasvant's (i.e., the sun's) birth occurs (*Harivaṃśa* 8) and the lunar lineage beginning with the story of Soma's (the

26. *viṣṇuśarīrajāṃ nirdeśakāriṇīm, Harivaṃśa* 48.10 (my translation).

moon's) birth (*Harivaṃśa* 20). The great progenitor Kaśyapa generated Vivasvant, who at his birth was dark (*śyāmavarṇa* 8.8). Actually, his own heat had completely burned his limbs off (8.3). Ignoring what had happened and wondering whether his son was not dead in the shell, his father called him Mārtaṇḍa. He finally married him to Saṃjñā, Tvaṣṭṛ's daughter, who could not stand an energy whose blaze was enough to consume the three worlds. She emitted a shadow of herself called Suvarṇā and ran to her father's house. This situation provoked a series of curses. In the end, Tvaṣṭṛ, resorting to a skillful means (*yoga*, 8.32), placed Vivasvant on a potter's wheel (*bhramin*) and cut off his over-blazing, so that he became pleasing to look at. Mārtaṇḍa's birth deals with the powerful *yoga* discovered by Tvaṣṭṛ to hide Vivasvant's excessive heat and makes it more friendly, exactly like several of the stories studied earlier.

The second story relates the birth of the moon and implies that a miscarriage took place. As such, it seems first attested to in the *Harivaṃśa*. The *ṛṣi* Atri generated a wonderful being who, as soon as he was born, reached the sky, illuminating the quadrants in ten different ways. Together, these ten goddesses carried the embryo for a time, but, unable to bear it, they miscarried (or "the embryo fell on the ground"). Brahmā placed him on his car and drove around the world. When praised by all the *ṛṣis*, Soma's energy increased and caused the growth of the three worlds. Flowing down on the earth, this energy became the plants. Soma was called the one who nourishes the world (*poṣṭā jagataḥ*, 20.16), and was made the king of seeds, plants, Brahmins, and waters (20.21; cf. 4.2, which adds constellations and planets, sacrifices and ascetic practices). Soma's birth is just the opposite of Vivasvant's birth. Whereas the latter implies a reduction of power, the former requires more power in order to fully exist. Soma's embryo miscarried, was taken into Brahmā's chariot, and developed under the praises of the sages. He was finally anointed king of all those temporal realities that wax and wane with the flux of time.

Tradition regularly speaks of Saṃkarṣaṇa as being as white as the rays of the moon and of Kṛṣṇa's complexion as being as black as the monsoon clouds. It is interesting to note that the black color in question here is also the color of the blazing sun. The child Kṛṣṇa can be terrible. When he was seven, packs of black wolves ran out from the hair of his body and destroyed the cows and their herders. The comparison of both Saṃkarṣaṇa and Kṛṣṇa with the sun and moon is not just one detail among others. It is embedded in the text itself and may well be of greater significance than is generally realized. Hidden in the forest, dwelling in a cow-settlement (*vraja*), the close relationship between the brothers is compared to that of the sun and the moon. "These two children were always one with the other. Since their childhood they were one and the same. They had the same form [according to the vulgate of the text]. They were beautiful and had the brilliance of the young moon and sun [*bālacandrārkavarcasau*]" (51.2). Also: "They were embellishing the cow-settlement with games that joined them one to the other like the sun and moon in the sky who swallow one another's rays [*anyonyakiraṇagrastau candrasūryāv ivāmbare*]" (51.6). When he saw these two extraordinarily wise boys, *guru* Sāṃdīpani imagined that the deities who had approached him were actually the moon and sun (*mene tāv āgatau devāv ubhau candradivākarau*, 79.7). After their initiation, the children returned to their father's house where once again they are compared to the sun and moon entering the [cave of] Mount [Meru] (*praviṣṭau . . . candrādityāv ivācalam*, 79.38).

Of course, I am not suggesting here that Soma manifested himself as Saṃkarṣaṇa, and Sūrya as Kṛṣṇa, which is clearly not the case (cf. *Harivaṃśa* 44.2,4). In the *Mahābhārata,* Karṇa is explicitly said to be the incarnation of Sūrya, and Abhimanyu the incarnation of Soma. Nevertheless, it seems that the *Harivaṃśa* uses the motif of a meeting between the sun and the moon which occurs during the period of a new moon (*amāvāsyā rātri*) as an aid in understanding the strange cohabitation of Saṃkarṣaṇa and Kṛṣṇa in the forest surrounding Mathurā. The easiest way to illustrate the simultaneous manifestation of Puruṣa Viṣṇu and the snake symbolizing the world of *saṃsāra* seems to use this astronomic code. The name of the goddess whose presence was necessary throughout the birth story adds further credence to this assumption. In fact, the name Ekānaṃśā has a strange ring to it. The best explanation of its meaning is still that it is the name of the new moon, a time during which both sun and moon are supposed to meet. "When looking for this goddess people ask 'where, where is she?,' whom they call Ekānaṃśā, 'the [only] One [night of the month] who is not provided with any portion [of the moon]'—Kuhū, the daughter of Aṅgiras."[27] Since the birth of the goddess Ekānaṃśā happens exactly at the same time as Kṛṣṇa's birth, and since the association of Kṛṣṇa with Saṃkarṣaṇa immediately follows, one may safely conclude that these similes fit together perfectly as they evoke the union of Puruṣa and Prakṛti, the Spiritual and the Material Principle.

Conclusion

This chapter has tried to show that, in the story of Kṛṣṇa's birth, no detail is arbitrary. If the presence of a seventh child named Saṃkarṣaṇa, the incarnation of Snake Śeṣa, is taken seriously, one is led to conclude that the sequence of the eight babies of Devakī was modeled on similar stories found in older Brahmanic texts and that it reproduces exactly those events associated with cosmic dissolution. The whole world was destroyed, reduced to the state of a remnant and united to the great Viṣṇu-Nārāyaṇa. The close relationship of Kṛṣṇa with Saṃkarṣaṇa means that Kṛṣṇa's presence on the earth goes hand in hand with a renewed relationship between the spiritual self and the material world. As the incarnation of Śeṣa, Saṃkarṣaṇa symbolizes a world that has been purified by the fire of asceticism, exactly as it is explained to Arjuna by the Kṛṣṇa of the Bhagavadgītā. It can be added that such a sequence of episodes is not isolated in the story of Kṛṣṇa's childhood. In addition to the birth story that could be interpreted as a sort of *dīkṣā*, the whole period of childhood is explicitly said to be a *mānuṣī dīkṣā*, a true initiation to Kṛṣṇa's life as a warrior (*kṣatriya*). After a period of seven years in a first forest, the cow-settlement (*vraja*) where his father Vasudeva brought him, packs of wolves

27. *yāṃ tu dṛṣṭvā bhagavatīṃ janaḥ kuhukuhāyate / ekānaṃśeti yām āhuḥ kuhūm aṅgirasaḥ sutām / Mahābhārata* 3.208.8. For this translation, see G. von Simson, "Sinīvālī und das aschgraue Mondlicht," *Acta Orientalia* 63 (2002): 63.

sprang from Kṛṣṇa's body, destroying all the cows and their herders. The herders decided to move to another marvelous forest called the Vṛndāvana where both brothers probably spent a couple of years (although the period remains indeterminate). Things occur as if this period were, in fact, a duplication of the fetal period, both sequences preparing the renewal of the world inaugurated by the presence of Kṛṣṇa. The comparison of the years of childhood with the months of gestation would certainly contribute to a better understanding of Kṛṣṇa's story, but that is a topic for another work.

WORKS CITED

Bhāgavata Purāṇa. Śrīmad Bhāgavatamahāpurāṇa, with Sanskrit text and English translation, parts 1 and 2. Gorakhpur, India: Gita Press, 1971.

Brahma Purāṇa. The Brahmamahāpurāṇam. Delhi: Nag Publishers, 1985.

Couture, André. *L'enfance de Krishna.* Traduction des chapitres 30 à 78 du *Harivamsha* (critical ed.). Paris: Les Éditions du Cerf, 1991; Québec: Les Presses de l'Université Laval, 1991.

Hara, Minoru. "A Note on the Buddha's Birth Story." In *Indianisme et bouddhisme: Mélanges offerts à Mgr. Étienne Lamotte*, 143–57. Louvain, Belgium: Université Catholique de Louvain, 1980.

The Harivaṃśa, Being the Khila or Supplement to the Mahābhārata. Critically edited by P. L. Vaidya. Vol. 1: *Introduction, Critical Text, and Notes*; Vol. 2: *Appendices*. Poona, India: Bhandarkar Oriental Research Institute, 1969 and 1971.

Harivaṃśa-parvan (Vulgate). Vol. 7 of *The Mahābhāratam.* Edited by Pandit Ramchandrashastri Kinjewadekar, with Nīlakaṇṭha's commentary *Bhāratabhāvadīpa*. Poona, India: Chitrashala Press, 1936.

Kapani, Lakshmi. *La notion de saṃskāra*, tome I. Paris: De Boccard, 1992.

The Mahābhārata. Critically edited by V. S. Sukthankar and S. K. Belvalkar. 19 vols. Poona, India: Bhandarkar Oriental Research Institute, 1933–1966.

The Mahābhārata I. The Book of the Beginning. Translated and edited by J. A. B. van Buitenen. Chicago: University of Chicago Press, 1973.

Matsyapurāṇa. Ānandāśrama Sanskrit Series 54. Poona, India, 1909.

Preciado-Solis, Benjamin. *The Kṛṣṇa Cycle in the Purāṇas.* Delhi: Motilal Banarsidass, 1984.

Rau, Wilhelm. "Twenty Indra Legends." In *German Scholars on India*, Vol. 1, 199–223. Delhi: Cultural Department of the Embassy of FRG, 1973.

The Rig Veda. An Anthology. One Hundred and Eight Hymns Selected, Translated, and Annotated by Wendy Doniger O'Flaherty. Delhi: Penguin Books India, 1981.

Ruben, W. *Krishṇa: Konkordanz und Kommentar der Motive seines Heldenlebens.* Istanbul: n.p., 1944.

The Śatapatha-Brāhmaṇa, according to the text of the Mādhyandina School. Translated by J. Eggeling. 5 vols. Delhi: Motilal Banarsidass, 1972.

Simson, Georg von. "Sinīvālī und das aschgraue Mondlicht," *Acta Orientalia* 63 (2002): 53–66.

Smith, Brian K. *Reflections on Resemblance, Ritual, and Religion.* Delhi: Motilal Banarsidass, 1998.

Taittirīya Saṃhitā. The Veda of the Black Yajus School entitled Taittirīya Sanhitā. 2 vols. Delhi: Motilal Banarsidass, 1967.

Thite, Ganesh Umakant. *Sacrifice in the Brāhmaṇa-Texts.* Poona, India: Poona University Press, 1975.

Upaniṣads. Translated by Patrick Olivelle. Oxford: Oxford University Press, 1996.
Varenne, Jean. *Cosmogonies védiques*. Paris: Les Belles Lettres, 1982.
The Viṣṇu Purāṇa. Sanskrit text and English translation by H. H. Wilson. Delhi: Nag Publishers, 1989.
Viṣṇu Purāṇa. The Critical Edition of the Viṣṇu Purāṇam. 2 vols. Critically edited by Dr. M. M. Pathak. Vadodara, India: Oriental Institute, 1997 and 1999.

The Great Men of Jainism In Utero: A Survey

Eva De Clercq

Chapters of several other contributors to this volume attest to the notion in many South Asian religious traditions that the fetus is to be considered as an entity.[1] In the cycle of *saṃsāra*, "transmigration," a soul enters a new body through the workings of karmic bondage upon conception rather than birth.[2] This principle is also current in Jainism, the religion of the Jina, a "victor" who has defeated the cycle of *saṃsāra* and attained *mokṣa*, "final liberation." According to Jainism, twenty-four Jinas are born consecutively in every time period, to act as a kind of prophet who rediscovers and revives the eternal wisdom, the dharma, at a time when it has been forgotten and spreads it among the people. The Jinas are also known as the Tīrthaṅkaras, the "ford-makers," they who have created a ford through the ocean of *saṃsāra*, revealing the path to *mokṣa*. The last of these Jinas was Mahāvīra, a contemporary of the Buddha. Mahāvīra's predecessor, Pārśva, was also a historical figure who probably lived two centuries earlier, but the previous twenty-two Jinas are most likely mythological. Like the Buddhists, the Jainas refute the authority of the Vedas and reject the superiority of the Brahmin caste. They oppose Vedic ritual and do not believe in an immortal, superior god. Central to Jainism is the principle of *ahiṃsā*, nonviolence, manifested in strict measures to avoid harm to other life forms and extreme ascetic practice. In the centuries after Mahāvīra, the Jaina community became divided into two larger traditions: the Śvetāmbaras, the "white-clad," whose ascetics wear

1. See the chapters by André Couture, Vanessa Sasson, Robert Kritzer, Frances Garrett, and Justin McDaniel.

2. For different accounts of the transmigration of souls in South Asian traditions, see Wendy Doniger O'Flaherty, ed., *Karma and Rebirth in Classical Indian Traditions* (Berkeley: University of California Press, 1980).

a white cotton garment, and the Digambaras, the "sky-clad," whose ascetics are nude. This schism prevails to this day.[3]

Narratives concerning fetuses are found in the Jaina hagiographies of the Mahā-puruṣas or Śalākā-puruṣas, "great heroes." These mostly mythological heroes, generally sixty-three in number, consist of the twenty-four Tīrthaṅkaras, twelve Cakravartins, and nine triads of a Baladeva, Vāsudeva, and Prativāsudeva. The twelve Cakravartins are "universal monarchs," destined to become the rulers over the entire civilized world. Of the triads, the Baladeva and Vāsudeva are half-brothers, and the Prativāsudeva is their archenemy. Into these categories the well-known Indian heroes Rāma and Lakṣmaṇa of the popular Indian epic *Rāmāyaṇa* have been integrated as the eighth Baladeva and Vāsudeva. Another epic character, Kṛṣṇa, who has become the most famous manifestation of the Hindu god Viṣṇu, his brother Balarāma, and their enemy Jarāsandha form the ninth triad in these categories. The life stories of these Jaina heroes are typically the subject of the Jaina literary categories of Caritras or Purāṇas, yet the earlier texts of the Śvetāmbara canon already contain accounts of some of them.[4] It is thought these works were composed to offer an alternative for the world history of the Hindus as described in their epics and Purāṇas. The clearest indication of this is, of course, the Jaina adaptation of Rāma and Kṛṣṇa, the most popular of the epic and purāṇic heroes.[5] Jainas were prolific composers of Purāṇas, and a list of all the known Jaina Purāṇas would total several hundred.[6] The contents of the biographies differ slightly between the two Jaina sects, the Digambaras and Śvetāmbaras.

In this chapter, I examine and compare the intrauterine accounts of these sixty-three heroes in the two traditions. Given the relative similarity between Jainism and (early) Buddhism and the comparable status of a Buddha and a Jina, I will discuss, when appropriate, the resemblances and differences between the Jaina accounts and that of the Buddha. Parallels in Hindu literature will also be referred to.[7] For this study, I have selected two complete biographies of all the sixty-three Mahā-puruṣas, one for each sect. The oldest work, dating from the ninth century, is the *Mahā-purāṇa*, consisting of two parts: the *Ādi-purāṇa* of Jinasena, narrating the stories of the first Tīrthaṅkara, Ṛṣabha, and his son, Bharata, the first Cakravartin, and the *Uttara-purāṇa* of Jinasena's pupil Guṇabhadra, which gives the accounts of the remaining sixty-one characters. Jinasena and Guṇabhadra represent the Digambara tradition. The second text is the *Triṣaṣṭi-śalākā-puruṣa-caritra* by the

3. For more information on Jainism, see W. Schubring, *The Doctrine of the Jainas,* Lala Sundarlal Jain Research Series 15, trans. W. Beurlen (Delhi: Motilal Banarsidass, 2000); H. Glasenapp, *Jainism: An Indian Religion of Salvation,* trans. S. B. Shrotri (Delhi: Motilal Banarsidass, 1999); P. Dundas, *The Jains* (London: Routledge, 1992); P. S. Jaini, *The Jaina Path of Purification* (Delhi: Motilal Banarsidass, 1998).

4. Biographies of some of the Jinas are already found in the *Kalpa Sūtra,* and Kṛṣṇa occurs in the *Antagaḍadasāo.* See J. Cort, "An Overview of the Jaina Purāṇas," in *Purāṇa Perennis—Reciprocity and Transformation in Hindu and Jaina Texts,* ed. W. Doniger (Albany: State University of New York Press, 1993), 185–206, esp. 188–91.

5. P. S. Jaini, "Jaina Purāṇas: A Purāṇic Counter Tradition," in *Purāṇa Perennis—Reciprocity and Transformation in Hindu and Jaina Texts,* ed. W. Doniger (Albany: State University of New York Press, 1993), 207–49, esp. 207.

6. Cort, "An Overview," 185.

7. For the Buddhist material, my primary sources are Sasson's chapter in this volume and her book *The Birth of Moses and the Buddha: A Paradigm for the Comparative Study of Religions* (Sheffield, England: Sheffield Phoenix Press, 2007).

List of the Sixty-three Mahà-puruṣas

Tīrthaṅkara	*Cakravartin*	*Baladeva*	*Vāsudeva*	*Prativāsudeva*
Ṛṣabha	Bharata			
Ajita	Sagara			
Sambhava				
Abhinandana				
Sumati				
Padmaprabha				
Supārśva				
Candraprabha				
Suvidhi (Puṣpadanta)				
Śītala				
Śreyāṃsa		+Acala/*Vijaya	Tripṛṣṭha	Aśvagrīva
Vāsupūjya		+Vijaya/*Acala	Dvipṛṣṭha	Tāraka
Vimala		+Bhadra/*Dharma	Svayambhū	+Meraka/*Madhu
Ananta		Suprabha	Puruṣottama	+Madhu/ *Madhusūdana
Dharma	Maghavan	Sudarśana	Puruṣasiṃha	+Niśumbha/ *Madhukrīḍa
	Sanatkumāra			
Śānti	Śānti			
Kunthu	Kunthu			
Ara	Ara	+Ānanda/ *Nandiṣeṇa	+Puruṣapuṇḍarīka/ *Puṇḍarīka	+Bali/*Niśumbha
	+Subhūma/ *Subhauma	+Nandana	+Datta	+Prahlāda
Malli	*Padma	*Nandimitra	*Datta	*Balīndra
Munisuvrata	+Mahāpadma	Padma (Rāma)	Lakṣmaṇa	Rāvaṇa
	*Hariṣeṇa			
Nami	+Hariṣeṇa			
	Jayasena			
Nemi	Brahmadatta	Balarāma	Kṛṣṇa	Jarāsandha
Pārśva				
Mahāvīra				

Śvetāmbara, Hemacandra, dating from the twelfth century. The *Triṣaṣṭi-śalākā-puruṣa-caritra* was translated into English in its entirety by Helen M. Johnson between 1931 and 1962.[8]

To help the reader, I have listed the names of these heroes according to the two texts in the accompanying table. In cases where the accounts differ, the variants of Hemacandra are indicated with a plus sign (+), those of Jinasena or Guṇabhadra with an asterisk (*). In the vertical rows, the names of the different heroes are given chronologically, beginning with the earliest. The five horizontal columns

8. Johnson's translation is commonly employed as the basic source for Hemacandra's biographies of the Śalākā-puruṣas. Therefore I have made use of her translation, in addition to the original Sanskrit edition. The translation of the Sanskrit from the Digambara version is my own.

separate the different categories of heroes. Some vertical rows contain more than one name, indicating that these heroes, albeit of different categories, lived around the same time.

The Tīrthaṅkaras

The First Tīrthaṅkara, Ṛṣabha, the "Bull"

Because he is the first Tīrthaṅkara of our era, both authors accord considerable space to the biography of Ṛṣabha. Hemacandra devotes some fifty verses to the description of his conception, gestation, and birth. At the appropriate time, Ṛṣabha's soul descended from Sarvārthasiddhi, the highest heaven, immediately below the Siddha-loka, the abode of the liberated souls. We have here a noteworthy difference with the Buddhist accounts which state explicitly that every Bodhisattva must spend his penultimate existence in Tuṣita heaven, and not the highest heaven, a somewhat puzzling issue in the hagiographies of the Buddha.[9]

Ṛṣabha's soul entered the womb of Marudevī, the wife of Nābhi. Nābhi was the seventh Kulakara, "patriarch" of our era, a progenitor of the human race, comparable to the Manus of Hinduism. At the moment of his descent in Marudevī's womb "there was happiness for all creatures in the three worlds from the destruction of pain, and also a great light."[10] The manifestation of light at the time of conception and during gestation is very central in the prenatal account of the Buddha. Although it recurs regularly in the descriptions of other Jaina heroes in the selected texts, the theme of light is more developed in Buddhist narratives. Moreover, it appears to be a common element in many biographies of heroes.[11]

That night, Marudevī has a dream in which fourteen objects enter her mouth: (1) a white bull, (2) a four-tusked white elephant, (3) a lion, (4) the goddess Śrī, (5) a flower garland, (6) the moon, (7) the sun, (8) a banner, (9) a water pitcher, (10) a lotus pond, (11) an ocean of milk, (12) a *vimāna*, a heavenly abode, (13) a heap of jewels, and (14) a smokeless fire. At dawn, the queen narrates the dreams to Nābhi, who mistakenly interprets them as a prediction that their son will be the next Kulakara. Distraught by this faulty interpretation, the Indras, the leaders of the gods from the different heavens, come to Marudevī and explain the objects of which she dreamed one by one as indications that her son will be not only an extraordinary, powerful, heroic ruler, but also the reviver of the true dharma, the "faith," showing the way to salvation:

> O Mistress, from the sight of the bull in your dream—a son will be to you, able to lift up the chariot of dharma sunk in the mud of delusion. From the sight of the elephant, O Lady—your son will be the greatest of the great, and the sole abode of great power. From the sight of the lion—your

9. For a discussion on this subject, see Sasson, *Birth of Moses*, 92–93. Note that although the Buddha has to spend his penultimate life in Tuṣita, the heavens where the future Jinas reside prior to their final birth differ.

10. H. Johnson, *Triṣaṣṭiśalākāpuruṣacaritra*, Vol. 1: 100 (Baroda, India: Oriental Institute, 1931–62).

11. Sasson, *Birth of Moses*, 122–23, 127, and 161–63. See also Sasson's chapter in this volume.

> son will be a lion among men, resolute, always fearless, a hero with unflinching valor. From the fact that Śrī was seen, O Lady, is indicated that your son, the best of men, will be the Lord of the Śrī (Glory) of the sovereignty of the three worlds. From the sight of a wreath in a dream—the sight of your son will be auspicious, his rule worn on the head like a wreath by all the world. O Mother of the World, that a full moon was seen in your sleep means that your son will be pleasing, a joy to the eye. That you saw a sun means that your son will be the creator of the light of the world by destroying the darkness of delusion. That you saw a great banner in a dream, O Lady, that means that your son will be a dharma-banner, the founder of a great line. That you saw a pitcher full of water means that your son will be a vessel filled with all the supernatural powers (atiśayas). That you saw a lotus-pond, Mistress, means that your son will take away the pain of those who have fallen into the desert of saṃsāra. That your Ladyship saw an ocean means that your son will be inaccessible and accessible. That you saw a heavenly palace, a marvel to the earth, O Lady, means that your son will be worshipped even by Vaimānika gods. That you saw a heap of jewels with flashing light means that your son will be a heap of jewels of all the virtues. That you saw a flaming fire enter your mouth means that your son will absorb the dignity of other dignitaries. O Mistress, it is indicated by these fourteen dreams that your son will be Master in the world extending for fourteen rajjus.[12]

Several of the objects dreamed of by Marudevī are well known as omina predicting good luck. The *Agni Purāṇa*, an encyclopedic Hindu Purāṇa, describes a dream of an elephant, a bull, and gold as prophesying good fortune. It further mentions an elephant, full water pitchers, jewels, fire, and an image of a god among the items a prosperous king should preferably see upon returning from a journey.[13] Jainas seem to have a thorough tradition of divination in which dreams frequently occur as auspices. Dream science is elaborated on in the canonical texts and in Jaina epic and narrative literature descriptions and references abound.[14]

The white elephant entering the mother is well known from the fetal narrative of the Buddha. Though the Jaina accounts describe the dreams by summing up rather static images, in the Buddhist sources Māyā's pregnancy dream contains more action and flow: Māyā is taken to a lake where she is bathed, clothed, perfumed, and adorned and then laid down to sleep in a golden fairy palace near a mountain. The Bodhisattva, in the shape of a white elephant, arrives there, enters the palace and splits open her side, as if entering her womb. This elephant is in some texts described as having six tusks.[15] Bollée suggests these six tusks are "probably an

12. Johnson, *Triṣaṣṭiśalākāpuruṣacaritra*, Vol. 1: 102–103.

13. M. N. D. Shastrī, *Agni Purāṇa, A Prose English Translation*, Vol. 2: 823–25, Chowkhamba Sanskrit Studies 54 (Varanasi, India: Chowkhamba Sanskrit Series Office, 1967).

14. Glasenapp, *Jainism*, 449–50; Schubring, *Doctrine of the Jainas*, 25–26. For various accounts of dreams in Indian culture, see C. Bautze-Picron, ed., *The Indian Night, Sleep and Dream in India Culture* (New Delhi: Rupa, forthcoming).

15. Sasson, *Birth of Moses*, 113–14.

intended advantage" over Indra's four-tusked elephant Airāvata.[16] In the accounts of the selected Jaina texts the elephant in the dream is usually explicitly described as Indra's four-tusked mount, Airāvata himself. If we follow through Bollée's logic, this six-tusked elephant of the Buddhist accounts can be seen not only as a claim to the Bodhisattva's superiority over Indra, but over the Jina as well.

Another significant difference with the conception of the Buddha is that in the Jaina texts the elements dreamed of enter the mother through her mouth. The Buddhist account in which the elephant enters her womb through her side, as opposed to through her vagina, has been explained as eliminating any association of the Buddha with sexuality and freeing him from pollution through contact with bodily fluids.[17] The entrance through the mouth could be seen as a similar effort to create the idea of an "immaculate"—that is, asexual—conception for the Jina. This motif may further be connected with the many stories in Indian literature of women conceiving asexually through the oral ingestion of semen or another substance. Vālmīki's *Rāmāyaṇa*, for instance, narrates how the queens conceive from eating the celestial porridge procured by the king during a sacrifice for obtaining sons. In the Buddhist Jātakas we come across the story of a doe becoming pregnant by eating grass and drinking water mixed with the Bodhisattva's semen.[18]

During her pregnancy, Marudevī becomes beautified by the fetus in her womb: her naturally dark complexion becomes fairer, her breasts swell, her eyes and hips become wider, and her gait becomes slower. It is characteristic of the Jina that while residing inside the womb, he causes her no pain or fatigue. For Nābhi he brings about extraordinary honor, makes the wishing-trees especially fruitful and the earth free from hostility. The Buddhist accounts are very similar in this respect.[19]

The humane qualities of the future Jina influence Marudevī's behavior, making her especially compassionate toward all. Already as a fetus, the Jina embodies *ahiṃsā*. Moreover, his presence stimulates this nonviolence in his mother. The narratives of the Buddha are alike again describing how, in Sasson's words, he "radiated through her body and she became the expression of all that he was and would be."[20]

Jinasena's *Ādi-purāṇa* is entirely devoted to the biography of Ṛṣabha. It narrates the events of Marudevī's pregnancy in the twelfth and thirteenth *parvans* in more than two hundred verses. The miraculous events begin before the descent of the Jina in the womb of Marudevī, with the construction of the city of Ayodhyā by the gods (12.69–83) and a rain of gems (12.84–101).

One day Marudevī has sixteen dreams, which indicate she will give birth to a Jina.

> Then one day the queen was asleep in the palace on a soft bed, splendid with a colorful cover like the waves of the Gaṅgā. In the final three hours

16. W. Bollée, "Physical Aspects of Some Mahāpuruṣas, Descent, Foetality, Birth," *Wiener Zeitschrift für die Kunde Südasiens* 49 (2005): 10.

17. Sasson, *Birth of Moses*, 115–17.

18. Vālmīki's *Rāmāyaṇa* 1.15; M. Boisvert, "Conception and Intrauterine Life in the Pāli Canon," *Studies in Religion/ Sciences Religieuses* 29, 3 (2000): 305–306.

19. Sasson, *Birth of Moses*, 120, 129–30.

20. Ibid., 118.

> of the night she saw the following sixteen auspicious dreams, which praised the birth of the Jina. She saw Indra's huge elephant, muttering and roaring, rutting from three places, like a thundering autumn cloud filled with rain. She saw a huge, thundering, drum-necked bull, white and bright like a lotus, like a pool of nectar. She saw a lion, its body glittering like the moon, its head blood-red, as if its body was made up of the moonlight and the twilight. She saw Padmā [Lakṣmī] on a high seat made of lotuses, bathed by divine elephants and golden pitchers, as if it were her [Marudevī's] own glory. She saw two garlands with bees intoxicated by the fragrance of the flowers, as if they were delightfully humming in a song they had commenced. She saw the moon radiating from its full disk with the stars, as if it were her own smiling lotuslike face with pearls. She saw the sun rising up from the Eastern mountain, removing darkness, as if it was that golden pitcher for her own blessing. She saw two golden pitchers, their surfaces covered with lotuses, as if they were her own prominent breasts with her hands as lotuses. She saw two fish in a pond with blooming lotuses, showing as it were, the breadth of her own eyes. She saw a divine lake, with water yellowed with the filaments of floating lotuses, as if entirely of liquid gold. She saw the unsteady, overflowing ocean, resounding with gushing waves, and drizzling, as if it were high laughter. She saw a leonine high throne with sparkling gems and gold, displaying the superior grace of the top of Mount Meru. She saw a heavenly palace, radiant with excellent gems, as if the gods gave her a birth house for her son. She saw a Nāga palace rise up, bursting through the ground, as if it had risen to rival the chariot of the sun it sees in front. She saw a heap of jewels filling the sky with its rising rays, as if it were the treasure of the goddess Earth that was displayed. She saw a blazing, shining, smokeless, beautiful, harsh fire, as if it were the corporeal splendor of her son. And she saw a high bull with a golden body and a thick neck entering her mouth at the end of her dreams. (12.102–20)

The seventeenth dream of the bull will determine the name of the child as Ṛṣabha, "bull." Marudevī awakes and goes to her husband, Nābhi, to whom she describes the dreams. Nābhi explains that they predict she will beget an extraordinary son (12.121–62).

Compared with Hemacandra's account, three dreams are different: the image of a banner has been dropped and those of two fish, of a throne, and of a Nāga palace have been added. The pitchers and wreaths have been doubled. The *Agni Purāṇa* mentions fish and a throne as prosperous images.[21] In Buddhist lore, inauspicious dreams numbering sixteen are at the center of the *Mahāsupina-Jātaka*. Except for the number, there seems to be no other connection between this Buddhist story and the dreams of the Jina's mother in Digambara literature.[22]

21. Shastrī, *Agni Purāṇa*, Vol. 2: 84–85.

22. E. B. Cowell, ed., *The Jātaka or Stories of the Buddha's Former Births*, trans. R. Chalmers (London: Pali Text Society, 1957), 187–94.

Indra sends six goddesses, the Dikkumārīs, to Marudevī to serve her during her pregnancy (12.163–255). In Hemacandra's version, Marudevī is attended by the Dikkumārīs after the birth of her son.[23] The Buddhist accounts too mention how the queen is served by goddesses who clean and massage her body.[24] Despite her condition, the queen suffers no discomfort, and here too the glow that radiates from her is emphasized:

> Then she bore a luminous radiance which had entered her body. She became utterly glowing like the East. (12.157)
>
> The fetus did not cause his mother any pain: does a fire, reflected in a mirror, burn? Her slender waist also remained as it was with its three folds. Nevertheless, the fetus and that superior glow grew. There was no pain in her belly. Her nipples did not become dark blue, nor did her face become pale. The fetus grew miraculously. (12.160–62)

Ajitanātha

Hemacandra's narration of Ajita in utero is substantial. Here we find some new narrative elements which were not present in the account of Ṛṣabha's conception and birth. At the appropriate time, Ajita's soul descends into the womb of Vijayā, wife of King Jitaśatru, causing happiness even for the beings in hell. Thereupon Vijayā has a dream in which she sees fourteen elements enter her mouth: (1) a white elephant, (2) a white bull, (3) a lion, (4) the goddess Śrī, (5) a flower garland, (6) the moon, (7) the sun, (8) banners, (9) a water pitcher, (10) a lotus pond, (11) an ocean, (12) a *vimāna*, a heavenly abode, (13) a heap of jewels, and (14) a smokeless fire. This version differs slightly from Hemacandra's description of the dreams of Ṛṣabha's conception, namely in the appearance of the elephant before the bull and no specification of the ocean as an ocean of milk as the eleventh. Thereupon Śakra's (Indra's) throne shakes and through clairvoyance he comes to know that the future Jina has been born. Together with the other Indras, he descends from the heavens to pay homage to Queen Vijayā and explains that the dreams signify that she will bear a Tīrthaṅkara. He then orders the god Dhanada (Kubera) to fill the city with jewels, gold, etc. as he did at the time of Ṛṣabha. Note here that in the Ṛṣabha story Hemacandra describes Dhanada building the city at his coronation as king. In Jinasena's version, he builds the city before the birth.[25] Buddhist parallels appear to be limited to the gods and goddesses adorning Lumbinī garden prior to the birth in one text.[26] Thereafter, in Hemacandra's account, King Jitaśatru explains the dreams as a sign that she will bear an eminent son, without further specification. Thus, here the order of Indra's explanation and the king's

23. Johnson, *Triṣaṣṭiśalākāpuruṣacaritra*, Vol. 1: 105.
24. Sasson, *Birth of Moses*, 137.
25. Johnson, *Triṣaṣṭiśalākāpuruṣacaritra*, Vol. 1: 149–50; for Jinasena's version, cf. *Ādi-purāṇa* 12.69–83.
26. Sasson, *Birth of Moses*, 135.

explanation has been switched compared to the Ṛṣabha story.[27] Then Śakra orders the goddesses to attend to Vijayā:

> Vāyukumāra-women always removed dust, grass, sticks, etc., from all parts of the house of the mistress. Meghakumāra-women, like slave-girls, sprinkled the ground of the court-yard of her house with perfumed water. The goddesses of the season rained five-colored flowers, as if eager to give a respectful reception to the Lord in embryo. The women of the Jyotiṣkas brought light at pleasure and at the right time, knowing the wishes of the mistress. Forest-goddesses made festoons, etc., like slave-girls, and goddesses praised her in song, like women-bards. In this way Queen Vijayā was served daily by the goddesses, like their own chief deity or like a superior one.[28]

This motif is absent from Ṛṣabha's intrauterine account; however, there the Dikkumārīs attend Marudevī and her son after the birth.[29] In his description of the pregnancy of Vijayā and of Vaijayantī, the mother of Sagara, the second Cakravartin, Hemacandra depicts the women as being beautified by the fetus in words resembling those describing Ṛṣabha's mother Marudevī.[30]

Unlike Hemacandra, Guṇabhadra is relatively brief about the conception of Ajita.

> In that [Jambū]dvīpa, in Bhāratavarṣa, lived the king of the city of Sāketa, an Ikṣvāku, named Jitaśatru, from the lineage Kāśyapa. In his house Ailavila [Kubera] for six months every day incessantly dropped three and a half crores of gems on Śakra's orders. In the month of Jyeṣṭha, with the rise of Rohiṇī and only one digit of the moon remaining before the Brahma-muhūrta, Queen Vijayasenā, her eyes perturbed by sleep and fear, saw a rutting elephant entering her mouth, preceded by sixteen dreams. In the morning King Jitaśatru, who could see with clairvoyant knowledge, explained to her the fruit of these dreams upon her request: the Lord, luminous through his clear and correct perception and his triple knowledge, had come from Vijaya [heaven] to that womb, pure as crystal. (48.19–24)

The only substantial change with regard to Ṛṣabha's account is that here an elephant, the supreme symbol of sovereignty, enters her mouth instead of a bull.

From Sambhava, the Third Tīrthaṅkara, up to Pārśva, the Twenty-third

Guṇabhadra is equally brief about the conception of the other Tīrthaṅkaras and more or less follows the same pattern throughout the *Uttara-purāṇa* as we find in

27. Johnson, *Triṣaṣṭiśalākāpuruṣacaritra*, Vol. 2: 29–33.
28. Ibid., 36.
29. Johnson, *Triṣaṣṭiśalākāpuruṣacaritra*, Vol. 1: 105.
30. Johnson, *Triṣaṣṭiśalākāpuruṣacaritra*, Vol. 2: 36–37.

his description of Ajita.[31] Six months prior to the descent of the Tīrthaṅkara's soul, the gods drop a rain of gems on the house of the king.[32] In the night of the incarnation the queen has the sixteen dreams, after which she sees an elephant enter her mouth. The motif of the elephant is not mentioned explicitly in the accounts of Candraprabha, Suvidhi, Vāsupūjya, Dharma, Śānti, and Ara. The dreams are interpreted by her husband, the king. In his portrayal of the descent of Candraprabha, Nami, and Nemi, Guṇabhadra adds some verses, describing the goddesses attending the mother, which conform to Jinasena's account of Ṛṣabha. A recurring motif is first found in the description of Śītala's descent in the womb, when the gods come to celebrate the occasion. "The gods came with love and performed austerities for the first auspicious event" (56.28a). This is repeated in the accounts of all the following Tīrthaṅkaras, except Vāsupūjya.

Hemacandra is very concise about Candraprabha, Śītala, Vāsupūjya, Vimala, Ananta, Dharma, and Munisuvrata, where he merely refers to the queens having fourteen auspicious dreams. For the other Tīrthaṅkaras, he gives some additional elements.[33] He lists all the dreams in the stories of Sambhava, Abhinandana, Śreyāṃsa, Śānti, Kunthu, and Nemi. As in the accounts of Ṛṣabha and Ajita, the dreams are interpreted by the king, sometimes assisted by astrologers, and by the Indras.[34] Similar to Ṛṣabha, Hemacandra describes how the fetus grows without causing any discomfort to his mother in the stories of Sambhava, Abhinandana, Sumati, and Nami. In the accounts of Sambhava and Nemi he mentions how the queen's beauty is increased by the presence of the fetus. Another recurring motif in Hemacandra's narratives, already present in Ṛṣabha's account, is the remark that upon the descent of the Tīrthaṅkara in the womb, the inhabitants of hell find comfort and a light flashes in the three worlds. We find this in the accounts of Sambhava, Abhinandana, Sumati, Śreyāṃsa, Nami,[35] and Nemi. Beside these recurring elements, Hemacandra includes some things specific for one Tīrthaṅkara. Thus, in the story of Padmaprabha, he mentions how the queen has a whim for a couch made of lotuses. This is gratified by goddesses. This whim later determines the name of the child, Padmaprabha, "beautiful as lotuses." The biography of Malli has a similar motif, where the queen has a whim for sleeping on garlands, leading to the name Malli, from the word *mālā*, "garland." This motif of *dohada*, the "pregnancy

31. Sambhava: 49.14–19; Abhinandana: 50.16–19; Sumati: 51.19–23; Padmaprabha: 52.18–21; Supārśva: 52.17–22; Candraprabha: 54.163–70; Suvidhi: 55.23–27; Śītala: 56.23–28; Śreyāṃsa: 57.17–22; Vāsupūjya: 58.17–20; Vimala: 59.14–21; Ananta: 60.16–21; Dharma: 61.12–18; Śānti: 63.388–97; Kunthu: 64.12–22; Ara: 65.16–21; Malli: 66.18–32; Munisuvrata: 67.18–26; Nami: 69.25–30; Nemi: 71.29–38; Pārśva: 73.74–90.

32. Note that this is only implied in the account of Śānti (63.397), when after the birth of the Tīrthaṅkara, the author states that it had rained gems for fifteen months: nine months during the pregnancy and six months prior.

33. Sambhava: Johnson, *Triṣaṣṭiśalākāpuruṣacaritra*, Vol. 2: 233–34; Abhinandana: Vol. 2: 258; Sumati: Vol. 2: 278–81; Padmaprabha: Vol. 2: 290; Supārśva: Vol. 2: 306; Candraprabha: Vol. 2: 316; Suvidhi: Vol. 2: 326; Śītala: Vol. 2: 339; Śreyāṃsa: Vol. 3: 3–4; Vāsupūjya: Vol. 3: 66; Vimala: Vol. 3: 94; Ananta: Vol. 3: 112; Dharma: Vol. 3: 136; Śānti: Vol. 3: 300–302; Kunthu: Vol. 4: 3; Ara: Vol. 4: 12–13; Malli: Vol. 4: 54; Munisuvrata: Vol. 4: 79–80; Nami: Vol 4: 354; Nemi: Vol. 5: 164; Pārśva: Vol. 5: 379–80.

34. This is not mentioned in the accounts of Sumati, Padmaprabha, Supārśva, Suvidhi, Śreyāṃsa, Ara, Malli, Nami. In the account of Śānti, Kunthu, and Nemi, nothing is mentioned about the Indras. In the account of Nemi, the dreams are interpreted by Kroṣṭuki and a Muni.

35. In Nami's account, only the light is referred to.

longing," which must be fulfilled by the husband, is well known in Indian literature.[36] In the narrative of Supārśva, Hemacandra mentions that his mother dreams of a couch of serpents with one, five, and nine hoods.

Sumati: Maṅgalā's Judgment

The biography of Sumati in Hemacandra's text further contains an interesting story of disputed parentage in which the queen performs a "Solomon's judgment." A rich man from the city had two wives who looked very similar. The first wife bore a son, but both women brought up the boy together. When the man died and the son was to inherit all his wealth, both women claimed to be the natural mother of the boy. Due to the women's strong resemblance, no court, not even that of the king, was able to decide to whom the boy and the property belonged. The text continues:

> The King gave the Queen an account of the dispute between the two women; and, wise from the power of her embryo, the Queen said, "It is certainly fitting for a dispute between women to be decided by women alone. Therefore I shall decide the dispute, Your Majesty." In astonishment the King accompanied the Queen to the assembly. The two women were summoned and questioned, and told the same stories as before. The Queen considered the complaint and the answer, and spoke as follows: "In my womb I have a Tīrthakara, the possessor of three kinds of knowledge. When the Lord of the World is born, he will give judgment at the foot of the aśoka tree. So have patience, both of you."
>
> The step-mother agreed, but the mother said, "I will not wait at all, O Queen. Let the mother of the All-knowing, Your Ladyship, give judgment right now. I will not make my own child subject to my co-wife for so long a time." Then Queen Maṅgalā gave her decision. "He is certainly her son, since she can not endure delay. The step-mother can bear delay in this case, indeed, because she considers that it is another's son and money that are subject to both. Unable to endure her own son being made subject to both, how can the mother endure a delay? My good woman, since you can not endure the least delay, it is evident that the boy is yours. Take him and go home. For he is not this woman's child, even though cared for and cherished (by her). The offspring of a cuckoo, even though nourished by a crow, is a cuckoo."[37]

This motif of the Solomon's judgment recurs in folklore worldwide and knows several versions in India.[38]

36. See also M. Bloomfield, "The Dohada or Craving of Pregnant Women: A Motif of Hindu Fiction," *Journal of the American Oriental Society* 40 (1920): 1–24.

37. Johnson, *Triṣaṣṭiśalākāpuruṣacaritra*, Vol. 2: 278–81.

38. S. Thompson, *Motif-Index of Folk-Literature* (electronic version) (Bloomington: Indiana University Press, 1955), entry J1171.1; S. Thompson and J. Balys, *The Oral Tales of India*, Indiana University Publications Folklore Series 10 (Bloomington: Indiana University Press, 1958), 261.

The notion that the behavior of the fetus and the mother are linked can be traced back in theoretical accounts on embryology. There it is described that from the third month onward, the mother and fetus are connected by the heart in a state called *dvaihṛdayya*, "the state of two hearts." Thus, the feelings and behavior of mother and fetus are identical.[39] Accounts of the Buddha show a similarity in their accordance of extraordinary healing powers to his mother because of the presence of the Buddha inside her. Just as Māyā became an expression of Buddhahood, so too is the mother of a Jina an expression of Jinahood during her pregnancy. Like in the Buddhist stories, however, the connection between mother and fetus is one-directional: the fetus thoroughly influences the mother's behavior, but the mother has no such effect on the child.[40]

Mahāvīra: Fetal Transference

The Śvetāmbara biography of the last Tīrthaṅkara, Vardhamāna Mahāvīra, contains a unique feature compared to the other Jinas and the accounts of the Digambaras. Hemacandra describes how the soul of Mahāvīra descends into the womb of a Brahmin woman, Devānandā. That night she dreams of the fourteen objects associated with the conception of a Jina. Her husband interprets the dream as an indication that she will bear a son learned in the four Vedas. Great wealth befalls the Brahmin family. However, after eighty-two days, Śakra's throne shakes. By clairvoyance he realizes that the future Jina has descended into the womb of a Brahmin woman. He reflects as follows:

> The Arhats, teachers of three worlds, are never born in an insignificant family, nor in a poor family, nor in a family that subsists on alms. Rather, they are born in warrior-lines, Ikṣvāku, et cetera, man-lions, like pearls originating in pearl-oysters, et cetera. It is not suitable for the Lord's birth to have fallen into a low family. Yet even Arhats are not able to change strong karma. This low-family-karma, which was acquired by the Lord showing family-pride in the Marīci-incarnation, has now matured. We always have authority to place elsewhere in a great family Arhats who have fallen into a low family from the power of karma. What king and queen of a great family are there now in Bhārata, to whom the Master can be transferred, like a bee from a jasmine to a lotus?
>
> Here in Bharata there is a well known city named Kṣatriyakuṇḍagrāma, which resembles my city, the ornament of the earth, the place of many shrines, the sole support of dharma, unstained by sins, purified by sādhus. That same city, free from the vices—hunting, wine-drinking, et cetera, is the means of purification of Bharatakṣetra, like a holy place of the earth. The king there is Siddhārtha of the Jñāta-line, a descendant

39. G. J. Meulenbeld, *A History of Indian Medical Literature*, 3 vols., Groningen Oriental Studies 15 (Groningen: Egbert Forsten, 1999–2002), Vol. 1A: 42.

40. Sasson, *Birth of Moses*, 120–21.

> of Ikṣvāku, who always considered himself to have his purpose accomplished (siddhārtha) by dharma alone. Knowing the Principles—soul, non-soul, et cetera, a traveler on the road of propriety, he has placed his subjects on the road, devoted to their interests like a father.
>
> He is a kinsman for the rescue of people who are poor, without a lord, et cetera; the refuge of those seeking a refuge, the crest-jewel of the warriors. He has a chief-queen, named Triśalā, the best of wives, the abode of merit, the embodiment of praise-worthy qualities. She, spotless by nature, now purifies the earth by her various qualities like the Mandākinī by its waves. Unspotted by deceit which is the accompaniment of a woman-birth, straightforward by nature, she is a goddess on earth whose name is pronounced auspiciously. Just now she is pregnant. I must make quickly a change by the transfer of her embryo and that of Devānandā.

Śakra then orders his general, the god Naigameṣin, to take the fetus from Devānandā's womb and exchange it with that from Triśalā's womb. That night Devānandā has a dream in which she sees the fourteen elements predicting the birth of a Jina issuing from her mouth. Triśalā dreams of the elements entering her mouth.[41]

The antiquity of the motif of fetus transference is evident from the representation of this legend in sculptures from Mathura, depicting the god transporting the fetus, probably dating from around 200 CE. It underlines the anti-Brahmanical attitudes of the Jainas and reflects a conviction that Kṣatriyas, the "warrior" caste, are the highest in the social hierarchy, instead of Brahmins, as is clearly described here: in Jaina tradition, a "monarch," spiritual or material, must be born in the warrior caste, not in a family that "subsists on alms," clearly referring to Brahmins.[42] In the Buddhist narratives, this aversion to Brahmins appears to be less profound. Although a birth in the warrior caste is preferred, three previous Buddhas were born as Brahmins. Brahmins also figure as the consultants for the interpretation of Māyā's dream.[43] Sasson further suggests that the spectacular life of the Buddha in the womb as described in some texts may be a kind of competitive response to this account of Mahāvīra's intrauterine life.[44] The motif of fetal transference was probably not original to the biography of Mahāvīra, since the Digambaras reject it. It has been suggested that Siddhārtha possibly had two wives, a Kṣatriya wife Triśalā and a Brahmin wife Devānandā, the biological mother of Mahāvīra, and that Mahāvīra was foisted upon the Kṣatriya wife to give him a greater status, dissociating him from a Brahmin heredity. The Digambaras simply omitted Devānandā from Mahāvīra's story, making him the biological son of Triśalā. The Śvetāmbaras solved the issue of this Brahmin connection by introducing the fetal transference motif, most likely adopted from the Hindu Kṛṣṇa story, where Kṛṣṇa's older brother,

41. Johnson, *Triṣaṣṭiśalākāpuruṣacaritra*, Vol. 6: 25–26.
42. Jaini, *Jaina Path of Purification*, 7–8.
43. Sasson, *Birth of Moses*, 98, 117-18.
44. Ibid., 124 n. 55.

Baladeva, was transplanted from Devakī's womb into that of Rohiṇī. An added bonus of the Śvetāmbara account is that it made the life in the womb for Mahāvīra all the more miraculous and spectacular.[45] As an explanation why Mahāvīra had to spend part of his gestation in a Brahmin womb, Hemacandra refers to his karma caused in a previous birth as Marīci. In that existence, the soul of Mahāvīra was the son of Bharata, grandson of Ṛṣabha, the first Tīrthaṅkara. When he heard the prophecy that he was to become the last Tīrthaṅkara of our era, Marīci became proud and subsequently acquired *nīca-gotra-karma*, "low-family-karma" which would ultimately lead him to be conceived in a Brahmin woman's womb.[46]

As in many of the other narratives, the fetus remains motionless to spare his mother from discomfort. However, unable to feel the presence of her baby, Triśalā became extremely upset:

> "Has my embryo fallen? Or has some one taken it away? Or is it dead? Or transfixed by a spell? If this has happened, then enough of life for me. For the pain of death is endurable, but not that caused by the loss of an embryo."
>
> With this painful thought, the queen, weeping, her hair disordered, ointments abandoned, resting her lotus-face on her lotus-hand, wearing no ornaments, her lips miserable from sighs, silent even with her friends, did not eat nor sleep. King Siddhārtha grieved when he learned about that; and his worthy children, Nandivardhana and Sudarśanā, too.

When the Jina understood the grief he caused his parents, he moved a finger to show that he was still there. Touched by his parents' grief, he reflected:

> "My father and mother have great affection for me, indeed, when they have never seen me. If I should become a mendicant while they are alive, they would certainly acquire much bad karma by indulging in painful meditation because of the delusion of affection." So in the seventh month, the Lord made the resolution, "I will not become a mendicant during the lifetime of my parents."[47]

This resolution of Mahāvīra and the fulfillment thereof in his later life exemplifies Jainism's extreme efforts to implement the vow of *ahiṃsā*, nonviolence. Jaini points out the sharp contrast with Buddhism, which emphasizes the need to abandon worldly life despite familial pressures.[48] Nevertheless, as far as the prenatal

45. See also Couture's chapter in this volume; Schubring, *Doctrine of the Jainas*, 32; Bollée, "Physical Aspects," 12–14. Note that Jaini disagrees with the idea of Triśalā and Devānandā as wives of Siddhārtha given the strict regulations forbidding marriage between Brahmin women and Kṣatriya men. See Jaini, *Jaina Path of Purification*, 8. Jain suggests Mahāvīra was the biological child of the Brahmin couple Devānandā and Ṛṣabhadatta given up for adoption to Siddhārtha and Triśalā. See K. C. Jain, *Lord Mahāvira and His Times*, Lala Sundar Lal Jain Research Series 6 (Delhi: Motilal Banarsidass, 1991), 32–33.

46. Johnson, *Triṣaṣṭiśalākāpuruṣacaritra*, Vol. 6: 3–6.

47. Ibid., 28.

48. Jaini, *Jaina Path of Purification*, 9.

accounts of the Buddha are concerned, the texts agree that the queen suffered no discomfort, apart from the baby's foot pushing against her womb when she tried to sit squatting in Buddhaghoṣa's narrative.[49]

In the Digambara versions of Mahāvīra's biography this element is absent. They state that Mahāvīra renounced the world when his parents were still alive, though he did so only after receiving their explicit permission. Also, no mention is made of the transference of the embryo. Guṇabhadra devotes a mere ten verses to the description of Mahāvīra's life, prior to his birth:

> When he had six months of his life span left before leaving heaven, a wide stream of wealth, with seven crores of gems, fell down every day in the courtyard of the palace of King Siddhārtha, lord of Kuṇḍapura, in Bharata, in a kingdom called Videha. In the white half of Āṣāḍha, on the sixth day, while the moon was in Uttarāṣāḍhā, in a palace, situated inside a seven story building, lit up with jewel-lamps, on a jewel couch, decorated with goose-cotton, etc., at the end of the fourth night-watch called Manohara, the triad Raudra, Rākṣasa and Gandharva having already passed, his beloved, Priyakāriṇī, with her graceful mind, lightly asleep, beheld sixteen separate dreams, giving excellent fruits. After these, she also saw an elephant enter her mouth. Awakened by the sound of the morning drums and by the prayers recited by the bards, she quickly bathed and put on her ornaments, and went to King Siddhārtha with a bow. She was offered half a seat and related the dreams in succession. He informed her of the future fruit of these as she told them. When she had heard the fruits of the dreams, the queen was delighted, as if she herself had obtained that fruit. Then all the kings of the gods came to them in full glory. They performed an ablution for the auspicious occasion, as it is customary in these instances. They coerced the gods and goddesses and each went to their own dwellings. (74.251–61)

The Cakravartins

Bharata

In Hemacandra's biography of Ṛṣabha, the birth of his son Bharata, the first Cakravartin, is foretold by fourteen dreams of his mother. "Then Lady Sumaṅgalā, like Marudevā, saw fourteen great dreams, indicating the importance of the embryo. The Mistress related the dreams to the Master, who said unhesitatingly, 'Your son will be a Cakrabhṛt.'"[50]

Jinasena gives a longer account of Bharata's conception. He describes how his mother has dreams of six items. Here the Digambara tradition differs from the Śvetāmbaras, who describe the same dreams for a Cakravartin as those for a Jina.

49. Sasson, *Birth of Moses*, 120.
50. Johnson, *Triṣaṣṭiśalākāpuruṣacaritra*, Vol. 1: 148.

"One day Queen Yaśasvati was asleep in the palace. In her sleep she saw the earth eclipsed, the Meru, the sun and the moon, a lake with swans, and a wavy ocean" (15.100–101a). The king, Ṛṣabha, interprets the dreams as follows.

> O queen, from [seeing] that king among mountains, you will beget a son, a Cakravartin. The sun indicates his splendour, the moon his lustre. O lotus-eyed woman, from seeing the lake, he will marry [a woman] fragrant of lotuses. His body, with a broad chest, will be marked with auspicious signs. From the eclipsing of the earth, o queen, your son will be a universal monarch, ruling the entire earth with its oceans. From the ocean, he will be in his last body, swimming across the ocean of rebirth. (15.123–126a)

After the dreams the soul of Bharata enters the womb of Yaśasvati. During her pregnancy Yaśasvati displays some strange behavior, indicating influence by the haughty warrior instincts of her unborn child. "Because of that [unborn child] she could not tolerate the sun rising in the sky. That proud woman looked at the reflection of her face in the blade of a sword as a mirror, and could not even bear her own reflection in it" (15.129b–30). Jinasena further describes Yaśasvati's beauty during her pregnancy (15.131–39).

Sagara and the Other Ten Cakravartins

Guṇabhadra gives no account of the circumstances of Sagara's time in utero, or that of any of the other Cakravartins aside from Śānti, Kunthu, and Ara, who are not only Cakravartins but also Tīrthaṅkaras. The mothers of these three have sixteen dreams, as is usual for a Tīrthaṅkara, instead of six as in the case of the other Cakravartins in Digambara tradition. Hemacandra describes how Sagara's mother has the same dreams as the mother of the second Tīrthaṅkara, the nephew of Sagara. Sagara's father goes to his brother, Jitaśatru, Ajita's father, and relates to him the dreams of his wife.[51] Jitaśatru's wife and his sister-in-law have experienced identical dreams in the same night. Puzzled by this, the king questions some astrologers who are experts in dream-science. They explain them as follows:

> Your Majesty, seventy-two dreams are described in dream-science. Of these, thirty are pre-eminent like planets among heavenly bodies. Among these thirty dreams fourteen are called "great dreams" by the experts in dream-science. When a Tīrthaṅkara or a cakravartin is in the womb, his mother sees these in succession in the fourth watch of the night. The mother of a Hari (Vāsudeva) sees seven of them; the mother of a Sīrin (Balabhadra) sees four; and the mother of a king one. There are never two Arhats nor two cakrins at the same time. So the son of one is a Tīrthakṛt and of the other a cakrabhṛt. The teachings of the Arhats say, "Bharata is cakrin in the time of Ṛṣabha; and Sagara, the son of Sumitra,

51. Ibid., Vol. 2: 34.

in the time of the Tīrthaṅkara Ajita, son of Jitaśatru." The son of Queen Vijayā must surely be known as a Tīrthaṅkara, and the son of Vaijayantī as the lord of six-part Bharata.[52]

The identical dreams of the Śvetāmbara sources for a Cakravartin and a Tīrthaṅkara is very significant, as is the fact that three Tīrthaṅkaras of the current era were at the same time Cakravartins. It highlights their close relationship and the notion of the Tīrthaṅkara as a spiritual king and of his asceticism as a spiritualized martial virtue. The strict requirement of his birth into a warrior clan is also to be seen in this perspective.[53] Likewise, the Buddha too is described as a potential Cakravartin.[54] In the Digambara texts, the status of the Cakravartin is lowered significantly by the mention of merely six dreams, illustrating the Tīrthaṅkara as a being far superior to even the supreme "worldly" ruler, the Cakravartin. This gave rise to some inconsistency in the pattern of the intrauterine life of the Cakravartins as three later become a Tīrthaṅkara, and their mother thus has sixteen dreams instead of six.[55]

Hemacandra further describes how the beauty of Sagara's mother increases at the same time as Ajita's mother, because of the fetus. Of the following ten Cakravartins, except the three Cakravartin-Tīrthaṅkaras, Hemacandra merely states that their mothers have the fourteen auspicious dreams.[56] In the case of Maghavan and Sanatkumāra, he specifies that the elements dreamed of entered the mothers' mouth.

The Baladevas, Vāsudevas, and Prativāsudevas

A final category of Mahā-puruṣas are the triads of Baladevas, Vāsudevas, and Prativāsudevas. The Baladeva and Vāsudeva are heroic brothers. The Prativāsudeva is their enemy. Guṇabhadra hardly gives any information on the Baladevas, Vāsudevas, and Prativāsudevas prior to their birth. In the biography of Tripṛṣṭha (57.83–85) and Dharma (59.71) he implies that the mother has some auspicious dreams.

Hemacandra gives more information. The mother of the first Baladeva, Acala, dreams of four auspicious elements entering her mouth: (1) a four-tusked elephant, (2) a white bull, (3) a moon, and (4) a lotus pond. Her husband interprets that she will bear a Baladeva.[57] From the first Vāsudeva, Tripṛṣṭha, Hemacandra

52. Ibid., 35–36.

53. L. A. Babb, *Ascetics and Kings in a Jain Ritual Culture*, Lala Sunder Lal Jain Research Series 11 (Delhi: Motilal Banarsidass, 1998), 82.

54. S. J. Tambiah, *World Conqueror and World Renouncer: A Study of Buddhism and Polity in Thailand against a Historical Background*, Cambridge Studies in Social Anthropology 15 (Cambridge: Cambridge University Press, 1976).

55. Despite this inconsistency it is not impossible that in the Śvetāmbara accounts an originally far lower status of the Cakravartin was raised, perhaps through analogy with the Cakravartins of Buddhism, instead of the Digambaras reducing his significance.

56. Maghavan: Johnson, *Triṣaṣṭiśalākāpuruṣacaritra*, Vol. 3: 164; Sanatkumāra: Vol. 3: 172; Subhūma: Vol. 4: 45; Mahāpadma: Vol. 4: 89; Hariṣeṇa: Vol. 4: 362; Jaya: Vol. 4: 365; Brahmadatta: Vol. 5: 323.

57. Johnson, *Triṣaṣṭiśalākāpuruṣacaritra*, Vol. 3: 13–14.

describes seven elements as entering her mouth in a dream: (1) a lion, (2) Lakṣmī, (3) the sun, (4) a water pitcher, (5) an ocean, (6) a heap of jewels, and (7) a smokeless fire. The king gave his interpretation of the dreams first. "'Your son will surely be an Ardhacakrin, queen,'" he said. Then the "experts" were polled. "The astrologers, questioned by the king who had summoned them at once, also explained the dreams in the same way. There is no disagreement among the wise."[58] In the Jaina hagiographies the Vāsudeva is always an Ardhacakravartin, a monarch who rules half of the civilized world. In Hemacandra's version, the number of elements dreamed of corresponds to this: fourteen for a Cakravartin and seven for an Ardhacakravartin. Hemacandra does not describe the birth of the first Prativāsudeva, Aśvagrīva. He further mentions that the conception of the following six Baladevas is preceded by four dreams[59] and that the conception of the following six Vāsudevas is preceded by seven dreams, sometimes specified as entering the mother's mouth.[60]

The Epic Heroes

The eighth and ninth triad represent the adaptations of the Indian epic heroes in the Jaina world history. The eighth Baladeva is Rāma, the hero of the *Rāmāyaṇa*. His brother Lakṣmaṇa and their enemy Rāvaṇa are the Vāsudeva and Prativāsudeva. The ninth triad entails some characters from the *Mahābhārata* and its appendix, the *Harivaṃśa-purāṇa*. Kṛṣṇa is the Vāsudeva, his brother Balarāma is the Baladeva, and Jarāsandha is the Prativāsudeva. The accounts of these popular characters are longer than those of the other triads in both texts. Hemacandra gives the following on the conception of Rāma: "Then Aparājitā one day saw the elephant, lion, moon, and sun in a dream, which indicated the birth of a Bala, in the last part of the night."[61] Before the descent of Lakṣmaṇa's soul in his mother's womb, he gives the following: "Sumitrā saw an elephant, lion, sun, moon, fire, Śrī, and ocean in a dream at dawn, which indicated the birth of a Viṣṇu."[62] The conception of Rāvaṇa is described in a relatively large portion:

> One day in a dream Kaikasī saw a lion, in the act of tearing an elephant's boss, enter her mouth. At dawn she related the dream and Ratnaśravas interpreted, "You will have a son, who will be arrogant to all, powerful." From the time of that dream the wife of Ratnaśravas constantly made offerings in the shrines and carried her very precious embryo. From the time of the embryo's conception Kaikasī's speech became very harsh and her body firm, free from fatigue. She looked at her face in a sword,

58. Ibid., 16–17.

59. Vijaya: Johnson, *Triṣaṣṭiśalākāpuruṣacaritra*, Vol. 3: 78; Bhadra: Vol. 3: 99; Suprabha: Vol. 3: 117; Sudarśana: Vol. 3: 139; Ānanda: Vol. 4: 38; Nandana: Vol. 4: 50.

60. Dviprṣṭha: Johnson, *Triṣaṣṭiśalākāpuruṣacaritra*, Vol. 3: 78; Svayambhū: Vol. 3: 99; Puruṣottama: Vol. 3: 118; Puruṣasiṃha: Vol. 3: 140; Puruṣapuṇḍarīka: Vol. 4: 38; Datta: Vol. 4: 50. For the first three Hemacandra specifies that the elements enter her mouth.

61. Johnson, *Triṣaṣṭiśalākāpuruṣacaritra*, Vol. 4: 193.

62. Ibid.

> even if a mirror were at hand; she began to give orders fearlessly even in dominion over the gods. Without any cause she spoke harshly with contemptuous expressions. She did not bow her head at all even to gurus. For a long time she wished to put her foot on the heads of the wise. From the power of her embryo she acquired cruel characteristics such as these.[63]

Guṇabhadra is again briefer. He mentions that Rāma's mother experiences auspicious dreams (67.148–50). For Lakṣmaṇa he sums up six items dreamed by his mother: "Then the king begot [a son] from Kaikeyī, after seeing auspicious dreams, a lake, a son, a moon, a paddy field, and a lion" (67.150a–51). He gives no account of Rāvaṇa's conception, nor of the conception of Balarāma or Jarāsandha. Hemacandra gives the following on Balarāma's conception: "Rohiṇī saw an elephant, ocean, lion, and moon entering her mouth in a dream in the last part of the night, indicating the birth of a Halabhṛt."[64] He mentions the dreams of Kṛṣṇa's mother: "Then Devakī, after her purificatory bath, saw a dream at dawn—a lion, sun, fire, elephant, banner, aerial car, and a lotus-pool."[65]

Both Jaina texts include a parallel account to the popular Hindu story in which Balarāma is transferred from the womb of Devakī to Rohiṇī. Here, however, it does not concern Balarāma, who is the son of Rohiṇī plain and simple, but Devakī's six other children. As in the Hindu story, Devakī's brother-in-law, Kaṃsa, intends to kill her children as soon as they are born. The god Naigameṣin, well known as the executor of Mahāvīra's fetal transference, exchanges her six firstborns immediately after birth with the stillborns of Sulasā, a woman cursed by an ascetic in her childhood.[66] This modification in the Jaina texts in which the exchange happened after the children were born instead of before was deliberate. It was Sulasā's curse that she give birth to stillborn children. Therefore the exchange could occur only afterward. The miraculous event of a fetal transfer remains reserved only for the greatest hero, namely the Jina. The exchange of Devakī's children, who are of no importance other than their being the brothers of the Vāsudeva Kṛṣṇa, is still noteworthy, yet much less spectacular, and conforms to their lower status.

Conclusion

If we look at the accounts of the Mahā-puruṣas' prenatal biographies, we see well established patterns returning in both traditions. We even get the impression of a "Jina-life blueprint," "Cakravartin-life blueprint," and other different categories under the one "Mahā-puruṣa-life blueprint," to use J. S. Strong's terms for Buddha's

63. Ibid., 116.
64. Ibid., Vol. 5: 154.
65. Ibid., 159.
66. Ibid.; Guṇabhadra's *Uttarapurāṇa* 70. 384–86. In Guṇabhadra's version, the woman is called Alakā, and the god who transfers the children is called Naigamārṣa.

biography.[67] However, these blueprints do not seem to be followed precisely, and there is no consistency among different authors.

The most significant and recurring motif is that of the mothers' dreams, foretelling the destiny of her unborn child. In fact, if anything is mentioned in the sometimes very concise accounts of the conception and gestation of the heroes, it is these dreams. Their recurrence in Jaina ritual underscores their great importance.[68] The texts describe them rather statically as objects entering the mouth of the mother. The Digambaras and Śvetāmbaras differ in the number and nature of these dreams. The Digambara narrative of Jinasena and Guṇabhadra presupposes sixteen dreams for a Tīrthaṅkara, six for a Cakravartin and an unspecified number for the Baladeva and the Vāsudeva. Hemacandra's Śvetāmbara version is more consistent, describing fourteen dreams for the Tīrthaṅkara and the Cakravartin, seven for the Vāsudeva, and four for the Baladeva. The importance of the hero appears to correspond to the number of dreams described by the mother. In the Digambara version these dreams are interpreted by the father of the hero. Hemacandra varies: in some stories, it is the father who explains the dreams; in others, astrologers are consulted. In the case of a Tīrthaṅkara, sometimes the gods come from heaven to reveal their meaning. In the accounts of the Buddha, the king seeks the advice of Brahmins to expound the dream, though an intervention of the gods is sometimes also incorporated.[69]

A second motif is a change in the mother's behavior, ascribable to the character of her unborn child—for instance, in the wise judgment made by Sumati's mother and in the warriorlike behavior of Bharata's and Rāvaṇa's mothers. This is related to the belief that the heart of mother and fetus are connected as described in Indian embryological theory.

A motif occurring only in the cases of the Tīrthaṅkaras concerns various divine and supernatural events. One such event is a light that shines in the three worlds. The manifestation of light during the Buddha's conception, gestation, and birth is amply attested in different accounts, where it appears to emanate from the Buddha, or rather Bodhisattva, himself. As in the Jaina accounts, the light permeates the entire universe, including hell.[70] Other such elements, such as the visits of gods and celestial beings to mother and child as in Buddhist accounts, appear to be archetypal for biographies of heroes.[71]

The events in utero of the Jaina Mahā-puruṣas parallel their future feats. The higher the status of the hero, the more spectacular his intrauterine life.

WORKS CITED

Texts and Translations

Bhatt, G. H. *The Bālakāṇḍa: The First Book of the Vālmīki-Rāmāyaṇa, The National Epic of India.* Baroda, India: Oriental Institute, 1960.

67. J. S. Strong, *The Buddha: A Short Biography* (Oxford: Oneworld, 2002), 10–14.
68. Babb, *Ascetics and Kings*, 82.
69. Sasson, *Birth of Moses*, 117–18.
70. Ibid., 126-27.
71. Ibid., 122, 128–30, 168–69.

Charaṇavijaya, Muni. *The Trishashtisalākāpurushacharitram-Mahākāvyam by Śrī-Hemachandra-Āchārya.* 2 vols. Śrī-Jaina-Ātmānanda-Śatābdi Series 7 and 8. Bhāvnagar, India: Śrī-Jaina-Ātmānanda-Sabhā, 1936–50.

Cowell, E. B., ed. *The Jātaka or Stories of the Buddha's Former Births,* Vol. 1. Translation by R. Chalmers. London: Pali Text Society, 1957.

Goldman, R. *The Rāmāyaṇa of Vālmīki: An Epic of Ancient India.* Book 1: *Bālakāṇḍa.* Princeton, N.J.: Princeton University Press, 1984.

Jain, P., ed. *Ādipurāṇa of Āchārya Jinasena.* 2 vols. Jñānapītha Mūrtidevī Jaina Granthamālā Sanskrit Granth nos. 8–9. Kāshī, India: Bhāratīya Jñānapītha, 1963–65.

———, ed. *Mahāpurāna.* Vol. 2: *Uttar Purāna of Acārya Gunbhadra—with Hindi Translation.* Jñānapītha Mūrtidevi Jaina Granthamālā—Sanskrita Grantha no. 14. Kāshī, India: Bhāratīya Jñānapitha, 1954.

Johnson, H. *Triṣaṣṭiśalākāpuruṣacaritra.* 6 vols. Gaekwad's Oriental Series 51, 77, 108, 125, 139, and 140. Baroda, India: Oriental Institute, 1931–62.

Rāybudhasiṃhjī, B. *Śrītriṣaṣṭiśalākāpuruṣacaritra—parva 1, 2, 7, 8, and 9.* 4 vols. Bhāvnagar, India: Śrījainadharmaprasāraka Sabhā, 1903–1907.

Shastrī, M. N. D. *Agni Purāṇa, A Prose English Translation.* 2 vols. Chowkhamba Sanskrit Studies 54. Varanasi, India: Chowkhamba Sanskrit Series Office, 1967.

Secondary Sources

Babb, L. A. *Ascetics and Kings in a Jain Ritual Culture.* Lala Sunder Lal Jain Research Series 11. Delhi: Motilal Banarsidass, 1998, 82.

Bautze-Picron, C., ed. *The Indian Night: Sleep and Dream in India Culture.* New Delhi: Rupa, forthcoming.

Boisvert, M. "Conception and Intrauterine Life in the Pāli Canon." *Studies in Religion/Sciences Religieuses* 29, 3 (2000): 300–11.

Bollée, W. "Physical Aspects of Some Mahāpuruṣas, Descent, Foetality, Birth." *Wiener Zeitschrift für die Kunde Südasiens* 49 (2005): 5–34.

Cort, J. "An Overview of the Jaina Purāṇas." In *Purāṇa Perennis—Reciprocity and Transformation in Hindu and Jaina Texts,* edited by W. Doniger, 185–206. Albany: State University of New York Press, 1993.

Doniger O'Flaherty, W., ed. *Karma and Rebirth in Classical Indian Traditions.* Berkeley: University of California Press, 1980.

Dundas, P. *The Jains.* London: Routledge, 1992.

Glasenapp, H. *Jainism: An Indian Religion of Salvation.* Translated by S. B. Shrotri. Delhi: Motilal Banarsidass, 1999.

Hardy, R. S. *A Manual of Buddhism.* Chowkhamba Sanskrit Studies 56. Varanasi, India: Chowkhamba Sanskrit Series Office, 1967.

Jain, K. C. *Lord Mahāvira and His Times.* Lala Sundar Lal Jain Research Series 6. Delhi: Motilal Banarsidass, 1991.

Jaini, P. S. *The Jaina Path of Purification.* 2nd ed. Delhi: Motilal Banarsidass, 1998.

———. "Jaina Purāṇas: A Purāṇic Counter Tradition." In *Purāṇa Perennis—Reciprocity and Transformation in Hindu and Jaina Texts,* edited by W. Doniger, 207–49. Albany: State University of New York Press, 1993.

Lipner, J. *Hindus—Their Religious Beliefs and Practices.* London: Routledge, 1994.

Meulenbeld, G. J. *A History of Indian Medical Literature.* 3 vols. Groningen Oriental Studies 15. Groningen, Netherlands: Egbert Forsten, 1999–2002.

Sasson, V. R. *The Birth of Moses and the Buddha: A Paradigm for the Comparative Study of Religions.* Sheffield, England: Sheffield Phoenix Press, 2007.

Schubring, W. *The Doctrine of the Jainas.* Lala Sundarlal Jain Research Series 15. Translated by W. Beurlen. Delhi: Motilal Banarsidass, 2000.

Strong, J. S. *The Buddha: A Short Biography.* Oxford: Oneworld, 2002.

Tambiah, S. J. *World Conqueror and World Renouncer: A Study of Buddhism and Polity in Thailand against a Historical Background.* Cambridge Studies in Social Anthropology 15. Cambridge: Cambridge University Press, 1976.

Thompson, S. *Motif-Index of Folk-Literature* (electronic version). Bloomington: Indiana University Press, 1955.

Thompson, S., and J. Balys. *The Oral Tales of India.* Indiana University Publications Folklore Series 10, 261. Bloomington: Indiana University Press, 1958.

A Womb with a View: The Buddha's Final Fetal Experience

Vanessa R. Sasson

The most famous early biography of the Buddha, Aśvaghoṣa's *Buddhacarita*,[1] begins with the story of a young queen who dreamed of a white elephant painlessly entering the right side of her body. Ten lunar months later, she gave birth to a beautiful and luminous son while standing in a garden grasping a branch. He slipped out of her right side, took seven steps and proclaimed his future Buddhahood. Many modern biographies of the Buddha tell a similar tale, and this is ascribable, in part, to the importance of the *Buddhacarita* in Buddhist literature.[2] Most early Buddhist hagiographies, however, have more to say on the subject. A number begin their narratives with descriptions of the Buddha's previous incarnations; others begin with his descent from Tusita heaven. Either way, these early texts make clear that the Buddha's final rebirth was not the beginning of his story.[3] Rather, it was the first scene in the last leg of a very long journey.[4]

Early texts such as the *Acchariyābbhūtasutta* of the *Majjhimanikāya*, Buddhaghosa's commentaries, the *Lalitavistara*, the *Abhiniṣkramaṇasūtra*,

1. Dated by Johnston to approximately the first century CE. See *Aśvaghoṣa's Buddhacarita or Acts of the Buddha*, trans. E. H. Johnston (New Delhi: Motilal Banarsidass, 1995), xvii.

2. See, for example, H. Oldenberg, *Buddha, His Life, His Doctrine, His Order*, trans. W. Hoey (London: Williams and Norgate, 1882); A. Foucher, *La vie du Bouddha d'après les textes et monuments de l'Inde* (Paris: Adrien Maisonneuve, 1949); H. W. Schumann, *The Historical Buddha: The Times, Life, and Teachings of the Founder of Buddhism*, trans. M. O'C. Walshe (London: Arkana, 1982); M. Carrithers, *The Buddha* (New York: Oxford University Press, 1983).

3. John Strong and Richard S. Cohen have been instrumental in reminding readers of this facet of Indian Buddhist hagiography. See J. S. Strong, *The Buddha: A Short Biography* (Oxford: Oneworld, 2001); and R. S. Cohen, "Shakyamuni: Buddhism's Founder in Ten Acts," in *The Rivers of Paradise: Moses, Buddha, Confucius, Jesus, and Muhammad as Religious Founders*, ed. D. N. Freedman and M. J. McClymond (Grand Rapids, Mich.: William B. Eerdmans, 2001), 121–232.

4. I would like to thank both Jason Kalman and Mathieu Boisvert for their comments on this chapter. Their contributions were invaluable.

and the *Mahāvastu*, suggest that the Buddha's life story was remarkable at every stage of his life—including his time in the womb before his final rebirth. He was extraordinary in the beginning, the middle, and the end. His fetal life was no exception. He is described as having been ablaze with light to the point that his mother's womb shone with brilliance and the outside world could see him seated therein. He is said to have resided in a jeweled palace that was brought down by the gods for his stay in the womb. He was bathed by deities, and he even gave teachings to his visitors.

This chapter argues that these stories serve a number of important hagiographic purposes. They give voice to the views of the time, such as the emerging Trikāya doctrine, Āyurvedic medicine, and the doctrine of karma. They distinguish the future Buddha from ordinary beings by rendering him independent and invulnerable, and they foreshadow all the qualities he would eventually manifest as the Buddha he would become. In short, these fetal narratives tell us everything we need to know about the Buddha and the role he comes to play. The womb functions as a perfect metaphor for the cosmos—a legend at the microcosmic level that speaks of something far greater to come.

The Bodhisattva in the Womb

According to the *Acchariyābbhūtasutta*, the in utero life of the Bodhisattva (the future Buddha) was rather unusual. While pregnant with him, his mother was endowed with a supersensory power that allowed her to watch him therein.[5] The queen sat contentedly gazing at her navel as she watched her son grow inside of her. Buddhaghosa likewise states that she could see her son while pregnant, but not because of any supernatural powers; rather, the skin around her womb became magically thin and translucent, providing her with a view.[6] Indeed, he claims that by looking upon her child during her pregnancy through this translucent belly, she was spared of whatever suffering or discomfort her pregnancy would have otherwise generated.

Clearly, however, a translucent belly alone cannot make a fetus visible. The light must have been projected from within for those outside to see him. Although Buddhaghosa is not explicit in this regard, the queen would likely have had to develop an illuminated belly along with her translucent skin for the Bodhisattva to be seen. This light, according to many of the Sanskrit sources, was not generated by the mother's body, but rather by the son's. Buddhaghosa does not make an explicit association between light and the Bodhisattva's body in his commentary

5. *Majjhimanikāya* iii 121. Pāli Canon translations are my own. For the Pāli text, see *Majjhima-nikāya*, 4 vols., ed. V. Trenckner (Oxford: Pali Text Society, 1991–1994). For a discussion of the Buddha's birth from beginning to end, see also V. R. Sasson, *The Birth of Moses and the Buddha: A Paradigm for the Comparative Study of Religions* (Sheffield, England: Sheffield Phoenix Press, 2007).

6. *Majjhimanikāyaṭṭhakathā* iii 121.19. Translations of Buddhaghosa's commentaries are my own. See Buddhaghosācariya. *Papañcasūdanī Majjhimanikāyaṭṭhakathā*, parts 4 and 5, ed. I. B. Horner (London: Pali Text Society, 1977).

to the *sutta*, but he does link the two at the time of delivery. He claims that, as the Bodhisattva emerged, light poured out of her womb "like water pouring out of a water pot."[7] This poetic image connects the Bodhisattva with light in the womb, and thus it is possible that the Bodhisattva was alight while his mother looked through her translucent skin. The Sanskrit sources develop this imagery to a greater extent, rendering the association unambiguous and central to the Buddha's fetal hagiography.

The *Mahāvastu*, for instance, describes the Bodhisattva as exploding with radiance "like a body of pure gold"[8] while in his mother's womb, and, according to the *Lalitavistara*, the Bodhisattva was a brilliant star that illuminated the queen from within:

> When the Bodhisattva had entered his mother's womb, his body assumed a form which appeared like a grand fire on the top of a mountain—a mountain fire which is visible even in a densely dark night at a distance of a yojana—and visible from a distance of five yojanas. Thus did his effulgence spread from the womb of his mother. His complexion was luminous, pleasing, agreeable; and seated on the bedstead in the pavilion, he looked exceedingly beautiful, like the lapis-lazuli set on native silver; and remaining in her fixed position, his mother could always see him in her womb. As the lightening flashing from the clouds enlightens everything, even so did she see the Bodhisattva in his mother's womb.[9]

Whereas Buddhaghosa may have only implied that light emanated from the Bodhisattva, these texts make the association unequivocally clear. The queen's son was aflame with light to the point that he shone through her womb like the sun in the dark universe. The implication here is that the queen was not the only one to partake in this visual pleasure. Her son, exploding with light through her body, was visible to everyone, rendering her pregnancy a much more public event than is normally the case. This is a significant point: because the world outside could gaze upon his radiance, he did not belong to his mother alone. Fetuses have very particular relationships with their mothers. They are the only ones with whom the fetuses interact to any significant extent, and they do so on a profoundly intimate level. The Bodhisattva, however, demonstrated his difference right from the beginning of his final sojourn on earth. He did not limit himself to his mother, but rather expressed himself outward beyond his mother's sphere. Buddhaghosa would have probably agreed with this view, as he comments elsewhere that the Bodhisattva became so visible to the outside world, he was looked upon by others

7. *Majjhimanikāyaṭṭhakathā* iii 122.21.

8. *Mahāvastu* ii 16. For the *Mahavāstu*, see the following translation: *The Mahāvastu*, 3 vols., trans. J. J. Jones (London: Pali Text Society, 1949).

9. *Lalitavistara* 96. For the *Lalitavistara*, see the following translation: *The Lalita Vistara: Memoirs of the Early Life of Sakya Sinha*, chaps. 1–15, trans. R. L. Mitra (Delhi: Sri Satguru Publications, 1998).

"as though he were standing outside the womb."[10] The Bodhisattva would soon become the Buddha, a being with cosmic significance. He could not belong to his mother alone, nor could she expect him to. He belonged to the ten thousand world systems, to history, to the present, and to the future. His fetal life is a microcosmic symbol of his significance on a macrocosmic scale, and, as such, he—as a fetus—had to be available to everyone. He belonged to the universal family and not just to his biological relatives. Moreover, by appearing as though he were standing "outside the womb," he was, in a sense, symbolically standing outside *saṃsāra*. He was a universal being, and he was free.

The light emanating from the future Buddha also highlights the tension he embodied between centrality and selflessness. The Buddha was at the center of the Buddhist universe, the most important and most spiritually advanced being in the ten thousand world systems. He was higher even than the gods. As he glowed inside his mother's belly, he stood alone and above all others as a shining lamp illuminating a path out of the darkness of cyclical existence. And yet, his light also symbolizes his compassion and selflessness, as he showed himself to the world rather than immersing himself in self-absorption. Fetuses are prime examples of self-absorption and self-centeredness. They feed off of their mothers, and as such, can be categorized as human parasites par excellence. But not this fetus. The future Buddha engaged with the world and shone for the benefit of others. He did not use his mother, but rather was of benefit to her. The *Mahāvastu* even remarks that, not only could his mother see him, but he could see her.[11] In other words, he was aware of the outside world, shining upon it and paying attention to it. The Bodhisattva offered himself to others with light and awareness as no other fetus could. He was at the center of his universe, but he was there for the benefit of those around him—the perfect symbol for a being caught between cosmic centrality and absolute selflessness.

What the queen saw inside her womb as a result of his light was no ordinary fetus. This, of course, is to be expected. His glow-in-the-dark feature gave him away. But other elements similarly distinguished his experience from ordinary beings. According to Buddhaghosa, for example, fetuses normally lie in their mothers' wombs curled up like monkeys with their jaws in their fists. The Bodhisattva, however, sat in her womb with his back against her backbone, cross-legged "like an expounder of the Dhamma on his seat, facing East."[12] Fetuses normally resemble primitive animals, but not the Bodhisattva. He sat elegantly in the lotus position, an indication of the Buddha he would eventually become. She therefore did not see within her an ordinary fetus, but beheld a miraculous being who sat with the dignity reserved for awakened beings. The *Mahāvastu* agrees and explains that, when the Bodhisattva entered his mother's womb, "he [did] not occupy a position that

10. *Majjhimanikāyaṭṭhakathā* iii 121.19.

11. *Mahāvastu* ii 16. Buddhaghosa explicitly disagrees with this view (*Majjhimanikāyaṭṭhakathā* iii 121.19). He does not accept that the Bodhisattva could see his mother while still in the womb. He is not willing to attribute to the future Buddha powers that he believes exceed the appropriate. The *Mahāvastu*, however, readily paints the picture of an all-seeing fetal future Buddha.

12. *Majjhimanikāyaṭṭhakathā* iii 121.19.

is either too high or too low. He [did] not lie on his face, nor on his back, nor on his left side, nor squatting on his heels. But he [sat] in his mother's right side with his legs crossed."[13] He sat in the posture of *samādhi*, foreshadowing what he would eventually accomplish.

The Bodhisattva also appeared in his mother's womb in an advanced stage of development. According to a few sources, he did not enter her body as a microscopic collection of cells, but as a fully formed child. The *Abhiniṣkramaṇasūtra* explains that he entered his mother's womb "perfectly formed," experiencing no physical changes from one stage of development to the next.[14] The *Lalitavistara* concurs, stating that the Bodhisattva was not born as a fetus "made of consolidated bubbles and fleshy fibers. No, he appears with all his body and its members fully developed and marked with all auspicious signs, and in a seated position."[15] Moreover, the palace the Bodhisattva resided in while in his mother's womb was made for a six-month-old infant.[16] It may therefore be concluded that the Bodhisattva did not descend in the shape of a fetus, but appeared as a child. Early Indian embryology did recognize that a fetus slowly takes shape over the period of gestation until it is fully formed and ready for birth.[17] Indeed, both Robert Kritzer and Frances Garrett have amply demonstrated this in their articles in this volume. The Bodhisattva, however, did not need to undergo such changes and development. He appeared in the womb prepared to partake in the world. He did not require physical development just as he did not require spiritual development. Although fetuses may be the perfect expression of transformation, this fetus required none. He had reached his full potential even before he was born, and thus, in a sense, never really was a fetus. In fact, it should be noted that he is rarely, if ever, actually described as a fetus in the literature. He is usually referred to as the Bodhisattva (or a similar type of epithet), but almost never as a fetus (i.e., *gabbha* in Pāli, or any of the many other terms employed by the literature for the various stages of embryological development). The Bodhisattva simply resided in the womb. He was a being placed in utero, but a fetus he was not.

The above discussion is obviously rooted in the docetic two-body theory of early Buddhism, which eventually led to the Mahāyāna Trikāya doctrine or the doctrine of "the three bodies" of the Buddha.[18] Evidence of this doctrine can be

13. *Mahāvastu* ii 16. Marten Stol, in his article in this volume, notes that, in ancient Near Eastern literature as well, male fetuses were believed to reside on the right side of the womb. Whether this is a coincidence or a result of cross-cultural influence cannot be known at this time.

14. *Abhiniṣkramaṇasūtra* 41. For the *Abhiniṣkramaṇasūtra*, see the following translation: *The Romantic Legend of Śākya Buddha: A Translation of the Chinese Version of the Abhiniṣkramaṇasūtra*, trans. S. Beal (Delhi: Motilal Banarsidass, 1875).

15. *Lalitavistara* 96.

16. Ibid., 94.

17. The *Sārīra-Sthāna* of the *Suśruta Saṃhitā* describes the various embryonic stages of an ordinary fetus. For a translation of the text, see *Anatomical and Obstetric Considerations in Ancient Indian Surgery: Based on Sārīra-Sthāna of Suśruta Saṃhitā*, ed. G. D. Singhal and L. V. Guru, 3:1–34. Allahbad, India: G. D. Singal, 1973. See also, J. H. Sanford, "Wind, Waters, Stupas, Mandalas: Fetal Buddhahood in Shingon," *Japanese Journal of Religious Studies* 24, 1 (1997): 2–4.

18. For discussion of the Trikāya doctrine, see P. Williams, *Mahāyāna Buddhism: The Doctrinal Foundations* (London: Routledge, 1989), 167–84; and W. Lai, "The Humanity of the Buddha: Is Mahayana 'Docetic'?" *Ching Feng* 24, 2 (1981): 97–107.

found in the earliest sources, in which a dual notion of Buddhahood was invoked: Buddhahood as an abstract reality and Buddhahood embodied in human form. Clearly, the Sanskrit sources were written with this dual perspective in mind, describing a Buddha figure that was, on the one hand, a real human being conceived and developed as all beings are and do, but who was also an illusion, expressing ultimate awakening but never struggling to reach it. All of his actions were, therefore, merely plays put on for the benefit of others. From this perspective, the Buddha was never a fetus, never gestated in his mother's womb, was not delivered ten months later. He never *did* anything, but he *appeared* as though he was acting and participating in the world for the benefit of others. Indeed, the very title of the *Lalitavistara* alludes to this doctrine, as it is a play (*līlā*) of the Buddha's life.

In "The Fruits of Paradox: On the Religious Architecture of the Buddha's Life Story," Jonathan Silk deftly demonstrates the nature of this paradox, which he believes is built into the Buddha's hagiography for literary as well as doctrinal purposes. The paradox, as we have seen, is that the Buddha appeared as someone who needed to experience the world and learn from it in order to discover the truths of Buddhism, and yet he also appeared as a fully awakened being from the moment of his birth (and obviously even earlier than that). This paradox, according to Silk, is not merely the product of the docetic philosophy of Buddhism; it may also be understood as being the result of two simultaneous hagiographic models intertwined into a single narrative. On the one hand, his hagiography was propelled by the authors' desire to relate to him, and thus he was described as a man who achieved awakening after having made concerted efforts for countless lifetimes. With this model, the Buddha was reachable, his life story "re-enactable," to use Ernst Kris's expression.[19] But the Buddha also had to go beyond human potential and dreams; his hagiography was necessarily inadequate, because it could never capture the transcendent nature of Buddhahood. The Buddha therefore also became a magical being putting on a show or play for the world, his every action "enacted in order to conform to the expectations of the world but actually not at all reflective of his true, supramundane, and entirely transcendent character."[20]

No greater illustration of the Buddha's play can be found than in the palace the Bodhisattva is said to have resided in while waiting in his mother's womb. According to the *Lalitavistara*, the gods refused to allow the Bodhisattva to reside in the "stinking human abode"[21] that is a woman's womb for ten unimaginably long months. They therefore brought the Bodhisattva Enjoyment Palace down from the highest heaven and placed it inside the queen's womb. This remarkable palace is described in great detail:

> The mansion was in every way worthy of the Bodhisattva. It was a handsome palace, four-sided, four-cornered, with a pavilion on its top, of the height worthy of an infant six months old. In the middle of the

19. E. Kris, *Psychoanalytic Explorations in Art* (New York: International Universities Press, 1952), 83.
20. J. Silk, "The Fruits of Paradox: On the Religious Architecture of the Buddha's Life Story," *Journal of the American Academy of Religion* 71, 4 (2003): 875.
21. *Lalitavistara* 92.

> pavilion there was a bedstead fit for an infant six months old. The house was so painted that the equal of it could not be found in the regions of the Devas, of the Maras, or of the Brahmas. The Devas were struck with wonder at the sight of its shape and color. Their eyes were quite dazzled. Brought to the side of the Tathagata, it looked exceedingly lustrous, radiant and effulgent. Glowing like a thing made by a skillful goldsmith, and devoid of every defect, the pavilion verily appeared at that time most splendid. Therein appeared the bedstead of Bodhisattva enjoyment, the like of which in make and color nowhere in the regions of the Devas was to be seen, except in the three dimpled lines on the neck of the Bodhisattva. The cloth in which the Mahabrahma (the great Brahma), was arrayed appeared dim in the presence of the Bodhisattva's bedstead—it seemed very like a weather-beaten black blanket.
>
> Within the first pavilion there was another jeweled pavilion made of sandalwood, which was worth as much gold as would equal in bulk a thousand earths;—it was with such wood that the whole of the pavilion was veneered—such was the second pavilion. It stood firm but detached. Within it there was a third pavilion of the same kind. In that pavilion, redolent with exquisite aroma, was the bedstead placed and arranged. Of that sandalwood the color was like that of lapis-lazuli. The redolent pavilion again was covered on the outside with exquisite flowers, which seemed as if the merit of the Bodhisattva's former good acts had been smeared on it.[22]

The Bodhisattva not only resided comfortably in his mother's womb, but according to this source, he did so in the greatest of all palaces, the likes of which had never been seen before on this earth. Surrounded by jeweled walls and exquisite aromas, the Bodhisattva was enveloped in his mother's womb as a future Buddha ought to be. Moreover, all kinds of beings approached him while he was in the womb, and he welcomed them, offered them seats in his enchanted palace, and spoke virtuously to them.[23] His mother likewise welcomed them, as they entered his world through her womb (although how exactly they did this is not clear!).

This scene makes beautiful use of the symbols encountered thus far. He dwelt at the center of his magical universe, hosting guests and giving teachings. Free of self-absorption and isolation, he made himself available to the world, and the universe responded by offering him the most splendid amniotic palace in the universe to dwell in. Although he was living inside a woman's womb, this narrative illustrates, without any ambiguity, that the Bodhisattva was never a fetus or in any way a being requiring development and transformation. He was an awakened being already in the womb, manifesting himself in the world for the benefit of others. His fetal life was merely a play.

His residing in a magical palace also serves a new and very important function: it severs and radically separates the Bodhisattva from his mother. Fetuses

22. Ibid., 94.
23. Ibid., 97.

are normally deeply intertwined with their mothers' bodies. Indeed, it is literally impossible to separate them for quite some time (although this time period is getting shorter as medicine advances). The fetus is wholly dependent upon the mother for survival and its heartbeat is linked to hers. By isolating the Bodhisattva in a jeweled mansion, he was made free of any physical contact or dependency on her. This is further emphasized by the nectar the Bodhisattva was said to have fed himself with while in the womb. Normally, fetuses feed off of their mothers' bodies, nourishing themselves with the fabric of their mothers' insides. According to the *Lalitavistara*, however, the Bodhisattva sustained himself with the nectar of a magical lotus flower that embodied the essence of three thousand realms, provided for him by the Indian god Brahmā as an offering. And he did not even require this to survive, but only accepted the offering "out of favour to Mahābrahma,"[24] thereby highlighting yet again his absolute independence and self-reliance as a fetus. He needed nothing as a fetus, not even food, but the food he did consume was not of his mother's body. He relied upon her least of all. He never touched her body, encased as he was by his jeweled palace, he was not polluted by her bodily fluids, and he did not even feed off of her to survive gestation. His mother was thoroughly eliminated from the equation—something modern medicine is presently striving to achieve as well.

Another layer of maternal elimination can be found in the gender symbolism of the narrative. More than twenty years ago, Helen Hardacre explored the gender issues that emerged from a particular Japanese ritual in which both men and women climb Omine-san Mountain as a reenactment of entering the "womb world,"[25] and her findings can be applied to the Bodhisattva's scenario. The rite is meant to help the pilgrim reenter and then reemerge from the womb with new knowledge and powers. The point is not so much to reenact the birthing process as it is to reenact gestation, for through gestation, the pilgrim can transform him- or herself into a new being, just as a lotus flower can emerge from the mud. Hardacre explores how this ritual is experienced by men and women and notes that, for men, entering the womb implies uniting with difference, whereas for women, it implies returning to a source that is already theirs. Either way, each sex experiences the ritual in a particular way that enables them to be transformed by it. Drawing a parallel with the Bodhisattva's fetal life, we find that he never united with his mother's opposite sexual identity. He was most certainly a male fetus, but he did not require union with his mother's femaleness to complete him. He was safely encased in his amniotic palace like a relic in its own chamber, never needing his mother for food, gestation, or even gender development. He was well beyond all of these needs long before he was born.

A Glimpse into Indian Embryology

The Bodhisattva's fetal experience as described in these early sources, albeit extraordinary by any standard, cannot really be appreciated without some understanding

24. Ibid., 95.
25. H. Hardacre, "The Cave and the Womb World," *Japanese Journal of Religious Studies* 10, 2–3 (1983): 149–76.

of early Indian embryology. In his *Abhidharmakośabhāsyam*, for example, Vasubhandu describes the womb as a hideous wound, "bad-smelling, and wet with all sorts of impurities."[26] These impurities are a result of the various fluids, particularly semen and blood, that permeate the womb and eventually contaminate the fetus residing therein. The future Buddha could not possibly be expected to dwell in such an odious laboratory for ten months. The Bodhisattva Enjoyment Palace brought down from the heavens in the *Lalitavistara* saved the Bodhisattva from any possible association with his mother's inner organs, containing and protecting his purity. But even without the palace, all the sources are quite clear that somehow, the Bodhisattva's fetal life was easy, as he sat with his back straight unencumbered by his environment. When Vasubhandu's description of the womb is considered, the Bodhisattva seems to have had nothing in common with ordinary beings. The only thing he apparently shared with other fetuses was that he resided on the right side of his mother's womb, where, Vasubhandu explains, male fetuses normally reside.[27] Otherwise, he was in a category all his own.

In his *Visuddhimagga*, Buddhaghosa provides a much more vivid description of life in the womb:

> When this being is born in the mother's womb, he is not born inside a blue or red or white lotus, etc., but on the contrary, like a worm in rotting fish, rotting dough, cess-pools, etc., he is born in the belly in a position that is below the receptacle for undigested food (stomach), above the receptacle for digested food (rectum), between the belly-lining and the backbone, which is very cramped, quite dark, pervaded by very fetid draughts redolent of various smells or ordure, and exceptionally loathsome. And on being reborn there, for ten months he undergoes excessive suffering, being cooked like a pudding in a bag by the heat produced in the mother's womb, and steamed like a dumpling of dough, with no bending, stretching, and so on. . . .
>
> When the mother suddenly stumbles or moves or sits down or gets up or turns round, the extreme suffering he undergoes by being dragged back and forth and jolted up and down, like a kid fallen into the hands of a drunkard, or like a snake's young fallen into the hands of a snake-charmer; and also the searing pain that he undergoes, as though he had reappeared in the cold hells, when his mother drinks cold water, and as though deluged by a rain of embers when she swallows hot rice gruel, rice, etc., and as though undergoing the torture of the "lye-pickling" when she swallows anything salty or acidic, etc.—this is the suffering rooted in gestation.[28]

26. *Abhidharmakośabhāsyam* III 19c. For a translation, see *Abhidharmakośabhāsyam*, ed. L. de La Vallée Poussin, trans. L. M. Pruden (Berkeley, Calif.: Asian Humanities Press, 1988).

27. Ibid., III 15a. See also *Mahāvastu* ii 16 and *Lalitavistara* 96.

28. *Visuddhimagga* 500. For a translation, see *Visuddhimagga: The Path of Purification*, trans. Bhikkhu Ñāṇamoli (Seattle: BPE, 1999).

Buddhaghosa obviously felt that life in the womb was one of great torment and pain.[29] The fetus is cramped in a dark and disgusting place where it is jostled with each of his mother's movements and tortured with each bite of food she swallows. This is particularly relevant when we consider the *Abhiniṣkramaṇasūtra* statement that the Bodhisattva never moved during his stay in his mother's womb: "Such movement, from right to left, [gives] constant pain and anxiety to the mother. But Bodhisatwa remains ever at rest, whether the mother rise, or sit, or sleeps."[30]

Both Vasubhandu and Buddhaghosa developed their ideas in an Indian context that understood fetal life as a highly polluting and uncomfortable event. In an article on the Buddha's birth story, Hara Minoru explores Purāṇic descriptions of life in the womb, and demonstrates how similar these notions were to Buddhaghosa's and Vasubhandu's descriptions. Consider the following example: "He [the fetus] experiences severe pains, while being tormented immensely by the foods his mother takes, which are (to him) extremely acid (*amla*), bitter (*katu*), pungent (*tiksna*), hot (*usna*) and saline (*lavana*). Incapable of extending (*prasarana*) or contracting (*akuncana*) his own limbs and reposing amidst a mud of feces and urine, he is in every way incommoded. He is unable to breathe."[31] The Buddha's hagiography is both miraculous and extraordinary, but it is also a response to the developing embryological notions of the time. Although fetuses were believed to suffer unimaginable discomfort and torment, the Bodhisattva experienced only pleasure. He sat comfortably in his mother's womb, cross-legged, straight-backed, and immersed in light. He dwelled, moreover, in a palace surrounded by jewels and perfume according to the *Lalitavistara*, and he did not move. His experience was by no means ordinary, and the hagiographic literature emphasizes this point repeatedly.

His experience was also free of bodily pollution, as noted briefly above. Early Indian society allocated most elements and experiences into one of two categories: purity and pollution. Bodily fluids were considered particularly polluting, rendering all natural human functions and biological processes dangerously contaminating. Birth was (and remains) one of these processes as it involves significant quantities of blood and other bodily fluids.[32] It would hardly be appropriate

29. For further discussions of fetal life in early Indian literature, see M. Boisvert, "Conception and Intrauterine Life in the Pāli Canon," *SIR* 29, 3 (2000): 300–11; J. P. McDermott, "Abortion in the Pāli Canon and Early Buddhist Thought," in *Buddhism and Abortion*, ed. D. Keown (Honolulu: University of Hawaii Press, 1999), 157–82; R. P. Das, *The Origin of the Life of a Human Being: Conception and the Female according to Ancient Indian Medical and Sexological Literature* (Delhi: Motilal Banarsidass, 2003); S. Hamilton, "From the Buddha to Buddhaghosa: Changing Attitudes toward the Human Body in Theravāda Buddhism," in *Religious Reflections on the Human Body*, ed. J. M. Law (Bloomington: Indiana University Press, 1995), 48–63; and E. Wilson, "The Female Body as a Source of Horror and Insight in Post-Ashokan Indian Buddhism," in *Religious Reflections on the Human Body*, 76–99.

30. *Abhiniṣkramaṇasūtra* 41. The author of this text clearly did not understand pregnancy and its effects on women. Far from causing a woman anxiety, a fetus's movement in the womb is normally reassuring as it confirms the health of the being inside her. The fact that the Bodhisattva did not move in his mother's womb may have caused her less physical discomfort, but it could not have been particularly reassuring for her. Perhaps this is why her belly became translucent: if she could neither see him nor feel him move, she would have had no way of knowing he was alive.

31. M. Hara, "A Note on the Buddha's Birth Story," in *Indianisme et Bouddhisme: mélanges offerts a Mgr. Etienne Lamotte* (Louvain, Belgium: Université Catholique de Louvain, 1980), 148–49.

32. For discussion of pollution surrounding childbirth, see D. Jacobson, "Golden Handprints and Red-Painted Feet: Hindu Childbirth Rituals in Central India," in *Unspoken Worlds: Women's Religious Lives*, ed. N. A. Falk and R. M. Gross (Toronto: Wadsworth, 2001), 83–102; R. Jeffrey, P. Jeffrey, and A. Lyon, "Only Cord-Cutters? Midwifery

for the Bodhisattva to be immersed in light, but ritually toxic. He was thus encased in a jeweled palace in part to isolate him from the bodily fluids lurking dangerously without. The *Mahāvastu* is similarly concerned with attributing him a hygienic fetal life by advocating that he was "not polluted by bile, phlegm, blood or any other foul matter, but remain[ed] clean. For while the Bodhisattva [was] in his mother's womb, he ha[d] his body rubbed with perfumes and washed clean."[33] Add to these descriptions the consistent claim in almost all of the early sources (as well as in most of the early iconographic depictions) that the Bodhisattva emerged from the womb through his mother's right side, thereby avoiding the polluting vaginal canal, and we have a fetal hagiography that ensured his purity.[34]

Gods and Demons

The presence of gods in the womb also speaks of the Bodhisattva's significance and distinction. Whether they appeared in order to purify the Bodhisattva, bring him offerings or receive teachings from him, their presence and actions deftly illustrate the new spiritual hierarchy of early Buddhism: that, contrary to contemporary indigenous belief, the Buddha ranked higher than all others. Just as a king is pampered, protected, and bathed by his servants, so was the Bodhisattva by the gods. The gods, however, did not merely function as his personal attendants. Even more scandalous is that they are also depicted as his devotees.

These narratives of divine attendants likewise respond to the Indian medical views of the day. The Bodhisattva's fetal narratives are packed with appearances made by the gods, and this is probably a response to the contemporary medical tradition of demonology. In "Miscarriages of Justice: Demonic Vengeance in Classical Indian Medicine,"[35] Dominik Wujastyk describes the prevalence of demons in Āyurvedic literature, and more specifically in this case, demonic violence against fetuses and children. According to the *Suśruta Saṃhita*, one of the founding classical texts of the North Indian medical tradition, the primary objective of certain demons is to attack children whose mothers or nurses have not kept them clean or who have failed to fulfill the proper ritual requirements surrounding childbirth and the early years. Mothers who have failed in these regards have left themselves open and vulnerable to demonic attack. As Wujastyk so aptly puts it, "This is medical justice: disease as retribution."[36] In the *Kaśyapa Saṃhita*, an entire section is

---

and Childbirth in Rural North India," *Social Action* (1984) 34: 229–50; P. Jeffrey, R. Jeffrey, and A. Lyon, "Contaminating States: Midwifery, Childbearing, and the State in Rural North India," in *The Daughters of Harītī: Childbirth and Female Healers in South and Southeast Asia*, ed. S. Rozario and G. Samuel (London: Routledge, 2002), 90–108; S. Rozario and G. Samuel, "Tibetan and Indian Ideas of Birth Pollution: Similarities and Contrasts," in *The Daughters of Harītī: Childbirth and Female Healers in South and Southeast Asia*, 182–208. For a survey of pollution in world cultures, see M. Douglas, *Purity and Danger: An Analysis of Concepts of Pollution and Taboo* (New York: Frederick A. Praeger, 1966).

33. *Mahāvastu* ii 14.

34. See, for example, the *Buddhacarita* i 10–11.

35. D. Wujastyk, "Miscarriages of Justice: Demonic Vengeance in Classical Indian Medicine," in *Religion, Health, and Suffering*, ed. J. H. Hinnells and R. Porter (London: Kegan Paul, 1999), 256–75.

36. Ibid., 260.

devoted exclusively to demonology, and a number of the demons described in these passages are occupied with causing harm to pregnant women and the fetuses they carry. The most important of these is the demon Revatī, who is described as extremely violent, with wings, a beak, fangs, and eyes that burn like gems.[37] Revatī is committed to killing fetuses that carry the souls of evil demons to protect the world from further violence. In such cases, a miscarriage is understood as being the result of a demon protecting the mother and her family from the evil lurking within her. And, it must be pointed out, the mother would not have been chosen as the vessel for such a creature had she not been susceptible to it. The miscarriage is, therefore, in part at least, a reflection of her moral standing. Sin and disease are inextricably intertwined. Consider the following description:

> Now, consider a woman who has given up righteousness, pious behavior, purity and devotion to god. She hates the gods, cows, priests, gurus, elders, and good people, she is badly behaved, egotistical, and fickle. She loves quarrels, strife, meat-eating, cruelty, sleep and sex. She is vicious, spiteful, voracious, garrulous, nonchalant, and she laughs, bawls or laments for no apparent reason. She tells lies, is a greedy eater, is rumored to be prepared to eat anything, does whatever she wants, and rejects appropriate food and conversation. She is fiercely impious. She is cruel to other people's children, only cares about her own business, and is negligent about helping others. She is contrary with her husband, has no love for her children, and constantly curses them. She deeply despises her father-in-law, her sister-in-law, her brother-in-law, priests, and others who hold such positions. She may devastate them with her fury, or curse them. She is wicked and puts the evil eye on her co-wife, or she does black magic on her using mantras, evil herbs and rituals. And she drops the baby on his head! She doesn't know these people's joys and sorrows. She is malicious towards her friends, what she says is jinxed. She never makes peace offerings, she never does rituals, or meditates, or gives to charity, or makes offerings to her ancestors, or congratulates anyone, or spits, or kisses or hugs anyone, even when it is appropriate.[38]

As a result of this woman's behavior, "she creates openings, caused by the unrighteousness, through which Childsnatcher fastens on to her."[39] In other words, Childsnatcher attacks those women who deserve it. And presumably, such evil women attract fetuses vulnerable to demonic possession that will inevitably be destroyed by way of miscarriage.

If we incorporate this worldview into our understanding of the Buddha's fetal life, yet another layer of his hagiography emerges: the Buddha's mother must have been morally magnificent to have carried him to term; demons would have

37. Ibid., 266.

38. D. Wujastyk, *The Roots of Āyurveda: Selections from Sanskrit Medical Writings* (London: Penguin, 2003), 172–73.

39. Ibid., 173. For descriptions of demonic attacks on pregnant women in the Purāṇas, see S. A. Dange, *Encyclopedia of Puranic Beliefs and Practices*, Vol. 2 (New Delhi: Navrang, 1987), 384–85.

otherwise successfully intervened. The Bodhisattva was an extraordinary fetus, but she too deserves praise, and his famous five great investigations support this view. According to most of the early sources, while still a god in the Tusita heaven, the Bodhisattva scanned the many thousand world systems looking for the ultimate vessel for rebirth. Out of all the women in all the universes, only one qualified to play this cosmically significant role: Māyā alone was born in the right time, continent, country, and family; she alone could boast of an exemplary record of virtuous behavior over a period of countless lifetimes.[40] Because she alone qualified, she was chosen to carry him in her womb. And demonic violence *was* attempted, according to Buddhaghosa. He reports that they lurked in her chambers during her pregnancy, but the Four Great Kings kept them at bay, guarding her and her precious cargo with valiance and enthusiasm.[41] The demons therefore were a concern, but both mother and fetus were shielded by merit and celestial bodyguards.

The Indian medical literature is concerned not only with demons, but with bipolar divinity as well. Pregnant women are vulnerable creatures, easy prey for the evils lurking without, and thus they have to be particularly diligent about protecting themselves through ritual and moral behavior.[42] Demons are a risk to be taken seriously, but the gods are similarly elements to contend with. Divine forces (more commonly female ones) appear to counteract many of these demons, to fight the pregnant woman's fight for her. But sometimes, a goddess may also *be* the demon in an expression of divine bipolarity. Consider Bemata, for example—a goddess found in certain rural areas of Northern India. She is described by Janet Chawla as the goddess of female reproductive physiology.[43] She is responsible for the creation and healthy development of fetuses, but she also embodies the violence of destruction, responsible, as she is, for the death of fetuses and young children. Bemata is, therefore, both the goddess and the demon of fetuses and childbirth. Hāritī may be Bemata's Buddhist equivalent. According to the *Mūlasarvāstivāda Vinaya*, she began as a child-eating ogress, but the Buddha was eventually able to persuade her against her evil ways. To ensure that she never slip back into her bad habits, the Buddha enthroned her as a child-granting goddess.[44] Like Bemata, she embodies both the violence of a demon and the benevolence of a goddess.[45]

40. *Majjhimanikāyaṭṭhakathā* iii 119.29.

41. Ibid., 120.22; the *Mahāvastu* likewise makes reference to these cosmic guardians, but not to the attacks they were employed to deflect. See *Mahāvastu* ii 11.

42. The *Kaśyapa Saṃhita* gives a long description of the rituals a woman is expected to fulfill in order to ensure a safe pregnancy and delivery. I see little evidence in the early hagiographic literature of Māyā performing these. See Wujastyk, *Roots of Āyurveda*, 185–89; and P. Kolenda, "Pox and the Terror of Childlessness: Images and Ideas of the Smallpox Goddess in a North Indian Village," in *Mother Worship: Themes and Variations*, ed. J. J. Preston (Chapel Hill: University of North Carolina Press, 1982), 242.

43. J. Chawla, "Negotiating Narak and Writing Destiny: The Theology of Bemata in Dais' Handling of Birth," in *Invoking Goddesses: Gender and Politics in Indian Religion*, ed. N. Chitgopekar (New Delhi: Shakti Books, 2002), 175. For further discussion on this phenomenon, see also D. Kinsley, *Hindu Goddesses: Visions of the Divine Feminine in the Hindu Religious Tradition* (Berkeley: University of California, 1986), 151–60.

44. For Hāritī's story, see J. Strong, *The Legend and Cult of Upagupta: Sanskrit Buddhism in North India and Southeast Asia* (Princeton, N.J.: Princeton University Press, 1992), 36. See also N. Peri, "Hāritī, la mère des demons," *Bulletin de l'Ecole Française d'Extrême Orient* 17, 3 (1917): 1–15.

45. Sīitalā, the goddess of smallpox, is another example of this phenomenon. See Kolenda, "Pox and the Terror of Childlessness."

Given this complex system of bipolar divinity, and given pregnant women's particular susceptibility to demonic or even divine attacks, it is clear that fetuses require all the protection they can get to make it through the dangerous journey of gestation and birth. Gods and goddesses were with the Bodhisattva in the womb, and one of these may have easily turned on him therein. Fetuses represent ultimate vulnerability, susceptible as they are to the dangers of both the material and the supernatural world, and they can do nothing to protect themselves other than attempt survival—and even this they often cannot manage. The future Buddha, however, was not a vulnerable being. The joy at his birth described in the literature was not an expression of relief that he survived his ordeal, but rather was the sound of celebration for the long-awaited near-Awakened One. He was not prey to demonic attack, nor indeed was he in danger of divine upset. Gods shared the womb with him, both to guard him from the violence of others, and to articulate his own strength as he rested unconcerned by their bipolar identity. He was not at risk in the womb; he was not defenseless.

The gods, therefore, serve a number of functions in his hagiography. They express the new spiritual hierarchy of Buddhism; they guard and attend to him during what is normally a tenuous time; and they illustrate his absolute transcendence over all things ordinary. Perhaps their most important function, however, was as a source of devotion: by showering the future Buddha with celestial attendants, these gods presented the authors with an opportunity to express their devotion to the Awakened One.

Karma

A discussion about the Buddha's fetal life is not complete without addressing karma. According to the *Suśruta Saṃhitā*, the mother, the fetus, her morality, her karma, and the fetus's karma are all deeply intertwined.[46] If she miscarries or produces a deformed or sickly child, the cause is to be found either in a demonic attack, her karma, the fetus's karma, or in her behavior while pregnant—or any of these causes combined.[47] And if the fetus's experience in the womb was blissful and even luminous, as in the Buddha's case, it was the consequence of divine protection, someone's karma, and/or of the mother's exemplary behavior and mental state throughout the process.

Much of the early hagiographic literature depicted the Bodhisattva's stay in the womb as having been comfortable for both the mother and the fetus. According to the *Acchariyābbhūtasutta*, the queen was healthy and happy throughout her pregnancy and was never tired. Buddhaghosa agrees and adds that her hands and

46. *Sārīra-Sthāna* 3:18–28.

47. It was also believed that a mother experiences a series of cravings (*dohada*) during her pregnancy, and that, should these not be fulfilled, the fetus could be seriously endangered. For a discussion of Māyā's cravings during her pregnancy with the Bodhisattva, see H. Durt, "The Pregnancy of Māyā: The Five Uncontrollable Longings (*dohada*)," *Journal of the International College for Advanced Buddhist Studies* 5 (2002): 43–66.

feet were not even bloated.[48] According to the *Lalitavistara*, the queen was healthy and energetic during her pregnancy. She knew none of the pains of pregnancy, experiencing only happiness and a feeling of lightness.[49] The Bodhisattva, moreover, obviously had a pleasurable experience, what with being bathed and perfumed by goddesses and contained in a jeweled amniotic palace. We may therefore conclude that both she and the fetus she was carrying were virtuous beings, free from demonic possession and accompanied by positive karma.

To reinforce this point, we may consider the Buddha's son, Rāhula, and his experiences in the womb. According to a number of sources, Rāhula spent six years inside his mother's womb, and the explanation for this extraordinary length of time is to be found in the karma produced by both him and his mother in their past lives. One version describes Rāhula as a prince named Candra in a past life. His older brother, Suriya, relinquished the throne for a life of homelessness, and as a result, Candra became king. Suriya became a hermit and took a vow to never take anything that was not freely given to him. He was deeply committed to this vow, but one day found that he needed medicinal herbs, but there was no one around to give them to him. He therefore broke his vow and took them himself. On another occasion, he was thirsty and drank water from a pitcher. The owner of the pitcher discovered the theft and accused him of being a fraud. This pained Suriya deeply, as he realized that he had not fulfilled his vow as purely as he had intended. He turned himself over to his brother the king as a thief. Candra refused to charge him with the crime and insisted that hermits are permitted to take water and herbs without asking. Still, Suriya was not satisfied. He believed that his brother established this new rule to appease his guilt, and he was certain the rule did not exist when he committed his crimes. Eventually, Candra accepted Suriya's "guilt" and ordered him to the royal garden to live as a prisoner. Six days passed before Candra remembered his brother in the royal garden. He asked his servants if Suriya was still there or if he had left.[50] Upon discovering that his brother was still there, he set him and all other prisoners free, and offered Suriya a variety of gifts in apology. The text explains that, because he forgot his brother for six days in the garden, Rāhula was left for six years in the womb.[51]

The *Abhiniṣkramaṇasūtra* provides a second explanation. It focuses on the karmic history of the Buddha's wife and Rāhula's mother, Yaśodharā. In a past life, Yaśodharā was the daughter of a milkmaid. Every day, she and her mother went to milk their cows and brought the milk home in pails. One day, her mother gave her the heavier pail of milk to carry. The girl complained and eventually put it down. She walked away, leaving her mother behind to carry the pail for the length of six

48. *Majjhimanikāyaṭṭhakathā* iii 121.18.

49. *Lalitavistara* 99.

50. He was obviously not bound physically to the garden.

51. *Abhiniṣkramaṇasūtra* 361–63. See also *Mahāvastu* iii 172–75. Strong refers to this story as it appears in the *Mūlasarvāstivadā Vinaya* in his article, "A Family Quest: The Buddha, Yaśodharā, and Rāhula in the *Mūlasarvāstivadā Vinaya*," in *Sacred Biography in the Buddhist Traditions of South and Southeast Asia*, ed. J. Schober (Honolulu: University of Hawaii Press, 1997), 116–24.

yojanas.[52] Because the girl made her mother carry the pail for six *yojanas*, she was made to carry Rāhula for six years.[53]

Both of these stories demonstrate karmic influence over pregnancy. Both mother and fetus generated a particular karma to warrant this extraordinary gestation period. Rāhula was to be abandoned in the womb just as he had abandoned his brother, and Yaśodharā had to carry a burden[54] for an extended period of time to repay the debt she incurred by making her mother do the same. Their karma shaped this pregnancy just as it shapes all pregnancies—Māyā's included.

Conclusion

The Buddha's final fetal experience was an extraordinary adventure. Although ordinary beings suffer, trapped deep inside their mothers' bodies between the different tracts of the digestive system constantly wet with impurities, the Bodhisattva did not. His experience was blissful, surrounded by gods and goddesses, dwelling in a palace with jeweled walls and exquisite aromas, and he never had to endure any contact with his mother's bodily fluids. All of these miraculous features emerge as a result of the hagiographical need to separate the Buddha from his mother and to raise him in stature above ordinary mortals.

Moreover, these fetal narratives function as a microcosm for his hagiography as a whole. Everything one needs to know about the Buddha can be learned from these narratives—his cosmic centrality, his superiority over the gods, his selflessness, his willingness to teach, his invulnerability, his independence, and his accumulated store of positive karma. Further, his mother's womb became a mini-universe in which the Buddha demonstrated his playfulness. He was not like other fetuses because he did not share their needs. Indeed, he was not really a fetus after all. He was a dharma being, presenting himself in utero to inspire his audience. The view from this womb—and the view into it!—were extraordinary indeed.

WORKS CITED

Abhidharmakośabhāsyam. Edited by L. de La Vallée Poussin. Translated by L. M. Pruden. Berkeley, Calif.: Asian Humanities Press, 1988.

Anatomical and Obstetric Considerations in Ancient Indian Surgery: Based on Sārīra-Sthāna of Suśruta Saṃhitā. Edited by G. D. Singhal and L. V. Guru. Allahbad, India: G. D. Singal, 1973.

Aśvaghoṣa. *Buddhacarita or Acts of the Buddha*. Translated by E. H. Johnston. New Delhi: Motilal Banarsidass, 1995.

52. A *yojana* is defined by the Pali-English dictionary as "a measure of length: as much as can be traveled with one yoke (of oxen); a distance of about 7 miles." See *The Pali-Text Society's Pali-English Dictionary*, ed. T. W. Rhys-Davids and W. Stede (Oxford: Pali Text Society, 1998), 559.

53. *Abhiniṣkramaṇasūtra* 363. Also appears in the *Mūlasarvāstivadā Vinaya* as reported by Strong in "A Family Quest," 116–17.

54. Hence the name *Rāhula*, which means, among other things, "burden" in Pāli.

Boisvert, M. "Conception and Intrauterine Life in the Pāli Canon." *Studies in Religion / Sciences Religieuses* 29, 3 (2000): 300–11.
Buddhaghosācariya. *Papañcasūdanī Majjhimanikāyaṭṭhakathā*. Parts 4 and 5. Edited by I. B. Horner. London: Pali Text Society, 1977.
Carrithers, M. *The Buddha*. New York: Oxford University Press, 1983.
Chawla, J. "Negotiating Narak and Writing Destiny: The Theology of Bemata in Dais' Handling of Birth." In *Invoking Goddesses: Gender and Politics in Indian Religion*, edited by N. Chitgopekar, 165–99. New Delhi: Shakti Books, 2002.
Cohen, R. S. "Shakyamuni: Buddhism's Founder in Ten Acts." In *The Rivers of Paradise: Moses, Buddha, Confucius, Jesus, and Muhammad as Religious Founders*, edited by D. N. Freedman and M. J. McClymond, 121–232. Grand Rapids, Mich.: William B. Eerdmans, 2001.
Dange, S. A. *Encyclopedia of Puranic Beliefs and Practices*. Vol. 2. New Delhi: Navrang, 1987.
Das, R. P. *The Origin of the Life of a Human Being: Conception and the Female according to Ancient Indian Medical and Sexological Literature*. Delhi: Motilal Banarsidass, 2003.
Douglas, M. *Purity and Danger: An Analysis of Concepts of Pollution and Taboo*. New York: Frederick A. Praeger, 1966.
Durt, H. "The Pregnancy of Māyā: the Five Uncontrollable Longings (*dohada*)." *Journal of the International College for Advanced Buddhist Studies* 5 (2002): 43–66.
Foucher, A. *La vie du Bouddha d'après les textes et monuments de l'Inde*. Paris: Adrien Maisonneuve, 1949.
Hamilton, S. "From the Buddha to Buddhaghosa: Changing Attitudes toward the Human Body in Theravāda Buddhism." In *Religious Reflections on the Human Body*, edited by J. M. Law, 48–63. Bloomington: Indiana University Press, 1995.
Hara, M. "A Note on the Buddha's Birth Story." In *Indianisme et Bouddhisme: mélanges offerts à Mgr. Etienne Lamotte*, edited by D. Donnet, A. Bareau, and H. Bechert. Louvain, Belgium: Institut Orientaliste, Université Catholique de Louvain, 1980.
Hardacre, H. "The Cave and the Womb World." *Japanese Journal of Religious Studies* 10, 2–3 (1983): 149–76.
Jacobson, D. "Golden Handprints and Red-Painted Feet: Hindu Childbirth Rituals in Central India." In *Unspoken Worlds: Women's Religious Lives*, edited by N. A. Falk and R. M. Gross, 83–102. Toronto: Wadsworth, 2001.
Jeffrey, P., R. Jeffrey, and A. Lyon. "Contaminating States: Midwifery, Childbearing, and the State in Rural North India." In *The Daughters of Harītī: Childbirth and Female Healers in South and Southeast Asia*, edited by S. Rozario and G. Samuel, 90–108. London: Routledge, 2002.
Jeffrey, R., P. Jeffrey, and A. Lyon. "Only Cord-Cutters? Midwifery and Childbirth in Rural North India." *Social Action* 34 (1984): 229–50.
Kinsley, D. *Hindu Goddesses: Visions of the Divine Feminine in the Hindu Religious Tradition*. Berkeley: University of California, 1986.
Kolenda, P. "Pox and the Terror of Childlessness: Images and Ideas of the Smallpox Goddess in a North Indian Village." In *Mother Worship: Themes and Variations*, edited by J. J. Preston, 227–50. Chapel Hill: University of North Carolina Press, 1982.
Kris, E. *Psychoanalytic Explorations in Art*. New York: International Universities Press, 1952.
Lai, W. "The Humanity of the Buddha: Is Mahayana 'Docetic'?" *Ching Feng* 24, 2 (1981): 97–107.
The Lalita Vistara: Memoirs of the Early Life of Sakya Sinha. Chaps. 1–15. Translated by R. L. Mitra. Delhi: Sri Satguru Publications, 1998.
The Mahāvastu. 3 vols. Translated by J. J. Jones. London: Pali Text Society, 1949.

Majjhima-nikāya. 4 vols. Edited by V. Trenckner. Oxford: Pali Text Society, 1991–1994.

McDermott, J. P. "Abortion in the Pāli Canon and Early Buddhist Thought." In *Buddhism and Abortion,* edited by D. Keown, 157–82. Honolulu: University of Hawaii Press, 1999.

Oldenberg, H. *Buddha, His Life, His Doctrine, His Order*. Translated by W. Hoey. London: Williams and Norgate, 1882.

Peri, N. "Hāritī, la mère des démons." *Bulletin de l'Ecole Française d'Extrême Orient* 17, 3 (1917): 1–15.

The Romantic Legend of Śākya Buddha: A Translation of the Chinese Version of the Abhiniṣkramaṇasūtra. Translated by S. Beal. Delhi: Motilal Banarsidass, 1875.

Rozario, S., and G. Samuel. "Tibetan and Indian Ideas of Birth Pollution: Similarities and Contrasts." In *The Daughters of Harītī: Childbirth and Female Healers in South and Southeast Asia,* edited by S. Rozario and G. Samuel, 182–208. London: Routledge, 2002.

Sanford, J. H. "Wind, Waters, Stupas, Mandalas: Fetal Buddhahood in Shingon." *Japanese Journal of Religious Studies* 24, 1 (1997): 1–38.

Sasson, V. R. *The Birth of Moses and the Buddha: A Paradigm for the Comparative Study of Religions*. Sheffield, England: Sheffield Phoenix Press, 2007.

Schumann, H. W. *The Historical Buddha: The Times, Life and Teachings of the Founder of Buddhism*. Translated by M. O'C. Walshe. London: Arkana, 1982.

Silk, J. "The Fruits of Paradox: On the Religious Architecture of the Buddha's Life Story." *Journal of the American Academy of Religion* 71, 4 (2003): 863–81.

Strong, J. S. *The Buddha: A Short Biography*. Oxford: Oneworld, 2001.

———. *The Legend and Cult of Upagupta: Sanskrit Buddhism in North India and Southeast Asia*. Princeton, N.J.: Princeton University Press, 1992.

Visuddhimagga: The Path of Purification. Translated by Bhikkhu Ñāṇamoli. Seattle, Wash.: Paryatti Editions, 1999.

Williams, P. *Mahāyāna Buddhism: The Doctrinal Foundations*. London: Routledge, 1989.

Wilson, E. "The Female Body as a Source of Horror and Insight in Post-Ashokan Indian Buddhism." In *Religious Reflections on the Human Body,* edited by J. M. Law, 76–99. Bloomington: Indiana University Press, 1995.

Wujastyk, D. "Miscarriages of Justice: Demonic Vengeance in Classical Indian Medicine." In *Religion, Health and Suffering,* edited by J. H. Hinnells and R. Porter, 256–75. London: Kegan Paul, 1999.

———. *The Roots of Āyurveda: Selections from Sanskrit Medical Writings*. London: Penguin, 2003.

Life in the Womb: Conception and Gestation in Buddhist Scripture and Classical Indian Medical Literature

Robert Kritzer

The first Noble Truth of Buddhism asserts that all is suffering. In this context, the word "all" means all conditioned things, that is to say, all worldly things. Hence anything that perpetuates the cycle of rebirth in this world can be considered antithetical to liberation and subject to condemnation.

A number of Buddhist *sūtras*, meditation manuals, and doctrinal texts, probably written before the third century, describe in various degrees of completeness the stages between one lifetime and the next. The process of rebirth begins at the moment of death in one life, continues through the intermediate existence or *antarābhava*, the moment of conception, and the period of gestation, and culminates in the moment of birth in the next life. Among the Buddhist texts that take up the topic, the *Garbhāvākrāntisūtra* presents the most detailed description of conception and gestation.

Little has been written about this fascinating *sūtra*. In this chapter, I compare its accounts of the crucial moment of conception and the period of gestation with accounts in Indian medical literature, particularly the *Carakasaṃhitā*. On the one hand, there are many similarities, which may be the result of mutual influence between the Buddhist *sūtra* and the medical texts as well as possible borrowing from a now-lost common source. On the other hand, there are also considerable differences, which can be explained at least in part by the fact that the *sūtra* and the medical texts have different purposes.

This is an expanded version of the 2006 Numata Lecture at McGill University, a transcript of which is being published in *ARC: The Journal of the Faculty of Religious Studies, McGill University*. I am indebted to Professor Elizabeth Kenney for her invaluable criticism and suggestions.

Before examining the *Garbhāvakrāntisūtra*, I will start out by briefly discussing some non-Buddhist Indian religious texts that include descriptions of the rebirth process so that the special features of the *sūtra* will stand out in contrast. The texts that I mention are not particularly old; in fact, they are all probably more recent than the *sūtra*. But we cannot conclude that they are based on the *sūtra*. It is more likely that they borrow from the same common sources as the *sūtra* and the medical literature.

Rebirth Accounts in Non-Buddhist Religious Texts

In stories of the Buddha's birth, the Buddha, unlike ordinary people, is said to be born in a state of complete purity, unblemished by the messy fluids that normally characterize birth. Furthermore, he causes his mother none of the usual discomforts of pregnancy and childbirth, and he emerges from her side rather than be born in the conventional way. As a result, he completely avoids the "suffering at birth" (*janmaduḥkha*) and is able to remain conscious for the entire period of conception, gestation, and birth.[1] Uniquely, the Buddha remembers all his past lives and embarks upon his last birth confident that he will achieve enlightenment.

The experience of ordinary people is quite different. Because of the oppressive environment of the womb and the narrowness of the vagina, they lose consciousness when they are born and, with it, all memory of their past lives. As a result, they are doomed to ignorance and to continued suffering in *saṃsāra*. A number of non-Buddhist texts, summarized by Hara, describe how the fetus is folded and distorted in the womb, how it is tormented by contact with the food the mother consumes and with her feces and urine, how it is squeezed unbearably by the vagina, and how it is shocked unconscious when it touches the outside air.[2]

Other texts go into some detail regarding the development of the fetus in the womb. According to the *Agnipurāṇa*, the soul (*jīva*), after entering the womb, first becomes *kalala* (liquid in consistency). In the second month, it becomes *ghana* (a solid mass). In the third month, the limbs develop; in the fourth, bones, skin, and flesh. In the fifth month, body hair appears. In the sixth, consciousness develops. In the seventh month, the fetus experiences suffering. Its body is covered with the placenta, and its hands are folded on its forehead. If it is female, it is positioned on the left, if male, on the right, and it faces its mother's back. If it is neuter,[3] it is positioned in the middle of the belly. The fetus knows without doubt in whose

1. The Indian religious literature on the rebirth process has been explored by Hara Minoru, who is especially interested in the notion of *janmaduḥkha*. This literally means "suffering at birth" but can also be loosely applied to the period immediately before birth. See M. Hara, "Shō ku," in *Hotoke no Kenkyū: Tamaki Kōshirō Hakushi Kanrekikinenronshū* (Tokyo: Shunjūsha, 1977), 667–83; M. Hara, "A Note on the Buddha's Birth Story," in *Indianisme et Bouddhisme: Mélanges offerts à Mgr Étienne Lamotte* (Louvain, Belgium: Université Catholique du Louvain, 1980), 143–57. See also Sasson's chapter in this volume.

2. M. Hara, "Note on the Buddha's Birth Story," 146–51.

3. The Sanskrit word here is *klīva* ("neuter"). In other texts, the word *napuṃsaka* is used, probably suggesting an intermediate gender rather than a lack of sex organs (S. Smets, "Le développement embryonnaire selon la *Jaiminīyasaṃhitā* du *Brahmāṇḍapurāṇa*: Étude sur l'intertextualité," *Studia Asiatica* 4–5 [2003–2004]: 313–330).

womb it is. Furthermore, it knows its past lives since it was first born as a human, and it experiences darkness and great pain. Also in the seventh month, the fetus obtains nourishment consumed by its mother. In the eighth and ninth months, it is greatly afflicted, receiving pain when the mother has sex or is very active and being ill when she is ill. A moment seems like a hundred years; the fetus is tortured by its karma, and it wishfully vows, "Brahman, freed from the womb, [I] will achieve knowledge of liberation." The fetus is finally turned head downward by the birth-wind and goes out, being pressed by the restraint of the vagina, and, for the first month of life outside the womb, it is pained by the mere touch of a hand.[4]

The *Garbhopaniṣad* also gives a brief, month-by-month description: During the first month, the fetus passes through the stages of *kalala, budbuda* (bubble-like), and *piṇḍa* (a roundish lump), becoming solid by the end of the first month. By the end of two months, the head has developed; after three months, the feet; four, the ankles, belly, and hips; five, the back; six, the mouth, nose, eyes, and ears. In the seventh month, the fetus is joined with the soul (*jīva*). In the eighth month, it is complete in its parts, the sex and certain birth defects are determined, and the senses and consciousness can operate. In the ninth month, it is complete in all its qualities and knowledge, and it remembers its past births and its good and bad karma. After this, the fetus contemplates the suffering of repeated births and deaths and resolves to study Sāṃkhya and Yoga in order to achieve emancipation, but when it is born, it forgets its rebirths and karma.[5]

Another account is found in a Jaina text, the *Tandulaveyāliya*.[6] This work consists of groups of verses separated by prose passages, and there are some minor differences between the verses and the prose. According to the prose account, in the first month, the fetus weighs three-quarters of a *pala* (about 75 grams). In the second month, it is called *pesī,* which is described as being *ghaṇa*, or solid. In the third month, two-heartedness (*dohala*) develops. This is the condition in which the fetus influences the mother, who develops inexplicable whims. In the fourth month, the fetus causes the mother's body to swell up. In the fifth month, five lumps, namely the hands, feet, and head, develop. In the sixth month, bile and blood accumulate. In the seventh month, the fetus develops seven hundred veins, five hundred muscles, nine arteries, and 35 million pores. The fetus is complete in the eighth month, and birth takes place in the ninth.[7]

These accounts display some differences, as can be seen in the accompanying table. One thing we notice in comparing these three texts is that there is little agreement regarding the precise terms assigned to each of the earliest stages of the fetus, although similar words appear in all texts, such as *kalala* and *ghana.* However, the most striking difference among the texts is that the description in the *Tandulaveyāliya,* the shortest of the three, does not refer to the subjective experience

4. *Agnipurāṇa* 3: 398.19–27. Hara, "Shōku," 673. Manmatha Nāth Dutt Shastri, *Agni Purāṇam* (Varanasi: Chowkhamba Sanskrit Series Office, 1967), 2: 1288–1289.

5. *Garbha-Upanisad (Garbhopanisad).* Available at www.sub.uni-goettingen.de/ebene_1/fiindolo/gretil/1_sanskr/1_veda/4_upa/garbhupu.htm.

6. I am grateful to Professor Nalini Balbir for bringing this text to my attention.

7. *Tandulaveyāliya*: 5.6–12.

A Comparison of the Development of the Fetus in the *Agnipurāṇa*, *Garbhopaniṣad*, and *Tandulaveyāliya* [Jaina]

Month	*Agnipurāṇa*	*Garbhopaniṣad*	*Tandulaveyāliya* [Jaina]
1	soul enters the womb, becomes *kalala*	*kalala, bubuda, piṇḍa*; becomes solid (*kaṭhina*)	verse *kalala, abuya, pesī, ghaṇa* prose weight: 3/4 *pala*
2	becomes solid (*ghana*)	head develops	becomes *pesī*, which is solid (*ghaṇa*)
3	limbs develop	feet develop	two-heartedness (*dohala*) develops
4	bones, skin, flesh develop	ankles, belly, hips develop	the mother's body swells up
5	body hair appears	back develops	hands, feet, and head develop
6	consciousness appears	mouth, nose, eyes, ears develop	bile and blood accumulate
7	fetus experiences suffering, knows its career	fetus is joined with soul	700 veins, 500 muscles, nine arteries, 35 million pores develop
8	receives pain from mother's activities, vows to attain liberation after birth	complete in all parts, consciousness can operate	fetus is completed
9	head turned downward by the birth-wind, pressed by the vagina, experiences pain after birth	complete in all qualities, remembers past births and karma, resolves to achieve emancipation, forgets past births and karma upon being born	birth takes place

of the fetus. However, the group of verses that are found at the end of the first section of the text elaborates on the suffering of birth in a way similar to the other texts.[8] Thus, although the month-by-month account in the *Tandulaveyāliya* is more neutral and, as we shall see, closer to accounts found in the medical texts, it is put to use in the same way as those of the other religious texts in emphasizing the ills of *saṃsāra* and encouraging the pursuit of liberation.[9]

The most dramatic religious account of the rebirth process, however, is found in the Buddhist *Garbhāvakrāntisūtra*. Although it shares many features with the non-Buddhist texts mentioned here, it is far richer in medical or pseudo-medical detail, and, especially in the later version, it is far more insistent on its religious message, intent upon illustrating the first Buddhist Noble Truth of suffering in every stage of the rebirth process.

8. Ibid., 18–21 (6.23–30).

9. C. Caillat. "Sur les doctrines médicales dans le *Tandulaveyāliya* 1. Enseignements d'embryologie," *Indologica Taurinensia* 2 (1974): 51.

Next, I will analyze the descriptions of conception, gestation, and childbirth in the *Sūtra* in comparison with corresponding material from the *Carakasaṃhitā* to show how the Buddhist and medical traditions draw on a common store of information about the facts of life for their very different purposes. First, I will briefly introduce these two texts.

The *Garbhāvakrāntisūtra*

The *Garbhāvakrāntisūtra* is a rather long *sūtra* that includes an account of the mechanism of rebirth. The account begins before conception, when the being about to be reborn is in the intermediate state (*antarābhava*). The text is best known for its week-by-week description of the development of the fetus, but it also details the ills to which the newly born being is subject.

There are several extant versions of the *sūtra*. The earliest is a translation by Dharmarakṣa titled *Pao-t'ai ching* (Taishō edition, Buddhist canon [T.], 317), dated 281 or 303. A translation by Bodhiruci titled *Fo wei a-nan shuo ch'u-t'ai hui* (T. 310 n. 13), dated 703–713, is found in the *Ratnakūṭasūtra*. I-ching also translated the *sūtra*, and his translation (dated 710) can be found in two different places, in the *Ratnakūṭasūtra* (T. 310 n. 14), titled *Fo shuo ju-t'ai-tsang hui*), and in the *Mūlasarvāstivādavinayakṣudrakavastu*, titled *Ju-mu-t'ai ching* (T. 1451: 251a14–262a19). I-ching's version is much longer than Dharmarakṣa's or Bodhiruci's. It consists of three parts: (1) an account of the instruction of Nanda; (2) an account of conception and gestation that generally corresponds with Bodhiruci's version, followed by various teachings related to suffering and how to overcome it; (3) an account of Nanda's previous lives. There is no extant Sanskrit for the portion of the *Mūlasarvāstivādavinaya* in which the *sūtra* is found, but there is a ninth-century Tibetan translation. The other Tibetan translations of the *sūtra* are from the Chinese translations, not from a Sanskrit original.

The *Carakasaṃhitā*

The *Carakasaṃhitā* is the earliest of the Indian medical texts that Kenneth Zysk calls "the classical compilations," which also include the *Suśrutasaṃhitā*, the *Aṣṭāṅgahṛdayasaṃhitā*, and the *Aṣṭāṅgasaṃgraha*. As is the case with Indian Buddhist texts, it is difficult to establish the dates of Indian medical texts. According to Zysk, the *Carakasaṃhitā* and the *Suśrutasaṃhitā* probably date from a few centuries before or after the beginning of the common era,[10] whereas the *Aṣṭāṅgahṛdayasaṃhitā* and the *Aṣṭāṅgasaṃgraha* are from around the seventh century, with the *Aṣṭāṅgahṛdayasaṃhitā* probably being slightly older.[11]

10. K. G. Zysk, "Mythology and the Brāhmaṇization of Indian Medicine: Transforming Heterodoxy into Orthodoxy," in *Categorization and Interpretation*, ed. Folke Josephson (Göteborg, Sweden: Meijerbergs institut för svensk etymologisk forskning, Göteborg universitet, 1999), 125.

11. Ibid., 139.

Clearly, the authors of Indian medical texts share a certain pool of knowledge with authors of religious texts, both Buddhist and non-Buddhist. I am primarily concerned with the different emphases and the uses to which this knowledge is put in the *Garbhāvakrāntisūtra*, which includes the most prominent Buddhist treatment of the subject of conception and gestation, and the *Carakasaṃhitā*, which I have chosen as a representative of the classical medical tradition.

Conception

Since both the *Garbhāvakrāntisūtra* and the *Carakasaṃhitā* presuppose a belief in rebirth related to, if not directly resulting from, karma, it is not surprising that their accounts of conception are generally quite similar. According to both texts, the mother must be at the proper time of her menstrual cycle, and her reproductive organs must be healthy. Naturally, the father and mother must have sex. Finally, the entity that will be reborn as the new baby must be present in the form of the intermediate being (*antarābhava*) at the time of intercourse; this is crucial if moral continuity is to be preserved from one lifetime to the next.[12]

Not surprisingly, given the different purposes of the two texts, there are also some differences. The *Garbhāvakrāntisūtra* specifies that the parents must have a "defiled thought," that is to say, a lustful thought. This reflects the Buddhist conviction that desire, because it leads to rebirth, is essentially defiling and is, as the second Noble Truth implies, the cause of suffering. Like the non-Buddhist religious texts discussed above, the *Garbhāvakrāntisūtra* describes the rebirth process in detail, not as a disinterested explanation of the facts of life, but for the sake of arousing or confirming disgust in *saṃsāra*. Its audience was probably the meditating monk.

The *Carakasaṃhitā*, on the other hand, is not addressed to monks, and it passes no moral judgment on socially acceptable sexual activity. Rather, its aim is to encourage a successful pregnancy and a healthy birth. In addition to instructions regarding the best position for intercourse, the sensibilities of both partners are taken into account. The couple is recommended to wear white clothes and garlands, to have pleasant dispositions, and to have sexual desire for one another. They should be stimulated, ready for intercourse, and well fed, and their bed should be sweet smelling and comfortable. For a week after intercourse, the woman is to be pampered with various soothing and nutritious drinks, all white in color, and all of her surroundings should be white. She should have a large white bull or a decorated horse to look at, morning and evening. She should be told pleasant stories and look upon men and women of agreeable form, speech, and behavior as well as other pleasant sense-objects. Far from evoking disgust, these passages emphasize

12. *Garbhāvakrāntisūtra* (T. 1451: 253a23–26; Peking 120a6–7; Derge 249.3–4; not discussed in T. 317); *Carakasaṃhitā* 4.3.3 (1: 419).

the pleasantness of the process, and the frequent mention of the color white suggests purity, not defilement.[13]

The other obvious difference is that the *Garbhāvakrāntisūtra* refers to the about-to-be-reborn being as *antarābhava*, or intermediate being. The *Carakasaṃhitā*, on the other hand, calls it the "soul" (*jīva*), the same word that is used in the Brahmanical and Jaina texts mentioned earlier. Despite the difference in terminology, the *Garbhāvakrāntisūtra* and the *Carakasaṃhitā* agree that something in addition to the material contributions of the father and mother is required for conception to occur. Thus, in both these systems, which take rebirth for granted, a conscious entity accompanied by previously accumulated karma seems to be necessary for the mixture of semen and blood to become animated.

After the explanation of the conditions for entering the womb, the *Mūlasarvāstivādavinaya* version of the *Garbhāvakrāntisūtra* (but not the version translated by Dharmarakṣa) describes some features of the *antarābhava*. The *Carakasaṃhitā* similarly includes a description of the *jīva* as it is being reborn.

Next, the *Garbhāvakrāntisūtra* discusses the arrival of a woman's period of fertility each month and explains the connection between a woman's condition and the duration of her period of fertility.[14] Some women take three days to become fertile, others five days or half a month or a month, while others become fertile only after a long time depending on conditions. If a woman does not have much power, if she undergoes a lot of suffering and misfortune, if she is ugly, or if she does not have pleasant food and drink, her period of fertility, even though it arrives, will quickly stop, just as water, when it is sprinkled on parched earth, quickly dries up. If she is powerful, always receives pleasure, has an elegant appearance, and gets pleasant food and drink, her period of fertility does not quickly stop, just as water, when it is sprinkled on moist earth, does not quickly dry up. While a number of other medical texts have various views regarding the duration of the period of fertility, the *Carakasaṃhitā* seems to be silent about this.

The *Garbhāvakrāntisūtra* then enumerates the reasons why a woman might fail to conceive.[15] If the seed of either the mother or father is not emitted, or if either partner is impure, conception will not occur. Next follows a long list of graphically described "faults" of the vagina that can prevent conception from occurring. The first three are diseases caused by imbalances in the three humors, wind, bile, and phlegm. In their sections on gynecology, the medical texts similarly classify the diseases of the vagina according to the three humors.

Other faults mentioned by the *sūtra* include diseases characterized by obstruction due to blood and, perhaps, fat, conditions such as being overweight or applying medicine, and a disease that resembles an ant's waist (perhaps by making the vagina very narrow at some point). Still other faults are identified by the appearance of the vagina: like a camel's mouth, like a tree with many roots, like a plough

13. *Carakasaṃhitā* 4.8.5–4.89 (1: 462–64).
14. *Garbhāvakrāntisūtra* (T. 1451: 253b6–13; Peking 120b2–8; Derge 249.7–250.6; not discussed in T. 317).
15. *Garbhāvakrāntisūtra* (T. 1451: 253b13–27; Peking 120b8–121a9; Derge 250.6–251.7; T. 317: 886a13–b3).

head, like a cart, like a cane stalk, like a tree leaf, like the hair on barley. Furthermore, the uterus may be too deep at the bottom or too deep at the top. It may bleed or drip water. It may be always open, like a crow's mouth. Its dimensions may be uneven in all directions. It may have raised and depressed areas. Finally, it may harbor worms that eat putrefied filth.

Although a few of these conditions may correspond more or less closely with the diseases of the vagina described in the medical texts, most of them do not. The medical texts formally name the disorders and explain their causes and symptoms. The *sūtra*, on the other hand, generally goes no further than the fanciful similes listed above. The language used to describe these "faults" resembles that used in a description of the vagina in a passage found later in the *sūtra*: "that hole, which is a wound on the body that has arisen from the maturation of past *karma*, very nauseating like a toilet, foul-smelling, a dungeon, heaped up with filth, home of many thousands of types of worms, always dripping, continually in need of being cleaned, vile, always putrid with semen, blood, filth, and pus, thoroughly putrefied, slimy, covered with a perforated skin, frightful to behold."[16] This is the language of two traditional Buddhist meditations, the meditation on unpleasant things and the meditation on the body, both of which are intended to arouse feelings of disgust and thereby remove attachment to the body.

After enumerating the faults of the vagina, the *sūtra* states that if the parents are exalted and the *antarābhava* is low, or vice versa, conception cannot occur. There is no further explanation, but the meaning seems to be that an *antarābhava* will not be reborn in a family whose karma is strikingly different from its own. Furthermore, even if the parents and the *antarābhava* are all exalted or are all low, conception still will not occur if the parents have not amassed the appropriate karma to have a child, or if the *antarābhava* has not amassed the appropriate karma to be born to the parents, and thus the *antarābhava* does not have the appropriate thought of hatred toward the father and lust toward the mother or lust toward the father and hatred toward the mother.

The medical texts do not subscribe to this Buddhist oedipal theory. Instead, sex differences are explained by the predominance of semen or blood in the fetus; the *jīva*, unlike the *antarābhava*, has no gender. However, the *Carakasaṃhitā* shares the same general model of the necessary conditions for conception, and it devotes a chapter to a defense of the Sage Ātreya's position that the fetus is produced by a combination of factors: father, mother, self, suitability, nutrients, and mind. If any of these is not present, conception will not take place.[17] This notion that a number of different causes need to come together for conception to occur seems quite similar to the Buddhist account. Furthermore, the *Carakasaṃhitā* specifically mentions the importance of the parents' karma in producing the fetus. It also attributes to the *jīva* a number of factors, including birth in a certain species and a given life span,[18] both of which Buddhist texts consider to be the result of karma.

16. R. Kritzer, "Childbirth and the Mother's Body in the *Abhidharmakośabhāṣya* and Related Texts," in *Indo tetsugaku bukkyō shisō ron shū: Mikogami Eshō kyōju shōju kinen ronshū* (Kyoto: Nagatabunshodō, 2004), 1089.

17. *Carakasaṃhitā* 4.3 (1: 418–27).

18. *Carakasaṃhitā* 4.39–10 (1: 422–23).

The *sūtra* next explains how the *antarābhava* enters the womb. If the mother's uterus is clean, the *antarābhava* is present, the faults mentioned above are absent, and the parents and the *antarābhava* all have the appropriate karma, then conception can take place. First, the *antarābhava* has the misguided thoughts of lust for the parent of the opposite sex and hatred for the parent of the same sex mentioned above. Next, it has the false idea that it is very cold, that there is wind, rain, clouds, and fog, and that it hears the sound of a great, clamoring crowd. Thereupon, according to its past karma, the *antarābhava* imagines that it is escaping into one of ten types of shelters, ranging from very elegant to very primitive. With one of these mistaken notions, it thus enters the womb.[19] Since the medical texts are not concerned with the spiritual development of the *jīva*, it is not surprising that no corresponding passages can be found in them.

Finally, before the week-by-week account of the fetus, the *sūtra* contains an elaborate description of the composition of the earliest stage of the new life, the *kalala*.[20] This is said to be neither the same as nor different from the semen and blood of the parents; rather, the body of the *kalala* is formed on the basis of the semen and blood but with the cooperation of various causes and conditions. There follows a long series of similes, all of which stress that the material elements of the new being arise because of the confluence of causes and conditions.

These elements are the necessary constituents of the embryo, and their functions are described: earth contributes hardness; water, wetness; fire, hotness; and wind, fluidity. If there is earth without water, the *kalala* will dry up and fall apart, like a handful of dry flour or ashes. In similar fashion, the *sūtra* describes what will happen if various combinations of the other elements are absent. It is only because of past karma that the elements are able to perform their functions and that the embryo can grow properly.

The same subject is treated in the *Carakasaṃhitā*, where the embryo is defined as the combination of the semen, blood, and self in the womb; this is further analyzed in terms of the elements, which are said to be the base of consciousness and to produce the various parts and features of the body.[21]

The large number of similes in the *Garbhāvakrāntisūtra* and the imagery employed are quite different from the matter-of-fact discussion in the *Carakasaṃhitā* of the same biological phenomena and causal principles. Although it would be misleading to say that the *Carakasaṃhitā* is totally unconcerned with religion or philosophy, its section on embryology consists largely of what Mitchell Weiss has described as "detailed directives for promoting fertility and the birth of a healthy, intelligent male child" and a presentation of the medical knowledge on which these directives are based.[22]

The *sūtra*, on the other hand, appears to be an extended meditation on one aspect of the first Noble Truth of suffering (*duḥkhasatya*), namely the suffering

19. *Garbhāvakrāntisūtra* (T. 1451: 253b28–c9; Peking 121a9–122a1; Derge 251.7–253.4; T. 317: 886b3–10).

20. *Garbhāvakrāntisūtra* (T. 1451: 253c10–254a22; Peking 122a1–124a4; Derge 253.4–257.6; T. 317: 886b11–887a14).

21. *Carakasaṃhitā* 4.4.5–12 (1: 428–40).

22. M. G. Weiss, "*Caraka Saṃhitā* on the Doctrine of Karma," in *Karma and Rebirth in Classical Indian Traditions*, ed. W. Doniger O'Flaherty (Berkeley: University of California Press, 1980), 97.

of birth, and the summary of the first part of the *sūtra*, before the week-by-week account of gestation, declares that the essential nature of the birth process is suffering:

> Nanda, I do not extol the production of a new existence even a little bit; nor do I extol the production of a new existence for even a moment. Why? The production of a new existence is suffering. For example, even a little [bit of] vomit stinks. In the same way, Nanda, the production of a new existence, even a little bit, even for a moment, is suffering. Therefore, Nanda, whatever comprises birth, [namely] the arising of matter, its subsistence, its growth, and its emergence, the arising, subsistence, growth, and emergence of feeling, conceptualization, conditioning forces, and consciousness, [all that] is suffering. Subsistence is illness. Growth is old age and death. Therefore, Nanda, what contentment is there for one who is in the mother's womb wishing for existence?[23]

Gestation

To the best of my knowledge, the *Garbhāvakrāntisūtra* is the first text that mentions each week of the development of the fetus. In Tibet, however, week-by-week accounts are standard in medical texts, notably in the *Rgyud bźi*, although there are differences in the total number of weeks as well as in the sequence of development. Most scholarly interest in the account in the *sūtra* focuses on Tibetan medicine and Tibetan Buddhism, for which the *sūtra* is a source. In the following, however, I am more interested in the *sūtra* itself and its relationship to the Indian medical tradition.

I now compare the accounts of gestation in the *Garbhāvakrāntisūtra* and in the *Carakasaṃhitā*. I should note at the outset that the *sūtra* account is considerably longer and more detailed than that in the *Carakasaṃhitā*.

Month 1

First of all, the *sūtra*, in its description of each of the first four weeks, stresses the suffering of the embryo, which is said to lie in filth, like a lump. The sense organs and consciousness are all in the same place, as if in a pot, and the embryo is very hot and in great pain. Each week the *sūtra* designates the embryo by one of the terms that we have seen used in the non-Buddhist religious texts: *kalala, arbuda, peśī, ghana.*

The *Carakasaṃhitā*, in contrast to the *sūtra*, does not use such terms for the stages of the embryo, nor does it dwell on the embryo's suffering. Furthermore, during the first month the *sūtra* envisions a faster development of the fetus than does

23. *Garbhāvakrāntisūtra* (T. 1451: 254a22–29; Peking 124a4–7; Derge 257.6–258.2; T. 317: 887a15–20).

the *Carakasaṃhitā*. By week four of the *sūtra* account, the embryo has hardened to the extent that it can be likened to distinct objects, such as a metal cylinder or a shoe last, whereas according to the *Carakasaṃhitā*, it is still semi-liquid and shapeless.

However, perhaps the most striking difference between the *sūtra* and the various Indian medical accounts is the winds that feature in the *sūtra* descriptions of almost all of the first thirty weeks and in the thirty-eighth week. Although "bodily winds" are an important feature of Indian medical theory, winds are generally absent from the accounts of the development of the fetus. The *Carakasaṃhitā*, as far as I can tell, does not mention any winds that provoke changes in the fetus. It is true that, according to the *Suśrutasaṃhitā*, wind *(vāyu)* is instrumental in causing the male to discharge semen, the *jīva* to enter the uterus, and the menstrual blood, after it has collected for a month, to move to the opening of the vagina, but these are not directly related to fetal development. *Vāyu* is also mentioned regarding the production of various body parts and functions, but always in connection with the other humors, and in these cases, the winds are not differentiated or named, as in the *sūtra*. In one verse, the blowing of wind (*māruta*) is said to cause the growth of the fetus. However, the wind is not named, nor is any specific developmental feature identified.

The manifold winds of the *sūtra*, each with its imaginative name, do not seem to be derived from the Indian medical tradition of the time. However, they do seem to have been absorbed from the *sūtra* into the Tibetan medical system, where they are found in many texts, although not in the *Rgyud bźi*. For now, the question of the winds' origin must remain unanswered.[24]

Month 2

Again, the embryo is developing faster in the *sūtra*'s account than in the *Carakasaṃhitā* version. In the *sūtra*, the limbs appear gradually during this month, impelled by the sequence of winds. For each week, a botanical simile is provided to describe the function of the winds in producing the various features. For example, in week six a wind causes the fetus to manifest its elbows and knees, just as spring rain falling on edible plants produces branches. During this month, the outline of the body seems to take shape, but its contents—bones, blood, organs, and skin—will not appear until later.

In the *Carakasaṃhitā*, on the other hand, there is no differentiation of body parts; the embryo is simply a congealed mass. The term *ghana* is used at this point as a general description of the embryo at this stage, whereas the terms *peśī* and *arbuda* refer respectively to female and neuter embryos. A third term, *piṇḍa*, is introduced to designate the male embryo. These terms do not refer to separate stages of the fetus here.[25]

24. Ibid. (T. 1451: 254b2–17; Peking 124a7–125a5; Derge 258.2–260.1; T. 317: 887a21–b13); *Carakasaṃhitā* 4.4.9 (1: 429–30).

25. *Gārbhāvakrāntisūtra* (T. 1451: 254b18–c1; Peking 125a5–b8; Derge 260.1–261.4; T. 317: 887b14–c1); *Carakasaṃhitā* 4.4.10 (1: 430).

Month 3

In the ninth week, according to the *sūtra*, a wind causes the fetus to manifest the signs of the nine orifices (eyes, ears, etc.). In the tenth week, one wind makes the fetus firm, while another one expands the womb. In the eleventh week, a wind causes the fetus to be penetrated by nine holes, presumably the same nine mentioned before, which it then enlarges as the mother moves. In the twelfth week, intestines and joints are produced by another wind. The process of filling in the outline of the body has begun.

The *sūtra* describes a more gradual process than does the *Carakasaṃhitā*, which states that the sense organs and the parts of the body are all formed at once. This may be in part ascribable to the fact that a week-by-week account will naturally seem more gradual than a month-by-month one. However, the use of the word "all at once" (*yaugapadyena*) in the *Carakasaṃhitā* leaves no doubt that sometime in the third month the featureless embryo suddenly gains the features that make it recognizable as an incipient human being. On the other hand, it is important to note that both accounts are at odds with the Western medical belief in "preformation," prominent in the seventeenth century, according to which the fetus was "preformed, a fully fashioned though tiny adult that simply grew in size."[26]

The *Carakasaṃhitā* says that feelings (*vedanā*) appear at the same time, the fetus becomes animated, and its influence on its mother, which is called "two-heartedness" (*dvaihṛdayya*, equivalent to *dohala*), commences. However, in the *sūtra* two-heartedness is not mentioned, nor are feelings. The *sūtra* describes only external physical features in this month.[27]

Month 4

In its account of the fourth month, the *sūtra* includes many interesting details. In week thirteen, the fetus is said to be hungry and thirsty, and it receives nourishment through its navel from the food consumed by the mother. In weeks fourteen and fifteen, winds produce large numbers of sinews and blood vessels. In week sixteen, a wind, which is said to result from karma, establishes the eyes, ears, nostrils, mouth, throat, and heart in their proper places and makes digestion and respiration possible, just as a potter takes a lump of clay, puts it on his wheel, and shapes it into a vessel.

Similar details are not included in the month-by-month account in the *Carakasaṃhitā*, which simply says that the fetus becomes thick and the mother feels heavy. In fact, after the third month, the text hardly describes any developmental details and focuses more on the pregnant woman and her interaction with the fetus.[28]

26. K. Newman, *Fetal Positions: Individualism, Science, Visuality* (Stanford, Calif.: Stanford University Press, 1996), 33.

27. *Gārbhāvakrāntisūtra* (T. 1451: 254c2–18; Peking 125b8–126b1; Derge 261.4–262.6; T. 317: 887c2–24); *Carakasaṃhitā* 4.4.11–15 (1: 430–31).

28. *Gārbhāvakrāntisūtra* (T. 1451: 254c19–255a14; Peking 126b1–127b2; Derge 262.6–265.1; T. 317: 887c25–888b3); *Carakasaṃhitā* 4.4.20 (1: 432).

Month 5

In the seventeenth week, according to the *sūtra*, a wind first cleanses and arranges the digestive and respiratory systems, as well as the parts of the body with which, in the nineteenth week, the sense organs will be associated. The simile is drawn to a skillful person cleaning a dirty mirror with a cloth. In the eighteenth week, another wind purifies the six bases (the meaning of which is unclear), "as when the sun and the moon are obscured by a great cloud, and a strong wind arises and disperses the cloud." In the twentieth week, still another wind causes the bones to be produced and arranges them, just as a sculptor shapes a sculpture.

According to the *Carakasaṃhitā*, in the fifth month flesh and blood appear, and the mother becomes thin. The *sūtra*, however, assigns these developments to the sixth month and as usual does not worry about the mother's condition.[29]

Month 6

According to the *sūtra*, following the production of flesh and blood, skin is produced and then "brightened" in the sixth month. In the description of the twenty-first week, another interesting simile is made: a wind makes flesh grow on the body just as when a plasterer spreads mud on a wall. As for the *Carakasaṃhitā*, it states that strength and complexion develop in the fetus, while the mother loses strength and complexion.

There seems to be some agreement here if we can assume that the production and brightening of skin correspond to developing complexion. As in the previous month, the *Carakasaṃhitā* envisions the fetus's development at the expense of the mother. This aspect is totally absent from the *sūtra* although it would seem to be a good basis for meditation on suffering: the condition of the fetus improves at its mother's expense.[30]

Month 7

In its description of the seventh month, the *sūtra* portrays the fetus as nearing completion. Its blood and flesh become increasingly moist, and hair, body hair, and fingernails appear. But the striking feature here is the sudden introduction, in the account of the twenty-seventh week, of a discussion of the karma of the fetus (this is found in all versions of the *sūtra* so there can be no question of its being a later interpolation). If the fetus has done bad things in a previous life, it will receive various bad results: its attributes will all be the opposite of what is desirable in the world into which it will be reborn; it will have various disabilities, such as deafness, and even its relatives will hate it. If the fetus has done good things in a previous life, the opposite will happen.

29. *Gārbhāvakrāntisūtra* (T. 1451: 255a15–b9; Peking 127b2–128b1; Derge 265.1–267.1; T. 317: 888b4–c2); *Carakasaṃhitā* 4.44.21 (1: 433).

30. *Gārbhāvakrāntisūtra* (T. 1451: 255b10–18; Peking 128b1–5; Derge 267.1–5; T. 317: 888c3–15); *Carakasaṃhitā* 4.4.22 (1: 433).

Furthermore, in the description of the twenty-seventh week, it is said that if the fetus is male, he will squat on the mother's right side, his hands covering his face, facing his mother's back. If the fetus is female, she will squat on the mother's left side, her hands covering her face, facing her mother's belly. The fetus is situated between the stomach and the intestines, the contents of which respectively press down on and poke up at the fetus, causing pain. When the mother eats too much or too little, it causes pain, as does food that is too oily or too dry, too cold or too hot, salty or bland, bitter or acidic, sweet or hot. The various actions of the mother, such as having sex and walking fast, all cause pain. Nanda, the interlocutor of the *sūtra*, is then reminded of the various sufferings that humans experience in the womb and exhorted to avoid the endless sea of sufferings of *saṃsāra*.

Also, in the twenty-eighth week, eight mistaken ideas are said to arise in the fetus: a house, a vehicle, a park, a tower, a grove, a seat, a river, a pond. There is no further explanation, but it seems as though these are mistaken notions because the fetus thinks it is dwelling in one of these places rather than in the place where it really is, namely its mother's womb.

According to the *Carakasaṃhitā*, the fetus develops in every respect, and the mother becomes generally exhausted. The details of growth enumerated in the *sūtra* are left unspecified. Like the *sūtra*, the *Carakasaṃhitā* ascribes a role to karma in both embryology and disease, a topic explored by Weiss. However, Weiss points out that in many passages, particularly those with practical applications, the influence of karma is rather downplayed (106–107). In its month-by-month account of gestation, the *Carakasaṃhitā* explains the two-heartedness of the third month as resulting from past karma and mentions the self (with which karma is associated) as one of the factors in determining sex, but it does not associate karma with the further development of the fetus. Nor does it claim, as the *sūtra* does at a later point, that karma causes defects that lead to the premature death of the fetus.[31]

Month 8

According to the *sūtra*, winds apply the finishing touches to the external features of the fetus, and the effects of karma on its appearance are mentioned. This is a continuation of the development in the twenty-seventh week, when the effects of karma on the fetus are first mentioned. The *Carakasaṃhitā* still focuses on the relationship between mother and fetus, both physical and mental. It says that they exchange *ojas* (vital fluid), as a result of which their moods can be unstable.[32]

Months 9–10

During the thirty-first through thirty-fifth weeks, according to the *sūtra*, the fetus gradually grows and reaches its full size and complete development. In the

31. *Gārbhāvakrāntisūtra* (T. 1451: 255b19–256a5; Peking 128b5–130b1; Derge 267.5–271.2; T. 317: 888c16–889b6); *Carakasaṃhitā* 4.4.23 (1: 433).

32. *Gārbhāvakrāntisūtra* (T. 1451: 256a6–14; Peking 139b1–8; Derge 271.2–272.1; T. 317: 889b7–21); *Carakasaṃhitā* 4.4.24 (1: 433).

thirty-sixth week, it becomes unhappy inside its mother's belly, and in the thirty-seventh week, it has three unmistaken notions, of uncleanliness, a bad smell, and darkness. This seems to be in contrast to the mistaken notions in the twenty-eighth week: now it realizes how unpleasant the womb is and presumably is ready to come out. Finally, in the thirty-eighth week, a wind directs the fetus toward the vagina, and another wind, compelled by the force of karma, turns the fetus so that its head is pointing downward ready for birth.[33]

The *Carakasaṃhitā* simply states that these are the months of childbirth, and it mentions elsewhere that the fetus turns over so that it can be born headfirst.[34] Again the *sūtra* invokes the agency of winds, this time to move the fetus into position for birth, whereas the *Carakasaṃhitā* does not. As we have seen above, at least one other religious text, the *Agnipurāṇa*, also mentions a wind that turns the fetus over into position to be born headfirst. It appears as though all the accounts have finally converged at this point.

Conclusion

The *Garbhāvakrāntisūtra* and the *Carakasaṃhitā* share an epigenetic model of fetal development unlike the preformationist one common in seventeenth- and eighteenth-century Europe. They do not imagine that a homunculus is implanted in the womb at conception and needs only to bide its time and grow in size during the nine or ten months of gestation. Rather, they describe a process in which the material contribution of the two parents, once animated by the *antarābhava* or the soul, develops gradually, its various parts becoming differentiated and growing month by month. The *Carakasaṃhitā* is rather terse in its account and goes into few details, giving the impression of an abrupt development, with the sense organs and body parts all being formed at once in the third month, the flesh and blood developing in the fifth, and the fetus growing and gaining strength in the remaining months. The *sūtra*, on the other hand, goes into far greater detail. It gives the impression that in the earlier months the outline of the fetus is being sketched in. As time goes by, the contents—the internal organs—appear, and the structure of the fetus is literally fleshed out. Finally, the most external parts of the body, the hair and nails, become completely visible as the fetus attains its full size.

It is perhaps surprising how similar these two ancient accounts are to modern medical descriptions of gestation. One major difference is that development, generally speaking, occurs earlier according to modern medicine, with many things happening during the first month, whereas in the Indian accounts the fetus is little more than a lump or an even more shapeless blob. This may be explained by the available technology: there was obviously no ultrasound technology in ancient India, nor were there scanning electron microscopes for conducting meaningful

33. *Gārbhāvakrāntisūtra* (T. 1451: 256a13–b9; Peking 130b7–131b3; Derge 272.1–273.4; T. 317: 889b21–c6); *Carakasaṃhitā* 4.4.25 (1: 433).

34. *Carakasaṃhitā* 4.6.24 (1: 452).

dissection. From the second month, however, the account in the Buddhist *sūtra* seems to move along similarly to that of modern medicine, although often perhaps a month behind. Of course, the details differ, and the *sūtra* is not as sophisticated. Nevertheless, the epigenetic model is the same.

This is not to say that the *sūtra* is scientific. The winds it mentions are mythical and magical, corresponding to nothing in medicine, either ancient Indian or modern Western. The account of gestation occurs in the context of a sermon on the suffering inherent in rebirth, and the emotion elicited by the physiological details is neither scientific detachment nor wonder at the miracle of life. We are reminded of the filth in which the fetus grows and the pain that it experiences, at both the embryonic stage and in the seventh month, when it is fully capable of appreciating its predicament. In the Buddhist meditation on the body, the practitioner is explicitly told that the enumeration of the hairs, sinews, guts, bones, etc., is for the "direction of attention to repulsiveness." In this *sūtra*, Nanda is not meditating, but the message that he is hearing is that the body, beginning from the porridge-like liquid in the hot, filthy pot-like womb, is an unsatisfactory, suffering mess, consisting of vast numbers of components, formed and arranged by often grotesquely named winds.

This contrasts strikingly with the neutral description found in the medical literature. However, perhaps the same imaginative prowess that the unknown author or authors of the Buddhist *sūtra* employ to disgust the listener with the rebirth process enabled them to visualize more completely than the medical texts, and surprisingly accurately, the development of life in the womb.

Finally, it must be emphasized that in the *Garbhāvakrāntisūtra*, the embryo and the womb are viewed totally negatively. Elsewhere in Buddhist literature, the womb comes to have positive connotations, as in the doctrine of Tathāgatagarbha, where the "womb of the Tathāgatas" refers to the inherent potential in all beings to become Buddhas. In Tantric texts, as Frances Garrett points out, spiritual development is likened to the development of the embryo.[35] But this *sūtra* is clearly an example of what Alan Sponberg refers to as ascetic misogyny in early Buddhist literature.[36] Here the womb, as well as the vagina and the woman to whom they belong, are all considered to be agents of *saṃsāra*. And as the Buddha tells Nanda in the account of the twenty-seventh week: if even in good rebirths, one is born in such an unclean and awful place and suffers so much pain, how much worse will it be in bad destinies such as those of hungry ghosts, animals, and hell-beings? The only way out is to give up the pursuit of pleasure so that one can eventually escape the suffering that begins in the womb in every lifetime.

WORKS CITED

Agnipurāṇa. Edited by R. Mitra. Bibliotheca Indica 65.1–3. Osnabrück: Biblio Verlag, 1985.

Caillat, C. "Sur les doctrines médicales dans le *Tandulaveyāliya* 1. Enseignements d'embryologie." *Indologica Taurinensia* 2 (1974): 45–55.

35. F. Garrett, "Ordering Human Growth in Tibetan Medical and Religious Embryologies," in *Textual Healing: Essays on Medieval and Early Modern Medicine*, ed. E. Furdel (Leiden, Netherlands: Brill, 2005), 37.

36. A. Sponberg, "Attitudes toward Women and the Feminine in Early Buddhism," in *Buddhism, Sexuality, and Gender*, ed. J. Cabezon (Albany: State University of New York Press, 1992), 18–24.

Carakasaṃhitā: Agniveśa's treatise refined and annotated by Caraka and redacted by Dṛḍhabala (Text with English Translation). Edited and translated by P. Sharma. Jaikrishnadas Ayurveda Series 36. Varanasi: Chaukhamba Orientalia, 1981.
Fo shuo ju-t'ai-tsang hui (T. 310 n. 14). Translated by I-ching = *Garbhāvakrāntisūtra.*
Fo wei a-nan shuo ch'u-t'ai hui (T. 310 n. 13). Translated by Bodhiruci (P'u-t'i-liu-chih) = *Garbhāvakrāntisūtra.*
Garbha-Upanisad (Garbhopanisad). Based on the edition by R. Tarkaratna in *The Atharvana-Upanishads,* Calcutta: Ganesha Press, 1872 (Bibliotheca Indica 76). Available at www.sub.unigoettingen.de/ebene_1/fiindolo/gretil/1_sanskr/1_veda/4_upa/garbhupu.htm.
Garrett, F. "Ordering Human Growth in Tibetan Medical and Religious Embryologies." In *Textual Healing: Essays on Medieval and Early Modern Medicine,* edited by E. Furdel, 31–52. Leiden, Netherlands: Brill, 2005.
Hara, M. "A Note on the Buddha's Birth Story." In *Indianisme et Bouddhisme: Mélanges offerts à Mgr Étienne Lamotte.* Publications de l'Institut Orientaliste de Louvain 23, 143–57. Louvain, Belgium: Université Catholique du Louvain, 1980.
———. "Shō ku." In *Hotoke no Kenkyū: Tamaki Kōshirō Hakushi Kanreki kinen ronshū,* 667–83. Tokyo: Shunjūsha, 1977.
Ju-mu-t'ai ching (T. 1451: 251a14–262a19). Translated by I-ching = *Garbhāvakrāntisūtra.*
Kritzer, R. "Childbirth and the Mother's Body in the *Abhidharmakośabhāṣya* and Related Texts." In *Indo tetsugaku bukkyō shisō ron shū: Mikogami Eshōkyōju shōju kinen ronshū,*1009–85. Kyoto: Nagatabunshodō, 2004.
Mūlasarvāstivādavinaya(kṣudrakavastu) (Peking *'dul ba* de 114a3–149b7; Derge *'dul ba* tha 248.6–316.5) = *Garbhāvakrāntisūtra.*
Newman, K. *Fetal Positions: Individualism, Science, Visuality.* Stanford, Calif.: Stanford University Press, 1996.
Pao-t'ai ching (T. 317). Translated by Dharmarakṣa (Chu fa-hu) = *Garbhāvakrāntisūtra.*
Shastri, M. *Agni Purāṇam.* 2 vols. Chowkhamba Sanskrit Studies 54. Varanasi: Chowkhamba Sanskrit Series Office, 1967.
Smets, S. "Le développement embryonnaire selon la *Jaiminīyasaṃhitā* du *Brahmāṇḍapurāṇa*: Étude sur l'intertextualité." *Studia Asiatica* 4–5 (2003–2004): 313–30.
Sponberg, A. "Attitudes toward Women and the Feminine in Early Buddhism." In *Buddhism, Sexuality, and Gender,* edited by J. Cabezon, 3–36. Albany: State University of New York Press, 1992.
Tandulaveyāliya: Ein Paiṇṇaya des Jaina-Siddhānta: Textausgabe, Analyse und Erklärung. Edited by W. Schubring. Abhandlungen der Geistes- und Sozialwissenschaftlichen Klasse 6. Mainz, Germany: Akadmie der Wissenschaften und der Literatur, 1970.
Weiss, M. G. "*Caraka Saṃhitā* on the Doctrine of Karma." In *Karma and Rebirth in Classical Indian Traditions,* edited by W. Doniger O'Flaherty, 90–115. Berkeley: University of California Press, 1980.
Zysk, K. G. "Mythology and the Brāhmaṇization of Indian Medicine: Transforming Heterodoxy into Orthodoxy." In *Categorization and Interpretation,* edited by F. Josephson, 125–45. Göteborg, Sweden: Meijerbergs institut för svensk etymologisk forskning, Göteborg universitet, 1999.

Philosophical Embryology: Buddhist Texts and the Ritual Construction of a Fetus

Justin Thomas McDaniel

Sang Thong was a born a beautiful boy with golden skin. He was a kind son. His heart was filled with compassion for his mother who, once a queen, was now living in exile in the jungles of Siam. Sang Thong was troubled also because he was the cause of his mother's exile and suffering, for he had been born in a conch shell. This shell, although it protected him, hid him from his mother and had led the king to exile both him and her. Eventually, his compassion overwhelmed his fear, and he emerged from his shell. Sang Thong and his mother won the kingdom back.

Southeast Asian literature is populated by an assembly of stories like Sang Thong, which feature characters who have long periods of fetal development within fruit, stone eggs, and conch shells. Heroes, whether Buddhist bodhisattvas or royal princes and warriors, emerge from their mothers' wombs as gourds or watermelons and spend their early years locked within the walls of these solid calyxes. They walk around in the eggs and watermelons, speak to their mothers, and listen to the chaotic voices of the outside world before emerging as enlightened beings who transform the world through their heroic acts of bravery, dazzling physical beauty, and selfless qualities. Stories emerging from the literary world of Burma, Laos, and Thailand such as *Sang Thong, Om Kaeo, Wok Khai Hin*, and the various versions of the founding myth of the Lao people emphasize the importance of the heroes' birth and the formative periods of their postuterine fetal adventures. Though these stories are well known among Southeast Asian children, adults, and scholars alike, they do not constitute the only genre of fetal narratives in Southeast Asia. There is a tradition of stories about fetal development which crosses from the world of mythology to that of ritual and science.

This short study examines premodern and modern rituals that involve the creation of ephemeral fetuses through the power of Buddhist philosophical texts and protective science. This chapter will emphasize that, although Abhidhamma texts often say absolutely nothing about fetal development, motherhood, and birth, male monks use them to invoke the generative power of a mother. They are used to metaphorically and, many believe, actually create new life. The Abhidhamma texts that these rituals are based on are not mythological stories. They are detailed psychological and philosophical treatises. However, in Southeast Asia these psychophilosophical treatises have been transformed into fantastic stories that describe how new fetuses are created using words from the Abhidhamma. The *Nissaya Atthakathā Mātikā*, the *Abhidhamma Cet Gambhī*, and the *Abhidhamma-atthasaṅgaha* (three commentaries on the canonical Abhidhamma—the "philosophical" section of the Theravada Buddhist canon) offer instructions on how to ensure favorable rebirth through refined and ritually protected new fetuses.[1] In this way, Buddhist philosophy moves from the realm of cerebral reflection, psychological and epistemological taxonomies, and ethical/psychological speculation to ritual technology and physical transformation. It shows that the fetus is not simply a biological entity but a powerful metaphorical tool in ritual life. This chapter demonstrates a unique way Abhidhamma texts are read, transformed, taught, and applied in matters of life and death by Southeast Asian Buddhists.

The Texts: The Abhidhamma Genre

Scholars have long argued over the origin, dating, canonical status, mode of compilation, method of recording, linguistics, and provenance of the texts collectively called the Abhidhamma. There is no doubt among practitioners that they represent the pinnacle of the Buddha's own insight into the complexity of the human mind. According to most scholarly and traditional descriptions of the Abhidhamma there are seven sections (alternatively called groupings, treatises, or volumes) that are listed in different sequences depending on the school of Buddhism. In most indigenous descriptions, catalogues, and summaries of the teachings of the Buddha, these seven sections comprise the third "basket" of the *Tipiṭaka* (Buddhist canon). Locally they are largely considered, despite scholarly reservations, the actual words of the Buddha.

These seven sections are the *Dhammasaṅgaṇī, Vibhaṅga, Dhātukathā, Puggalapaññatii-pakaraṇa, Kathāvatthu, Yamaka*, and *(Mahā)paṭṭhāna*. They were most likely compiled over several centuries by a diverse group of commentators

1. There was a lively debate in the first few decades of Buddhist Studies over the classification of Abhidhamma as "philosophy." Many scholars refer to it as "psychology" or "applied philosophy" versus "speculative philosophy." This debate over terms is not my concern here. Commentators gloss the word "Abhi-dhamma" as "things related to the teaching" or "higher teaching." Basically, the Abhidhamma consists of seven volumes which break down the teachings found in the Sutta and Vinaya sections of the Buddhist "canon" into taxonomies and short explications of the various "components" of the mind, the operation of the senses, the elements, and the interaction among them. See Oskar von Hinüber, *A Handbook of Pali Literature* (Berlin: Walter de Gruyter, 1996), chapter 3, for a good introduction to the Abhidhamma.

more than two thousand years ago, and they reflect different stages of language, doctrinal development, and rhetorical styles. Traditional accounts state that the Buddha proclaimed the seven sections while residing in the Tāvatiṃsa heaven over a period of three months. The Buddha's original audience for this oral exposition was his mother, who lived among the world of the deities. In fact, in rituals in Southeast Asia, the mother's generative power is more important than the philosophical and psychological content of the Abhidhamma. In these seven treatises, the Buddha, according to local interpretations, taught his mother about ideal "motherhood."

The seven sections are characterized by long taxonomic lists that cover a wide range of subjects generally relating to the relationships among the sense receptors; emotions; mental states; analytical modes; physical elements; the nature of perception; conditional relationships among thought, sense, and action; and the genesis and result of these conditional relationships. They also include early Buddhist debates, the refutation of heretical views, and specific commentaries on passages from the other sections of the *Tipiṭaka*.

Quite simply, these massive tomes, equaling several thousand pages in Pali, attempt to describe in detail the psychological nature of the individual and link that nature to virtuous/nonvirtuous actions and soteriological potentials. Generally, these are complex and highly scholarly texts that offer an exegesis of the Buddha's teachings. Mastery of them, if possible, is a mark of intellectual, ethical, and social prestige for teachers and students.

The contents of these sections have been the subject of commentary and debate in Southeast Asia. Not surprisingly, none of these commentaries include instructions on how to generate ephemeral fetuses. None discuss the nature of motherhood. None promote the recitation of Abhidhamma texts at cremation ceremonies or state that individual syllables from the Abhidhamma can be used for ritual protection. Nevertheless, Lao and Thai monastic teachers have used the Abhidhamma in just these ways. An education on the Abhidhamma in Laos and Thailand is an education not only on the ethical and mental nature of the individual, but also on ritual birth and death.

Mātikā/Matrix/Mother: A Manuscript from Northern Thailand

I first came across the ritual and embryological way of reading Buddhist philosophy while translating a palm-leaf manuscript of the *Nissaya-Atthakathā-Mātikā* composed in 1569 in northern Thailand.[2] I was immediately struck by the strange use of language and the abbreviated structure. This commentary could not possibly have been a useful resource for instructing monks and laity on philosophy (the *mātikā* establishes the subjects for the Abhidhamma's description of the mind's

2. *Nissaya-Atthakathā-Mātikā* (Title on Manuscript: *Nisai Mātikāṭṭhhakathā)*, Social Research Institute Chiang Mai University 81.146.11F.006–006. 1 fascicle, 24 folios, dated Cūḷa Sakkarāja 931 (CE 1569), National Museum (Chiang Mai Branch). Script, Tai Yuan; material, palm leaf.

intentions, influences, and moral and immoral tendencies). The *mātikā* is a table of contents of sorts that seeks to establish the important subjects for those beginning a study of higher Buddhist philosophy of mind. I supposed the commentary would quickly move from the discussion of this "table of contents" to the actual content of the Abhidhamma. However, it remained at the level of the table and seemed to be more of a technical vocabulary lesson than a work of philosophical reflection and analysis. I later discovered that this vocabulary was essential not only for explaining (often orally) the nature of the senses, intentions, and so on, but also for creating a ritual fetus.

The choice of the *mātikā* for a commentator is itself strange.[3] Although the *mātikā* of the *Dhammasaṅgaṇī* (the first book of the Abhidhamma) is one of the most important parts of any text in the Theravada Buddhist canon, its contents are simply short phrases and terms. There is no explanation of the terms; there are no pronouns, speakers, narrative, and so on. As K. R. Norman states, "The *mātikā* is an outline of a universal system of classification comprising the whole analytical teaching of the Buddha. . . . The greater part of the *Dhammasaṅgaṇī* is an expansion of the *mātikā*."[4] Shwe Zan Aung wrote in 1908 that in Burma the *mātikā* was "considered by scholars as indispensable to the study of the remaining six books."[5]

The *mātikā* is thus a list of terms useful for memorizing the text and commentaries, and translations of it are guides explaining certain basic terms that are essential for understanding the complex psychological analyses of the *Dhammasaṅgaṇī* and the Abhidhamma as a whole. Northern Thai pedagogical manuscripts based on the *mātikā* isolate and repeat terms, seemingly to serve as triggers and guides for those giving a sermon or teaching a class; the *mātikā* is thereby rendered a platform, or index cards, on which teachers could create their own speech. When I first read through the 1569 manuscript of the *Nissaya-Atthakathā-Mātikā,* I was struck by the way the author repeated certain terms but did not translate them. However, when the *mātikā* is viewed as a lexical foundation upon which expansions are based, repetition of important and powerful terms makes perfect sense. The authors of the 1569 manuscript would have wanted to emphasize the terms in the *mātikā* through repetition, rather than translation, because they were technical terms students would need to be familiar with in order to comprehend teaching based on material from the Abhidhamma. However, it is not just the semantic meanings that unlock ultimate truths. The terms are also transformative ritual terms used in constructing an ephemeral fetus. Therefore, as the text states in several places, the *mātikā* can be expanded by commentators over time term by term, and thus could be "endless and immeasurable."

3. For a good introduction to the *mātikā* in Southeast Asia, see Shwe Zan Aung, "Abhidhamma Literature in Burma," *Journal of the Pali Text Society* 6 (1978 [1910]), 106–23.

4. K. R. Norman, "Pali Literature," in *A History of Indian Literature*, Vol. 7.2., ed. Jan Gonda (Wiesbaden, Germany: Otto Harrassowitz, 1983), 99.

5. Shwe Zan Aung, "Abhidhamma Literature," 115.

The most recent study of the *mātikā* tradition, by Rupert Gethin, offers an intriguing and convincing suggestion that the *mātikā* should be seen as a "matrix" or "mother" (which follows the actual etymology of the term, from the Sanskrit—*mātṛkā*). *Mātikā* can be translated as "having the qualities of a mother." Gethin notes that the "translators of Buddhist texts have often taken the word to mean something like 'summary' or 'condensed content.' . . . It is the underlying meaning of 'mother' that seems to inform the use of the term here. A *mātikā* is seen not so much as a condensed summary, as the seed from which something grows. A *mātikā* is something creative—something out of which something further evolves. It is, as it were, pregnant with Dhamma and able to generate it in all its fullness." Gethin cites a passage from Kassapa of Cola, who writes:

> In what sense is it a *mātikā*? In the sense of being like a mother. For a *mātikā* is like a mother as a face is like a lotus. For as a mother gives birth to various different sons, and then looks after them and brings them up, so a *mātikā* gives birth to many different dhammas and meanings, and then looks after them and brings them up so that they do not perish. Therefore, the word mātikā is used. For in dependence on the *mātikā*, and by way of the seven treatises beginning with the *Dhammasaṅgaṇī*, dhammas and meaning without end or limit are found as they are spread out, begotten, looked after and brought up, as it were, by the *mātikā*.[6]

The *Nissaya-Atthakathā-Mātikā* manuscript from northern Thailand, and *nissayas* in general, work very much like this matrix. Teachers based lectures on the gloss of terms from a Pali source text and expanded on the terms and their glosses in oral performance. Every teacher could add to the matrix of terms as he saw fit, making the chosen set of terms a deep font of subject headings in which to creatively expand. The *nissaya* writers of Thailand certainly realized and emphasized the text's importance and sought to expand on it. We can therefore see not only why it would not be strange to devote an entire commentary to a "table of contents" or a lexical matrix of one book of the Abhidhamma, but also the origins of using the Abhidhamma as ritual text to create new ephemeral fetuses. To this use of the Abhidhamma as a ritual mother we now turn.

The Rituals: The *Abhidhamma Cet Ghambhī* and Funerary Rites

The most obvious time to construct a new fetus is at a funeral. Death demands new birth. The popularity of commentaries and vernacular glosses (*nissayas*) of the

6. Rupert Gethin, "The Mātikās: Memorization, Mindfulness, and the List," in *The Mirror of Memory: Reflections on Mindfulness and Remembrance in Indian and Tibetan Buddhism*, ed. J. Gyatso (Albany: State University of New York Press, 1992), 163.

mātikā is connected not only to the pedagogical explanation and expansion of philosophical terms, but also to funerary rituals that are designed to create new fetuses. Knowing the foundational "motherlike" words from which the entire Theravada Buddhist philosophical complex arises not only enables a teacher to transmit information about the nature of thought, desire, sensory perception, emotion, and intention but also enables him to create new life. This is explicitly seen in the *Abhidhamma Cet Gambhī (Seven Books of the Abhidhamma)*, a genre of Abhidhamma commentaries well known to both the elite and the common people in Thailand. There are several types of texts included under this genre rubric. These various texts were most likely composed long before the eighteenth century, but few copies have survived. Although their origins are largely unknown, they have been used as funerary texts for centuries.

This title is misleading: this genre of texts does not contain the entire seven volumes of the Abhidhamma. I consulted several palm-leaf and modern pulp-printed paper editions, and I will discuss three in particular. One is a palm-leaf manuscript of four fascicles from 1771. It was composed at the Wat Sung Men monastery in Phrae (a small province in present-day northern Thailand) and is the longest and most detailed version.[7] It starts by relating the story of the Buddha residing near Benares with five disciples, then discusses the first time the Buddha orally delivered the seven books of the Abhidhamma to his mother in the heavenly realm (*devaloka*). From this story it moves on to offer the first few verses from each book of the Abhidhamma in Pali, followed by a short (often only a few words) gloss in Northern Thai (Yuan). Occasionally the first verse of each chapter of each book is discussed, but many verses are skipped, and some are only partially cited. The discussion of the first few verses of the *mātikā* of the *Dhammasaṅgaṇī* is the longest. As in our first manuscript from 1569, this manuscript concentrates on the connection between the "philosophical" text and the generative qualities of the ideal mother. Here, however, there is explicit connection to the fact that in Buddhism death precedes new life.

According to Abhidhamma teachings, human life can be reduced to certain mental and physical conditions (actions, sense objects, association, disassociation, dependence, practice, previous birth, etc.). However, these seven short passages in this manuscript do not explicitly discuss conditions. In fact, the text is very simple and repetitive, and it would seem senseless—merely a list of similar-sounding words—to the untrained ear. The words either have to be expanded upon in oral vernacular commentary or listened to not for their semantic meaning but for their meritorious power at the time of death. Most often they are chanted in Pali at a funeral, and then the words are "lifted" and used as the basis for a vernacular sermon after the funeral.

The verses are chanted while monks stand in front of the funeral pyre (*sūt nā fai*). Sections from the longer *Abhidhamma-atthasaṅgaha*, discussed below, are chanted

7. Title on Manuscript: *Abhidhamma Cet Gambhī*, Center for the Preservation of Art and Culture, Chiang Mai University 010301800, 4 fascicles, 102 bi-folios, dated Cuḷa Sakkarāja 1133 (CE 1771). Wat Sung Men, Phrae Province, northern Thailand. Script, Tai Yuan; material, palm leaf. The colophon provides little information except for the date and a standard dedication.

at the beginning of the funeral, also in Pali. Funerals are perhaps the most common occasion for public Pali chanting in Thailand; indeed, it is at funerals that lay people most commonly come in contact with monks. But because the vast majority of lay people and monks do not understand Pali, the Abhidhamma, though one of the most commonly heard texts, is also one of the least understood. The semantic meaning of the chanting matters little compared to its powerful ritual value, however.

A Fetus Made of Syllables

Another manuscript I found is quite different from the *Abhidhamma Cet Gambhī* from Phrae and brings us closer to an understanding of the connection between philosophy and fetal generation.[8] Instead of citing verses sequentially, it cites only the titles of the books of the Abhidhamma and then links those titles to parts of the mind and body. So rather than serve as a guide to a reciter or to a teacher trying to briefly explain the main contents of the Abhidhamma, it is designed to be a ritual guide to the text. However, despite this difference, it too is used at funerals. This manuscript is titled the *Abhidhamma Cet Gambhī Ruam*. Like the Phrae manuscript from 1771, it has Pali and northern Thai sections. It draws Pali terms from the Abhidhamma and breaks them down into syllables to be used in protective incantations and to connect the sounds of the words to particular parts of the body. One example particularly interesting for our purposes is that given from the breakdown of the word *Dhammasaṅgaṇī*. It begins: "*San* [from *Dhamma-SAN-gani*] . . . It refers to the thirty-three factors of the mind in the *Dhammasaṅgaṇī*. *San* was in the right side of the first man for seven days. Then, departing from the left side, it entered the womb of the first woman through the top of her head. . . . *i* [final vowel of *Dhammasaṅgaṇī*] became the waist [of the first child]."

In nineteenth century versions of this text, these syllables are associated with the body of the Buddha and with gaining the Buddha's power and protection. Today these syllables are still important for chanting a protective incantation. For example, "Vi" from *Vibhaṅga* is traditionally associated with a drop of sesame oil, which was on the tail of a deer at the beginning of time. This drop of oil eventually led, through processes represented by the five other syllables, to the formation of the ideal human body. Without this body, neither the Buddha nor any other human being would have come into existence. Therefore, the seven books of the Abhidhamma are directly connected to the first human being. When chanting these books (made easy by chanting only the first syllables), the body is protected and released from suffering. Specifically, each of these syllables relates to a particular

8. I thank Donald Swearer for providing me with a copy of this manuscript from his personal library. The manuscript's colophon does not provide a date, but it was most likely copied in the mid-nineteenth century. Although my translation is different at points, Swearer translated this manuscript for the first time in his "Summary of the Seven Books of the Abhidhamma," in *Buddhism in Practice*, ed. Donald Lopez (Princeton, N.J.: Princeton University Press, 1996), 336–42.

form of bodily protection. For example, "san" of the *Dhammasaṅgaṇī* is related to the "eye." Therefore, if a person is born or dies on Sunday and chants or hears the *Dhammasaṅgaṇī* (a person's "ghost" can do this after death), then she or he will be protected from "demerit accrued through the eye [faculty of sight]."[9] Therefore, that person will have a good rebirth in a heavenly realm. If a person is born or dies on Monday, the *Vibhaṅga* should be chanted, and so on. One version of this text states that if a monk does not know the seven books of the Abhidhamma (presumably through the syllables), he will go to hell after he dies and will be considered a "fool" by the Buddha.[10]

This helps us understand why lifting and explaining (or chanting) words from the *mātikā* was so important in the 1569 and 1771 manuscripts. This vocabulary was invoked ritually to protect the body at the time of death and ensure a favorable rebirth through a newly created fetus. Here vocabulary from the Abhidhamma is broken down into syllables. This emphasis on the syllables of the Abhidhamma book titles is also expanded into other syllables related to the thirty-two parts of the ideal human body, the five *khandhas*, and the five elements (water, earth, fire, wind, atmosphere). They are connected to persistent ideas in Southeast Asian Theravada Buddhism of the relationship between the human body and the words spoken by the Buddha. They are also related to the origin of human kind and the protection of the body in this world and the next.

Today the *Abhidhamma Cet Gambhī* or sections of the Abhidhamma are still used as the common text for a sermon at a funeral. Here the syllables help guide the body to a good rebirth. This tradition of chanting the Abhidhamma syllables at funerals is also related to a little-known funerary custom in which monks write the four syllables of the four major subjects of the Abhidhamma (as outlined in the *Abhidhamma-atthasaṅgaha*): "cī" for *citta* (mind), "ce" for *cetasika* (mental factors or concepts), "rū" for *rūpa* (material form), and "ni" for *nibbana* on a piece of paper. This piece of paper with the four syllables is placed inside the corpse's mouth to guide the dead person to a favorable rebirth.[11] Because these four subjects were important for chanting or at least abbreviating at funerals, it became standard to study them in the major monasteries of Bangkok. It is also common for sections of the Abhidhamma to be chanted as monks walk alongside the corpse being taken for cremation. Of course, this is all nominally related to the belief that the Buddha himself chanted the entire Abhidhamma in the *Tāvatiṃsa* heaven to his mother

9. Swearer, "Summary," 340.

10. Ibid., 342.

11. K. E. Wells, *Thai Buddhism: Its Rites and Activities* (Bangkok, 1974), 214–16. There has been little historical or anthropological work in English on funerary rites in Thailand of any real value since classics by B. J. Terweil, *Monks and Magic: An Analysis of Religious Ceremonies in Central Thailand* (Bangkok: White Lotus, 1975; rpr. 1994), and (Phya) Anuman Rajadhon, *Life and Ritual in Old Siam: Three Studies of Thai Life and Customs*, trans. William Gedney. New Haven: HRAF Press, 1961). Charles Keyes and (Phrakhru) Anusaranasasanakiarti, "Funerary Rites and the Buddhist Meaning of Death: An Interpretative Text from Northern Thailand," *Journal of the Siam Society* 68, 1 (January 1980): 1–28, is very useful. There are too many Thai sources to list. They range from close descriptions of funerals in different regions to cremation volumes published at the time of important monks and lay persons.

after her earthly death. The Abhidhamma is certainly not just useful for teaching Buddhist "philosophy" or psychology.

Ancient Science for Modern Funerals: The Liang Jiang Manuscript

The last *Abhidhamma Cet Gambhī* version I will look at is published by Liang Jiang in Bangkok. There have been several printings, the most recent in 2001. It is meant for oral performance and reflects similar pedagogical methods to the previous manuscripts. The first seven sections have the titles of the seven volumes of the canonical Abhidhamma (*Dhammasaṅgaṇī, Vibhaṅga, Dhātukathā, Puggalapaññati, Kathāvatthu, Yamaka*, and *Mahāpaṭṭhāna*). These are not brief summaries of the contents of these canonical texts, as I first suspected, but actually short narratives of when the Buddha preached the contents originally, followed by the first three lines of the canonical text and then by an explanation of some of the important terms in the text. At the beginning of each section, there are also instructions to the monk using this text to give a sermon. Following this, the syllables representing the seven books are given. These syllables are important at funerary rites. The text is actually sold in modern Thailand to those who want to donate it to monasteries at the time of a funeral. This manuscript is a blend of the first two. It is a guide to a preacher and briefly explains the main contents of the seven books of the Abhidhamma in vernacular. This system of connecting syllables to the sense organs and parts of the body and mind has been a central feature of Abhidhamma teaching in the region for more than four hundred years. François Bizot notes that the syllables from the title of the Abhidhamma are essential for drawing *yantras* (usually by placing the syllables in circles which we will see below) as well as for recitation at a funeral. He writes that "the recitation of the Abhidhamma at the moment of death is indispensable for giving birth to the new body."[12] The seven syllables marking the seven books of the Abhidhamma: "sam [for DhammaSAMgani], vi, dhaa, pu, ka, ya, pa," he states, "mark the beginning of the development of the fetus through the production of the mental faculties . . . the seven books are pronounced at the time of death, these books are the *mātikā*, or the mother, that enable rebirth." Here Bizot shows the connection between syllables (often placed inside drawn circles on *yantras*) of the Abhidhamma, the body, senses, and death.

Another Cambodian ritual that Bizot observed in the 1970s takes place in a cave which is a simulacrum of a womb. The body of the ill person is tied with sacred string as it lies in the cave. In the ritual, the syllables of the Abhidhamma are chanted over the body. The books of the Abhidhamma are said to be connected to the naval of a woman. The way to access the womb and unlock its generative powers was through meditation, especially the control of the breath. After controlling the breath and associating different parts of the body with different Pali syllables,

12. François Bizot and François LaGirarde, *La pureté par les mots* (Paris: École française d'Extrême-Orient, 1996), 44; translation mine.

each participant takes part in ensuring a successful rebirth.[13] Although in these Cambodian rites the Abhidhamma is not the only text invoked, it is the one text (or, at least, the syllables or titles of the seven texts) that connects them all.

The Abhidhamma is not just informative and descriptive, it is transformative and protective. It is necessary not just for being a well-educated student of Buddhism, but also for the amelioration and ultimate liberation of one's mind and body. The connection between the *Abhidhamma Cet Gambhī* from 1771 and the nineteenth century and the modern Liang Jiang version from Bangkok becomes apparent through an understanding of the Abhidhamma as a life-giving mother. It was, and is, important for monks to understand the grammar, the words, and the syllables to help the laity at the time of death, to put their training to practical and existential use. As we can see, there are fundamental continuities in the epistemological approach to the Abhidhamma and the way it has been taught in Thailand despite the changes brought by modernity to the study and teaching of Buddhism.

Memory Circles in Modern Bangkok: The Abhidhamma Jotika's Guidebook to the *Abhidhamma-atthasaṅgaha*

This continuity is not only a persistent "folk" tradition in rural Cambodia, Laos, and northern Thailand but is also taught at the central monastic universities of Bangkok and Chiang Mai and more than a hundred other participating monasteries throughout the country. This continuity is clearly seen in the last example of an Abhidhamma in this study. It is a modern handbook used at the Abhidhamma Jotika College and Mahāchulalongkorn Rājavidyālaya, the largest monastic university in Thailand. One of the most basic and popular textbooks is the "Handbook for the Study of the Abhidhamma" (*Gū Meu Kānseuksā Phra Abhidhamma*) by Phra Platavisut Guttajayo. It is a study of the *Abhidhamma-atthasaṅgaha*, the most ubiquitous commentary on the entire Abhidhamma in Buddhist Southeast Asia. The *Abhidhamma Cet Gambhī* is not the only type of Abhidhamma text chanted or used at funerary rites. The *Abhidhamma-atthasaṅgaha*, a twelfth-century Pali commentary on the Abhidhamma, has long been associated with funerals in Thailand. The *Abhidhamma-atthasaṅgaha*, or at least the "sī nā" (four subjects), is chanted at the beginning of the funerary rites when the corpse has yet to be removed from the home.[14] The *Abhidhamma Cet Gambhī* is chanted at the time of the actual cremation. These subjects were important to study at elite royal monasteries, as is seen in monastic university textbooks published as early as 1926 (the year of the earliest edition I could find; the first edition was probably published in 1912) just as they

13. François Bizot, "La grotte de la naissance," in *Recherches sur le bouddhisme khmer II, Bulletin de l'École française d'Extrême-Orient* 67 (1980): 240–73.

14. See K. E. Wells, *Thai Buddhism: Its Rites and Activities*. 3rd ed. (Bangkok, 1974), 226; and C. Keyes and (Phrakhru) Anusaranasasanakiarti. "Funerary Rites and the Buddhist Meaning of Death: An Interpretative Text from Northern Thailand." *Journal of the Siam Society* 68, 1 (January 1980): 8.

were in rural northern Thailand in 1771 because of their connection to a ceremony that neither the rich nor poor can avoid.

This way of presenting the titles—short sections, and selected verses from the Abhidhamma and *Abhidhamma-atthasaṅgaha* at funerals—has persisted over time throughout the region despite the rise in Theravadin canonicity and elite institutional curricular reforms. The first seven chapters of the handbook contain a study guide to the *cetasikas* (group of mental factors) that are outlined in the first part of the *mātikā* and that form the primary subject of the *Dhammasaṅgaṇī.*

The final section of the handbook is drawn from a standard modern biology textbook that describes the process of procreation and birth. This section comes complete with detailed drawings of fetal development, the umbilical cord, the uterus, and so on. Here ovulation, chromosomes, genes, and spermatozoa are mentioned as the origin of the process that leads to sense faculties, mental formations, perception, and other cognitive events. The process of death is connected to the process of life both cognitively and physically.

This handbook describes the cognitive evolution from life to death, as well as the physical. The original *Abhidhamma-atthasaṅgaha* has been long abandoned by the end of the handbook. However, this final chapter relates to the *Abhidhamma Cet Gambhī*'s use at funerals to ensure a good rebirth. In fact, the guide to chanting the Abhidhamma at a funeral is not taken directly from the canonical Abhidhamma, but from the *Abhidhamma-atthasaṅgaha.* The syllables representing the four central terms of the *Abhidhamma-atthasaṅgaha* are those placed in the mouth of the corpse. Moreover, the introduction to the Thai script edition of the nine chapters of the *Abhidhamma-atthasaṅgaha* explicitly connects this commentary to funerals and to the death of the Buddha's mother. The introduction states that the Abhidhamma "contains teachings which ordinary men cannot easily understand"; therefore, the *Abhidhamma-atthasaṅgaha* is chanted instead, and short sections from the *Abhidhamma-atthasaṅgaha* are often heard at funerals instead of canonical passages. The Abhidhamma Jotika guide to the *Abhidhamma-atthasaṅgaha* is designed not only to teach the Abhidhamma in brief but also to help monks understand the basis of their chanting at one of the most common Thai Theravada rituals—the funeral.

This handbook is also associated with the different versions of the *Abhidhamma Cet Gambhī* through its use of syllables. These are the primary pedagogical methods of the text and form the basis of examinations on this handbook. The handbook emphasizes the syllables of the core text. First, one of the first verses from the *Abhidhamma-atthasaṅgaha* is cited: "tattha cittaṃ tāva catubbidhaṃ hoti kāmāvacaraṃ rūpāvacaraṃ arūpāvacaraṃ lokuttarañceti" (First, therefore, mind is fourfold: the mental abode that is characterized by desire, the mental abode that is characterized by material form, the mental abode that is characterized by formlessness, the supramundane mental abode.) This passage is translated into Thai literally. From there, this one verse is expanded and each of the four abodes of the mind are broken down. When I say "broken down," I do not mean explained. The term *citta* is followed by a list of six *cittas* in Palized Thai (*akusalacit, ahetukacit, kāmāvacarasobhanacit, rūpāvacaracit, arūpāvacaracit, lokuttaracit*: unwholesome mind (or consciousness), causeless mind, a wholesome mind characterized by the senses, mind characterized by material form, mind characterized by formlessness, supramundane mind). Each term from this list is further broken down into a list of three or four terms, each according to its ethical import. For example, the term *akusalacit* (unwholesome mind) is broken down into eight types of mind characterized by greed, two types of mind characterized by delusion, and two types of mind characterized by hatred. The last member of the first list (*lokuttaracit*/supramundane mind) is further broken down into two lists each with four members. The first list consists of the well-known four paths of a nearly enlightened being (stream-enterer, once-returner, non-returner, enlightenment). The second consists of the well-known four fruits (ends of the four paths) of enlightenment. There is little surprise here for a student of the *Abhidhamma-atthasaṅgaha*. After these lists are established, each member of the list is further broken down into their member's first syllables.

Their first syllables are "so, sam, a; so, sam, sa; so, vip, a; so, vip, sa; u, sam, a; u, sam, sa; u, vip, a; u, vip, sa." These syllables are then placed in drawn circles divided into three sections. These circles are placed in a row, and then placed in alternative assemblages. They are shuffled around like billiard balls. These syllables in circles are reminiscent of *yantra* mystical drawings mentioned above. They are useful as mneumonic triggers, but also for training in the epistemological and technical foundation of protective incantations and for the practical act of transforming a dead body into a new ephemeral body reborn into a new life. These syllables are important not just as signs of longer words, but as symbols of conceptual ways of approaching the contents and power of the Abhidhamma as life-giving. That is why this handbook not only abbreviates the words of the Abhidhamma (as summarized in the *Abhidhamma-atthasaṅgaha*) associated with the mystical syllables placed inside the mouth of a corpse, chanted at a funeral, or drawn on a *yantra*, but also has a chapter describing the biological processes of birth. The Abhidhamma is the mother who bears new children.

This handbook is a modern repository of pedagogical techniques and rhetorical approaches used as early as the sixteenth century in Thailand. Just as the *Abhidhamma Cet Gambhī* is used to chant at a funeral, the *Abhidhamma Jotika Handbook* is used to help students learn the major Pali terms for sermon giving and funeral chanting. The students are given a basic list of terms and clauses from which to expand orally. They use the syllable method to memorize these verses or groups of verses. The verses serve as the basis to chant these sections of the text, and they also can be used as triggers for vernacular exegesis in a sermon. The students are tested on their ability to memorize these syllables; however, in practice they need to be able to chant the initial verses of all seven books of the Abhidhamma (based on the *Abhidhamma-atthasaṅgaha* interpretation), as well as to offer sermons explaining their import to nuns, monks, and the laity at funerals. The process of memorizing the syllables in the circles, although not explicitly taught in connection to drawing *yantras*, most likely grew out of a long tradition of memorizing, chanting, and drawing syllables for the sake of protective rituals. The ritual to create a new fetus specifically involves the Abhidhamma's syllables. This tradition is seen most clearly in the inclusion of biological sketches describing the development of an actual fetus in the Abhidhamma handbook. In order to create an ephemeral fetus, you need to understand how a biological fetus develops.

Conclusion

At first glance the versions of the *Abhidhamma Cet Gambhi* and the *Abhidhamma Jotika Handbook* for the *Abhidhamma-atthasaṅgaha* are so different in form that it would seem to confirm the general scholarly consensus that there was a massive rupture between premodern and modern Buddhism. Physically, the texts are on palm leaf in Yuan script, on cardboard libretto, and in modern paper-pulp codex. The Abhidhamma Jotika draws on modern biology textbooks to explain some Abhidhamma concepts and is replete with scientific sketches of the ovaries and spermatozoa. Institutionally, the 1771 Phrae manuscript was taught unsystematically in various independent northern monasteries and did not form part of an official royal-sponsored curriculum that was aimed at passing state examinations. The *Abhidhamma Jotika Handbook* is an official textbook used in the central monastic university and many participating Abhidhamma education centers. The *Abhidhamma Cet Gambhī* is a sermon and ritual guide for funeral rites, which are neither nationally consistent nor monitored.

These texts were composed at different times in different scripts in different regions by monks in very different institutional settings. However, rhetorical features and pedagogical methods tie these texts together and reflect a regional epistemological approach to studying, teaching, and ritually using the Abhidhamma. These texts do not see the contents of the seven volumes of the Abhidhamma as the sole reason for studying them. Ritual is also important. Ritual and cognitive philosophy are partners in creating ephemeral fetuses at the time of death. Abhidhammic funerary rituals bridge the study of Buddhist philosophy and embryology. Philosophy in this case does not simply describe or speculate, but, like a mother, creates.

BIBLIOGRAPHY

Abhidhamma Cet Gambhī. Bangkok: Liang Jiang, 2001.

Alsdorf, L. "The Akhyana Theory Reconsidered." In *Kleine Schriften Herausgegeben von Albrecht Wezler*. Wiesbaden, Germany: Franz Steiner Verla GMBH, 1974.

(Phya) Anuman Rajadhon. *Life and Ritual in Old Siam: Three Studies of Thai Life and Customs*. Translated by W. Gedney. New Haven, Conn.: HRAF Press, 1961.

Anuson Bhuribhiwatanakun. *Abhidhamma-Atthasaṅgahādipakaraṇa, lem thi 3*. Bangkok: Mahachulalongkorn Mahavidayalai, 2001.

(Phra) Ariyamuni [Chaem]. *Suat mon blae*. Bangkok: Rong phim phisalapanani, 1913.

Becchetti, C. *Le mystere dans les lettres*. Bangkok: Editions des cahiers de France, 1991.

Bizot, François. *Le chemin de Lankâ*. École français d'Extrême-Orient, Paris, 1992.

———. "La consecration des statues et le culte des morts." In *Recherches nouvelles sur le Cambodge*. École français d'Extrême-Orient, Paris, 1994.

———. *Le donne de soi-même*. Publications de l'École français d'Extrême-Orient Monographies 130. Paris, 1981.

———. *Le figuier à cinq branches*. Publications de l'École français d'Extrême-Orient Monographies 107. Paris, 1976.

———. "La grotte de la naissance." *Recherches sur le bouddhisme khmer II, Bulletin de l'École français de Extrême-Orient* 67 (1980).

———. "Notes sur les yantra bouddhiques d'Indochine." In *Tantric and Taoist Studies in honour of R. A. Stein. Melanges chinois et bouddhiques XX*. Vol. 1. Edited by M. Strickmann. Brussels, Belgium: Institut Belge des Hautes Etudes Chinoises, 1981.
Bizot, François, and François LaGirarde. *La Pureté par les mots*. Paris: École française d'Extrême-Orient, 1996.
Bode, M. *The Pali Literature of Burma*. London: Royal Asiatic Society, 1966.
Buddhaghosa Acariya. *Atthasālinī-atthayojanā*. Edition of the Munidhi Bhumiphalobhikkhu. Bangkok: Wat Srakhet, 1982.
Ca Brian. *Anisong 108 Kan chabab poem toem mai*. Bangkok: Amnuisasana, 1966.
A Comprehensive Manual of Abhidhamma: The Abhidammattha Sangaha of Ācariya Anuraddha. Bhikkhu Bodhi, general editor. Pali text originally edited and translated by Mahāthera Nārada. Translation revised by Bhikkhu Bodhi. Introduction and explanatory guide by U. Rewata Dhamma and Bhikkhu Bodhi. Abhidhamma tables by U. Sīlānanda. Kandy, Sri Lanka: Buddhist Publication Society, 1993.
Frauwallner, E. *The Earliest Vinaya and the Beginnings of Buddhist Literature*. Translated from the German by L. Petech. Rome: L'Istituto italiano per il Medio ed Estremo Oriente, 1956.
———. *Studies in Abhidharma Literature and the Origins of Buddhist Philosophical Systems. Translated from the German by S. F. Kidd under the supervision of Ernst Steinkellner*. Albany: State University of New York Press, 1995.
Gethin, R. "The Mātikās: Memorization, Mindfulness, and the List." In *The Mirror of Memory: Reflections on Mindfulness and Remembrance in Indian and Tibetan Buddhism*, 149–72. Edited by J. Gyatso. Albany: State University of New York Press, 1992.
Hayashi, Y. *Practical Buddhism among the Thai-Lao*. Kyoto: Kyoto University Press, 2003.
Hinüber, O. von. "Chips from Buddhist Workshops: Scribes and Manuscripts from Northern Thailand." *Journal of the Pali Text Society* 22 (1996): 35–57.
———. *A Handbook of Pali Literature*. Berlin: Walter de Gruyter, 1996.
———. "Pāḷi Manuscripts of Canonical Texts from Northern Thailand." *Journal of the Siam Society* 71 (1983): 75–88.
———. "Die Sprachgeschichte des Pāli im Spiegel der südosrasiastischen Handschriftenüberlieferung," *Untersuchungen zur Sprachgeschichte und Handschriftenkunde des Pāli I*. Stuttgart, Germany, 1988.
Ishii, Y. *Sangha, State, and Society: Thai Buddhism in History*. Translated by P. Hawkes. Honolulu: University of Hawaii Press, 1986.
Jory, P. "Thai and Western Scholarship in the Age of Colonialism: King Chulalongkorn Redefines the Jatakas." *Journal of Asian Studies* 61, 3 (2002): 99–124.
Keyes, C., and (Phrakhru) Anusaranasasanakiarti. "Funerary Rites and the Buddhist Meaning of Death: An Interpretative Text from Northern Thailand." *Journal of the Siam Society* 68, 1 (January 1980): 1–28.
Kieffer-Pulz, P. *Die Sīm: Vorschriften zur Regelung der Buddhistischen Gemeindegrenze in älteren Buddhistischen Texten*. Berlin: D. Reimer, 1992.
LaGirarde, F. "Gavampati-Kaccayana: Le culte et la legende du disciple ventripotent dans le bouddhisme des Thais." Vols. 1–2. Ph.D. diss. Sorbonne, Paris, 2001.
Lamun Canhom. *Wannakam Thong Thin Lanna*. Chiang Mai, Thailand: Suriwong Book Center, 1995.
Law, V. *The Insular Latin Grammarians*. Totowa, N.J.: Distributed by Biblio Distribution Services, 1982.
A Manual of Abhidhamma; being Abhidhammattha-Sangaha of Anuruddhācariya. Pali text translated and edited by Mahāthera Nārada. Colombo, Sri Lanka: Vajirārāma, 1956.

McDaniel, J. "Creative Engagement: The Sujavanna Wua Luang and Its Contribution to Buddhist Literature." *Journal of the Siam Society* 88 (2000): 156–77.

———. "The Curricular Canon in Northern Thailand and Laos." *Manusya: Journal of Thai Language and Literature Special Issue* (2002): 20–59.

Norman, K. R. "Pali Literature." *A History of Indian Literature.* Vol. 7.2. Edited by J. Gonda. Wiesbaden, Germany: Otto Harrassowitz, 1983.

(Phra) Platavisut Guttajayo. *Guu Meu Kanseuksa Phra Abhidhamma Chan Chulabhidhammikatri.* Bangkok: Mahachulalongkorn Rajavidyalaya, 2001.

Pruitt, W. *Étude linguistique de nissaya Birmans: traduction commentee de Textes Bouddhiques.* École française d'Extrême-Orient, Paris, 1994.

———. "Un Nissaya Birman de la Bibliotheque Nationale, le Patimokkha. Étude linguistique. Part 1. *Cahiers de l'Asie du Sud-Est* 19 (1986): 84–119.

———. "Un Nissaya Birman de la Bibliotheque Nationale, le Patimokkha. Étude linguistique. Part 2. *Cahiers de l'Asie du Sud-Est* 21 (1987): 7–45.

———. "Un Nissaya Birman de la Bibliotheque Nationale, le Patimokkha. Étude linguistique. Part 3. *Cahiers de l'Asie du Sud-Est* 22 (1987): 35–57.

Reid, Anthony. *Charting the Shape of Early Modern Southeast Asia.* Chiang Mai, Thailand: Silkworm Books, 1999.

———. *Southeast Asia in the Age of Commerce, 1450–1680.* New Haven, Conn.: Yale University Press, 1993.

———, ed. *Southeast Asia in the Early Modern Era: Trade, Power, and Belief.* Ithaca, N.Y.: Cornell University Press, 1993.

Reynolds, Craig. "The Plot of Thai History: Theory and Practice." In *Patterns and Illusions: Thai History and Thought in Memory of Richard B. Davis*, edited by Gehan Wijeyewardene and E. C. Chapman. Melbourne: Australian National University Press, 1992.

Reynolds, Suzanne. *Medieval Reading: Grammar, Rhetoric, and the Classical Text.* New York: Cambridge University Press, 1996.

Rhys-Davids, C. *A Buddhist Manual of Psychological Ethics: Being a Translation, Now Made for the First Time, from the Original Pali, of the First Book in the Abhidhamma Pitaka Entitled Dhammasangani, Compendium of States or Phenomena.* 3rd ed. London: Pali Text Society; distributed by Routledge and Kegan Paul, 1974.

Rhys-Davids, C., and Shwe Zan Aung. *Compendium of Philosophy: Being a Translation Now Made for the First Time from the Original Pali of the Abhidhammatthasangaha.* London: Published for the Pali Text Society by Luzac, 1972.

(Phra) Sasanasobhon. *Suatmon chapap Luang.* Bangkok: Mahamakut University Press, 1975, 1986.

Shwe Zan Aung, "Abhidhamma Literature in Burma." *Journal of the Pali Text Society* 6 (1978 [1910]): 106–23.

Siriwat Khamwansa. *Song Thai nai 200 pi.* Bangkok: Mahachulalongkorn, 1981.

Swearer, D. "A Summary of the Seven Books of the Abhidhamma." *Buddhism in Practice.* Edited by D. Lopez. Princeton, N.J.: Princeton University Press, 1996: 336–42.

Terwiel, B. J. *A History of Modern Thailand, 1767–1942.* Lucia, N.Y.: University of Queensland Press, 1983.

———. *Monks and Magic: An Analysis of Religious Ceremonies in Central Thailand.* 3rd rev. ed. Bangkok: White Lotus, 1994.

Warder, A. K., ed. *Mohavicchedani.* London: Pali Text Society, 1961.

Wells, K. E. *Thai Buddhism: Its Rites and Activities.* 3rd ed. Bangkok: Suriyabun, 1974.

Wutichai Mulasilpa. *Kan patirupakanseuksa nai samai phrapansomdej phrachulachom klao chao yu hua.* Bangkok: Thai Wattana Panich, 1995.

Tibetan Buddhist Narratives of the Forces of Creation

Frances Garrett

The effort to explain the nature of phenomena without positing their permanent existence led to highly developed theories of causality in Buddhist literature. In this essay I will consider the mechanics of causation in Tibetan narratives of human gestation. Buddhists throughout history have concerned themselves with describing how change occurs in the various realms of human experience, and embryology is fundamentally about change. From India, accounts of early human development traveled to Tibet with other sorts of Buddhist literature, and they were embellished by Tibetans in religious and medical circles over the centuries to follow. This essay will consider how embryological accounts interacted with each other and with their literary environments throughout Tibetan history, asking more widely what embryology may tell us about the intertwining of religion and medicine in Tibet.

In the doctrines of the early Buddhist canon, humans are said to be composed of five components, or "aggregates" (in Pāli, *khandha*), the proportions and nature of which are continually shifting, such that an individual cannot be, in reality, a stable entity, unchanging from moment to moment. Misperception of the basic fact of substantial instability, or impermanence, and the imposition of a stable, constant "self" upon this shifting configuration of aggregates is in Buddhism considered the central downfall of humankind. Belief in a self that underlies or unites the aggregates into one, the Buddha taught, is the root of all human suffering. The trouble with this theory, however, is the continuity across multiple lifetimes asserted by the process of rebirth. According to

This chapter is an extraction of chapter 6 of my book *Religion, Medicine and the Human Embryo in Tibet*, Critical Studies in Buddhism series (New York: Routledge, 2008).

Buddhist doctrine, the world is created by the actions (in Sanskrit, *karman*) of sentient beings. All actions leave upon the actor an imprint that has an effect on the actor's future, dictating the direction of his or her rebirth. The issue of how these imprints are transferred over lifetimes, however, is complicated by theories of impermanence and no-self, and this problem has been one of the central topics of debate in Buddhist philosophy over the centuries.[1]

Karmic causality is thus a historically and systematically complex notion. Although it is but one aspect of Buddhist causal theory overall, karmic causality is at the root of much of Buddhist thought and practice. In Tibetan discussions of the body at the level of fetal development, concerns with the workings of karma are at the heart of debates in both medical and religious systems. Many of these systems award karma a significant, motivationally shaping role in the creation of a new human body. In this essay, I will discuss how embryology is used in Tibetan literature to express a range of Buddhist notions of causation, change, and growth. I will focus on four models of causation found in twelfth- to sixteenth-century Tibetan embryological narratives: a model in which the primary causal force is karma, another in which the primary forces of growth are the body's energetic winds, yet another in which the primary forces are all of the natural elements together, and, finally, a model in which the primary force of growth is the wisdom of a Buddha. Over the course of this essay, by examining the presence in embryological discourse of competing models for causation and human growth, we will see that while karma was vital to some models, others emphasized the power of other psychosomatic features of the individual. We will observe that embryology is at the center of a fundamental Buddhist concern, explored here through discussion of the role of karma in becoming human and disagreement over the primary forces that motivate human development.

Competing Models of Growth: The Force of Karma

How karma works, and how exactly karmic causality can be effective from one lifetime to the next is an issue that has been debated since the beginning of Buddhism. Buddhist texts as far back as the *Saṃyuttanikāya* feature philosophical dialogues between the Buddha and his students on the topics of causality in the context of rebirth specifically; this topic has been well summarized by Surendranath Dasgupta, James McDermott, and others.[2] Karmic causality is an integral part of both Āyurvedic

1. For a brief overview of such debates in Tibetan Buddhism, see Lobsang Dargyay, "Tsong-Kha-Pa's Concept of Karma," in *Karma and Rebirth: Post Classical Developments*, ed. Ronald W. Neufeldt, SUNY Series in Religious Studies (Albany: State University of New York Press, 1986), 169–71. For a discussion of medieval Theravāda views on karma's relationship to rebirth, see Bruce Matthews, "Post-Classical Developments in the Concepts of Karma and Rebirth in Theravada Buddhism," in *Karma and Rebirth: Post-Classical Developments*, ed. Ronald W. Neufeldt, SUNY Series in Religious Studies (Albany: State University of New York Press, 1986).

2. See summaries in Surendranath Dasgupta, *A History of Indian Philosophy*, 5 vols. (New Delhi: Motilal Banarsidass, 1975); and James P. McDermott, *Development in the Early Buddhist Concept of Kamma/Karma* (New Delhi: Munishiram Manoharlal, 1984), and "Karma and Rebirth in Early Buddhism," in *Karma and Rebirth in Classical Indian Traditions*, ed. Wendy Doniger (Delhi: Motilal Banarsidass, 1983).

medical and Indian Buddhist sources on rebirth, and all Tibetan authors who write on embryology—whether affiliated with medical or religious traditions—acknowledge the role of karma in human conception and development. Karma plays a role in embryology on two levels: first, in the larger context of the Buddhist law of interdependent origination (*rten cing 'brel bar 'byung ba*; Skt. *pratītyasamutpāda*), and, second, in the context of the specific causes of conception and fetal growth.

The law of interdependent origination is a doctrine of causality that explains the ultimately interdependent nature of all phenomena in the world, a notion that is the basis of the Buddhist thesis that all phenomena are impermanent, arising through causes and conditions. It is interpreted variously by all schools of Buddhism and is arguably the philosophical helm of Buddhist thought. Traditions such as the Mādhyamika used the twelve sequential stages of interdependent origination to justify their position that because all phenomena are interdependent, they must therefore be intrinsically selfless or empty.[3] From this perspective, there *are* no things causally connected—ultimately there is only causal connection. The doctrine of interdependent origination serves as a mediating concept, a "middle way," between the two extremes of eternalism, in which one believes that the individual, or an essential portion of the individual, continues unchangingly throughout a series of lifetimes, and nihilism, in which one believes that an individual is completely annihilated at death. The doctrine allows Buddhists to speak of a causal chain connecting actions and their effects, without asserting a permanent transmigrating entity. Significantly, it also explains that the cause of ultimate liberation is the cessation of the mechanics of karma, which means the end of the cycle of rebirth. This places embryology—where the mechanics of rebirth is taught—at the center of Buddhist soteriology.

Within embryological accounts, the problem of karma is addressed in the context of explaining both the causes of conception and the course of fetal development. All accounts of human development agree that conception is caused by three main factors: the joining of the two healthy reproductive substances of a man and a woman in intercourse and the consciousness of the transmigrating sentient being, which is generally said to be propelled toward that particular copulating man and woman by its own karmic imprints. This basic model of conception arrived in Tibet in the eleventh century with Vāgbhaṭa's Indian medical text, the *Eight Branches*, which was widely influential in the subsequent development of Tibetan medical literature; it is the model present in the Buddhist sūtra, *Teaching Nanda about Entering the Womb*, the most widely cited source for Tibetan embryology; and it can be seen in the earliest of Buddhist texts, such as the *Majjhima Nikāya* and the Abhidhamma.[4] There is little disagreement among Tibetan religious or

3. The twelve stages are explained clearly in Jeffrey Hopkins, *Meditation on Emptiness* (London: Wisdom Publications, 1983), 275–83. The doctrine of interdependent origination is also represented iconographically by the "wheel of life" (*srid pa'i 'khor lo*). See, for example, Geshe Sopa, "The Tibetan Wheel of Life: Iconography and Doxography," *Journal of the International Association of Buddhist Studies* 7, 1 (1984). See also David M. Williams, "The Translation and Interpretation of the Twelve Terms in the Paticcasamuppada," *Numen* 21 (1974).

4. In Tibet, the most influential Indian medical text with a presentation of embryology is Vāgbhaṭa's *Aṣṭāṅgahṛdayasaṃhitā* (*Yan lag brgyad pa'i snying po bsdus pa*, referred to in this article in English as the *Eight Branches*). On the *Sūtra of Teaching Nanda about Entering the Womb* (*Āyuṣmannandagarbhāva-krāntinirdeśa-sūtra*), see Robert

medical writers on these key features of conception. Although we will see that in other aspects of gestation the issue of causality is more problematic, to this degree and in this context, karma is important to all.

In the earliest extant examples of Tibetan embryology in medical texts, such as in the *Four Tantras* and its first commentaries,[5] conception is a significant, heavily commented-upon topic. As above, the factors required for conception are typically listed as nondefective male reproductive substance (*khu ba*), nondefective female reproductive "blood" (*khrag*), a transmigrating consciousness (*rnam shes*) that is drawn from the space where it waits between lifetimes toward a man and woman in sexual union, plus, in some sources, the five natural elements (*'byung ba*), earth, fire, water, wind, and space. Menstruation is also discussed in this context to explain exactly when a woman is fertile. According to medical traditions, if these necessary factors are defective or not present, conception will not take place. Defects in either the female or male reproductive substances will make them unsuitable to cause normal development, resulting either in unsuccessful conception or in a fetus that is severely deformed. If the reproductive substances are not defective but there is no karmic connection between the transmigrating consciousness and the potential parents, it is said that there will be nothing to draw the consciousness to those parents—thus in this case also, conception will not occur. Early Buddhist scriptures are cited as evidence for this view. Some sources note that the presence of each of the five natural elements is also required for successful conception and growth.[6] The elements provide the material and energetic opportunity for development: the substance of the body is composed by the earth element, its fluidity and flexibility by the water element, its maturation by the fire element, its growth by the wind element, and the space in which it grows is provided by the space element. Each of these conditions must be in place for gestation to occur. The developing embryo is thus bound by the same laws of natural physics, as it were, as every other impermanent phenomenon in the natural world. Other requirements for successful conception include the woman's fertility: she must be at the proper phase of her menstrual cycle. When the "womb is open" (*mngal kha bye*), conception can occur. The womb is open for up to twelve days per month—menstrual blood is collected in the womb during the first three of these days, and conception can occur there

---

Kritzer, "Garbhāvakrāntisūtra: A Comparison of the Contents of Two Versions," *Maranatha: Bulletin of the Christian Culture Research Institute (Kyoto)* 6 (1998); and Marcelle Lalou, "La version Tibetain du Ratnakūṭa," *Journal Asiatique* (October–December 1927). For more on the sources for embryology available to Tibetans, see Frances Garrett, "Ordering Human Growth in Tibetan Medical and Religious Embryologies," in *Textual Healing: Essays on Medieval and Early Modern Medicine*, ed. Elizabeth Lane Furdell (Leiden, Netherlands: Brill, 2005).

5. The *Four Tantras*, still today considered the principal medical text in Tibetan medicine, was arranged in the twelfth century by the Tibetan physician Yuthog Yonten Gonpo (*g.yu thog yon tan mgon po*, 1112–1203), probably following several centuries of development. The earliest commentaries on the *Four Tantras* date to the time of Yuthog himself. Portions of the *Four Tantras, Bdud rtsi snying po yan lag brgyad pa gsang ba man ngag gi rgyud*, (Delhi: Bod kyi lcags po ri'i dran rten slob gner khang, 1993) are available in translation as *The Quintessence Tantras of Tibetan Medicine*, trans. Barry Clark (Ithaca, N.Y.: Snow Lion Publishers, 1995).

6. Skyem pa tshe dbang, *Mkhas dbang skyem pa tshe dbang mchog gis mdzad pa'i rgyud bzhi'i 'grel pa bshugs so*, Vol. 2 (New Delhi: bod gshung sman rtsis khang, n.d.), 125.

up to the eleventh day. After this time, the "old blood" is eliminated and the womb "closes."[7]

In his treatise, *Transmission of the Elders*, the sixteenth-century medical scholar Zurkhar Lodro Gyalpo (b. 1509) condemns those who only make passing note of the causes of conception, stating that simple explanations do not adequately explain how the consciousness enters the womb or how precisely the body is established.[8] He insists that one should describe the causes of conception fully as follows: one, the healthy wind (*lung*), bile (*khris pa*), and phlegm (*bad kan*) humors that are present in the father's and mother's reproductive substances; two, the transmigrating consciousness that is impelled toward human rebirth by its karma; and three, the very subtle forms of the five natural elements that exist within the reproductive substances and the consciousness. Only with these causes in place, if the healthy man and woman copulate, will a transmigrating consciousness be able to enter the womb.

Whereas the commentaries on the *Four Tantras'* terse statements on the *causes* for conception emphasize karma's role in conception, when addressing *how* conception occurs, the causal significance of the winds is also introduced. Lodro Gyalpo contends that the transmigrating consciousness, driven by its karmic imprints, is caused by the winds to observe a man and woman in copulation, whereupon karma impels the consciousness into the womb. At the time the consciousness melts into the mixture of male and female substances, it experiences a moment of senselessness, as if intoxicated.[9] Lodro Gyalpo cites tantric accounts, the *Guhyasamāja* tantra and a work by the fourteenth-century tantric writer Rangchung Dorje (1284–1339), to emphasize the role of the winds as well as the karmic imprints in bringing the transmigrating mind into the womb.[10] He also describes an alternative Indian Buddhist tradition in which the transmigrating being enters the mixture of reproductive substances and immediately reacts to one or the other substance in a way that instantaneously determines its sex—attracted to the mother's substance, it becomes male; attracted to the father's substance, it becomes female. This early Buddhist Abhidhamma account makes sex identification central to conception itself.

Karma is given responsibility for more than pushing the transmigrating consciousness toward the copulating man and woman. Citing the *Entering the Womb* sūtra, Lodro Gyalpo explains that the transmigrating being must possess an adequate level of virtuous karma to be born as a human and that the karma of the transmigrating being and that of the parents must be equivalent in "type" or "class" (*rigs*) and level of meritorious distinction. In this case, therefore, karma also plays an important role in what *type* of rebirth one obtains. Lodro Gyalpo summarizes

7. Ibid., 128.

8. The *Transmission of the Elders*, by Zurkhar Lodro Gyalpo (zur mkhar blo gros rgyal po, 1509–1579), is a famous commentary on the *Four Tantras*. Zur mkhar pa blo gros rgyal po, *Rgyud bzhi'i 'grel pa mes po'i zhal lung*, 2 vols. (krung go'i pod kyi shes rig dpe skrun khang, 1989), 103–105.

9. Ibid., 116.

10. Ibid., 117. The text referred to by Rangchung Dorje (*rang byung rdo rje*, 1284–1339) is the *Profound Inner Meaning* (*zab mo nang don*), a text on yogic physiology and practice.

a tradition present in the *Entering the Womb* sūtra that is maintained by various Tibetan religious scholars, such as Gampopa (1079–1153), in which transmigrating beings entering the womb are of two types, some possessing more merit, others possessing less merit. Gampopa's narrative explains that all transmigrating beings possess miraculous abilities before taking rebirth, such as being able to walk on air and see with divine eyes, but after a period of time the strength of their karma causes them to have frightening visions, such as that of a storm, heavy rain, a darkening sky, or the roar of a crowd of people. As they approach the womb of their rebirth, they envision entering a place such as the second story of a house, a throne, a thatched hut, a leaf house, a shelter of grass, a jungle, or a rocky crevice. Those with exceptional merit will see palaces or mansions, while those with low merit will be directed toward rocky crevices. Arriving at their envisioned destination, they are immediately attracted to either the father's or the mother's reproductive substance. Colored by this emotional reaction, the consciousness enters into the mixture of the reproductive essences, whereupon conception has occurred.[11]

Lodro Gyalpo explains that, according to sūtric traditions, ordinary beings experience a loss of awareness upon entry into the womb, whereas the classes of beings with higher levels of spiritual realization have different experiences.[12] Advanced Buddhist spiritual figures known as universal monarchs (*'khor los sgyur ba*, Sanskrit *cakravartin*) and stream-enterers (*rgyun du zhugs pa*, Sanskrit *shrotāpanna*) are aware of their entry into the womb, but then lose awareness for the duration of gestation. Even more advanced first-level bodhisattvas (*byang chub sems dba' las dang po*) and solitary realizers (*rang sangs rgyas*, Sanskrit *pratyekabuddha*) also are "unconscious" during gestation, but they are aware of entering the womb and leaving the womb at birth. Higher level bodhisattvas are aware of the entire process.[13] Tibetan authors in both religious and medical traditions thus used embryology to perpetuate Buddhist taxonomies of embodiment, conceptual systems that organize bodies by their moral status.

Methods for Overpowering Karma

Following models inherited from Indian texts, for Tibetan authors karma plays a critical role in causing rebirth and in directing the type of rebirth one takes. Some of these authors admit, however, that the effects of karma may be overwritten by ritual intervention or medicinal application. In some contexts, therefore, one's karmic destiny can be overcome by human intervention. Medicinal or ritual intervention is said to be able to affect the health of one's reproductive substances, for example. For conception to occur successfully, male and female reproductive substances must

11. Gampopa, *The Jewel Ornament of Liberation by Sgam.po.pa*, trans. Herbert V. Guenther, The Clear Light Series (Berkeley, Calif.: Shambala Publications, 1971), 63–64; Zur mkhar pa blo gros rgyal po, *Mes po'i zhal lung*, 106–107 and 116–17.

12. Zur mkhar pa blo gros rgyal po, *Mes po'i zhal lung*, 106–107 and 116–17.

13. Ibid., 119–20.

not possess humoral disorders, and these defects may be caused by karma. Lodro Gyalpo says that one can observe the many signs of texture, color, and taste that are adequate indications of the condition of these substances. When the reproductive substances are defective, conception will not be possible, and yet some types of defects can be treated medicinally. Lodro Gyalpo refers the reader to the texts of Vāgbhaṭa and his commentators in which appropriate treatments are described. He notes that these texts also provide rituals that men and women can do themselves to promote healthy qualities in their own reproductive substances.[14]

More dramatically, medical texts claim that the very sex identification of the fetus can be changed medico-ritually. The issue of how to guarantee the birth of a male child is of great importance in Tibetan medical embryological works, although this is a matter ignored by the embryological accounts of religious texts. Rituals to transform the sex of the fetus described in the *Four Tantras* and its commentaries, as derived from Vāgbhaṭa's *Eight Branches*, are alchemically and astrologically oriented.[15] Such rituals are not described in the *Entering the Womb* sūtra, and the issue of sex transformation is not mentioned. The *Four Tantras* and its commentaries state that these rituals should be performed during the third week of gestation, and they summarize various methods for ensuring the development of a male child. Fifteenth-century commentator Kyempa Tsewang argues that although generally the sex of the fetus depends on its karmic inheritance, because additional factors do play a role in development, rituals should still be performed.[16] Clearly, although karma is accepted as a primary cause of rebirth and cited by many as the determinant of body type, there is nonetheless a conflict between the apparent predeterminism of the karmic model of causality, on the one hand, and the need for medical systems to assume that intervention can be efficacious, on the other. Medical interventions are in fact regularly cited as strategies that have the power to override the effects of karma, even in the matter of forming the human body.

The Role of the Energetic Winds

The firm foundations of karma's predeterministic role in rebirth is shaken by more than this, however. Despite the ubiquitous presence of karma as a force of conception and growth in these accounts of creation, some medical commentators use tantric texts as authorities for attributing a role to the energetic winds in conception. Beyond the moment of conception, there are numerous disagreements in Tibetan texts over the relative importance of karma and other factors, such as the winds, during gestation. By the eleventh century, Tibetans had available to them two Indian textual models for the function of the winds in embryology. The Indian

14. Ibid., 104.
15. *Vāgbhaṭa's Aṣṭāṇga Hṛdayam Sūtrasthāna* (Varanasi, India: Krishnadas Academy, 1996), 365–66.
16. Skyem pa tshe dbang, *Rgyud bzhi'i 'grel pa*, 133–34.

medical model, on the one hand, ignores the role of the winds in favor of karma, even during the process of gestation. On the other hand, the Buddhist canonical model, as revealed in sūtras and tantras, emphasizes the causal function of the winds over that of karma. These narratives offer intricate schemes for attributing growth during gestation to a host of variously named winds.

In Tibetan medical and religious embryological narratives alike, various Buddhist sūtras are referred to as authorities on the process of transmigration, the nature of the transmigrating entity, the workings of karma and the four elements, the relationship between the mind and the body, and other topics relevant to human growth. The *Entering the Womb* sūtra, for instance, makes note of independently named winds that are responsible for fetal growth during each week of gestation. These details are extensively cited by many Tibetan authors who write about embryology in both medical and religious traditions. In the early twelfth century, the religious writer Gampopa utilizes such details in his *Jewel Ornament of Liberation*, crediting the sūtra specifically. Citing the *Entering the Womb* repeatedly, the medical commentator Lodro Gyalpo states that it is very important in embryology to get the names of the weekly winds correct, and that this is an issue about which other scholars are often mistaken. The names and functions of the winds, as taken from Buddhist sūtra, are the most prominent and consistent details that medical commentators add to their accounts of the body's weekly development.

Another tradition of embryology in which specific causal forces for fetal development—that is, forces other than karma—occur is that of the tantras, which outline ten winds that play a role in tantric psychophysiology. In the context of his embryology, the twelfth-century scholar Drakpa Gyeltsen (1147–1216) explains that when discussing winds functionally, tantric traditions generally describe five primary winds, also called the five "outer" winds (*phyi'i rlung lnga*), and five subsidiary winds. The life-sustaining (*srog 'dzin*) wind originates at the heart and is generally responsible for the integrated relationship between mind and body. The downward-clearing (*thur sel*) wind originates near the anus and is responsible for waste elimination. The fire-accompanying (*me mnyam*) wind is at the navel, aiding in the digestive process. The upward-upholding (*gyen rgyu*) wind is at the throat, allowing speech, laughter, or vomiting. The all-pervasive (*khyab byed*) wind, finally, pervades the entire body. Drakpa Gyeltsen's embryology also describes five subsidiary winds, located at the sense organs and the joints and responsible for interacting with external objects.[17] Tantric texts discuss these winds in various ways in the context of embryology. Some narratives link each of the five primary and five branch winds of tantric physiology to each of ten months in the womb. Others simply note the general role of the five primary winds throughout fetal growth. Still others attribute fetal growth to each of the four natural elements, one of which is wind. While tantric narratives do discuss the causal relationship

17. This discussion about the winds is at Grags pa rgyal mtshan, "Rgyud kyi mngon par rtogs pa rin po che'i ljon shing," in *The Complete Works of Grags pa rgyal mtshan*, ed. bsod nams rgya mtsho, *Sa skya bka' 'bum (The Complete Works of the Great Masters of the Sa skya Sect of the Tibetan Buddhism)*, Vol. 3 (Tokyo: Toyo Bunko, 1968), 63a–65b.

between the winds and the general *stages* of fetal growth, however, it is primarily the sūtric tradition in which separate winds are enumerated for each *week* of development.[18]

As in the Buddhist sūtras and tantras, many Tibetan religious and medical scholars felt that intermediary causal forces—that is, forces other than karma—were essential to the growth of the body. Other scholars in Tibet who wrote about embryology did not mention such intermediary forces at all, by contrast, leaving karma as the sole causal force. In the *Eight Branches'* model of embryology, it is karma alone that provides the impetus, at the time of conception, for the growth of the body, and over the course of fetal growth no other force, not even that of the winds, has any causal function. The *Four Tantras* is also largely silent on the role of the winds in the body's development. The earliest extant commentaries of the *Four Tantras'* embryology, three small medical texts likely authored by students of Tibetan physician and editor of the *Four Tantras* Yuthog Yonten Gonpo, also do not mention the weekly winds. It is clear that the winds played a larger role than karma in theories of the developing body that are based on Buddhist canonical materials, than in those closer to Indian medical models. There is a historical aspect to this: given the evidence available to us today, earlier accounts of embryology—those from the eleventh or twelfth centuries—are significantly less likely to attribute causality to the winds than are later embryological accounts, where doing so becomes almost ubiquitous, especially in the case of medical texts. What is interesting here is the absorption of the Buddhist canonical model into the Tibetan medical commentaries. By the fifteenth century, medical texts focus heavily on the intermediary causal role of the winds during gestation. In the matter of identifying causal forces responsible for the growth of the body, over time the Buddhist canonical model—emphasizing the causal influence of the winds—won out in Tibet over the early medical model, which left developmental causality up to karma.

The Role of the Natural Elements

For some authors, wind is not the only natural element playing a role in human growth. Whereas most accounts state that the natural elements are essential to the process of creating a new human life, Tibetan descriptions of the precise role of the four or five natural elements in embryology are far from consistent. Some authors emphasize the essential role of all the elements, others ignore most elements in favor of the wind element alone, and yet others neglect to mention the elements at all. The three earliest extant commentaries on the *Four Tantras,* for example, do not mention the role of the elements in embryonic development. Other authors, such as Gampopa, provide details on the activities of the wind element, but overlook the activities of other elements. The *Entering the Womb* sūtra does discuss the

18. Further discussion of the winds in various sources can be found in Frances Garrett, *Religion, Medicine and the Human Embryo in Tibet,* Critical Studies in Buddhism series (New York: Routledge, 2008).

importance of the elements for conception, but it downplays the role of all but one of the elements in the subsequent process of fetal growth.

As noted above, in his *Transmission of the Elders*, Lodro Gyalpo is highly critical of those who question the need for all the elements in embryology (despite the absence of the elements in Vāgbhaṭa's *Eight Branches*, one of his primary medical sources).[19] Both the reproductive substances of the parents and the transmigrating consciousness, he argues, are necessarily possessed of subtle forms of the five elements, and therefore it is logically impossible for conception to occur without the presence of all elements. The natural elements refer not to static material elements, he says, but rather to qualitative, dynamic functions. For instance, the earth element refers to the quality or function of hardness, and the water element refers to the quality or function of cohesiveness, flexibility, or coolness. The natural elements are thus the very functional interactivity that makes change and growth possible. Acknowledging the *Eight Branches'* neglect of this matter, Lodro Gyalpo looks to another Indian source, noting that the *Entering the Womb* does clearly state that each element is essential.[20] Lodro Gyalpo defends the presence of the elements in the transmigrating consciousness especially, maintaining that consciousness and the five elements necessarily exist interdependently. He asserts that conception is the role of the earth element, generating the embryonic form is the role of the water element, ripening the fetus is the role of the fire element, growing the fetus larger is the role of the wind element, and providing the opportunity for all of this is the role of the space element. The elements are also held responsible for the development of the sense powers and other aspects of the body. Unlike the majority of Tibetan embryologists, who only discuss the functions of the elements at the time of conception, Lodro Gyalpo also maintains that the five elements are responsible for generating various aspects of the body throughout the course of its development. Intrinsically part of the reproductive substances and the mind that join in the womb at conception, the initially subtle elements grow stronger during gestation because of the power of the nutrients consumed by the mother.[21] As the fetal body grows, supported by the mother's supply of nutrients, the strength of the elements increases.

The description of fetal development by the fourteenth-century religious scholar Longchenpa (1308–64) is dominated by the activities of all the natural elements to a far greater degree than other Tibetan presentation of embryology.[22] Longchenpa organizes the first two weeks of development into seven-day cycles according to the functions of the elements: during days one through four, each of the four elements is sequentially predominant; on days five and six they operate

19. Zur mkhar pa blo gros rgyal po, *Mes po'i zhal lung*, 107.

20. Lodro Gyalpo also explains here why the *Entering the Womb* mentions four elements, and the *Four Tantras* and other Tibetan sources describe have five. Ibid., 108.

21. Ibid., 120.

22. Klong chen pa, *Tshig don mdzod, Mdzod chen bdun* (Gangtok, Sikkim: Sherab Gyaltsen and Khyentse Labrang, 1983), 188ff. The *Tshig don mdzod* is translated in David Germano, "Poetic Thought, the Intelligent Universe, and the Mystery of Self: The Tantric Synthesis of rdzogs chen in Fourteenth-Century Tibet (Buddhism)," Ph.D. diss., University of Wisconsin, 1992. My discussion of Longchenpa's work in this article relies upon Germano's extensive research, and I am grateful to him for generously sharing his manuscripts.

in pairs; and on the seventh day they function together as a group. This organizational principal is said to pertain to the entire period of gestation, although Longchenpa provides details only for the first two weeks. His account of the first week of development describes the four elements' activation of four very subtle circulatory channels in the embryo's body: named for the elements themselves, these are a water channel, an earth channel, a fire channel, and a wind channel. The space element operates on the seventh day to provide a place for the four elements to gather together. In the second week, the work of the elements continues as the embryo is dissolved, compacted, baked, and scattered about, dispersing "like fluffy clouds in the sky." On the eighth evening, by the power of karma and predispositions, these fragments are gathered by the water element. In the third and fourth weeks, the embryo is again sequentially destroyed and reconstituted, as new structures and energies of the subtle body are formed within the embryo.

In this quite unusual presentation of the role of the elements in embryology, Longchenpa also distinguishes between conventional (*kun rdzob*) and ultimate (*don dam*) elements. Through the male and female substances, the conventional elements become functional—these conventional elements are responsible for the development of physical features during gestation. The activity of the conventional elements thus generates the body's blood, flesh, breath, as well as many of the mental abilities of cognition, perception, and awareness. Through the mind and wind, which are the contributions of the transmigrating being, the ultimate elements become functional—these allow the consciousness to take hold of its new body, and they initiate the maturing dynamic energies of differentiation and assimilation that cause embryonic development. The ultimate elements thus generate the eyes, four wheels (*'khor lo*, Sanskrit *chakra*), and three circulatory channels of the embryo. With the parents' reproductive substances causing physical development and the consciousness's contribution causing the organizational impulse for development, the role of the natural elements is discussed in a unique and much more subtle and detailed way in Longchenpa's writings than in any other tradition. In the case of Longchenpa's tradition, the emphasis on the activities of the natural elements during gestation is justified by the tradition's overall philosophical and soteriological system. The significance of the natural elements here, then, goes far beyond their role as the building blocks of material reality.

The Power of Gnosis

Up to this point I have argued that, as in the Buddhist sūtras and tantras, many important Tibetan religious and medical scholars felt that causal forces other than karma were essential to the growth of the human body. Those other forces—the winds alone, or all of the natural elements—were themselves integral components of the newly developing body of the ordinary human fetus. In these models, the various features of the growing body themselves thus served to cause further development, in a gradually accumulative way. Notably, however, these forces are impure, part of the world of *saṃsāra*. There is another model of causation in human growth, however, one that differs quite radically from other presentations, and one in which change is motivated by an eminently pure phenomenon, the wisdom of a Buddha.

Longchenpa's narrative of embryology is unusual not only for its particular attention to the role played in growth by the natural elements; also remarkable is his discussion of the formation of the eyes in the embryo. His theory of fetal development describes the formation of two tiny "eye-like" features, called the "eye of the lamps" (*sgron ma'i spyan*) and the "eye of the elements" (*'byung ba'i spyan*). Whereas in other Tibetan embryological accounts the eyes are said to appear only much later in gestation, in Longchenpa's account these eyes appear within the circulatory channels during the first week of gestation. The "eye of the elements" directs the development of the physical body, and the "eye of the lamps" is given ultimate responsibility for the subtle body, and therefore also, later on in life, for the visionary experiences felt during specific forms of contemplative practice in Longchenpa's tradition. The designation of these forces as "eyes" and their placement in the very earliest stages of human development is dictated by the importance of vision in his contemplative system. In this context it is also notable that, by attributing the force of causality in embryonic growth to these "eyes," which are explicitly correlated to innate wisdom (*ye shes*), Longchenpa has effectively given the Buddha's wisdom the power to cause human growth. In this model, therefore, a purified form of knowing is explicitly the operative causal agent of human existence. Contrasting this model with the earlier model valuing the role of karma, here we see a primacy of epistemology over ethics—in other words, a valorization of cognitive over moral transformation. The wisdom of a Buddha—not karma—is the primary causal dynamic operative in this notion of generation.

Forces of Creation

Embryology is a means for Tibetan authors to define human bodies, and to say something about what it is, or what it should be, to be human. In addition to deciding what counts as a body, embryology divides bodies into a range of body types. A typology of bodies is done according to some underlying organizational principle; in our society, for example, bodies may be sorted by explicitly racist or sexist schemas. The problem of how bodies are differentiated is one that all religions try to solve. Why are some born healthy, some beautiful, some ugly, some into poverty and distress? Why do illness and misfortune strike some and not others? Why do they strike when they do?

An answer is provided in Buddhism by the concept of karma, which rationalizes and moralizes that which otherwise would seem random, instructing humans to cherish their human embodiment as a precious opportunity to generate good karma and obtain a better rebirth. It is also karmic merit or demerit, however, that keeps one locked in the perpetual cycle of rebirths until ultimate salvation. In early Indian Buddhism, one's karmic destiny is largely only a matter of one's own concern—that is to say, one's karmic effects are carried solely within one's own lineage of rebirths and do not affect to a significant extent the rebirth paths of others. With the Mahāyāna bodhisattva ideal, the notion of karmic destiny is expanded beyond one's own line of lifetimes: the bodhisattva generates a karmic force powerful enough to liberate all beings from their own karmic destinies. In Vajrayāna Buddhism, the emphasis on ritual action is seen as an essential intervention, as many traditions rely on the power of the divine—whether embodied within oneself or called upon as an external force—on the path to enlightenment.

In this essay we have seen that for Tibetan authors, karmic causality is far from the only pattern of thinking about the causation of the human individual. I began by explaining that karma as articulated in embryological accounts—both in its involvement with the Buddhist law of interdependent origination, and in its specific role as a causal agent in conception and fetal growth—is held by some early Tibetan embryologists to be the sole causal agent in human rebirth and development. Karma is an integral part of the law of interdependent origination, propelling the transmigrating being along the path toward physical embodiment and defining the nature of that embodiment. Karma is also responsible for the type of body a transmigrating being could obtain: transmigrators carrying superior moral achievements could obtain psychophysiologically and soteriologically superior bodies. I also demonstrated that a karmic theory of causality was not enough for all embryologists, and that for some authors other factors, such as winds, natural elements, or one's Buddha-nature, are the dominant causal contributors to the formation of the new human being. Medieval Tibetans seemed little constrained by the authorities of scripture or empiricism, apparently free to write the details of embryonic growth as they liked. Tibetan embryology germinated the individual human body with a scholar's own specialized narrative about causation and growth. Embryological accounts defined certain acceptable paradigms for change and growth. Change and growth happen in stages, as for Drakpa Gyeltsen and other writers who outline the religious path structure; they are completely integrated with both the emotions and the workings of the natural elements, as for Longchenpa, and in his tradition they are ultimately driven by an enlightened form of knowing. In some accounts, change and growth are innately present as potentials within the fetus; in others, they require the successful workings of an intricately coordinated complex of sequentially generated causal forces. In Tibetan literature, embryology thus imbues religious doctrines with specific, personified models of temporality.

WORKS CITED

Bdud rtsi snying po yan lag brgyad pa gsang ba man ngag gi rgyud. Delhi: Bod kyi lcags po ri'i dran rten slob gner khang, 1993.

Dargyay, Lobsang. "Tsong-Kha-Pa's Concept of Karma." In *Karma and Rebirth: Post Classical Developments*, edited by Ronald W. Neufeldt. Albany: State University of New York Press, 1986.

Dasgupta, Surendranath. *A History of Indian Philosophy*. 5 vols. New Delhi: Motilal Banarsidass, 1975.

Gampopa. *The Jewel Ornament of Liberation by Sgam.po.pa*. Translated by Herbert V. Guenther. The Clear Light Series. Berkeley, Calif.: Shambala Publications, 1971.

Garrett, Frances. *Religion, Medicine and the Human Embryo in Tibet*, Critical Studies in Buddhism series. New York: Routledge, 2008.

———. "Ordering Human Growth in Tibetan Medical and Religious Embryologies." In *Textual Healing: Essays on Medieval and Early Modern Medicine*, edited by Elizabeth Lane Furdell, 32–52. Leiden, Netherlands: Brill, 2005.

Germano, David. "Poetic Thought, the Intelligent Universe, and the Mystery of Self: The Tantric Synthesis of rdzogs chen in Fourteenth-Century Tibet (Buddhism)." Ph.D. diss., University of Wisconsin, 1992.

Grags pa rgyal mtshan. "Rgyud kyi mngon par rtogs pa rin po che'i ljon shing." In *The Complete Works of Grags pa rgyal mtshan*, edited by bsod nams rgya mtsho, 1–139. Tokyo: Toyo Bunko, 1968.

Hopkins, Jeffrey. *Meditation on Emptiness*. London: Wisdom Publications, 1983.

Klong chen pa. *Tshig don mdzod, Mdzod chen bdun*. Gangtok, Sikkim: Sherab Gyaltsen and Khyentse Labrang, 1983.

Kritzer, Robert. "Garbhāvakrāntisūtra: A Comparison of the Contents of Two Versions." *Maranatha: Bulletin of the Christian Culture Research Institute (Kyoto)* 6 (1998): 4–13.

Lalou, Marcelle. "La version Tibetain du Ratnakūṭa." *Journal Asiatique* (October–December 1927): 233–59.

Matthews, Bruce. "Post-Classical Developments in the Concepts of Karma and Rebirth in Theravada Buddhism." In *Karma and Rebirth: Post-Classical Developments*, edited by Ronald W. Neufeldt, 123–43. Albany: State University of New York Press, 1986.

McDermott, James Paul. *Development in the Early Buddhist Concept of Kamma/Karma*. New Delhi: Munishiram Manoharlal, 1984.

———. "Karma and Rebirth in Early Buddhism." In *Karma and Rebirth in Classical Indian Traditions*, edited by Wendy Doniger, 165–92. Delhi: Motilal Banarsidass, 1983.

The Quintessence Tantras of Tibetan Medicine. Translated by Barry Clark. Ithaca, N.Y.: Snow Lion Publishers, 1995.

Skyem pa tshe dbang. *Mkhas dbang skyem pa tshe dbang mchog gis mdzad pa'i rgyud bzhi'i 'grel pa bshugs so*. Vol. 2. New Delhi: bod gshung sman rtsis khang, n.d.

Sopa, Geshe. "The Tibetan Wheel of Life: Iconography and Doxography." *Journal of the International Association of Buddhist Studies* 7, 1 (1984).

Vāgbhaṭa's Aṣṭāñga Hṛdayam Sūtrasthāna. Varanasi, India: Krishnadas Academy, 1996.

Williams, David M. "The Translation and Interpretation of the Twelve Terms in the Paticcasamuppada." *Numen* 21 (1974).

Zur mkhar pa blo gros rgyal po. *Rgyud bzhi'i 'grel pa mes po'i zhal lung*. 2 vols. Beijing: krung go'i bod kyi shes rig dpe skrun khang, 1989.

Female Feticide in the Punjab and Fetus Imagery in Sikhism

Nikky-Guninder Kaur Singh

Plato has it backwards; the search for the wholly transcendent is, historically and psychologically, the search for the remembered state of union with the wholly immanent.

—Naomi Goldenberg, "The Return of the Goddess"

Currently, sex-specific abortions eliminating female fetuses are rampant in the Punjab. From time immemorial, the patriarchal society of northern India has been obsessed with sons: the region resounds with the blessing "May you be the mother of a hundred sons!"[1] The great Rig Veda, one of the earliest textual pieces produced in India, begins with Agni granting many "heroic sons" to his worshippers. Over the centuries, this wish has only deepened. The rich soil of Punjab, literally the land of the "five rivers," has attracted many outsiders including the Indo-Aryans, the Greeks, the Afghans, Persians, Turks, Mughals, and the British. Both these geohistorical contingencies—the settled agricultural communities and the constant waves of invasions—have reinforced the wish for heroic sons who will plow the land and fight the enemy.

The Sikh religion was birthed in this geographical landscape, and it developed within a doubly patriarchal milieu. Between the birth of the founder (Guru Nanak in 1469) to the death of the tenth guru (Guru Gobind Singh in 1708), the Hindu society of North India succumbed to

In this chapter, I draw upon my previous work, *The Birth of the Khalsa: A Feminist Re-Memory of Sikh Identity*, chapter 5, and *The Feminine Principle in the Sikh Vision of the Transcendent*, chapter 2.

1. See Elisabeth Bumiller's *May You Be the Mother of a Hundred Sons* (New York: Random House, 1990).

Muslim rulers from outside—Turks, Afghans, and the Mughals. In the old Hindu caste system, women were subjugated to their husbands, and under the new Muslim regime, women had to stay in purdah. The gurus tried to free their society from such oppressions, but instead of heeding the words of the gurus, the Sikhs retained the patriarchal values they were surrounded by and even reinforced them. British colonialism provided yet another oppressive layer, producing a hypermasculine culture. The Punjab was annexed by the British in 1849, and the imperial masters greatly admired the martial character and strong physique of Sikh men; they recruited them in disproportionately large numbers to serve in the British army. A vigorous new patriarchal discourse with its patriotism and paternalism was thereby attached to the "brotherhood of the Khalsa." Sikhs formed approximately one fifth of the imperial army in World War I, with numbers reaching one hundred thousand by the end of the war. They valorously fought for the empire in Europe, Africa, West Asia, Burma, Malaysia, and China. The Sikhs won fourteen of the twenty-two military crosses awarded to Indians for conspicuous gallantry. From Shanghai to Mesopotamia, Sikhs heroically guarded the outposts of the empire. In return, they received honors and handsome grants of land in the new canal colonies in the Punjab (that they had helped to build) and thus became the richest agriculturists in Asia.[2]

The momentum continues. With the Green Revolution and the enterprising spirit of its people, postcolonial Punjab has become the breadbasket of India. Today it is in the ferment of globalization. All these economic and technological priorities have made the patriarchal compulsion for sons even stronger. Parents regard sons as their social security, financial insurance, and religious functionaries who will eventually perform their funeral rites. Sons are deemed essential for carrying on the family name, property, and land. When a son marries, he brings his wife into the family home, and she takes care of her in-laws into their old age. With *his* wife comes *her* dowry adding to the economic resources of his family. Simple marriage ceremonies have become extremely opulent, dowries extravagant, and gifts to the daughter and her in-laws for every rite, ritual, and festival exorbitant. Both in India and in Sikh diasporas, marriages are transformed into elaborate affairs, and the quantity and quality of what is hosted for or given to the daughter reinforces the power and prestige of her father. Daughters have no rights over their natal homes; they are viewed as beautiful commodities and investments in their father's status and honor. The not-so-wealthy feel extreme pressure to squeeze out their hard-earned money to keep up with the cultural norms. Whereas the son is desired for the accretion of his father's assets, the daughter is rejected because she represents its depletion. The economic and social demands of contemporary Sikh culture are extremely demanding.

With the combination of ancient patriarchal values and new globalization, the proportion of baby girls is declining rapidly. In India's population of 1.027 billion, a recent census showed only 927 girls for every 1,000 boys—down from 945

2. For many of the historical details, I have relied on Khushwant Singh's *History of the Sikhs,* Vol. 2 (Princeton, N.J.: Princeton University Press, 1966); see esp. p. 160.

ten years ago. Neonatal sex identifications through ultrasound have made gender-selective abortions increasingly easy. Female fetuses are being aborted to preserve the legacy, business, property, and status of fathers and their sons. With technological and economic advancements, Punjab, the home of the Sikhs, is ironically facing a terrible situation. In the West, newspaper reports like "Abortions in India Spurred by Sex Test Skew the Ratio against Girls" in the *New York Times* focus on the tragedy of female feticide in the affluent agrarian Punjab.[3] Such alarming news items also appeared on the front pages of local Indian newspapers when I was in Patiala, Amristar, and New Delhi in January 2006. A "diabolic link" exists between sex-selection technologies and the abortion of female fetuses, with the result that there is an increasing imbalance in the ratio of males to females in the population of the Punjab. Since immigrant Sikhs maintain transnational ties with their families and friends in the Punjab, the customs and values from home are quickly exported to diasporic communities across the globe.[4]

The government of India banned the use of sex determination techniques more than a decade ago. The prohibitions against it are coming primarily from the Sikh governing body, the Shromani Gurdwara Prabandhak Committee. Recently, in the city of Fatehgarh Sahib in the Punjab—where the ratio of females is 750 per 1,000 males!—about 250 Sikh religious leaders discussed ways to outlaw female feticides. The general population has not confronted this situation seriously, and the laws are obviously not working. As we all know, rules and regulations fail if the community is not ready for them. The dedicated activist and founding editor of *Manushi* (a leading Indian journal about women and society), Madhu Kishwar, has been proclaiming that laws and regulations are useless gestures and concessions by governments.[5] Kishwar is extremely familiar with a modern-day India in which women are granted equal rights on paper but not in reality.

Can literature succeed where laws are failing? Yes, I believe it can. Literature has the capacity to reach our inner recesses and change our conscience and consciousness. The land where female fetuses are being aborted is also the land of Sikh scripture, the Guru Granth, which resonates with powerful fetal imagery. But unfortunately, for various reasons, neither Sikhs nor outsiders have had sufficient access to it. Clearly, the text does not outlaw feticides. It is sheer poetry that offers only intimations. Here the Sikh gurus voice their passionate longing for the divine. This scripture does not set up a strict deontology. It is not prescriptive; it is not proscriptive. Yet, in a poignant way, the Guru Granth draws our attention to our contemporary tragedy. Pulling us away from death and "necrophilic" ideologies, its fetus imaginary leads us to the origins of life, to the world around us, and, most significantly, to the *mother's* body in which fetuses are lodged. This literary symbol has tremendous potential to activate our imagination and sensibility and to transform sexist attitudes and practices. My chapter therefore functions a bit like

3. Celia Dugger, "Abortions in India Spurred by Sex Test Skew the Ratio against Girls," *New York Times*, April 22, 2001.

4. See C. C. Fair, "Female Foeticide among Vancouver Sikhs: Recontexualizing Sex Selection in the North American Diaspora," *International Journal of Punjab Studies* 3, 1 (1996): 1–44.

5. For example, see M. Kiswhar, *Off the Beaten Track* (Delhi: Oxford, 1999).

a sonogram—a device that not only helps us identify some of the complex literary frequencies rhythmically beating within the Sikh sacred text, but also enables us to envision a new egalitarian world. As the exciting fetal nuances tucked in the folds of the Guru Granth reveal some essential values of the Sikh religious tradition, they motivate us to rectify existing patriarchal structures. Generally, this North Indian tradition is ignored in the study of religion and society, and its potential to raise our awareness about our common humanity remains unrecognized.

At the outset we must realize that for the Sikhs (who are a majority population in the Punjab) the Guru Granth is the quintessence of their philosophy and ethics, the center of all their rites and ceremonies. I cannot fully underscore its importance. Sikh weddings consist of the bride and groom walking around the holy book four times. No vows are exchanged, no rings exchanged. Bowing before the Guru Granth—with their foreheads touching the ground in unison—is an outward sign of the couple's acceptance of a life-long commitment. When the couple has a child, the Guru Granth is again central. For the naming ceremony, the book is opened at random, and whatever letter the left-hand page begins with becomes the first letter of the child's given name. During all events of joy and sorrow there is a continuous reading of the Guru Granth. Sikhs pay utmost reverence to their scripture: it is always placed on a pedestal, adorned in silks and brocades; devotees have their feet bare, heads covered, and sit on the floor when in its presence. Guru Arjan, the fifth Sikh guru, who compiled the Guru Granth in 1604 and put most of it in musical measures, did not make any religious demarcations: whatever was in harmony with the vision of Guru Nanak (1469–1539), the founding guru, he included in the book. The Granth includes the poetry of Hindu Bhaktas and Muslim Sufis, and words rooted in Arabic, Sanskrit, and Persian language flow freely into its placental waters nurturing generations of Sikh men and women. A day before he passed away, Guru Gobind Singh (Nanak X, 1666–1708) endowed the Granth with guruship, and so it is revered as the "Guru" eternal. The Guru Granth has a sensuous quality; it is not simply the "soul" of the guru poets but their very body: it palpitates with their inhaling and exhaling, it resounds with their diastolic and systolic movements, it flows with the flow of the gurus' blood.

In spite of its centrality in Sikh life, the feminist import of Sikh scripture has not been recognized, and as a result the literary symbols and social reality of the community exist in opposition The vital poetic images revered on the Punjabi soil need to be concretized in Punjabi habits and customs. We must explore Sikh literature and utilize its fetal imagery to end gender-specific feticides.

The Guru Granth offers us multivalent womb imagery. Conceived by different poets with different emphases and in different contexts, we find here an extremely fertile ground inspiring a wide range of responses. The womb is celebrated as the matrix for all life and living. However, it also serves as an eschatological expression for the return of the self. According to Sikh scripture, birth is rare and precious like a diamond, but it can be flitted away for naught. An immoral life generates a negative rebirth, and the mother's womb in that instance is pictured as a scorching and painful mode of being—empty of the Divine. Under positive circumstances, however, the womb becomes a vital space for the Divine, and the fetus functions as a symbol for cultivating Sikh morality, spirituality, and aesthetics. Indeed, this textual body takes female genealogy seriously, and affirms the category of birth that feminist theologians, philosophers, and psychologists find so critical. Sadly, Sikh scholarship today, being the domain of "minds and men," finds little importance in the creative and sustaining powers of the mother's body. In the course of Sikh exegesis, translation, and communal memory, the unique female organ is neglected. Our primal home is neither remembered nor celebrated, and at times it even gets turned into a generic stomach! It is imperative, then, that we return to it and recover its full potential. Through graphical representations of sound, and its dimensions of frequency and intensity, our sonogram reveals many exciting features of the fetus tucked warmly in her body.

1

First of all, the embryonic figure reveals the complexity of female biology, reminding us immediately of the significance of menstruation in the creative process. Her monthly period indicates that she has the potential to create new life, and serves as a healthy marker for the origin of life. Unfortunately, this unique female phenomenon explodes with negative connotations. Considered a private, shameful process, it is equated with being ill or weak, and has been used across cultures to justify women's subordination and oppression. Feminist scholars have studied the degradation of menstruation and how the disdain for this natural feminine phenomenon has led to the lowering of women's status. To quote Judy Grahn: "The status and social control women have had has fallen with the fall of menstruation."[6]

A very different perspective emerges from Sikh scripture—one that acknowledges menstrual bleeding as an essential, natural process. We hear the founding guru reprimand those who stigmatize a blood-stained garment as polluted.[7] Guru Nanak strongly questioned the legitimacy and purpose of devaluing women on the basis of their reproductive energy: "How can we call her polluted from whom the great ones are born?"[8] Clearly, the Sikh guru was aware of the sexism prevalent in his society, and he denounced taboos against women. The fear of the gaze, touch, and speech of a menstruating woman had been internalized by Indian society for centuries. These deeply rooted negative attitudes to women have seeped into all of India's religious traditions. In the Hindu tradition, for example, they are expressed in the Laws of Manu (second century BCE–second century CE): Any touch of the "untouchable, a menstruating woman, anyone who has fallen (from his caste), a woman who has just given birth, a corpse, or anyone who has touched any of these objects" is deemed polluted.[9] Food touched by a menstruating woman is forbidden.[10] To even lie down in the same bed as a menstruating woman is forbidden.[11]

6. J. Grahn, "From Sacred Blood to the Curse Beyond," in *The Politics of Women's Spirituality*, ed. C. Spretnak (Garden City, N.Y.: Anchor, 1982), 275.

7. Guru Granth, 140.

8. Ibid., 473.

9. *The Laws of Manu*, trans. W. Doniger (New York: Penguin, 1991), 5:85.

10. Ibid., 4:208.

11. Ibid., 4:40.

Manu's injunctions also include: "A man who has sex with a woman awash in menstrual blood loses his wisdom, brilliant energy, strength, eyesight, and long life. By shunning her . . . he increases his wisdom, brilliant energy, strength, eyesight, and long life."[12] These misogynistic views transcend religious boundaries; they prevail through space and time, and were prevalent in Nanak's society.

But the more closely we examine the Sikh sacred text, the farther such negative social meanings and harmful stereotypes recede. How can we undermine a process that is the prime sign of women's generative power? Had it not been for her monthly cycles, the mother would not have been able to conceive. Menstruation represents the possibility of pregnancy. So the embryo attached to the uterus has tremendous impact: it transforms feelings of shame and embarrassment into joy and pride; indeed, it shakes the very foundations of gender inequality entrenched in our patriarchal world.

2

The Guru Granth also discloses the equality of male and female in the creative process. It underscores that a fetus is created from *both* father and mother. The total equality and unity of *bindu* (semen) and *raktu* (blood) is the source of life: "Mother and father together form the fetus, and with blood and semen they make the body";[13] "From mother's blood and father's semen is created the human form."[14] Priority is given to the mother's blood consistently. Consider the following passages for further confirmation: "From blood and semen is one created";[15] "The union of mother and father earns us the body";[16] and Kabir categorically states, "Without mother or father there can be no children."[17] Feminist scholars have noted how Aristotelian doctrine attributes the father with the agency to create, and so the maternal womb is only a container of inert and cold matter to which the warm sperm gives life. In Aristotelian embryology, the mother's "container" merely holds what the father produces. Against androcentric perceptions of a temporary "little oven in which the paternal gene was nurtured and cozily leavened,"[18] the womb (*garbh* or *udar*) is claimed as the source of life in Sikh scripture: "In the first stage of life, o friend, you by the divine will, lodged in the womb . . . says Nanak, in the first stage of life, the creature by the divine will lodged in the womb."[19] In the Sikh metaphysical scheme, both parents are equally important in the gift of life, and the whole person is created in the womb.

Our focus on the initial shaping of the union of the mother and father in the uterus reinforces the generative power of the mother. She is the maternal

12. Ibid., 4:41–42.
13. Guru Granth, 1013.
14. Ibid., 1022.
15. Ibid., 706.
16. Ibid., 989.
17. Ibid., 872.
18. Adriana Cavarero, *In Spite of Plato: A Feminist Rewriting of Ancient Philosophy* (New York: Routledge, 1995), 74.
19. Guru Granth, 74.

continuum, one who retrieves the primacy of birth over death, and reaffirms the union of body and mind. The mother offers new openings to feminist perspectives that are underscored by scholars in their own and different ways. *Her* body connects each one of us with the two sequences of infinity: the past and future of every being, male or female. In her provocative book *In Spite of Plato*, Adriana Cavarero notes, "Both infinities, past and future, origin and perpetuation, always exist through the feminine."[20] At the outset of her study on Freud, Madelon Sprengnether makes the observation: "Whatever our other differences, as human beings we have one thing in common: we are all born of woman."[21] This is a vivid testimonial to the power of the mother's body. Sikh scripture illuminates the views of contemporary feminist scholars that we are rooted in female genealogy, and returns meaning to the basic fact that we are all born of woman. Rather than an abstraction, the fetus is firmly lodged and reveals to us a palpable portion of infinity in which each of us from every species becomes embodied and exists authentically.

The textual verses disrupt patriarchal dichotomies and direct us toward our earthly existence. Instead of fleeing the world and body, the fetal imagery inspires us with positive perceptions of ourselves to develop constructive relationships with the world around: "Amidst mother, father, brother, son, and wife, has the Divine yoked us," states the Guru Granth.[22] In these divinely bound relationships, mother and wife are both significant, and women's maternal and sexual proclivities are equally celebrated. The horizon of the physical, which has been severed by the patriarchal metaphysical order in which death functions as the fundamental paradigm, is protected by the mother's sexual and maternal powers. Feminist scholars criticize metaphysics as a form of matricide, and in Luce Irigaray's words, "Its soil has become culture, history, which successfully forgets that anything that conceives has its origins in the flesh."[23] For Cavarero, "Man, with a masculine—universal—natural valence, is a term from a language that has turned its gaze away from the place of birth, measuring existence on an end point that bears no memory of its beginning."[24] Grace Jantzen argues that the obsession with death is connected to an "obsession with female bodies, and the denial of death and efforts to master it are connected with a deep-seated misogyny."[25] For Jantzen, the various forms of dominance—racism, capitalism, colonialism, homophobia, ecological destruction—are manifestations of the need to conquer death.

In contrast with the necrophilic imaginary of the male symbolic, fetal imaginary affirms life and living in diverse forms. The Granth states, "You yourself are born of the egg, from the womb, from sweat, from earth: you yourself are all the continents and all the worlds."[26] The sacred text invokes the Transcendent as

20. Caravero, *In Spite of Plato*, 60.

21. Madelon Sprengnether, *The Spectral Mother: Freud, Feminism, and Psychoanalysis* (Ithaca, N.Y.: Cornell University Press, 1990), 1.

22. Guru Granth, 77.

23. Luce Irigaray, *Sexes and Genealogies*, trans. G. Gill (New York: Columbia University Press, 1993), 109.

24. Cavarero, *In Spite of Plato*, 69.

25. G. Jantzen, *Becoming Divine: Towards a Feminist Philosophy of Religion* (Bloomington: Indiana University Press, 1999), 132.

26. Guru Granth, 604.

an essential experience of everyday life. While reminding us of Julia Kristeva's principle that "the reproductive system is the essential link between the living individual and the species,"[27] Sikh scriptural images are vital reminders that we come into the world along with the Divine, and that we come into the world by a woman who could not be a man. The Guru Granth exalts, "Blessed are the mothers!"[28] The maternal power with her paradigm of natality overturns the male death-ideal as its fundamental paradigm. Indeed, "the womb of the mother earth yokes us together."[29] Birth becomes the absolute possibility of orienting ourselves in the physical world so that we experience fully—body and spirit together—the Absolute within the natural and social fibers of our being.

Fetal imagery in the Guru Granth constantly turns our gaze to our origin in the mother's body. She beckons us back to the womb, reminding us poignantly that it is the place where we become the self, both body and spirit. Even the pervasive usage of *rahime* ("compassionate"—an expression for the Divine) draws our attention to her maternal space. In the speculations of the Muslim philosopher Ibn Arabi, the root of the word *rahimat* is womb, and the meaning of compassion or mercy is derived from it.[30] Similarly, feminist scholars relate the Hebrew word *rachum* ("compassion"), with *racham,* the word for womb.[31] Sikh scripture continues to resonate with many positive memories of our lodging in the womb, the mother's creative organ: "In the mother's womb are we taken care of";[32] "In the womb you worked to preserve us";[33] and "In the mother's womb you nurture us."[34]

Her creative site of pregnancy is brilliantly photographed by the first Sikh guru. In a melody of phonetic sounds and a collage of visual images, Guru Nanak leads us to our primal lodging:

> Semen and blood came together to create the body;
> Air, water, fire came together to create life;
> And the One performs wonders in the colorful body;
>   all else is the expanse of illusion and attachment.
> In the rounded womb is the upside down thinker,
> And the knower knows every one's hearts;
> Each breath remembers the true name,
>   for inside the womb flourishes the One.[35]

This is no scopophilic or fetishistic construction. Focusing on the maternal organ, Nanak's semiotic lens takes us back to that magical location where womb, ovum,

27. Julia Kristeva, *In the Beginning was Love: Psychoanalysis and Faith,* trans. A. Goldhammer (New York: Columbia University Press, 1987), 45.

28. Guru Granth, 513.

29. Ibid., 1021.

30. Ibn al'Arabi, *The Bezels of Wisdom,* trans. R. W. J. Austin. *The Classics of Western Spirituality* (Mahwah, N.J.: Paulist Press, 1980), 29.

31. Phyllis Trible, *God and the Rhetoric of Sexuality* (Philadelphia: Fortress Press, 1978), 31–59.

32. Guru Granth, 1086.

33. Ibid., 177.

34. Ibid., 132.

35. Ibid., 1026–27.

and sperm come together making us mindful of the locus where life is produced—life that is the body, life that is the spirit. The founding Sikh guru's recollection of our first home forms a diametric contrast to male conceptions noted by Luce Irigaray: "The womb is never thought of as the primal place in which we become body. Therefore for many men it is variously phantasized as a devouring mouth, as a sewer in which anal and urethral waste is poured, as threat to the phallus or, at best, as a reproductive organ."[36] Her womb is no "devouring mouth," no "sewer," no mere "reproductive organ." The Sikh guru makes us cognizant of our ontological, epistemological, and aesthetic rootedness in women's physiology. "Woman is the stuff out of which all people are made."[37]

In Nanak's feminist photography we discover a maternal space pregnant with the Transcendent One, rooted fully and richly in her body. Hers is an active site where the One is dynamically present: "And the One performs wonders in the colorful body."[38] That One has not made the entry from the outside or above, but constitutes an essential part of her physiology: "Inside the womb flourishes the One."[39] With the Infinite delighting inside her body, the fetus grows, drawing upon the nutrients of the physical elements that the mother herself shares with the rest of the cosmos. The male Sikh guru seems to have used the lens of modern feminists for whom natural elements "constitute the origin of our bodies, of our life, of our environment, the flesh of our passions."[40] The tenth and final Sikh guru, Gobind Singh, likewise reminds us that we are created from the four elements, "a combination of earth, air, fire and water."[41] The Sikh gurus go further than our contemporary French feminist writer, for they even show us the Divine present visibly—performing wonders as Nanak says—within the walls of her uterus! That the Transcendent is not an extraneous addition but the very core of our physical self is highlighted in Sikh sacred verses. Being in the womb is therefore a most healthy and positive human condition, and the Guru Granth overall is full of palpable reminders that we are tenderly cared for by the Divine: "In the mother's womb you protect us with your hand."[42] Fetuses do not fall into the womb. They are lodged in the maternal space where the Transcendent exists simultaneously with the physical elements. In her biological foundations, we are somatically alive to the touch of the transcendent hand.

In fact we hear the Guru Granth honoring the maternal space as a social utopia in which the fetus is free from patriarchal designations of class, caste, and name: "In the dwelling of the womb, there is neither name nor caste."[43] The scriptural verses transparently reveal that the placental waters of the mother—primal and

36. Irigaray, *Sexes and Genealogies*, 16.

37. N. Goldenberg, "The Return of the Goddess: Psychoanalytic Reflections on the Shift from Theology to Thealogy," in *Religion and Gender*, ed. U. King (Cambridge: Blackwell, 1995), 154.

38. Guru Granth, 1026.

39. Ibid.

40. Irigaray, *Sexes and Genealogies*, 57.

41. Guru Gobind Singh in his hymn *Akal Ustat*, verse 86 (can be found in *Sabdarath Dasam Granth*, edited by Bhai Randhir Singh [Patiala, India: Punjabi University, 1985]), 16–52.

42. Guru Granth, 805.

43. Ibid., 324.

nourishing—are free of all distinctions and hierarchies. The Sikh gurus were acutely aware of their oppressive patrilineal North Indian society in which the family name, caste, and profession came down through birth. So the mother's pregnant body is envisioned as free from all sorts of "-isms" and social hegemonies. Her fetus is nurtured by *her* life-giving uterus; it is not suffocated by *his* hereditary names, caste, or professional ties.

Moreover, "in the womb is the thinker."[44] The womb is a region of self-cultivation. It is here that we hone our moral, aesthetic, intellectual, and spiritual faculties. It is here that we become fully human and gain our spiritual identity. The embryo lodged upside down is the guru's paradigm for one rapt in meditation and contemplation—its each and every heartbeat remembering the true Name. Several other scriptural verses resonate with this view of the womb as a locus for both biological and spiritual growth. "Upside down in the chamber of womb intense meditation is performed";[45] "you generated meditative heat in the womb";[46] and, "without remembrance, we rot in the womb."[47] Her womb is the space where body and spirit are harmoniously integrated. The embryonic unit is not split into the female body doomed to die as opposed to the male mind destined to live for eternity. Its upside-down posture graphically represents spiritual devotion since "each breath is that of the true name."[48] Indeed, the womb is the matrix for all mental and spiritual processes. Mind and body together grow and feed on the elements partaken by the mother.

So it is in *her* body, with *her* body, that we begin our immediate connections with the cosmos and come into the world with the "four objectives" identified in ancient Indian philosophy as *dharma, moksha, artha*, and *kama*. Each person comes into the world with the potential for moral commitments (*dharma*), the ability to work and earn money (*artha*), to enjoy sexual relations (*kama*), and experience spiritual freedom (*moksha*). Sikh scripture admires these four goals and celebrates their incubation right in the mother's body. It is the intrauterine phase where we all, men and women, begin to live intensely in all four dimensions. Birth—not death—is the absolute human possibility; the authenticity of Heidegger's *Dasein* is strongly established in the mother's womb.

3

When the fetus matures, its own glandular system sends messages into the mother's bloodstream and she goes into labor. The deep preverbal communication between the mother and fetus sets the intense process of utmost agony and exhilaration into motion. The uterus begins to contract and push out both the placenta and the

44. Ibid., 1026.
45. Ibid., 251.
46. Ibid., 337.
47. Ibid., 362.
48. Ibid., 1026.

transparent bag holding the precious fetus in its protective amniotic fluid. With its flow of blood, placenta, and milk, the birth phenomenon is most wondrous and complex. As feminist scholars have made us aware, the mother giving birth is a biologically natural and organic mode of creation. *Hers* is a model different from that of an omnipotent creator who simply makes his creation out of nothing, or even of an artist who admittedly "creates" but does not body forth his or her creation.[49] Yet birth, *every* mother's most fantastic miracle, is deemed dirty, with all sorts of lingering influences of fetal pollution feared. Like menstrual blood, blood of parturition is stereotyped as impure and dangerous, and is ritually avoided. No wonder only virgin births are considered miraculous! In medieval India, any home with a new birth was feared toxic for forty days, and only the performance of elaborate rituals would bring it back to normality. It is quite remarkable how publicly Guru Nanak condemned such notions of pollution:

> If pollution attaches to birth, then pollution is everywhere (for birth is universal).
> Cow-dung [used as fuel] and firewood breed maggots;
> Not one grain of corn is without life;
> Water itself is a living substance, imparting life to all vegetation.
> How can we then believe in pollution,
> when pollution inheres within staples?
> Says Nanak, pollution is not washed away by purification rituals;
> Pollution is removed by true knowledge alone.[50]

From the Sikh perspective, pollution is an inner reality, a state of mind, and not the product of a natural birth. Guru Nanak sought to remove false notions attached to the postpartum mother and her child.

4

Our fetus imaginary not only affirms the cosmic processes of conception, gestation, and birth, but also gives us an appreciation for lactation. Mother's milk is deemed very nutritious for it satisfies all hungers, and for me, Sikh scriptural poetry overflows with mother's milk. I can hear the language of the gurus joining in with the words of contemporary French feminist scholar Hélène Cixous, "Voice: milk that could go on forever. Found again. The lost mother/bitter-lost. Eternity: is voice mixed with milk."[51] The Guru Granth reminds us that every individual is formed from the physical and psychological sustenance provided by the mother. Her milk is inexhaustible. Not only does she feed her fetus with her nutrients, she also

49. See, for example, S. McFague, *Models of God: Theology for an Ecological, Nuclear Age* (Philadelphia: Fortress, 1987).

50. Guru Granth, 472.

51. Hélène Cixous and C. Clement, *The Newly Born Woman*, trans. B. Wing (Minneapolis: University of Minnesota Press, 1986), 93.

suckles the newborn with her life-giving milk. "The child's original attraction is to the mother's breastmilk,"[52] acknowledges Guru Nanak. The fifth guru recalls the experience of "her milk poured into the baby's mouth,"[53] and claims that satisfaction and fulfillment come from the mother pouring milk into her child's mouth.[54] The gurus compare the intensity of saintly devotion to that of an infant's love for the mother's milk.[55] In an unforgettable juxtaposition of analogies, the Divine is likened to a "cane for the blind" and "like mother's milk for the child."[56] In another tender passage, "says Nanak, the child, you are my father and my mother, and your name is like milk in my mouth."[57] Throughout the Guru Granth, the Sikh gurus unabashedly express their attachment to the Divine through an infant's attachment to the mother's breast: "My mind loves the Divine, O my life, like a child loves suckling milk."[58] In a plurality of sounds and rhythms, in a collage of artistic images, semiotic verse replays Guru Nanak's effervescent mnemonic, "that One is the calf, She is the cow, and She is the milk."[59] Sikh scripture is intrinsically written in "white ink," and we must absorb the maternal element in order to derive total nutrition and full benefit.

I find it truly amazing that, living within the parameters of patriarchal society of medieval India, Sikh male gurus possessed a "feminist" sensibility. The concerns and solutions articulated by contemporary feminists, such as the excerpt below, resound in their verses:

> Mother-*mater*-matter-matrix. "Woman" is the stuff out of which all people are made. In the beginning was her flesh, and, after the beginning, she continues to suggest human historicity, to suggest human connection to and dependence upon the outside world. It is this deep memory of birth union, I think, which turns any serious reflection on women into a reflection on the interconnection of human beings with each other and with all the things which make up the body of the world.[60]

The deep memory of birth union is vital to the Sikh gurus. Our spirituality is anchored in our bodies, and our physical and spiritual birth is from the mother's creativity. Her womb, the metonymic marker of woman, is not a passive receptacle but an active and powerful locus where our unified subjectivity is conceived and developed. Sikh scripture powerfully reminds us of our uterine relationship by which we are all siblings born of the same mother, and inspires us to reflect on our complex contingency.

52. Guru Granth, 972.
53. Ibid., 987.
54. Ibid., 1266.
55. Ibid., 613.
56. Ibid., 679.
57. Ibid., 713.
58. Ibid., 538.
59. Ibid., 1190.
60. Goldenberg, "Return of the Goddess," 154.

In fact, it is in the mother's womb, as Guru Arjan says, "that we acquire all recognition [*bhujan*] of relationships with mother, father, brother, friend."[61] Revealing the affinity between the male Sikh gurus and modern secular feminists, Sikh scripture inspires us to retreat to those initial moments and relearn the primal relationships we experienced in her oceanic womb, and from which we are now split and dichotomized. Our return would not constitute acts of regression, as our phallocentric psychoanalysts may speculate, but a real progression toward new forms of subjectivity and new avenues for discovering our human potential. We establish our identity not in opposition to, but pulling toward the mother. Sikh scripture resonates with the views of feminist theologians and object-relations psychoanalysts who posit the maternal-infant relationship at the heart of a person's psychological and social development. Instead of the Freudian oedipal conflict, castration complex, and individuality, such feminist theologians as Naomi Goldenberg and object-relations psychoanalysts as Melanie Klein and D. W. Winnicott shift the focus to the maternal-infant relationship. Both "thealogy" and object-relations theory "derive their insights into the matrices that support human life from an image of a woman-in-the-past."[62] The voice of the gurus displaces the father from his dominating symbolic and cherishes the body of the mother, the love of the mother, the care of the mother, the caresses of the mother, the transverbal communion with the mother. The male gurus remembered her prebirth and postbirth creativity, and our re-memories in turn can help us improve the individual and social fabric of our lives. "Just as the mother takes care of her children, so the One sustains us."[63] The abundant joy of envisioning the Ultimate is "like the look between a child and its mother."[64] Attaining divine bliss is like "the heart blossoming when it beholds the mother."[65] When we feel the Divine arms around us—"like a mother tightly hugs her child"[66]—we cannot but recharge the innermost batteries of our own selves and renew our relationships with our families, friends, and community.

Free of male symbolism, the sacred utterances reveal the organic process in which the embryo is consubstantial with the mother and the transcendent One. We see the wonderful delights performed by That One in the maternal womb, and feel the touch and warmth of the Divine "hand" by which we are primally held. Guru Nanak's reminder that we are brought into the world by our first principle, our original source brimming with dynamic physical and spiritual nutrients, flows vibrantly into the poetry of his successor gurus. The first guru's vivid cartography of the female body is reconfigured in Guru Gobind Singh's "salutations to the Mother of the cosmos!"[67] Female creatrix is central to the imagination and vision of the Sikh gurus from the first through the tenth. Connecting men and women with

61. Guru Granth, 1387.
62. Goldenberg, "Return of the Goddess," 155.
63. Guru Granth, 680.
64. Ibid., 452.
65. Ibid., 164.
66. Ibid., 629.
67. Jaap: 52—Guru Gobind Singh's hymn, which forms the opening of the Dasam Granth in *Sabdarath Dasam Granth*, ed. Bhai Randhir Singh (Patiala, India: Punjabi University, 1985).

each other, the "mother of the cosmos" (*lok mata*) connects us with all the other species which make up the body of our cosmos. When Sikh hymns are not simply recited but duly remembered, they send ripples of joy and strength into each of our bodies, male and female. Surely we are not thrown into the world but bring with every new birth—male and female—exciting beginnings and perspectives to develop intimate relationships with our mothers, our families, our friends, our pluralistic society, our variegated cosmos, and our singular Divine.

But as usual, the mother's body so boldly expressed and affirmed in the verses of the gurus is repressed or deleted in male hermeneutics. Sikh communal memory retains the paternal relationship but casts away the idyllic mother-child dyad. Translators abort the feminine import of Sikh scripture. For example, Guru Nanak's verse "that One is the calf, She is the cow, She is the milk,"[68] is oddly transformed in Gopal Singh's translation as, "Himself is the Lord the Cow, the Heifer, the milk."[69] Thus we are forced into a male world where cows are masculine lords and men lactate. Whereas the Guru Granth explicitly affirms that the divine permeates both the heart and the womb ("It pervades every heart and flourishes in the womb"[70]), the translators and commentators of Sikh scripture simply deem it unnecessary to remember her body or our origins, and so the unique emphasis of the Sikh gurus on the divine constitution of female physiology and of our integrated subjectivity is lost. In their English translations, both G. S. Talib and Gopal Singh register the heart (*ghat*) but utterly ignore the womb (*udar*) in Guru Nanak's feminist sensibility.[71] The unique female organ is even altered into a generic "stomach" or "belly." The authoritative and most popular exegetical text, the Sabdarath, refers to *udar* as *pet* (Punjabi word for "stomach"),[72] and a very useful new internet resource translates it as "belly."[73] The radical vision of the gurus and their invigorating overtures remain unseen, unheard.

Such a lack of attention has serious consequences. When Sikhs themselves are not receptive to their scripture's feminist imaginary, how can outsiders be expected to appreciate it? Their disregard keeps the global community from tapping into the womb-respecting, birth-oriented glimpses of the Sikh gurus, and deters any meaningful interreligious dialogue and engagement. As a result, the opportunity to pool our different religious, economic, social, and political resources is aborted; the opportunity to engage Western feminist perspectives with religion is aborted; the opportunity to break androcentric codes is aborted.

And the community suffers terribly. Both in India and in diasporic communities around the world, sexism festers in Sikh homes. It is extremely incongruous that Sikhs, who respect their scripture so reverently, are utterly oblivious to

68. Guru Granth, 1190.

69. Gopal Singh, *Sri Guru Granth Sahib: English Version* (Chandigarh, India: World Sikh University Press, 1978).

70. Guru Granth, 1026.

71. G. S. Talib, *Sri Guru Granth Sahib: In English Translation*, Vol. 3 (Patiala, India: Punjabi University, 1987), 2098: "In each being's heart pervasive." See also Gopal Singh, *Sri Guru Granth Sahib: English Version*, 4:979: "And he pervaded the hearts of all."

72. *Sabdarath Sri Guru Granth Sahib*, 4th ed., Vol. 3 (Amritsar, India: Shromani Gurdwara Prabandhak Committee, 1964), 1026.

73. See www.srigranth.org; for the most part, it is thorough and accessible. Nevertheless, it uses "belly" for "womb."

its celebration of the female principle. When the fetus is so strikingly honored, how could they be practicing consistent female feticides? Evidently, Sikh scripture treasures the fetus and the feminine; Sikh society aborts them both. How can a community that so reveres its sacred text pay such little heed to its words? Something is terribly out of joint. Why have I not heard Nanak's artistically beautiful fetus-affirming verses recited in public gatherings? Why did I have to do scholarly research to discover it? Why weren't such passages popularly recited so that they could have become a part of our psyches and personalities? Why didn't my sisters and I absorb them in our childhood and gain respect for our bodies? The tremendous feminist contributions made by the gurus in their oppressive milieu have been neither fully understood nor practiced. We must gain access to their empowering textual images and symbols. All that our sonogram has so graphically shown must be comprehended. Once we register the healthy fetus mentally, we may then find it easier to reproduce it in our visible social, cultural, and political realms. As I said at the beginning, feticides are illegal in India, and though they may be gravely prohibited on paper, they are extremely common. Real change in society can occur only through change within ourselves, and so if we hold on to our scriptural "fetus" and nourish it mentally and emotionally, it will surely birth a new world.

But a note of caution: we must not understand the Sikh maternal imaginary as a romantic exaltation of women as mothers. I do not want to equate womanhood with motherhood. Motherhood is one aspect of womanhood, and surely all women are not mothers, and may choose not to be mothers. Women who do not give birth—or in Sikh society who do not give birth to *sons*—are not failures, despite social pressure indicating the contrary. Woman's creative powers must not be construed as an automatic and mandatory process; they must not be tied down as reproductive machines to beget sons. There is no Sikh command that she be "the mother of a hundred sons." Nor should she be misinterpreted as fertile nature to be exploited by the sons for the profits of the fatherland. I do not in the least intend to equate the maternal with physical conception or limit the maternal to the domestic world; for me it is the germinative ocean, the formless potential which every female carries within her body. By focusing on the fetus we gain respect for the Subject who carries in her womb the power to produce—or refuse. The power of creation is her body, her womb, in which the conventional opposition between maternal love and sexual desire is washed away. It is not necessary that women give birth to children, they can give birth, as Luce Irigaray says, to many other things such as "love, desire, language, art, social things, political things, religious things." But Sikh society forces biological reproduction on women, and stifles all other forms of creativity in women, and so we must, as Irigaray exhorts, "take back this maternal creative dimension that is our birthright as women."[74] We can clearly see how the fetus confers a sense of authenticity on women's creativity, and as it grows for nine months or more, it is my hope that countless resources of our common humanity will also grow, and help us nurture and excel in literary, artistic, political, economic, scientific, and athletic fields with the "sky as the limit."

74. Irigaray, *Sexes and Genealogies*, 18.

WORKS CITED

Bumiller, Elisabeth. *May You Be the Mother of a Hundred Sons*. New York: Random House, 1990.

Cavarero, Adriana. *In Spite of Plato: A Feminist Rewriting of Ancient Philosophy*. New York: Routledge, 1995.

Cixous, Hélène, and C. Clement. *The Newly Born Woman*. Translated by B. Wing. Minneapolis: University of Minnesota Press, 1986.

Fair, C. C. "Female Foeticide among Vancouver Sikhs: Recontexualizing Sex Selection in the North American Diaspora." *International Journal of Punjab Studies* 3, 1 (1996): 1–44.

Goldenberg, Naomi. "The Return of the Goddess: Psychoanalytic Reflections on the Shift from Theology to Thealogy." In *Religion and Gender*, edited by U. King, 145–63. Cambridge: Blackwell, 1995.

Grahn, J. "From Sacred Blood to the Curse Beyond." In *The Politics of Women's Spirituality*, edited by C. Spretnak, 265–79. Garden City, N.Y.: Anchor, 1982.

Ibn al'Arabi. *The Bezels of Wisdom*. Translated by R. W. J. Austin. The Classics of Western Spirituality. Mahwah, N.J.: Paulist Press, 1980.

Irigaray, Luce. *Sexes and Genealogies*. Translated by G. Gill. New York: Columbia University Press, 1993.

Jantzen, G. *Becoming Divine: Towards a Feminist Philosophy of Religion*. Bloomington: Indiana University Press, 1999.

Kaur Singh, N. G. *The Birth of the Khalsa: A Feminist Re-Memory of Sikh Identity*. Albany, N.Y.: State University of New York Press, 2005.

———. *The Feminine Principle in the Sikh Vision of the Transcendent*. Cambridge: Cambridge University Press, 1993.

Kiswhar, M. *Off the Beaten Track*. Delhi: Oxford University Press, 1999.

Kristeva, Julia. *In the Beginning Was Love: Psychoanalysis and Faith*. Translated by A. Goldhammer. New York: Columbia University Press, 1987.

The Laws of Manu. Translated by Wendy Doniger. New York: Penguin, 1991.

McFague, S. *Models of God: Theology for an Ecological, Nuclear Age*. Philadelphia: Fortress, 1987.

Singh, Gopal. *Sri Guru Granth Sahib: English Version*. 4 vols. Chandigarh, India: World Sikh University Press, 1978.

Singh, Khushwant. *History of the Sikhs*. 2 vols. Princeton, N.J.: Princeton University Press, 1966.

Sprengnether, Madelon. *The Spectral Mother: Freud, Feminism, and Psychoanalysis*. Ithaca, N.Y.: Cornell University Press, 1990.

Talib, G. S. *Sri Guru Granth Sahib: In English Translation*. Patiala, India: Punjabi University, 1987.

Trible, Phyllis. *God and the Rhetoric of Sexuality*. Philadelphia: Fortress Press, 1978.

Embryology in Babylonia and the Bible

Marten Stol

The Beginnings

The average adult reader of this volume will be aware of the facts of beginning life. So were the Babylonians. They knew that pregnancy is caused by intercourse. A bilingual Sumerian-Babylonian proverb says: "Has she become pregnant without intercourse? Has she become fat without eating?"[1] Contrasting with the transports of lovemaking is the burden of bearing children. In the "Dialogue of Pessimism," the servant gives his master this advice: "Do not make loans, Sir, do not make loans. Making loans is like loving; getting them back is like having children."[2] The natural division of labor in these activities is as follows: "My father begot me, my mother bore me."[3]

Ubiquitous is the metaphor of the woman as a fertile field to be worked by the man. "That woman is a ploughed field is indeed familiar to the poetry of all ages and regions."[4] In Sumerian and Babylonian

Sections of this chapter appeared in chapter 1 of my book *Birth in Babylonia and the Bible: Its Mediterranean Setting* (Groningen, Netherlands: Styx, 2002).

1. W. G. Lambert, *Babylonian Wisdom Literature* (Oxford: Clarendon, 1960), 241, lines 40–42.
2. Ibid., 148, lines 66–67.
3. W. G. Lambert, "Dingirshadibba Incantations," *Journal of Near Eastern Studies* 33 (1974): 274; B. R. Foster, *Before the Muses* (Bethesda, Md.: CDL Press, 1996), 549.
4. G. Van der Leeuw, *Religion in Essence and Manifestation* (Princeton, N.J.: Princeton University Press, 1986), 95 (§10, 2); M. Eliade, *Traité d'histoire des religions* (Paris: Payot, 1964), 223–24 (§93, "Femme et sillon"). Among the Greeks: H. King, "Making a Man: Becoming Human in Early Greek Medicine," in *The Human Embryo: Aristotle and the Arabic and European Traditions*, ed. G. R. Dunstan (Exeter: University of Exeter Press, 1990), 17; and P. DuBois, *Sowing the Body: Psychoanalysis and Ancient Representations of Women* (Chicago: University of Chicago Press, 1988). See chapters 3 ("Field") and 4 ("Furrow"), in which DuBois discovers an estrangement from the spontaneously generating earth (parthenogenesis)

erotic lyrics, one can come across invitations like "Farmer, plough (my) field!"[5] or the declaration "Let me plough the field."[6] The goddess Inanna asks her lover, "Plough the gemstones"; the stones symbolize sexuality and fecundity.[7] In later songs, the "seeder plough" is the metaphor for the male's rod. This type of plough, typical of Babylonia, turned the soil and sowed at the same time; a literary text calls it "Fertilizer of the Plains."[8] In the letters written by the Phoenician king Rib-Addi of Byblos (ca. 1350 BCE), the following phrase occurs no less than four times: "My field, for lack of ploughing, is like a woman without a husband." The historical background is that enemy activity made it impossible for the fields to be cultivated; clearly, this simile reflects a local proverbial expression about woman and field.[9] This image is a few times found in Jewish literature. An addition to the chapter on women, the Wisdom of Sirach calls her a plot of field meant to yield noble offspring: "Single out from all the land a goodly field and there with confidence sow the seed of your increase—so shall you have your offspring around you."[10] The commentary *Genesis Rabbah* says that the remark, "Esau came in from the field" in Genesis 25:29 means that he had sexual relations with a betrothed girl. The Talmud gives the opinion that Esther, by conversing with a gentile, did not transgress because "Esther was merely natural soil."[11] The Qur'ān calls the wife the "tillage" of her man.[12]

Women without children were compared to an infertile field. "Abandoned (field)" is the literal meaning of the Akkadian word indicating a cloistered woman who was not to have children (*nadîtu*). The Hebrew word for an infertile woman, *galmûdâ*, means in Arabic, "stony (field)." In English, "barren" is said both of fields and of women.

Conception

According to an incantation in a medical text, the semen that does not beget is dry: "May your semen dry up like [that of] a eunuch who does not beget."[13] Most of the Mesopotamian men had not the elevated status of eunuch at court, and their generative excretions followed the ways that nature prescribes. Sumerian literary texts

ascribable to the development of the polis. For more on this aspect (and embryology in general), see M. Stol, *Birth in Babylonia and the Bible*.

5. Å. W. Sjöberg, "Miscellaneous Sumerian Texts," *Journal of Cuneiform Studies* 27 (1977): 24; he provides other examples as well.

6. B. Alster, "The Manchester Tammuz," *Acta Sumerologica* 14 (1992): 3 and 43 n. 10.

7. W. G. Lambert, "Devotion: the Languages of Religion and Love," in *Figurative Language in the Ancient Near East*, ed. M. Mindlin (London: School of Oriental and African Studies, 1987), 31–33.

8. W. G. Lambert, *Babylonian Wisdom Literature*, 178 and 332.

9. W. L. Moran, *The Amarna Letters* (Baltimore: Johns Hopkins University Press, 1992): 144, note on letter no. 74:17–19, etc.

10. Sirach 26:20–21.

11. Babylonian Talmud Sanhedrin 74b.

12. Sura 2:223.

13. *Cuneiform Texts from the Babylonian Tablets in the British Museum*, Part 23 (1906), plate 10:14. See also Isaiah 56:3: "Let not the eunuch say, Behold, I am a dry tree."

relish in telling more about those ways. The semen ("water") flows in the inside of the woman, and she "takes" it.[14] So conceiving is expressed by a verb meaning "to take." This is also the case in Akkadian terminology, where the words "to seize the seed" are used in a prayer to the moon god Sîn.

In Greek, too, conception is described as "to take, to seize"; as in Latin *concipere*. The texts are never precise about the place where the seed arrives. An Old Babylonian hymn says that the god Enlil "left his semen in her belly"; here a word is used that means "stomach" in other instances.[15]

The whole process, from lovemaking to birth, is described in an Ugaritic myth as follows: "He stooped and kissed their lips; behold, their lips were sweet, were sweet as pomegranates. By kissing, there was pregnancy, by embracing 'heating.' They crouched, they gave birth to Shahar and Shalim."[16] The problematical word is "heating." What does it mean here? A related word was used by David in Psalm 51:5, "Behold, I was brought forth in iniquity, and in sin did my mother conceive me." "Conceive" is here a related word in Hebrew meaning "to be hot," which usually refers to animals in sexual excitement ("heat," "rut"). We can translate the Ugaritic word as "heat" and assume that, according to those people, a female in this state easily gets pregnant.

In Hebrew, for conception or fertilization, passive forms of the common verb "to be pregnant" are used (*hârâ*). One could translate them as "to become pregnant." In several instances, the simple active form of the verb has the ingressive meaning "to become pregnant."[17] In Akkadian, there is an example for exactly the same use of the cognate verb *erû* in a wisdom text: "Where are the great kings, those from the former days until now? They are no more conceived, they are no more born."[18] A more literal translation would be "One does not get pregnant of them (anymore)." Hosea 9:11 gives the development of pregnancy in reverse order: "Ephraim's glory shall fly away like a bird—no birth, no pregnancy, no conception." The word translated as "pregnancy" literally means "belly."

It was commonly believed that the period after the menstrual flow is ideal for conception.[19] At that time, the mouth of the uterus is still open.[20] A remark in the David and Bathsheba story might suggest that the ancient Israelites had

14. H. Behrens, *Enlil und Ninlil* (Rome: Biblical Institute Press, 1978), 133–38.

15. *Cuneiform Texts from the Babylonian Tablets in the British Museum*, Part 15 (1902), plate 5 II 2, with W. H. Römer, "Studien zu altbabylonischen hymnisch-epischen Texten (2)," *Journal of the American Oriental Society* 86 (1966): 139.

16. M. Dietrich, O. Loretz, and J. Sanmartin, *Die keilalphabetischen Texte aus Ugarit* (Kevelaer, Germany: Verlag Butzon and Bercker, 1976), 1.23:49–52; D. T. Tsumura, "A Problem of Myth and Ritual Relationship—CTA 23 (UT 52): 56–57 Reconsidered," *Ugarit-Forschungen* 10 (1978): 387–95; compare *Texte aus der Umwelt des Alten Testaments* II/3 (1988): 355.

17. M. Ottoson, "Harah," *Theologisches Wörterbuch zum Alten Testament* II/4 (Stuttgart, Germany: Verlag W. Kohlhammer, 1975), 495ff.

18. D. Arnaud, *Recherches au pays d'Ashtata. Emar* VI/4 (Paris: Editions recherche sur les civilisations, 1987), 361 no. 767:18 (*erû* N). The text is bilingual.

19. For a Jewish perspective, see Leviticus Rabbah XIV, 5: "R. Hiyya b. Abba said: A woman absorbs [semen] only after her menstrual period, indeed shortly after, particularly if it is to be a male child." See D. Biale, *Eros and the Jews* (New York: Basic Books, 1992), 251 n. 141. For a Greek perspective, see Hippocrates in L. Dean-Jones, *Women's Bodies in Classical Greek Science* (Oxford: Clarendon, 1994), 170ff.

20. Hippocrates, *Diseases of Women* I, 24, 2; see H. Grensemann, *Hippokratische Gynäkologie* (Wiesbaden, Germany: Steiner, 1982), 114ff.

similar ideas about the moment of maximum fertility of the woman. We read, "So David sent messengers, and took her; and she came to him, and he lay with her. Now she was purifying herself from her uncleanness. Then she returned to her house. And the woman conceived; and she sent and told David, 'I am with child'" (2 Sam. 11:4,5). The seemingly irrelevant remark on her purification is meaningful, in the first place, because it wishes to prove that Bathsheba was at that moment not pregnant by her husband. But it also makes Bathsheba's immediate conception understandable.[21] We now know that the best moment is one week later. Jewish law requires that the married woman add seven "clean" days after the end of her days of menstruation. "Modern observers have repeatedly noted that the extension of the menstrual taboo to nearly two weeks means that the resumption of sexual activity coincides with the greatest moment of fertility: the laws of *niddah* seem almost tailor-made to promote procreation."[22]

Two passages show that the Bible does not consider the woman to be just a passive vessel in which the male semen develops. She actively contributes her own "seed." The literal translation of Leviticus 12:2 is, "If a woman gives seed and bears a male child, then she shall be unclean seven days." The old official Dutch translation of the Bible, completed in 1637 (the "Statenvertaling"), indeed gives this translation.[23] In the seventeenth century, people still believed in the existence of the "female seed." It is stored in the ovaries, which were considered to be the *testes mulieris*.[24] Those Bible translators had the same in mind when they rendered a difficult passage in the New Testament letter to the Hebrews as follows: "By faith also Sarah herself has received the strength to *give* seed" (Heb. 11:11).[25] The Greek expression is here *katabolè tou spérmatos*, literally "deposition of seed." It was Sarah who did this depositing. The commentary given with the "Statenvertaling" explained that Sarah "has given her own seed, as happens in every physical conception." It is remarkable that this insight has been lost over the centuries. Only a few have thought of the possibility of "female seed" in this verse, an oversight perhaps ascribable to the veiled terminology.[26]

The Bible translators of 1637 based their wording on a two-thousand-year-old scientific insight. Anybody who studies the Greek gynecological texts soon comes across the general idea of a female seed; it is also common knowledge in the Talmud and later.[27]

21. The commentary by Hugo Grotius was *hoc ideo additum ne mirareremur illico eam concepisse*.

22. D. Biale, *Eros and the Jews*, 55, 250 n. 139, and 241 n. 62. In the case of Bathsheba, Biale hesitates.

23. The English King James Version (1611) is vague: "If a woman has conceived seed."

24. G. A. Lindeboom, *Reinier de Graaf. Leven en werken* (Delft, Netherlands: Uitgeverij Elmar, 1973), 94ff.

25. The English King James Version (1611) offers here: "Sarah herself received the strength to conceive seed."

26. P. W. Van der Horst has taken all this up in his "Sarah's Seminal Emission: Hebrews 11:11 in the Light of Ancient Embryology," in *Greeks, Romans, and Christians: Essays in Honor of Abraham J. Malherbe*, ed. D. L. Balch, E. Ferguson, and W. A. Meeks (Minneapolis: Fortress, 1990), 287–302. Reprinted in P. W. Van der Horst, *Hellenism—Judaism—Christianity: Essays on Their Interaction* (Kampen, Netherlands: Kok Pharos, 1994), 203–23.

27. B. H. Stricker, *De geboorte van Horus II* (Leiden, Netherlands: Ex Oriente Lux, 1968), 125ff, § 36; D. M. Feldman, *Marital Relations, Birth Control, and Abortion in Jewish Law* (New York: Schocken, 1974), 135–40; G. E. R. Lloyd, "Alternative Theories of the Female Seed," in his *Science, Folklore, and Ideology* (Cambridge: Cambridge University Press, 1983); D. Nickel, *Untersuchungen zur Embryologie Galens* (Berlin: Akademie-Verlag, 1989), 189–92; Van der Horst, "Sarah's Seminal Emission."

It is striking that, according to Jewish scholarship, the child engendered by the female seed is male; one expects a girl. Indeed, the Greeks and the Romans were of the opinion that the child likens to the parent who happens to contribute the most powerful seed. To quote Lucretius: "And when at the mingling of the seed the female has happened to conquer the force of the male with sudden force and seize upon it, then children are made like their mothers by the mother's seed, as they are like their fathers by the father's seed."[28] The gender of the child is determined by the prevailing seed (Greek *epikráteia*).[29] The reason for the deviating Jewish opinion lies in Leviticus 12:2: "If a woman gives seed and bears a male child." Female seed engenders a boy. Clearly, the word of God forced the rabbis to reverse this accepted rule; the Talmud discusses this point.[30]

It is possible that the Babylonians, too, had some idea about female seed because the word "semen" is a few times said of women.[31] Furthermore, a woman is said "to beget" a male or female child. This normally is the part played by the male in procreation and attested in the Babylonian Diagnostic Handbook, Tablet 36, lines 100–102.

Embryology

A physical relationship between persons can be expressed by the Babylonian expression "flesh and blood." In letters one can find the exclamation, "I am no stranger; I am your flesh and blood."[32] In the Patriarchal narratives of the Bible, family relationships are expressed as follows: "Surely you are my bone and my flesh!" (Gen. 29:14). In the Mari letters, we read this phrase with the same implication: "The sons of Ekallatum are your brothers; they are your flesh and race [?]." The literal meaning of the word translated as "race" (*lipishtu*) is far from clear; it seems to be a membranous substance in the body, also meaning "offspring." Perhaps we can relate the Akkadian word with Sumerian *libish* which means "heart, inside." This reminds me of "the loins" from which humans originate, so often attested in the Old Testament. Does *libish/lipishtu* mean "loins" as the site of the male generative fluids?

The child is developing in the womb. Both words for "womb" in Akkadian and Hebrew can also have the metaphorical meaning "compassion, commiseration," as in New Testament Greek *splánchna*, literally "intestines." In Hebrew, the word "belly" often is used for the womb. The earth can also be seen as the womb to which

28. *De rerum natura* IV 1208–1212.

29. See also R. D. Brown, *Lucretius on Love and Sex* (Leiden, Netherlands: Brill, 1987), 320ff.

30. Babylonian Talmud Niddah 31a. See Van der Horst, "Sarah's Seminal Emission," 300 ("the theory of cross-wise sex determination").

31. R. D. Biggs, *Sha.zi.ga. Ancient Mesopotamian Potency Incantations* (Locust Valley, N.Y.: J. J. Augustin, 1967), 68a; R. Labat, *Traité akkadien de diagnostics et pronostics médicaux* (Leiden, Netherlands: Brill, 1968), 357a. The difficult word *su-'u-su* is now explained as "bed" (*suhsu*) by *Chicago Assyrian Dictionary* S (1984): 349.

32. K. Van Lerberghe and G. Voet, *Mesopotamian History and Environment I* (Ghent, Belgium: University of Ghent, 1991), 116, note to no. 29. In the Bible, "flesh and blood" has another connotation: it describes the fragility of a human being, in contrast to God; see Sirach 14:18 or Matthew 16:17 with the commentaries.

we all return.[33] Psalm 139:15 said, "Intricately I was wrought in the depths of the earth," and Job (1:21) complained of his fate in these words: "Naked I came from my mother's womb, and naked I shall return." Mishnaic and Talmudic literature speaks of the uterus with child as "the opened grave." The unborn child "is living in darkness." Babylonian incantations say, "and the House of Darkness will be our ultimate destination." The unborn demon *kûbu* lives in the underworld: he is a miscarriage.

Let us see how they felt about the development of the seed in the womb. According to a Sumerian incantation, the semen is clotting while the woman chews "Sweet Herb." This plant is well known from Sumerian literary texts; it is a water plant of which a specific fish particularly likes to eat. This could give us the clue: the fetus is in his mother's belly like a fish and needs food. This is why she craves Sweet Herb. If our interpretation of the passage is correct, the fetus really has the properties of a fish: he needs fish food. There is more evidence that they visualized the fetus as a fish. An Akkadian incantation to be translated below does this, in one interpretation of the word *dadum*. One name of the mother goddess is Nin-zizna, "Lady of the Brood"; and "brood" is specifically fish roe.

Another passage suggests that the fetus was coiled up like a snake, but the comparison with a snake is more apt when the child is born. An incantation says, "Let him come forth like a snake, let him slither like a serpent."[34]

The normal word for "embryo" in Akkadian is literally "that of her belly." Similar expressions exist in Sumerian and Hittite. The word "baby" is also used. More technical expressions are used for beings that are miscarried or stillborn.

Greek medical writers distinguished four stages in the development of the fruit: *gonè* (semen); *kúèma* (flesh and blood; days 7–40); *émbruon* (articulation of body parts); *paidíon* ("child": a moving human being).[35] Boys are supposed to be quicker in developing than girls. Modern embryology distinguishes three periods: pre-embryonic (two weeks); embryonic (six weeks of organogenesis; weeks 3–8); fetal (thirty weeks; grows in size and its basic pattern of organ systems matures; weeks 9–38). Birth takes place in the thirty-eighth week of development (forty weeks from the last menstrual period). By the end of the seventh week, the embryo is almost 2 cm (about three-quarters of an inch) long and has distinct fingers. Rudimentary genitalia are present, but the sex of the embryo is not yet distinguishable anatomically.[36]

Babylonian incantations, in fact literary texts, name the unborn child "sitting in darkness"; when born, it "sees the light of the sun."[37] A beautiful Old Babylonian incantation addresses the child as follows:

> In the waters of intercourse, the bone was created;
> In the flesh of muscles, the baby was created.

33. M. Krebernik, "Muttergöttin." *Reallexikon der Assyriologie* VIII/7–8 (1997): 516 § 7.12 (the mother goddess Mami is an underworld deity).

34. W. G. Lambert, "Dingirshadibba Incantations," 294, lines 3–5, and 274, line 4.

35. E. Nardi, *Procurato aborto nel mondo greco-romano* (Milan: Dott. A. Giuffrè Editore, 1971), 95ff.

36. P. R. Braude and M. H. Johnson, "The Embryo in Contemporary Medical Science," in *The Human Embryo: Aristotle and the Arabic and European Traditions*, ed. G. R. Dunstan (Exeter: University of Exeter Press, 1990), 208–27.

37. W. Farber, *Schlaf, Kindchen, Schlaf! Mesopotamische Baby-Beschwörungen und -Rituale* (Winona Lake, Ind.: Eisenbrauns, 1989), 34–36, 98, 110, 161–64; B. R. Foster, *Before the Muses*, 137, 896.

In the ocean waters, fearsome, raging,
In the far-off waters of the sea:
Where the little one is—his arms are bound!
Inside which the eye of the sun does not bring light.
Asalluhi, the son of Enki, saw him.
He loosened his tight-bound bonds,
He made him a path, he opened him a way;
"Opened are the paths for you, the ways are . . . for you.
The . . . is sitting for you,
She who creates . . . , she who creates us all.
She has spoken to the doorbolt: "You are released."
Removed are the locks, the doors are thrown aside.
Let him strike [. . .]; like a *dadum*, bring yourself out![38]

We see here the mythical picture of the child moving over a dark ocean; other incantations speak of a ship going from the "quay of death" to the "quay of life." Its cargo is unknown: lapis lazuli or cornaline? That is to say, boy or girl? It is possible that the Ugaritic text, too, describes the fetus as floating in the amniotic ocean.[39]

Not much is known about the ideas on the growth of the child. In the Babylonian myth on the creation of the world and man, Marduk says, "Let me knot [*katsâru*] blood, let me bring about bones, let me set up a human being—'man' be its name."[40] Many scholars take the verb *katsāru* to mean "to coagulate" or "to organize." The last proposal is too general, but the first looks attractive because of the reference to blood. However, in this meaning, blood itself would coagulate (the verb would be intransitive), and what is the purpose of coagulated blood? Another passage in this myth shows that "blood" can be used here for "blood vessels" ("they sliced open his blood," VI 32) and this gives the solution: "Arteries I will knot and bring bones into being."[41] The blood vessels are seen as a network knitted by the god.

The little that actually is known about the growth of the embryo is found in the middle of a mathematical text of the (late) Seleucid period.[42] This context implies that we have here an example of learned speculation, but even then, its ideas are interesting enough. The measures used are the "barleycorn" (2.7 mm; a tenth of an inch), "finger" (five barleycorns; 1.66 cm; about half an inch), "cubit" (30 fingers; 50 cm; 19.5 inches). The first lines run as follows: "The child, on the day that it is formed in the belly of its mother, has grown half a barleycorn. On the second day, it has grown one barleycorn. On the third day, it has grown one and a half barleycorns." The text goes on with this, assigning to the child one-half barleycorn of

38. My translation follows B. R. Foster, *Before the Muses*, 136, with a few modifications.

39. W. Watson, "Ugaritic and Mesopotamian Literary Texts," *Ugarit-Forschungen* 9 (1977): 280ff., on Shahar and Shalim, called the "splitters of the sea," or "sons of the sea" (lines 23, 58, 62).

40. *Enuma Elish* VI 5–6.

41. See T. Jacobsen, *The Treasures of Darkness* (New Haven, Conn.: Yale University Press, 1976), 180.

42. H. Hunger, "Wachstum eines Kindes vor der Geburt." *NABU* (1994) no. 34. Later, he discovered a similar passage in a contemporaneous text; H. Hunger, "Noch einmal: Wachstum eines Kindes vor der Geburt." *NABU* (1996) no. 39. It also reckons with ten months.

increase per day. After the tenth day, with five barleycorns, the text jumps to one month of thirty days; the child is now three "fingers" high, 5 cm (about 2 inches). Then follows the last line: "In the tenth month it has grown one cubit high." Do we observe here the influence of Greek science?

It was a common belief in antiquity that boys settle on the right side of the womb, and girls on the left. In general, the right was associated with male, and the left with female. The same obtains for Babylonian beliefs.

In the Hebrew Bible, the fetus is named "fruit," or "fruit of the belly." There are a few famous passages in the Bible hinting at the growth of the child in its mother. Job exclaims: "Remember that thou hast made me of clay; and wilt thou turn me to dust again? Didst thou not pour me out like milk and curdle me like cheese? Thou didst clothe me with skin and flesh, and knit me together with bones and sinews" (Job 10:9–11). We should not try to discover too much in a simile; still, behind this one on the cheese could lurk the idea that the male seed acts like the rennet that makes the milk curdle: it is the clotting agent.[43] This is how *Leviticus Rabbah* sees conception: "A woman's womb is full of blood, some of which goes out by way of her menstrual flow, and by the favor of the Holy One, blessed be He, a drop of white matter goes and falls into it and immediately the fetus begins to form. It may be compared to milk in a basin; if one puts rennet into it, it congeals and becomes consistent; if not, it continues to 'tremble.'"[44] This is indeed how Aristotle explained the process of conception, within his theory of the female seed: "The material secreted by the female in the uterus has been fixed by the semen of the male: this acts in the same way as rennet acts upon milk, for rennet is a kind of milk containing vital heat, which brings into one mass and fixes the similar material."[45] Latin authors like to use the word "coagulate,"[46] and Pliny speaks in fact of *coagulum* in the meaning of "rennet" in his remark that "the semen from the males, acting like rennet, collects this substance within it, which thereupon immediately is inspired with life and endowed with body."[47] The image of the embryo curdling like cheese is found in a few more texts. In the *Wisdom of Solomon*, the word "curdle" is used again: "curdled in blood from/by the seed of a man" (7:2). Mani, founder of the Manichean movement, tells in his autobiography with disgust how man is fashioned: "Through foulness it [the body] was made into cheese and, built, came into existence."[48] There is a village in the Pyrenees where the cheese image is still alive in people's thought and language.[49]

43. S. Kottek, "Embryology in Talmudic and Midrashic Literature," *Journal of the History of Biology* 14 (1981): 301.

44. XIV 9.

45. *De Generatione Animalium* II, 4 739b.

46. J. H. Waszink, *Q. S. Florentis Tertulliani de Anima: Edited with Introduction and Commentary* (Amsterdam: Meulenhoff, 1947), 343 (*coagulari*). The comparison with cheese and rennet is explicit in Tertullianus *De Carne Christi* XIX 1, 4.

47. *Historia naturalis* VII 15, 66.

48. L. Koenen and C. Römer, *Der Kölner Mani-Kodex* (Opladen, Germany: Westdeutscher Verlag, 1988), 58 (85.9–12).

49. S. Ott, "Aristotle among the Basques: The 'Cheese Analogy' of Conception," *Man*, n.s., 14 (1979).

Most famous is this passage from Psalm 139:

> For thou didst form my inward parts, thou didst knit me together in my mother's womb. I praise thee for thou art fearful and wonderful. Wonderful are thy works! Thou knowest me right well; my frame was not hidden from thee, when I was being made in secret, intricately wrought in the depths of the earth. Thy eyes beheld my unformed substance; in thy book were written, every one of them, the days that were formed for me, when as yet there was none of them. (13–16)

This translation in the Revised Standard Version is a little free. The Hebrew word, rendered as "inward parts," specifically means "the reins." For "womb" stands the word "belly." "Frame" is literally "bone(s)" in Hebrew. "Intricately wrought" is literally "weaved/stitched in variegated colors" (*meruqqam*). The Mishnah uses this word when discussing the miscarriage called "sac": in its first stage it is full of water or colored materials; when more developed, it is *meruqqam*.[50] One can recognize a human being in it. That the child is being wrought "in the depths of the earth" is a surprising metaphor which gives God's creation a cosmic dimension.[51] We are reminded of the earth as the mother in which the seed has been sown. The word "unformed substance" (*golem*) is attested only here; it is probably to be derived from a root of a verb once meaning "to fold up (a garment)."[52] Does the psalmist think of a fetus as "folded up"? The Talmud compares the child with "folded writing tablets."

Phasing and Duration of a Pregnancy

According to one influential ancient theory promoted by Aristotle, the embryo reached a new stage in its development after the fortieth day. In this, boys and girls were sharply distinguished, as girls were believed to take a longer time to fully develop.[53] The idea about forty days may even be older and looks like folk medicine.[54] Speculations working with the number "seven" led to such figures as forty-two or forty-nine.[55] Another matter has to do with the great philosopher's

50. M. Niddah III 3.

51. F. M. Th. De Liagre Böhl, H. A. Brongers, "Weltschöpfungsgedanken in Alt-Israel," *Persica* 7 (1975–78): 99ff.; G. Pettinato, *Das altorientalische Menschenbild* (Heidelberg, Germany: Winter 1971), 61ff.

52. The verb used, for example, in II Kings 2:8.

53. Forty days: B. H. Stricker, *De geboorte van Horus III* (Leiden, Netherlands: Ex Oriente Lux, 1975), 251–57; I. Jakobovits, *Jewish Medical Ethics* (New York: Philosophical Library, 1959), 174. Forty days, slower development of the female: U. Weisser, *Zeugung, Vererbung und pränatale Entwicklung in der Medizin des arabisch-islamischen Mittelalters* (Erlangen, Germany: Lüling, 1983), 322–32. For some graphs, see 339ff., and S. Kottek, "Embryology in Talmudic and Midrashic Literature," 306ff.

54. I. M. Lonie, *The Hippocratic Treatises "On Generation," "On the Nature of the Child," "Diseases IV"* (Berlin: Walter de Gruyter, 1981), 193.

55. L. Bourgey, *Observation et expérience chez les médecins de la collection hippocratique* (Paris: Librairie philosophique J. Vrin, 1953), 133ff.

prejudices about gender differences, and the reader may be surprised. Somewhat further on, Aristotle tells us that "as a general rule, women who are pregnant of a male child escape comparatively easily and retain a comparatively healthy look, but it is otherwise with those whose infant is a female; for these latter look as a rule paler and suffer more pain." The theory about the difference in development between boys and girls was accepted by almost everybody.[56] Pre-Socratic philosophers had laid its basis, and Hippocrates had worked it out. Amazingly, this view remains alive today in rural Egypt.[57]

When we read in the Talmud the following suggestions about prayers to be uttered during pregnancy, we realize that the Jews shared the convictions of their gentile fellow men: "Within the first three days a man should pray that the seed should not putrefy; from the third to the fortieth day he should pray that the child should be a male; from the fortieth day to three months he should pray that it should not be a *sandal*;[58] from three months to six months he should pray that it should not be still-born; from six months to nine months he should pray for a safe delivery."[59] The length of gestation is counted in months. An Egyptian text says that a child is born "after your months," and the verb "to be pregnant" in Hittite literally means, "to go through the months."[60]

The first chapter of the Gospel of Luke tells us how two expectant mothers met: Elizabeth and Mary. Here, I have made a discovery.[61] The author takes care to note in what month of their pregnancies both women were. I assume that this precise information on the two interlocking "chronologies" has a meaning which becomes clear when we look at Jewish time schedules. The point is that, in Jewish literature, the nine months of pregnancy are divided in three phases of three months each.[62] Such a phase is named "turn": four times in a year the sun makes a turn. The Hebrew Bible is still vague about this—so vague that modern translators have problems in rendering the word: "And Elkanah knew Hannah his wife, and the Lord remembered her; and in due time Hannah conceived and bore a son, and she called his name Samuel" (I Sam. 1:19–20). For "in due time," the Hebrew text has "and it happened at the turn of the days."[63] Are *three* "turns" meant? Or *two*, if Samuel was a seven months' child? It is certain that a first phase of three months

56. E. Nardi, *Procurato aborto nel mondo greco-romano,* 101ff.

57. S. A. Morsy, "Childbirth in an Egyptian Village," in *Anthropology of Human Birth,* ed. M. Artschwager Kay (Philadelphia: F. A. Davis, 1982), 154–57.

58. *Sandal*: a kind of miscarriage resembling a flat-shaped fish (*foetus compressus*); according to Babylonian Talmud Yebamoth 12b, the result of superfetation.

59. Babylonian Talmud Berakhot 60a.

60. H. Grapow, *Kranker, Krankheiten und Arzt: vom gesunden und kranken Ägypter* (Berlin: Akademie-Verlag, 1956), 11, with note b. Hittite: F. Starke, *Die keilschrift-luwischen Texte in Umschrift* (Wiesbaden, Germany: Harrassowitz, 1985), 204 n. 4, "in den (Schwangerschafts-) Monaten sein."

61. See M. Stol, *Zwangerschap en geboorte bij de Babyloniërs en in de Bijbel* (Leiden, Netherlands: Ex Oriente Lux, 1984), 44ff.

62. Cf. B. H. Stricker, *De geboorte van Horus II,* 273–76.

63. L. W. Koehler, W. Baumgartner, *Hebräisches und Aramäisches Lexikon zum Alten Testament IV* (Leiden, Netherlands: Brill, 1990), 1641–42: "zwei Möglichkeiten: a) um die Jahreswende, zu Beginn des neuen Jahres, b) an der Wende = am Ende der Tage der Schwangerschaft." "Seven full years, eight turns of time (nqpt 'd)" in Ugaritic shows that not a moment but a time span is meant; M. Dietrich, O. Loretz, and J. Sanmartin, *Die keilalphabetischen Texte aus Ugarit,* 1.23: 66–67, cited in L. W. Koehler and W. Baumgartner, *Hebräisches und Aramäisches Lexikon zum Alten Testament IV* 1604b.

is meant in Genesis 38:24: "About three months later Judah was told, Tamar had played the harlot; and moreover she is with child by harlotry." This was the moment she was aware of the child in her. This is why the Talmud says, "At what stage is the embryo discernable? Symmachus citing R. Meir replied: Three months after conception. And though there is not actual proof for this statement there is an allusion to it, for it is said in Scripture, 'About three months later,' etc."[64]

The Mishnah sees in the womb three "chambers": the child passes from one chamber to the other. The Talmud says, "During the first three months the embryo occupies the lowest chamber, during the middle ones it occupies the middle chamber and during the last months it occupies the uppermost chamber; and when it is time to emerge it turns over and then emerges, and this is the cause of the woman's pains."[65] The moment the child completes two phases (six months) is important: the fetus is viable and can be born.

One gets the feeling that all this is the frame of the chronology of Elizabeth's pregnancy. Luke 1:36 notes, "And this is the sixth month with her." Then Mary, hearing of this, "arose and went with haste into the hill country . . . and she entered the house of Zechariah and greeted Elizabeth. And when Elizabeth heard the greeting of Mary, the baby leaped in her womb; and Elizabeth was filled with the Holy Spirit and she exclaimed with a loud cry, Blessed are you among women" (1:39–42). Mary stayed with her three months and then Elizabeth's son, John the Baptist, was born. Clearly, this was the third phase. Our deduction is that John had just entered his seventh month when the two women met. He is now viable, has a deep understanding of what is going on, and jumps[66] with joy.

Did the Babylonians also have this division in periods of three months? Two myths indeed speak of a gestation period of gods of seven months.[67] There may be another indication. In their medical Diagnostic Handbook we read about a pregnant woman who is sick; the problem seems to be whether sexual intercourse is desirable from month 3 to month 9 or 10 (Tablet 37).[68] Does this mean that the first two or three months are the first phase when there is not yet any problem?

The full term of gestation is 280 days, that is to say, nine months and one week (forty weeks). To be more precise, birth normally takes place in the thirty-eighth week of development, forty weeks after the last menstrual period. A Babylonian horoscope, based on the moment of conception, presupposes 273 days or, according

64. Babylonian Talmud Niddah 8b.

65. M. Niddah II 5; Babylonian Talmud Niddah 31a, which adds an observation on the desirability of intercourse during the three phases: "During the first three months marital intercourse is injurious to the woman and it is also injurious to the child. During the middle ones it is injurious to the woman but beneficial for the child. During the last months it is beneficial for both the woman and the child, since on account of it the child becomes well-formed and of strong vitality." Cf. D. M. Feldman, *Marital Relations, Birth Control, and Abortion in Jewish Law*, 185–86; F. Rosner, *Medicine in the Mishneh Torah of Maimonides* (New York: Ktav, 1984), 138ff.

66. Greek *skirtáo*; compare Genesis 25:22 in the Greek translation (LXX): "and the children (Jacob and Esau) leaped within her."

67. K. Volk, "Vom Dunkel in die Helligkeit: Schwangerschaft, Geburt und frühe Kindheit in Babylonien und Assyrien," in *Naissance et petite enfance dans l'Antiquité*, ed. V. Dasen (Fribourg, Switzerland: Academic Press and Vandenhoeck and Ruprecht, 2004), 71–92, notably 79 n. 46.

68. Labat, *Traité akkadien de diagnostics et pronostics médicaux*, 212:1–7.

to some scholars, 279 days.[69] Other astrological texts reckon 277 days.[70] Classical and Ancient Near Eastern sources often speak of *ten* months; suffice it to quote this line from Virgil's famous fourth *Ecloga*, on the birth of the child: "Ten months have brought to your mother long qualms" (*matri longa decem tulerunt fastidia menses*, IV 61), or the verse in the apocryphal Wisdom of Solomon, "and in my mother's womb I was sculptured into flesh during a ten-month's space" (7:2).[71] The Sumerian myth "Enki and Ninhursag" presupposes a duration of nine months,[72] whereas the Old Babylonian Atra-hasis myth speaks of ten months: "And Nintu [sat rec]koning the months. [At the] destined [time] they summoned the tenth month. The tenth month arrived; . . . opened the womb."[73] In the chapter on pregnant women in the medical Diagnostic Handbook, the desirability of sexual intercourse from the third to the ninth or tenth month seems to be discussed.[74] The handbook on malformed babies says nothing about a woman giving birth in months 1–9 but does mention births in months 11 and 12; these are the unusual ones.[75] A Hittite myth says that the sons of Appu were born when the tenth month had arrived.[76] The Hittite Laws see as turning points in the gestation period the fifth and the tenth months (§ 17B). The fifth and the tenth months are also turning points in an Ugaritic myth: "By kissing there is pregnancy, by embracing there is 'heat.' He sat down and counted to five, for . .[. ; to t]en, the total completion [?]. They crouched and gave birth to the lovely [gods]."[77]

Why ten months? It has been suggested that these are ten lunar months of 28 days each, yielding the expected 280 days.[78] Is it not easier to solve our problem by realizing that a pregnancy actually lasts more than nine months? There was an understandable tendency to reckon with ten months, inclusively. Herodotus tells us that, in one case, they counted the months with their fingers to be sure: they were the normal ten months (VI 63). An ancient comment (*scholion*) to a

69. A. Sachs, "Babylonian Horoscopes," *Journal of Cuneiform Studies* 6 (1952): 59b.

70. Reiner, *Astral Magic in Babylonia,* 115; H. Hunger, "Ein astrologisches Zahlenschema," *Wiener Zeitschrift für die Kunde des Morgenlandes* 86 (1996): 192–95.

71. The evidence for ten months has been collected by Stricker, *De geboorte van Horus III,* 283 § 71 (cf. 247), and by D. Winston, *The Wisdom of Solomon: A New Translation with Introduction and Commentary,* Vol. 43 of the Anchor Bible (Garden City, N.Y.: Doubleday, 1979), 163ff. For Egypt, see J. Bergman, "Decem illis diebus. Zum Sinn der Enthaltsamkeit bei den Mysterienweihen im Isisbuch des Apuleius," in *Ex orbe religionum: Studia Geo Widengren I* (Leiden, Netherlands: Brill, 1972), 340–42; E. Feucht, "Der Weg ins Leben," in *Naissance et petite enfance dans l'Antiquité,* 43.

72. P. Attinger, "Enki et Ninhursaga," *Zeitschrift für Assyriologie* 74 (1984): 14.

73. W. G. Lambert and A. R. Millard, *Atra-hasis* (Oxford: Clarendon, 1969), 62 I 281; Foster, *Before the Muses,* 169.

74. Labat, *Traité akkadien de diagnostics et pronostics médicaux,* 210:106–13; 212:1–7. The text as the tradition has it must be a corrupted version of an Old Babylonian original. F. R. Kraus tried to read in it intercourse from three to nine or ten times "per month." But it is hardly a coincidence that the highest number is nine or ten. See his "Lexikalisches und Lexikographisches zu einem akkadischen Verbum," in *Im Bannkreis des Alten Orients: Studien Karl Oberhuber gewidmet,* ed. M. Meid and H. Trenkwalder (Innsbruck, Austria: Institut für Sprachwissenschaft, 1986), 131ff.

75. E. Leichty, *The Omen Series Shumma Izbu* (Locust Valley, N.Y.: J. J. Augustin, 1970), 70, Tablet IV 46.

76. H. A. Hoffner, "Birth and Name-Giving in Hittite Texts," *Journal of Near Eastern Studies* 27 (1968): 199.

77. M. Dietrich, O. Loretz, and J. Sanmartin, *Die keilalphabetischen Texte aus Ugarit,* 1.23:56–58, with D. T. Tsumura, "A Problem of Myth and Ritual Relationship—CTA 23 (UT 52): 56–57 Reconsidered."

78. For example, R. Barnett and F. Imparati, see H. A. Hoffner, "Birth and Name-Giving in Hittite Texts," 199. Ancient explanations: U. Weisser, *Zeugung, Vererbung und pränatale Entwicklung in der Medizin des arabisch-islamischen Mittelalters,* 337ff.

comedy of Aristophanes is explicit in its discussion of the line, "Yes, I have borne it during ten months: But women are not ten months pregnant, but nine. But they are wont, thus to use the full number instead of 'nine months'" (*Thesmophoriazousai* 741). The child that has entered its tenth prenatal month is called a "ten months' child" in Greek (*dekámènon*). Hippocrates speaks of "so-called ten months children" and adds that they are brought to completion within seven periods of forty days each.[79]

Women in the Southern Hemisphere still reckon with ten months. Women in Madagascar know that they are about to give birth when the moon is in the same position as at her last menstruation.[80] A German scholar reported of the Samoa islands that "the Samoan woman looks at the moon and expects the beginning of menstruation at a quite different position of that planet, each woman naturally having a different position of the moon in view. If menstruation does not take place then, she perceives that she is pregnant, and expects her confinement after ten moon-months."[81]

In two instances in the Hebrew Bible, a woman is promised a child after one year. At His momentous visit to Abraham, God promised a son: "I will surely return to you at the time of life, and Sarah your wife shall have a son" (Gen. 18:10). After Sarah had voiced her doubts, the Lord assured him again, "At the appointed time I will return to you, at the time of life, and Sarah shall have a son" (Gen. 18:14). The modern Revised Standard Version has rendered "at the time of life" as "in the spring." The second passage is 2 Kings 4:16 where Elisha foretells, "At this season, at the time of life, you shall embrace a son." In this case, that modern translation offers "when the time comes around." "At the time of life" means "after one year"; more precise is "in the next year." One expects nine or ten, not twelve months (a year). It is possible that we have here a solemn oracular phrase before us, and one is reminded of a very similar wording in Homer's *Odyssey*: "When the year has come round, you shall bear glorious children" (XI 248). However, it seems easier to connect the expression "at the time of life" with the Akkadian word for "life" in its special meaning "next year." "In the next year" sounds good for both Hebrew Bible passages.

Convictions among Jews and Arabs assert that birth can be delayed for quite some time. We read in the Babylonian Talmud that, according to "the majority," this is possible. The example is a woman who gave birth twelve months after her husband had gone to a country beyond the sea: the child is declared legitimate.[82] Widespread among Arab women of northern Africa is the belief that a child can

79. Hippocrates, *On the Eight-months' Child* X, 1. The discussion follows in XIII, 1–3.

80. L. Schomerus-Gernböck, *Die* Mahafaly: *eine ethnische Gruppe im Süd-Westen Madagaskars* (Berlin: Reimer, 1981), 152.

81. As rendered by M. P. Nilsson, *Primitive Time-Reckoning* (Lund, Sweden: C. W. K. Gleerup, 1920), 149. It is an almost literal translation of W. Von Bülow, "Beobachtungen aus Samoa zur Frage des Einflusses des Mondes auf terrestrische Verhältnisse," *Globus* 93 (1908): 251a.

82. Babylonian Talmud Yebamoth 80b. St. T. Newmyer, "Talmudic Medicine and Greco-Roman Science: Crosscurrents and Resistance," in *Aufstieg und Niedergang der Römischen Welt* Teil II, Band 37/3 (Berlin: Walter de Gruyter, 1996), 2908–909 (with data on long gestation periods taken from Hippocrates and Aristotle).

stay in his mother's body for years; this child is called "the sleeping" (*râqed*). This is an ancient belief firmly rooted in Islamic tradition and law, and said to go back to pre-Islamic times.[83] It came as a surprise to me to discover this very same belief in two entries of the Babylonian Diagnostic Handbook (Tablet 36). It is attested to in the chapter on pregnant women. Consider the two following cases: (5) "If a fertile woman is pregnant and the top of her forehead is multicolored [variant: *ba-ru-um*] her fetus sleeps." (94) "If a fertile woman, in the middle of her 'sickness,' steps to the right: she is pregnant of a sleeping [fetus]." The "sleeping fetus" is an unborn child not manifesting itself and staying in its mother for a long time. The meaning of "in the middle of her sickness" can now be explained. It should mean "her menstrual period": the woman has her period without knowing that she is bearing a child, and an uncommon experience makes her realize that she is carrying some burden. Undoubtedly, she warns her husband, and he awakens the child by having intercourse with her.

Infertility

Having children was a blessing in the ancient Near East. The word "fertile" refers to "giving birth" in Babylonian. A slave girl with a child is qualified as such.[84] Babylonian physiognomic omens related a woman's ability to get pregnant and to give birth to the appearance of her breasts or her navel; the expressions are, "she is child-bearing" (= fertile), "she is bringing to term." On the breasts: "If a woman's breasts are pointed, she cannot bear children. If a woman's breasts are sunken on [?] her chest, she cannot bear children."[85]

Being barren made life difficult. All births stop when "the womb is closed," like a door, as the Hebrew Bible has it; elsewhere, the word "to block" is used: Sarai and the wives in the palace of Abimelech had this experience.[86] "The key of the womb is in the hands of the Lord," the Talmud says.[87] Infertility is also a topic in myths, and it is the man who is disgraced by it. In the Hittite "Story of Appu," his wife says that it is his fault: "You have never taken [me correctly]." He reacts by saying, "You are [only] [a wom]an of the usual female sort and [consequently] don't know anything."[88] Basically, all infertility was ascribed to the woman; the English word "barren" is for that reason quite appropriate and reflects the same prejudice, or rather, antiquated medical opinion. The male's fault was impotency, and the Babylonians and Hittites cured this by rituals and incantations.[89]

83. O. Verberkmoes, R. Kruk, "Rakid," *Encylcopédie de l'Islam* VIII (Leiden, Netherlands: Brill, 1995); J. Colin, *L'enfant endormi dans le ventre de sa mère: étude ethnologique et juridique d'une croyance au Maghreb* (Perpignan, France: Presses universitaires de Perpignan, 1994).

84. S. I. Feigin, *Yale Oriental Series: Babylonian Texts,* Vol. 12 (New Haven, Conn.: Yale University Press, 1979), no. 185:33.

85. B. Böck, *Die babylonisch-assyrische Morphoskopie* (Horn, Austria: Selbstverlag des Instituts für Orientalistik der Universität Wien, 2000), 160ff., lines 160–66.

86. See Gen. 16:2 and 20:18.

87. Babylonian Talmud Ta'anith 2a.

88. Appu I 33–37, with G. Beckman, *Hittite Birth Rituals* (Wiesbaden, Germany: Harrassowitz, 1983), 2–3.

89. Biggs, *Sha.zi.ga. Ancient Mesopotamian Potency Incantations.*

Infertility is situated inside the belly.[90] Normally, "the womb is open and creates a child," the Atra-hasis myth says.[91] Elsewhere, it speaks of the reverse: "The womb was 'knotted' and did not deliver a child."[92] We learn from the ritual that a "knot" is to be loosened.[93] Being blessed with children ultimately depended on the gods. In a prayer to the god of the moon, Sīn, it is said, "Who has no son, you make acquire a son; without you a woman who does not bear will not get seed [= offspring] or pregnancy."[94] We humans can try to remedy barrenness by herbs, amulets, and magic. According to a late (Seleucid) speculative medical text, the origin of barrenness lies in "the kidneys—[it is] a stricture."[95]

The Egyptians knew methods to establish whether a woman could become pregnant or not. A woman would urinate on barley or wheat: she would be in a fertile period when it germinated. A modern test has shown that it works when a woman urinates on barley.[96] Even the gender of the child could be known this way: when the barley starts to germinate, it will be a boy; when the wheat, a girl.[97] We find similar methods in Greek medical literature, and western Europeans came to know these methods via the Byzantines. Erica Reiner has identified passages of a similar nature in one Babylonian text. It starts with the problem of whether a woman "will become pregnant" or not.[98] A wad of wool containing or saturated with medications is placed into her vagina and is removed after a certain time (three days, for example). It is then checked for any change of color, or an obscure water test is performed. One example: "If the wad is red or spotted with blood, she will become pregnant; if it is green, she will not."

Conclusion

We have come to the end of this survey of embryology in Babylonia and the Bible. We came across both sheer magic and the first dawning of science. Magic was found in the beautiful Babylonian incantations depicting the fetus as a ship on water, with an unknown cargo. In Psalm 139, God's "weaving" the child in his mother is pious fantasy. The Greeks developed theories on the formation of the child in phases

90. In the late medical text, H. Hunger, *Spätbabylonische Texte aus Uruk I* (Berlin: Gebr. Mann Verlag, 1976), no. 43:30, among problems originating in the kidneys.

91. A. R. George and F. N. H. al-Rawi, "Tablets from the Sippar Library VI: Atra-hasis," *Iraq* 58 (1996): 176:42.

92. Atram-hasis S iv 61; W. G. Lambert and A. R. Millard, *Atra-hasis*, 110.

93. R. Borger, "Einige Texte religiösen Inhalts," *Orientalia Nova Series* 54 (1985): 14–18, lines 29–30.

94. O. R. Gurney, *The Sultantepe Texts I* (London: British Institute of Archaeology at Ankara, 1957), no. 57 and dupls.; see M. J. Seux, *Hymnes et prières aux dieux de Babylonie et d'Assyrie* (Paris: Les Editions du Cerf, 1976), 281, with nn. 14 and 15.

95. H. Hunger, *Spätbabylonische Texte aus Uruk I*, no. 43:30: the *la a-li-du-ti* (lit., not bearing children) begins *ul-tu* BIR.ME *hi-niq-ti* (lit., from the kidneys—stricture).

96. R. Germer, "Untersuchungen über Arzneimittelpflanzen im Alten Ägypten," Ph.D. diss., Hamburg University, 1979, 143–46.

97. Feucht, "Der Weg ins Leben," 43.

98. E. Reiner, "Babylonian Birth Prognoses," *Zeitschrift für Assyriologie* 72 (1982): 124–38. A short summary can be found in E. Reiner, *Astral Magic in Babylonia* (Philadelphia: The American Philosophical Society, 1995), 41. See also K. Volk, "Vom Dunkel in die Helligkeit: Schwangerschaft, Geburt und frühe Kindheit in Babylonien und Assyrien," in *Naissance et petite enfance dans l'Antiquité*, 74 n. 16, and 77f.

but were not aware of their prejudices: the difference between quick boys on the right side and slow girls on the left side. In later Judaism and early Christianity (the Mishnah, the Talmud, and the Gospel of Luke), Greek insights were taken over and reconciled with information from the Bible. The Middle Ages and the early modern periods still followed those hallowed ancient traditions and did not make much progress. They stayed in the cradle of civilization.

WORKS CITED

Alster, B. "The Manchester Tammuz." *Acta Sumerologica* 14 (1992): 1–46.

Arnaud, D. *Recherches au pays d'Ashtata. Emar* VI/4. Paris: Editions recherche sur les civilisations, 1987.

Attinger, P. "Enki et Ninhursaga." *Zeitschrift für Assyriologie* 74 (1984): 1–52.

Beckman, G. *Hittite Birth Rituals.* Wiesbaden, Germany: Harrassowitz, 1983.

Behrens, H. *Enlil und Ninlil.* Rome: Biblical Institute Press, 1978.

Bergman, J. "Decem illis diebus: zum Sinn der Enthaltsamkeit bei den Mysterienweihen im Isisbuch des Apuleius." In *Ex orbe religionum. Studia Geo Widengren,* 332–46. Leiden, Netherlands: Brill, 1972.

Biale, D. *Eros and the Jews.* New York: Basic Books, 1992.

Biggs, R. D. *Sha.zi.ga. Ancient Mesopotamian Potency Incantations.* Locust Valley, N.Y.: J. J. Augustin, 1967.

Böck, B. *Die babylonisch-assyrische morphoskopie.* Horn, Austria: Selbstverlag des Instituts für Orientalistik der Universität Wien, 2000.

Borger, R. "Einige Texte religiösen Inhalts." *Orientalia Nova Series* 54 (1985): 14–26.

Bourgey, L. *Observation et expérience chez les médecins de la Collection Hippocratique.* Paris: Librairie philosophique J. Vrin, 1953.

Braude, P. R., and M. H. Johnson. "The Embryo in Contemporary Medical Science." In *The Human Embryo: Aristotle and the Arabic and European Traditions,* edited by G. R. Dunstan, 208–27. Exeter: University of Exeter Press, 1990.

Brown, R. D. *Lucretius on Love and Sex.* Leiden, Netherlands: Brill, 1987.

Colin, J. *L'enfant endormi dans le ventre de sa mère. Etude ethnologique et juridique d'une croyance au Maghreb.* Perpignan, France: Presses universitaires de Perpignan, 1994.

Dean-Jones, L. *Women's Bodies in Classical Greek Science.* Oxford: Clarendon, 1994.

De Liagre Böhl, F. M. Th., and H. A. Brongers. "Weltschöpfungsgedanken in Alt-Israel." *Persica* 7 (1975–78): 69–136.

Dietrich, M., O. Loretz, and J. Sanmartín. *Die keilalphabetischen Texte aus Ugarit.* Kevelaer, Germany: Verlag Butzon and Bercker, 1976.

DuBois, P. *Sowing the Body: Psychoanalysis and Ancient Representations of Women.* Chicago: University of Chicago Press, 1988.

Eliade, M. *Traité d'histoire des religions.* Paris: Payot, 1964.

Farber, W. *Schlaf, Kindchen, Schlaf! Mesopotamische Baby-Beschwörungen und -Rituale.* Winona Lake, Ind.: Eisenbrauns, 1989.

Feigin, S. I. *Yale Oriental Series. Babylonian Texts.* Vol. 12. New Haven, Conn.: Yale University Press, 1979.

Feldman, D. M. *Marital Relations, Birth Control, and Abortion in Jewish Law.* New York: Schocken Books, 1974.

Feucht, E. "Der Weg ins Leben." In *Naissance et petite enfance dans l'Antiquité,* edited by V. Dasen, 33–53. Fribourg, Switzerland, and Göttingen, Germany: Academic Press and Vandenhoeck and Ruprecht, 2004.

Foster, B. R. *Before the Muses*. Bethesda, Md.: CDL Press, 1996.
George, A. R., and F. N. H. al-Rawi. "Tablets from the Sippar Library VI. Atra-hasis." *Iraq* 58 (1996): 147–90.
Germer, R. "Untersuchungen über Arzneimittelpflanzen im Alten Ägypten." Ph.D. diss., Hamburg University, Germany, 1979.
Grapow, H. *Kranker, Krankheiten und Arzt: vom gesunden und kranken Ägypter*. Berlin: Akademie-Verlag, 1956.
Grensemann, H. *Hippokratische Gynäkologie*. Wiesbaden, Germany: Steiner, 1982.
Gurney, O. R. *The Sultantepe Texts I*. London: British Institute of Archaeology at Ankara, 1957.
Hoffner, H. A. "Birth and Name-Giving in Hittite texts." *Journal of Near Eastern Studies* 27 (1968): 198–203.
Hunger, H. "Ein astrologisches Zahlenschema." *Wiener Zeitschrift für die Kunde des Morgenlandes* 86 (1996): 191–96.
———. "Noch einmal: Wachstum eines Kindes vor der Geburt." *NABU* (1996) no. 39.
———. *Spätbabylonische Texte aus Uruk* I. Berlin: Gebr. Mann Verlag, 1976.
———. "Wachstum eines Kindes vor der Geburt." *NABU* (1994) no. 34.
Jacobsen, T. *The Treasures of Darkness*. New Haven, Conn.: Yale University Press, 1976.
Jakobovits, I. *Jewish Medical Ethics*. New York: Philosophical Library, 1959.
King, H. "Making a Man: Becoming Human in Early Greek Medicine." In *The Human Embryo: Aristotle and the Arabic and European Traditions*, edited by G. R. Dunstan, 10–19. Exeter: University of Exeter Press, 1990.
Koehler, L., and W. Baumgartner. *Hebräisches und Aramäisches Lexikon zum Alten Testament* IV. Leiden, Netherlands: Brill, 1990.
Koenen, L., and C. Römer. *Der Kölner Mani-Kodex*. Opladen, Germany: Westdeutscher Verlag, 1988.
Kottek, S. "Embryology in Talmudic and Midrashic Literature." *Journal of the History of Biology* 14 (1981): 299–315.
Kraus, F. R. "Lexikalisches und Lexikographisches zu einem akkadischen Verbum." In *Im Bannkreis des Alten Orients. Studien Karl Oberhuber gewidmet*, edited by M. Meid and H. Trenkwalder, 125–41. Innsbruck, Austria: Institut für Sprachwissenschaft, 1986.
Krebernik, M. "Muttergöttin." *Reallexikon der Assyriologie* 8, 7–8 (1997): 502–16.
Labat, R. "Review of Biggs 1967." *Bibliotheca Orientalis* 25 (1968): 356–58.
———. *Traité akkadien de diagnostics et pronostics médicaux*. Leiden, Netherlands: Brill, 1951.
Lambert, W. G. *Babylonian Wisdom Literature*. Oxford: Clarendon, 1960.
———. "Devotion: the Languages of Religion and Love." In *Figurative Language in the Ancient Near East*, edited by M. Mindlin, 25–39. London: School of Oriental and African Studies, 1987.
———. "Dingirshadibba incantations." *Journal of Near Eastern Studies* 33 (1974): 267–322.
Lambert, W. G., and A. R. Millard. *Atra-hasis*. Oxford: Clarendon, 1969.
Leichty, E. *The Omen Series Shumma Izbu*. Locust Valley, N.Y.: J. J. Augustin, 1970.
Lindeboom, G. A. *Reinier de Graaf. Leven en werken*. Delft, Netherlands: Uitgeverij Elmar, 1973.
Lloyd, G. E. R. "Alternative Theories of the Female Seed." In his *Science, Folklore, and Ideology*, 86–94. Cambridge: Cambridge University Press, 1983.
Lonie, I. M. *The Hippocratic Treatises "On Generation," "On the Nature of the Child," "Diseases IV."* Berlin: Walter de Gruyter, 1981.
Moran, W. L. *The Amarna Letters*. Baltimore: Johns Hopkins University Press, 1992.

Morsy, S. A. "Childbirth in an Egyptian Village." In *Anthropology of Human Birth,* edited by M. Artschwager Kay, 147–74. Philadelphia: F. A. Davis, 1982.
Nardi, E. *Procurato aborto nel mondo greco-romano.* Milan: Dott. A. Giuffrè Editore, 1971.
Newmyer, St. T. "Talmudic Medicine and Greco-Roman Science: Crosscurrents and Resistance." In *Aufstieg und Niedergang der Römischen Welt* Teil II, Band 37/3, 2895–2911. Berlin: Walter de Gruyter, 1996.
Nickel, D. *Untersuchungen zur Embryologie Galens.* Berlin: Akademie-Verlag, 1989.
Nilsson, M. P. *Primitive Time-Reckoning.* Lund, Sweden: C. W. K. Gleerup, 1920.
Ott, S. "Aristotle among the Basques: The 'Cheese Analogy' of Conception." *Man,* n.s., 14 (1979): 699–711.
Ottoson, M. "Harah." *In Theologisches Wörterbuch zum Alten Testament* II/4, 495–99. Stuttgart, Germany: Verlag W. Kohlhammer, 1975.
Pettinato, G. *Das altorientalische Menschenbild.* Heidelberg, Germany: Winter 1971.
Reiner, E. *Astral Magic in Babylonia.* Philadelphia: American Philosophical Society, 1995.
———. "Babylonian Birth Prognoses." *Zeitschrift für Assyriologie* 72 (1982): 124–38.
Römer, W. H. Ph. "Studien zu altbabylonischen hymnisch-epischen Texten (2)." *Journal of the American Oriental Society* 86 (1966): 138–47.
Rosner, F. *Medicine in the Mishneh Torah of Maimonides.* New York: Ktav Publishing House, 1984.
Sachs, A. "Babylonian Horoscopes." *Journal of Cuneiform Studies* 6 (1952): 49–75.
Schomerus-Gernböck, L. *Die* Mahafaly: *eine ethnische Gruppe im Süd-Westen Madagaskars.* Berlin: Reimer, 1981.
Seux, M.-J. *Hymnes et prières aux dieux de Babylonie et d'Assyrie.* Paris: Les éditions du Cerf, 1976.
Sjöberg, A. W. "Miscellaneous Sumerian texts." *Journal of Cuneiform Studies* 29 (1977): 3–45.
Starke, F. *Die keilschrift-luwischenTexte in Umschrift.* Wiesbaden, Germany: Harrassowitz, 1985.
Stol, M. *Birth in Babylonia and the Bible: Its Mediterranean Setting.* Groningen, Netherlands: Styx Publications, 2002.
———. *Zwangerschap en geboorte bij de Babyloniërs en in de Bijbel.* Leiden, Netherlands: Ex Oriente Lux, 1984.
Stricker, B. H. *De geboorte van Horus II.* Leiden, Netherlands: Ex Oriente Lux, 1968.
———. *De geboorte van Horus III.* Leiden, Netherlands: Ex Oriente Lux, 1975.
Tsumura, D. T. "A Problem of Myth and Ritual Relationship—CTA 23 (UT 52): 56–57 Reconsidered." *Ugarit-Forschungen* 10 (1978): 387–95.
Van der Horst, P. W. *Hellenism—Judaism—Christianity: Essays on Their Interaction.* Kampen, Netherlands: Kok Pharos, 1994.
———. "Sarah's Seminal Emission. Hebrews 11:11 in the Light of Ancient Embryology." In *Greeks, Romans, and Christians: Essays in Honor of Abraham J. Malherbe,* edited by D. L. Balch, E. Ferguson, and W. A. Meeks, 287–302. Minneapolis: Fortress, 1990.
Van der Leeuw, G. *Religion in Essence and Manifestation.* Princeton, N.J.: Princeton University Press, 1986.
Van Lerberghe, K., and G. Voet. *Mesopotamian History and Environment I.* Ghent, Belgium: University of Ghent, 1991.
Verberkmoes, O., and R. Kruk. "Râkid." In *Encyclopédie de l'Islam,* Vol. 3, 421. Leiden, Netherlands: Brill, 1995.
Volk, K. "Vom Dunkel in die Helligkeit: Schwangerschaft, Geburt und frühe Kindheit in Babylonien und Assyrien." In *Naissance et petite enfance dans l'Antiquité,* edited by

V. Dasen, 71–92. Fribourg, Switzerland, and Göttingen, Germany: Academic Press and Vandenhoeck and Ruprecht, 2004.

Von Bülow, W. "Beobachtungen aus Samoa zur Frage des Einflusses des Mondes auf terrestrische Verhältnisse." *Globus* 93 (1908): 249–54.

Waszink, J. H. *Q. S. Florentis Tertulliani De Anima: Edited with Introduction and Commentary*. Amsterdam: Meulenhoff, 1947.

Watson, W. "Ugaritic and Mesopotamian Literary Texts." *Ugarit-Forschungen* 9 (1977): 273–84.

Weisser, U. *Zeugung, Vererbung, und pränatale Entwicklung in der Medizin des arabisch-islamischen Mittelalters*. Erlangen, Germany: Lüling, 1983.

Winston, D. *The Wisdom of Solomon. A New Translation with Introduction and Commentary*. The Anchor Bible, Vol. 43. Garden City, N.Y.: Doubleday, 1979.

The Leaping Child: Imagining the Unborn in Early Christian Literature

Catherine Playoust
Ellen Bradshaw Aitken

Imagining the unborn is a task seldom undertaken in Christian literature of the first and second centuries CE. The chief artifacts from the foundational strata of Christianity, namely, the many preserved texts—whether narrative, epistolary, poetic, visionary, or discursive—contain few references to or descriptions of unborn children, whether they be major figures in the gospel tradition, humans in general, or Christian believers in particular. An important exception, the leap of joy by John the Baptist in his mother's womb (Luke 1:41), will be one of the points of focus in this chapter.

This is the case even for Jesus. In contrast to how other religious traditions reflect upon their foundational figures, it may be surprising to find little concern in early Christianity with the life of Jesus in the womb or even in his childhood. Of the four gospels in the canon of the New Testament, only the Gospels of Matthew and Luke include birth stories of Jesus, but neither of these explores Jesus' own activity prior to birth. In terms of the historical growth of the gospel tradition, the birth stories of Jesus were one of the final layers of the gospels to emerge and become attached to earlier traditions of the adult Jesus' sayings, deeds, suffering, death, and resurrection. The birth stories themselves developed as legendary material to satisfy narrative interest and expand upon what came to be perceived as biographical gaps, as well as to meet a range of apologetic needs. Similar interests account for the rise and circulation of stories about Jesus as a child, such as are found in some apocryphal gospels, notably the *Infancy Gospel of Thomas*, and in Luke's story of the twelve-year-old Jesus in dialogue with the elders in the Jerusalem temple (2:41–51).[1] Jesus in utero, however, appears not to have attracted the imaginative or midrashic activity of early Christian storytellers and authors.

This chapter will examine how certain Christian narrative texts from the first two centuries CE place interpretations upon unborns. The characters, and through them the implied audience, supplement the mere fact of the unborn's existence with ordinary and divinely revealed knowledge of its parentage and its destiny. Occasionally they also interpret sensations in the pregnant woman's womb as deliberate and profoundly significant actions by the unborn. We shall concentrate on the early chapters of the Gospel of Matthew, the early chapters of the Gospel of Luke, and passages from the *Protevangelium of James* (or *Infancy Gospel of James*, henceforth *Prot. Jas.*).[2] These three texts all tell of the circumstances surrounding the unborn Jesus. Jesus' mother, Mary, is betrothed to Joseph but not yet fully married to him, and thus how she became pregnant is a matter for speculation. Attention is drawn to the ancestry of Jesus as well, through both the maternal line and Joseph's line. The Gospel of Luke and the *Prot. Jas.* also speak of the unborn John ("John the Baptist"), whose parents are Elizabeth and Zechariah. According to these two texts, Elizabeth is Mary's cousin and the two women are pregnant at the same time. The *Prot. Jas.* begins with the unborn Mary, whose parents are Anna and Joachim, and proceeds to the time of John and Jesus. All these texts have had a strong impact on Christianity over the ages. The Gospels of Matthew and Luke, which are usually dated to the late first century CE, became part of the New Testament and have thereby been of great and continuing importance in Christianity. The *Prot. Jas.* is a second-century apocryphal gospel developing the Matthean and Lukan infancy accounts but starting the story a generation earlier. Although it was not canonized, it exerted direct or indirect influence for many centuries over the Christian imagination in texts and the visual arts.[3] Hence, although this chapter makes no attempt to speak of how the unborn is imagined in later periods of

1. These infancy narratives, especially the canonical ones, have attracted much scholarly attention. See Raymond E. Brown, *The Birth of the Messiah: A Commentary on the Infancy Narratives in the Gospels of Matthew and Luke*, 2nd ed., Anchor Bible Reference Library (New York: Doubleday, 1993); Helmut Koester, *Ancient Christian Gospels: Their History and Development* (Harrisburg, Pa.: Trinity, 1990), 303–14; Joseph A. Fitzmyer, *The Gospel according to Luke (I–IX)*, Anchor Bible 28 (Garden City, N.Y.: Doubleday, 1981), 305–309. For an introduction to earlier and later apocryphal infancy gospels, with translations of full texts and excerpts, see Wilhelm Schneemelcher, ed., *New Testament Apocrypha*, trans. R. McL. Wilson, 2 vols., rev. ed. (Cambridge: James Clarke, 1991–92), 1.414–69; J. K. Elliott, *A Synopsis of the Apocryphal Nativity and Infancy Narratives*, New Testament Tools and Studies 34 (Leiden, Netherlands: Brill, 2006).

2. All translations given in this chapter are our own. The New Testament Greek texts may be found in Nestle-Aland, *Novum Testamentum Graece*, ed. Eberhard Nestle and Erwin Nestle, rev. Barbara Aland, Kurt Aland, et al., 27th ed. (Stuttgart, Germany: Deutsche Bibelgesellschaft, 1993). The Septuagint (LXX, the principal ancient Greek translation of the scriptures of Israel) may be found in Alfred Rahlfs, ed., *Septuaginta* (Stuttgart, Germany: Deutsche Bibelgesellschaft, 1979). The Greek text of the *Protevangelium of James* is quoted from Ronald F. Hock, *The Infancy Gospels of James and Thomas*, The Scholars Bible 2 (Santa Rosa, Calif.: Polebridge, 1995).

3. For example, it provides details of the early life of Mary, including the names of her parents, and it contains the idea that when Joseph was betrothed to Mary he was an elderly widower who already had sons. For the influence of the *Prot. Jas.*, see Hock, *Infancy Gospels of James and Thomas*, 27–28; Elliott, *Synopsis*. In the visual arts, one of the most notable employments of noncanonical infancy narratives is in the fifth-century arch mosaic of the basilica Santa Maria Maggiore in Rome.

Christianity, it would be fair to say that the early Christian stories examined here contributed to the reflections of later times.

A few words about the limitations of this study are in order. First, as just noted, it is restricted to the first two centuries CE. A full exploration of how the unborn is imagined in Christianity as a whole would require an extensive collaborative project, examining many different historical periods and the multifold traditions of the Eastern and Western churches, as well as the spread of Christianity worldwide in recent centuries. Such a project would also take into account not only a wide range of written and oral texts, but also art and architecture. Prayer and other ritual practices related to pregnancy and childbirth would provide further material for analysis. Such research into the workings of Christian imagination would give considerable insight into lived religion and its conceptualizations, as well as into the interrelation between scriptural tradition, theological reasoning, and religious practice, but to our knowledge, no such study exists.

Second, this is a study of narrative texts only. At the heart of this project is the observation that, in a very few places in early Christian narratives, imagining the unborn becomes a means of exploring and establishing relationships between competing religious groups, as part of the negotiation of religious differences within formative Christianity. Separate examination of other types of texts from this period may illumine how imagining the unborn serves other rhetorical and social ends. For example, theories of development in utero play an important role in the arguments of Clement of Alexandria (ca. 150–215) about Christian formation and education, in which Christians are imaged as children of God.[4] Similarly, Tertullian (ca. 160–ca. 225) draws upon evidence from women about the experience of pregnancy in service of his philosophical-theological discussion of how the soul relates to the body, the mind, and divine inspiration.[5] Both of these theologians represent rather different—we might say, more scientific—treatments of the unborn from those in the narrative traditions of early Christian imagination.[6]

We have chosen in this chapter not to speak of "imagining the fetus," but rather of "imagining the unborn." We do so for two reasons. The stories explored here do not show the particular interest in precisely what is in the womb that the noun "fetus" would imply. Rather, they give a transitory glance at the existence and activity of what is soon to be born. Furthermore, these stories do not use a technical term for the unborn in utero, but rather the word for child or infant, as

4. Changes in utero are considered by Clement as part of the overall development from conception to the infant who sucks milk from the breast. Much of the emphasis is on transformation of bodily fluids. For the uterine phase, see Denise Kimber Buell, *Making Christians: Clement of Alexandria and the Rhetoric of Legitimacy* (Princeton, N.J.: Princeton University Press, 1999), 154–59 and 171–74, commenting on Clement of Alexandria, *Paidagōgos* 1.39.2–1.40.2 and 1.48.1–1.49.2.

5. Tertullian, *De Anima* 25. On Tertullian's rhetorical project in *De Anima*, see Laura Salah Nasrallah, *"An Ecstasy of Folly": Prophecy and Authority in Early Christianity*, Harvard Theological Studies 52 (Cambridge: Harvard Theological Studies, 2003), 95–127.

6. In regard to children in early Christianity, although mostly subsequent to their births, see O. M. Bakke, *When Children Became People: The Birth of Childhood in Early Christianity*, trans. Brian McNeil (Minneapolis: Fortress, 2005).

is common in Greek literature, or a circumlocution.[7] Introducing the term "fetus" to this discussion might thus falsely imply that these texts consider the moment of birth to change the nature or status of the being in question.

Notwithstanding this observation, there is a degree of discontinuity from unborn to born, as these texts recognize. The phase prior to birth is distinctive because so little is known about what is hidden inside the womb. Even if newborns often seem inscrutable, at least they can be perceived with all the senses. The unborn, being invisible and inaudible (in the absence of modern technology), is so close to unknown that it barely places any constraints on those who imagine it. It can make just two kinds of "self-revelations" to the world outside the womb. The simple fact of its existence is announced through the signs of pregnancy, first to the woman and later to those who view her swollen belly. The sensations that it causes in the mother, whether they be the child's own movements or the pains of labor, are the only other kind of data that it offers for interpretation, and these typically remain the private knowledge of the woman and those most intimate with her. With such a paucity of information available, the characters in these narratives attempt as best they can to interpret the unborns, often disagreeing with one another or acquiring new insights as time goes on. They engage in dialogue and reflection upon the origins, destiny, and significance of these unborns, on the divine and the human plane.

The shifting and uncertain ideas of the characters invite another kind of interpretation too, as those hearing the narrative try to decide which characters understand the truth. Furthermore, for the implied audience, the truth at issue is not merely the truth within the framework of the narrative. Early Christians who were sympathetic to the content and purpose of these works would have considered them neither fictional stories about fictional people, nor nonfictional stories about people of no great note, but revelatory texts about the key figure of Jesus and certain people closely associated with him. The preservation and transmission of these texts as holy writings demonstrates that a sufficient number of followers of Jesus valued them in this way in the early centuries. (At least a few in the ancient audiences would have recognized that imaginative development of traditions had taken place, to a greater or lesser extent, but this need not have impeded for them the capacity of the texts to convey religious truth.) Those for whom these texts were written would have marshaled all possible tools to help them interpret the narratives well: their theological understanding of Jesus (both who he was and what he had done); their awareness of how God had previously acted in history (as recorded in the scriptures of Israel—the Hebrew Bible or Old Testament); and their knowledge of which characters to consider reliable (namely, the angels as messengers of

7. Luke 1:41 refers to "the infant in her womb" (τὸ βρέφος ἐν τῇ κοιλίᾳ αὐτῆς); the noun βρέφος in earlier Greek tends to be restricted to mean "baby in the womb," but in the Septuagint and in later Greek literature it is regularly used to denote a newborn child. See Henry George Liddell, Robert Scott, and Henry Stuart Jones, *A Greek-English Lexicon*, 9th ed. with revised supplement (Oxford: Clarendon, 1996), s.v. βρέφος. The *Protevangelium of James* uses circumlocution for an unborn, such as "that which is within her" (τὸ ἐν αὐτῇ, *Prot. Jas.* 17). Other terms in Greek include ἐμβρύον ("young one, embryo, or fetus" for humans and livestock); κύημα ("that which is conceived"); κῦμα (anything swollen, as if pregnant; but frequently also "wave"); and βλαστός ("shoot, bud, embryo, germ").

God, and those who had the best reputations in Christian tradition or who were shown to be righteous and wise elsewhere in the narrative). Such hearers would have been open to letting the texts affect their belief and life.

It is no accident that these narratives about special unborns had such force: they were designed to act that way on their initial audience. More precisely, although no one can read the minds of the ancient authors, it can be said that the texts exhibit rhetorical features that would have been persuasive to at least some sectors of early Christianity; it should be recalled that every narrative account, no matter how factually based, is conformed by its teller to certain story patterns and shaped to certain ends.[8] In such a rhetorical context, the unborn is a potent symbol. Jesus and the other children in utero give out only limited signals and are thus wide open to interpretation; yet the stakes are high because the texts deal with matters of great religious importance. As a result, imagining the unborn does not remain a narrowly focused act, but becomes a useful and productive site for exploring other issues.

The principal leverage of the rhetoric surrounding the unborn in these texts is provided by the ancient Mediterranean presumption of continuity from generation to generation, whether the intergenerational connections are biological, adoptive, or teacher-disciple.[9] The twist, which poses a paradox if looked at too closely, is that it can be applied to the unborn in two ways. The unborn can be considered either as the offspring of previous generations (which emphasizes links with the past and the ancestors) or as the progenitor of a new family or movement (which presents the time in utero as the originary moment). Therefore the whole divine and human world through the whole course of history can be imagined, using any hint available from the unborn's existence and the sensations in the womb.

In the case of the texts examined here, all three unborns are depicted as Jewish children of Jewish parents, parents whose righteousness is highlighted. The children's existence demonstrates God's justice and saving fidelity to Israel through the provision of offspring to righteous Israelites over many generations. To the unborn-as-offspring pattern belong also the multiple revelations and testings showing that Jesus was virginally conceived and hence son of God in a special sense, for they serve to indicate that Jesus possesses divine qualities, like his divine Father. On the other hand, Jesus and John are depicted by these texts as progenitors, founder-figures of religious movements whose characteristics can be discerned in their founders. In this unborn-as-progenitor pattern, the metaphor of origins is literalized by dating the relationships and interactions of religious groups back to the time when their founding figures were still in the womb. The womb then becomes an important site for the conceptualization of origins; the practices and emotions of those in the womb accordingly denote the nature of the connection and divergence between groups as deriving from their inception.

8. For a now classic exposition of the narrative-rhetorical dimensions of historiography, see Hayden White, *Metahistory: The Historical Imagination in Nineteenth-Century Europe* (Baltimore: Johns Hopkins University Press, 1973), 5–11.

9. This is a simplified statement of a complex understanding that was current in various manifestations among Greeks, Romans, and Jews at the turn of the eras. For recent discussions, with certain differences in methodology, see Denise Kimber Buell, *Why This New Race? Ethnic Reasoning in Early Christianity* (New York: Columbia University Press, 2005) and Benjamin Isaac, *The Invention of Racism in Classical Antiquity* (Princeton, N.J.: Princeton University Press, 2004).

In the operation of both patterns, the narrative's imagining of the unborn makes rhetorical claims about religious groups whose interaction contributed to the formation of Christianity in the first centuries CE. It would be tempting to say that of the major religious communities relevant to these texts, the non-Christian Jews were an ancient group and the John-followers and Jesus-followers were new groups, but it is not so simple; all these groups partook of both venerability and novelty, and these mixtures are visible in how the unborns are depicted.[10]

The depiction of unborns in early Christian texts, particularly in the Gospel of Luke and the *Prot. Jas.*, draws in addition upon the cultural-religious practices of rejoicing and lamentation. As often in Jewish and Christian tradition, references to joy and grief do more than denote inner emotional response. Rather, as Gary A. Anderson has demonstrated, within both Israelite religion and rabbinic Judaism, joy and lamentation each designate a set of prescribed ritual practices. Joy can be commanded and is "the proper disposition before one's divine Lord."[11] The behaviors corresponding to such a joyful orientation include eating and drinking, making love, uttering praise, wearing festal attire, and anointing oneself with oil.[12] Mourning is the converse of joy and consists of such actions as fasting, abstaining from sex, reciting laments, tearing one's clothes or wearing sackcloth, and putting ashes or dust upon one's head.[13] The practices of mourning and lamentation entail a conceptual identification with the dead and a separation from God's presence. Thus Anderson outlines the following relationship: joy is to the presence of God as mourning is to the absence of God.[14] These connections are active as well in Israelite prophetic literature where lamentation and rejoicing are linked to the events of the destruction of the Jerusalem temple, the Exile, and the return to Israel, Judah, and Jerusalem. Lamentation signals a people, a land, and a temple bereft of God; rejoicing recognizes not only divine presence, but also divine blessing.[15]

Examining the lamentation and joy that are occasioned in these early Christian narratives by the existence of the unborn and the sensations during the pregnancy, this chapter will observe that they are not always simply responses to the coming of a child, as might first be expected. On occasion, the lamentation and joy can be interpreted as retrojections into the time in utero of later conflicts between these groups, and thus as attempts to address these vexed relationships. Thus the argument made here seeks to contribute to the understanding of not only how the

10. On the forms of Judaism in the Second Temple period and the emergence of formative Christianity and rabbinic Judaism in the next centuries, see Alan F. Segal, *Rebecca's Children: Judaism and Christianity in the Roman World* (Cambridge: Harvard University Press, 1986); Shaye J. D. Cohen, *The Beginnings of Jewishness: Boundaries, Varieties, Uncertainties*, Hellenistic Culture and Society 31 (Berkeley: University of California Press, 1999); Daniel Boyarin, *Border Lines: The Partition of Judaeo-Christianity* (Philadelphia: University of Pennsylvania Press, 2004).

11. Gary Anderson, "The Expression of Joy as a Halakhic Problem in Rabbinic Sources," *Jewish Quarterly Review* 80 (1990): 226. See also his *A Time to Mourn, A Time to Dance: The Expression of Grief and Joy in Israelite Religion* (University Park: Pennsylvania State University Press, 1991).

12. Anderson, "Expression of Joy," 224–25, and the specific references cited there.

13. Ibid., 225.

14. Ibid., 227.

15. See, for example, the laments for divine abandonment in Pss. 60(59) and 74(73), as well as the entirety of the Lamentations of Jeremiah. In addition, the prophecies to Jerusalem in Jer. 7 draw upon the relationship between divine abandonment and lamentation (see especially Jer. 7:29), as does God's lamentation over Jerusalem (Jer. 12:7–13).

unborn was imagined but also how the formation of Christian communities and identities proceeded in the first centuries of the common era.

We turn first to the Gospel of Matthew, in which the unborn Jesus addresses the world in only the most limited sense, by being present inside Mary's womb. The other two texts will involve slightly more agency by the unborn, when sensations inside the womb are interpreted as communication by the unborn or insight into its effect on the future. The Gospel of Luke highlights the leap of joy by one unborn, John, in recognition of the divine presence in Jesus. In the *Prot. Jas.*, shortly before the birth of Jesus, Mary has a vision of "two peoples" rejoicing and lamenting, which alludes to an account in Genesis of twins leaping in the womb. In all three cases, these clues for imagining the unborn need to be interpreted in light of the knowledge that the other characters possess, both their everyday knowledge and the revelations they receive, particularly in regard to the ancestry of the unborn.

The Gospel of Matthew

Probably the best-known part of Matthew's infancy account is the coming of the star-led magi to see Jesus. The visit of these sages from the East and the tragic aftermath of their discussion with King Herod take place once Jesus is already born, and so they will not be examined in detail here, but attention should be drawn to how they frame their quest as indicative of Matthew's depiction of Jesus. The magi call Jesus "the one born King of the Jews" (Matt. 2:2), and this designation is significant for the whole infancy narrative and indeed for all this gospel (e.g., Matt. 20:29–21:9; 27:11–56). Matthew's construction of Jesus and his early followers is situated within late-first-century controversies about how discipleship of Jesus relates to being a Jew.[16] The magi, as sympathetic "foreign" characters opposed to the wicked King Herod, are mobilized by the narrative as reliable outsiders with cosmic knowledge to testify to Jesus' true reign over the Jewish people. The scriptures consulted by Herod's scribes support this by recognizing Jesus' Judean birthplace of Bethlehem, the city of King David, as the proper place for such a king to be born (Matt. 2:1–6, with quotation of Mic. 5:2). Herod's phrasing to the scribes is not precisely "the king of the Jews" but "the Christ," but here it refers to the expectation by some Jews in this period that a royal messiah would come.[17]

Just before the meeting of Herod and the magi comes the only passage of the gospel set when Jesus is still unborn (Matt. 1:18–25). The focus is on Joseph, who

16. Daniel J. Harrington, *The Gospel of Matthew*, Sacra Pagina (Collegeville, Minn.: Liturgical Press, 1991), 1–22. Anthony J. Saldarini, *Matthew's Christian-Jewish Community*, Chicago Studies in the History of Judaism (Chicago: University of Chicago Press, 1994). Amy-Jill Levine, "Anti-Judaism and the Gospel of Matthew," in *Anti-Judaism and the Gospels*, ed. William R. Farmer (Harrisburg, Pa.: Trinity, 1999), 9–36.

17. "Christ" (the Greek translation of "the Messiah" or "the Anointed One") is a favorite title for Jesus in the Matthean infancy narrative and broadly in early Christianity. Various Jewish groups in the first century CE and earlier had hopes of one or more messiahs. John J. Collins classifies these messiah figures into Davidic-kingly, priestly, prophetic, and heavenly, and argues that a royal messiah in the Davidic line was the most common kind of messiah expected. See Collins, *The Scepter and the Star: The Messiahs of the Dead Sea Scrolls and Other Ancient Literature*, Anchor Bible Reference Library (New York: Doubleday, 1995).

discovers that Mary, his betrothed, is pregnant. Since Joseph has not had sexual relations with Mary, he plans to divorce her discreetly; this is portrayed by the text as a righteous gesture within the conventions of the day, a way of sparing Mary public humiliation. However, an angel of the Lord then appears to Joseph in a dream,[18] saying: "Joseph, son of David, do not fear to take Mary as your wife; for that which is in her is begotten from the Holy Spirit. She will bear a son, and you [singular] will call his name Jesus; for he will save his people from their sins" (Matt. 1:20b–21). Thus Mary has not conceived from some other man, but from the Holy Spirit, and Joseph should still marry her. Moreover, the child—who will become *their* child legally if Joseph marries Mary and acknowledges the child as his[19]—has a special destiny to bring salvation, and he should be named accordingly ("Jesus" being a form of "the Lord saves" in Hebrew). The advice and the prophecy constitute the core of the message, but the angelic diction deserves further attention. The angel greets Joseph as a son of David, and describes the people whom Joseph's "son" Jesus will save as Jesus' people. In this way, Jesus is cast as a Davidic king of Israel.

The narrator intrudes at this point with a reference to the scriptures, quoting Isa. 7:14:[20] "All this happened in order to fulfill the saying by the Lord through the prophet: 'Behold, the virgin [παρθένος] will be pregnant and bear a son, and they will call his name Emmanuel,' which means, 'God is with us'" (Matt. 1:22–23). Now, within the book of Isaiah itself, the prophecy quoted here has a specific historical application, unfolding over the space of a few years following its utterance, and there is no implication that a virginal conception occurs.[21] However, for the gospel text, which quotes the scriptures in Greek translation, Isaiah is looking ahead to the time of Jesus and prophesying an extraordinary event, conception by a virgin and thus necessarily through divine means, "from the Holy Spirit" (Matt. 1:18, 20). The quotation goes on to call the child Emmanuel, "God is with us." This will not be the everyday given name of the child—the audience knows that his name will be Jesus—but it highlights the consequences of Jesus' divine descent. Being God's son (cf. Matt. 2:15), Jesus will be the presence of God among humans.[22]

Taking the angel's advice, Joseph changes his plans and marries Mary after all. The text is careful to note that they did not have sexual relations during the pregnancy. In its immediate placement in the narrative, this comment ensures beyond

18. Since dreams were thought capable of being authentic channels of communication, this context in no way diminishes the seriousness and validity of the message the angel conveys. Indeed, in the following chapter of Matthew, there will be dream-messages to the magi and Joseph that save Jesus' life (Matt. 2:12–13). On ancient Mediterranean ideas about the possibility of revelation of divine matters in dreams, see Frances Flannery-Dailey, *Dreamers, Scribes, and Priests: Jewish Dreams in the Hellenistic and Roman Eras*, Supplements to the Journal for the Study of Judaism 90 (Leiden, Netherlands: Brill, 2004); Patricia Cox Miller, *Dreams in Late Antiquity: Studies in the Imagination of a Culture* (Princeton, N.J.: Princeton University Press, 1994).

19. Brown, *Birth of the Messiah*, 139.

20. On Matthew's technique of scriptural citation, see Krister Stendahl, *The School of St. Matthew and Its Use of the Old Testament*, 2nd ed., Acta Seminarii Neotestamentici Upsaliensis 20 (Lund, Sweden: Gleerup, 1968).

21. The Hebrew noun underlying the Greek παρθένος means "young woman" or "maiden" but does not place emphasis on virginity. Joseph Blenkinsopp, *Isaiah 1–39*, Anchor Bible 19 (New York: Doubleday, 2000), 232–34; Brown, *Birth of the Messiah*, 145–49.

22. This central theme is emphasized in the final scene of Matthew, in which Jesus, appearing after his resurrection from the dead, tells the eleven disciples, "All authority in heaven and on earth has been given to me. . . . And behold, I am with you always, until the completion of the age" (Matt. 28:18–20).

doubt that Joseph is not the biological father of Jesus.[23] Nonetheless, Matt. 1:18–25 overall articulates how Joseph came to be Mary's husband and, in a sense, Jesus' father, although Jesus was conceived of the virgin Mary through the Holy Spirit. By so doing, it explains how Jesus was both son of David (via Joseph) and son of God.

This brief but rich episode is preceded in the gospel by only one passage, a genealogy, which calls itself "the book of the genesis of Jesus Christ, son of David, son of Abraham" (Matt. 1:1). It is given on the side of Joseph, who is described with great nuance as "Joseph, the husband of Mary, she out of whom was born Jesus who is called Christ" (Matt. 1:16). This genealogy contains many stories simmering below its nonnarrative surface, since the names of several of Jesus' ancestors would have evoked stories well known to the initial hearers of the gospel. The list is artfully structured, periodizing Israelite and Jewish history in three phases, each of fourteen generations: from Abraham to David; from David through the Davidic royal line of Judah to King Jechoniah and the Babylonian exile; and finally from the exile to Joseph and thence Jesus.[24] Starting with Abraham places Jesus in the family of the Israelites and the nations most closely related to them. The emphasis is on the Davidic monarchy, however, as reinforced by the multiple references to Jesus as the Christ, thus establishing the royal tone for the forthcoming infancy narrative. The rhetorical effect of the thrice fourteen generations is to imply that Jesus' birth is another moment of great historical significance. Whereas the earlier punctuations of the genealogy, David and the exile, had marked the beginning and end of the Davidic monarchy as an earthly political power (notwithstanding some early postexilic attempts at its reestablishment), the birth of Jesus signals the rise of a new form of Davidic monarchy.

The genealogy for the most part lists only the males but occasionally draws attention to female ancestors as well. In this, too, it is skillfully constructed, for it turns out that each of the couplings highlighted in this manner is unusual in some way. For hearers familiar with the scriptures, the vestigial narratives would have been all that was required to activate these stories of the past. Tamar produced twins for her dead husband by tricking her father-in-law, Judah, into lying with her, when the more conventional route of levirate marriage proved impossible (Matt. 1:3; Gen. 38). Boaz's mother, Rahab, is presumably the same Rahab as the Canaanite prostitute who helped the Israelites conquer Canaan (Matt. 1:5; Josh. 6:17–25).[25] The Moabite woman Ruth was the widow of an Israelite who secured her future by marrying

23. Over the centuries, Christians have often interpreted the comment in keeping with the tradition that Mary remained a virgin always. On the development of Marian doctrine in the first five centuries CE, see J. N. D. Kelly, *Early Christian Doctrines*, rev. ed. (New York: HarperSanFrancisco, 1978), 490–99.

24. On this genealogy, see Harrington, *Gospel of Matthew*, 27–33; Elaine M. Wainwright, *Shall We Look for Another? A Feminist Rereading of the Matthean Jesus*, The Bible and Liberation (Maryknoll, N.Y.: Orbis, 1998), 55–58. The tally of fourteen generations in each of the three phases has been achieved only through some creative record-keeping and accounting.

25. The scriptures do not name the mother of Boaz, only his father Salmon (Ruth 4:21), who is also mentioned at this point of the genealogy. The reason the famous prostitute is presumed to be Matthew's referent is that she is the only woman called Rahab in the scriptures and in later centuries she had a high reputation among rabbinic Jews and early Christians. See W. D. Davies and Dale C. Allison, *A Critical and Exegetical Commentary on the Gospel according to Saint Matthew*, International Critical Commentary, Vol. 1 (Edinburgh: T. & T. Clark, 1988), 172–73.

Boaz, her kinsman by her first marriage (Matt. 1:5; Ruth). Bathsheba, called here only "Uriah's wife," conceived Solomon when already married to David, but their first child was conceived while she was still married to Uriah (Matt. 1:6; 2 Samuel 11–12). Considered individually, these instances are at least anomalous, and some have the taint of scandal. Gathered into a genealogy full of great Israelites, however, these apparent embarrassments are shown to have been providential moments in the history of Israel, occasions when God took special care for the future of the Jews. They invite the inference that Jesus' conception, which is similarly troublesome because his mother's husband has not fathered him in the normal sense, is also under God's gracious care and is to be beneficial to the Jewish people.

The tiny narrative about when Jesus was not yet born thus nestles between the declaration of his Davidic genealogy through Joseph and the birth narrative's emphasis on Jesus' Davidic heritage. In so doing, it places great dramatic tension on Joseph's decision. Confronted with the unexpected pregnancy of his betrothed, he initially interprets the unborn in her womb in the normal way, as the fruit of sexual intercourse outside marriage. Following the angel's dream-revelation, he reinterprets the unborn as the son of God, conceived by the Holy Spirit. Through his marriage to Mary, he provides the unborn with a Davidic lineage, thus placing a further interpretation on the unborn Jesus as the Christ, the king of the Jews. For Matthew, therefore, to know the human and divine ancestors of this unborn is to know his destiny.

The Gospel of Luke

The Gospel of Luke and the Acts of the Apostles together form a two-volume theological history which aims to supply a foundational epic for the early Christian movement.[26] At the outset, the author declares the intent of reckoning with sources and traditions so as to craft them into an orderly account (Luke 1:1–4). The first two chapters of Luke show this taking place: the infancy of Jesus is presented, but so is the infancy of John (the one who will become known as John the Baptist), and the two narratives are interwoven so as to present the two in harmony but Jesus as superior. In the present investigation the focus will be Luke 1, which includes the time when the two are not yet born.[27] According to many source critics, the traditions about the infancies of Jesus and John are likely to have been separate at first, preserved by followers of Jesus and followers of John, respectively. Certainly some of the details in Luke's infancy account of Jesus must be traditional, since it has elements in common with Matthew's infancy account and yet neither seems to have

26. We follow the majority view that Luke–Acts is a two-volume work by one author. See Robert C. Tannehill, *The Narrative Unity of Luke-Acts: A Literary Interpretation*, 2 vols. (Vol. 1, Philadelphia: Fortress, 1986; and Vol. 2, Minneapolis: Fortress, 1990). Regarding the genre and aims of Luke–Acts, see Marianne Palmer Bonz, *The Past as Legacy: Luke-Acts and Ancient Epic* (Minneapolis: Fortress, 2000).

27. The technique of showing Jesus to be superior to John by presenting their early lives in parallel continues in Luke 2, which is outside the scope of the present investigation. The newborn Jesus is hailed by angels, shepherds, and the prophets Simeon and Anna in the temple, and when Jesus is twelve he astonishes the religious teachers with his knowledge.

literary dependence on the other. So too, it is often speculated that Luke is using traditional materials about the infancy of John, presumably deriving from John's disciples, although all this must remain a hypothesis since there is no independent corroboration.[28] If this is true, then Luke has reshaped traditions that placed the principal focus on John into a narrative that retains an honored place for him but leaves him second to Jesus. In this reshaping, John is depicted as the willing forerunner of Jesus, prior but inferior to him, who recognizes Jesus as the Lord for whom he is preparing the way. All the canonical gospels find ways to negotiate the relationship of Jesus and John, and thereby they implicitly structure what they hold to be proper relations between followers of Jesus and followers of John. However, it is only Luke who has John recognize Jesus while they are still in utero, when he leaps with joy at the arrival of Mary, who is bearing Jesus in her womb.[29] The work's location of this recognition in utero befits its interest in the origins of early Christianity.

Before the interrelated infancy accounts can be considered, it will be helpful to sketch something of Luke's presentation of the adult John. In Luke 3, after John and Jesus have grown to maturity, John acts publicly before Jesus does. He preaches repentance to the Jewish crowds and baptizes many Jews in the Jordan River for the forgiveness of sins. The text characterizes him as a fulfillment of Isaiah's prophecy about a voice in the wilderness calling for the way of the Lord to be prepared (Luke 3:4–6, quoting Isa. 40:3–5). Jesus is one of those who come to be baptized. At Jesus' baptism, the Holy Spirit descends on him in bodily form and a voice from heaven, evidently God's voice, endorses him as "my beloved son." The text avoids saying outright that it is John who baptizes Jesus (Luke 3:21), despite its having been a strong early Christian tradition that this was the case (cf. Mark 1:9; John 1:24–34) and even though the logic of the narrative demands that John be the baptizer. The narrative even bends the time sequence a little for this purpose, mentioning John's imprisonment by Herod Antipas just before it recounts the baptism of Jesus. By not mentioning John's involvement in Jesus' baptism and by highlighting the divine manifestations at that time, the text minimizes the possibility that the one doing the baptizing would be seen as superior.

Other gospel traditions about John and Jesus as adults suggest that there was potential for rivalry among their respective followers who were trying to determine the relative significance of the two. The examples given here are drawn from Luke, but there are similar traditions in the other canonical gospels, and the presence of John in all these four gospels as well as in Josephus (*Antiquities* 18.116–119) suggests that John had a notable following for some time.[30] Jesus and John are both

28. This view is taken by Fitzmyer, *Gospel according to Luke (I–IX)*, 316–21 and by François Bovon, *Luke 1: A Commentary on the Gospel of Luke 1:1–9:50*, trans. Christine M. Thomas, ed. Helmut Koester, Hermeneia (Minneapolis: Fortress, 2002), 30–32. On source theories for Luke 1, see also Brown, *Birth of the Messiah*, 244–47, 622–23.

29. The two gospels with no infancy narratives necessarily structure the relationship between Jesus and John when the two are already adults: Mark 1:7–11 (with implicit recognition only) and John 1:19–41 (with elaborate recognition and proclamation, with renegotiation of discipleship). In Matthew, too, John recognizes Jesus only during their adulthood (Matt. 3:13–14), since John is not mentioned in that gospel's infancy narrative.

30. For further discussion of the historical John and how he was remembered by Christians, see Joan E. Taylor, *The Immerser: John the Baptist within Second Temple Judaism*, Studying the Historical Jesus (Grand Rapids, Mich.: Eerdmans, 1997) and Daniel S. Dapaah, *The Relationship between John the Baptist and Jesus of Nazareth: A Critical*

influential enough to be executed at the command of rulers in the region (Luke 9:7; 23:24–25). Both are placed in contrastive parallel on occasion (Luke 7:33–34), and so are their disciples (Luke 5:33). Both have disciples even after their deaths (for the legacy of John's baptism, see Acts 18:24–26; 19:1–7). John is questioned to see whether he is the Christ (Luke 3:15); John sends his disciples to ask whether Jesus is the coming one or whether they should wait for another (Luke 7:19–20); Jesus is thought by some to be Elijah, or else John raised from the dead (Luke 9:7–8, 19). Jesus acclaims John, saying that John is a prophet and more than a prophet, the messenger foretold in Mal. 3:1, and no one is greater among those born of women, but he then brushes him aside a moment later by adding that the least in the reign of God is greater than John (Luke 7:26–28). While handing on these traditions, Luke steps in to resolve them in a specific way, thus making implicit assertions about how John's and Jesus' followers should relate to one another too.

The key to Luke's resolution of the traditions is John's frequent characterization as the one who goes ahead and prepares the way for another who is coming (Luke 3:16–17; 7:19–20; 7:27), indeed, as the one who prepares the way for the Lord (Luke 3:4). What Luke emphasizes is that "the Lord" (κύριος) for whom John prepares is not so much YHWH, the Lord God of Israel—even though κύριος often means YHWH in Luke, not least in Luke 1—but the Lord Jesus Christ.[31] In broad terms, the other canonical evangelists make the same move in the course of their narratives, but for Luke the relationship is established at the very outset of the work, in Luke 1, as will now be seen.

Following a historiographical preface, Luke commences neither with Jesus' genealogy (which will be recounted at Luke 3:23–38, to be discussed below), nor with Jesus' conception and birth, but with a married couple. Zechariah and Elizabeth are righteous Jews, living according to the Torah, but they have no child, despite their prayers for offspring, and they are growing old. The scriptures taught that those faithful to God would be divinely blessed with fruitfulness (e.g., Pss. 127 and 128), so the audience would have expected their lack of children to have been a source of grief to them. Their situation resonates particularly with that of Abraham and Sarah, another couple who had grown old before they were blessed with a child (Gen. 17:15–22; 18:1–15; 21:1–7).

In time, God does reward Elizabeth and Zechariah with a child. Elizabeth interprets the conception and pregnancy as God's favor, saying, "Thus has the Lord done for me in the days when he looked upon me to remove my disgrace among people" (Luke 1:25). The first notice of the child's coming is given to Zechariah, however, while he is serving in the temple as a priest. The angel Gabriel appears

---

Study (Lanham, Md.: University Press of America, 2005). While the potential for rivalry between John's and Jesus' followers is evident in retrospect, there may have been first-century people who took interest in the two but did not attempt to rank their importance; for an argument that passages in the Sayings Source Q present John, Jesus, and their followers as Sophia-Wisdom's children, embedded in the same communal movement for the *basileia* of God, see Melanie Johnson-DeBaufre, *Jesus among Her Children: Q, Eschatology, and the Construction of Christian Origins*, Harvard Theological Studies 55 (Cambridge: Harvard Theological Studies, 2005).

31. The ambiguity in early Christian usage between κύριος as YHWH and as the Lord Jesus enriches early Christian scriptural interpretation (e.g., Phil. 2:9–11, alluding to Isa. 45:21–23) and helps to propel the emerging understanding of Jesus Christ as divine.

and announces that Elizabeth and Zechariah will have a son, to be called John (Luke 1:13–17). John will be filled with the Holy Spirit and will turn many of the Israelites to the Lord their God and prepare the people for the Lord. Here Gabriel identifies John's role as that of Elijah, while also alluding to the Second-Temple Jewish idea that Elijah would be the messenger who acts as forerunner of the eschatological Day of the Lord (Mal. 3:1–4; 4:1–6).[32] John will also be like Samuel, the first child of the previously barren Hannah and her husband, Elkanah (1 Samuel 1), for he will abstain from wine and strong drink; this is a sign of his dedication to the Lord (cf. Num. 6:3). Zechariah doubts the prophecy and is therefore struck dumb until the child's naming.

Once the child is born and is named John, Zechariah bursts forth with the hymnic passage known in later Christian tradition as the Benedictus (Luke 1:68–79). The Benedictus deserves particular attention in regard to the use of sources by Luke, as does the other canticle in the chapter, the one known as the Magnificat (Luke 1:46–55). Both canticles are steeped in allusions to the scriptures of Israel, and for the most part they would have functioned well in a non-Christian Jewish setting. Thus they have frequently been analyzed as preexisting texts lightly redacted for their inclusion in the gospel.[33] Opinions vary as to whether the canticles come from the same source as the traditions about John do, but there are several reasons to think that this is the case. In the Benedictus, Zechariah blesses God for his salvation of Israel in covenant fidelity. He then hails his son as the prophet who goes before the Lord to prepare his ways (Luke 1:76). These elements of the hymn are quite consistent with its possible origin among Jewish disciples of John who had no particular attachment to Jesus, and they make no suggestion in themselves that "the Lord" whose ways are being prepared is other than YHWH. However, the Benedictus also contains Davidic messianic allusions in the closing verses (Luke 1:78–79)[34] and the Davidic horn of salvation (Luke 1:69), and while it is just tenable that these Davidic elements are pre-Lukan and even non-Christian, they are more likely to be Lukan additions. Certainly, the Davidic Messianic material refers to Jesus when read in the overall context of Luke 1, for between the conception and the birth of John, the coming of Jesus, a Davidic child, has been announced. Thus, by Luke 1:76, the Lord for whom John will prepare the way (Luke 1:17) is identified through the narrative context as the Lord Jesus.[35]

The account of John's infancy, from the announcement of his conception to his naming and maturity, stretches over Luke 1, but it is interrupted by a story

32. The adult John's preaching will indeed emphasize eschatological judgment (Luke 3), and Jesus will identify John with the Malachi messenger figure (Luke 7:27).

33. There are many hypotheses in circulation about the origin of the Magnificat and the Benedictus. For examples and discussion, see Fitzmyer, *Gospel according to Luke (I–IX)*, 358–62, 378; Bovon, *Luke 1*, 64, 68–69; and Brown, *Birth of the Messiah*, 346–55, 377–78. Such hypotheses frequently allow for redaction of earlier versions of the canticles, and so a wide range of theories can be constructed, depending on what changes are thought to have been made. It is not possible to weigh up the relative merits of various redactional theories in detail here. The present analysis aims to argue the plausibility that the Benedictus and Magnificat once belonged to a John-source that was primarily interested in John rather than Jesus.

34. On the Messianic and Davidic cast of these verses, see Brown, *Birth of the Messiah*, 373–74, 390–91; Bovon, *Luke 1*, 76.

35. Regarding κύριος in Luke 1:76 as compared with Luke 1:17, see Fitzmyer, *Gospel according to Luke (I–IX)*, 385–86.

of another unborn, Jesus. As with Matthew's account, Jesus is virginally conceived through the Holy Spirit; his mother is Mary and her betrothed is Joseph, a descendant of David. However, Luke tells the events from Mary's perspective. Gabriel appears to Mary and announces the impending conception. Their conversation clarifies that Mary is a virgin and will conceive in this way. Similarly to the Matthean announcement to Joseph, Gabriel explains that Jesus will be both a king over Jacob (i.e., Israel) in the line of David (presumably through Joseph's ancestry, mentioned shortly before) and the son of God (because the power of the Most High will overshadow Mary for the conception). Mary assents to what the angel announces, calling herself "the slave of the Lord" (ἡ δούλη κυρίου, Luke 1:38).

Although Luke shares with Matthew an emphasis on Jesus' Davidic ancestry through Joseph and often mentions it during the infancy narratives, it is worth noting that when Luke provides Jesus' genealogy in chapter 3, the Davidic emphasis is not as strong; indeed, there is more interest in non-Israelite aspects of his ancestry.[36] As in Matthew, the genealogy is on Joseph's side (with a demurral that Jesus was the "son, as was thought, of Joseph," Luke 3:23) and follows the male line, but it is an unadorned list of male names only. David is one of the ancestors, but the ancestors do not include the whole string of Davidic kings of Judah, unlike in Matthew's version. Furthermore, the genealogy goes back past David and past Abraham, all the way back to Adam and his father God. This is to go back so far that it becomes slightly absurd, for everyone is a child of Adam and a child of God in this sense. Its effect, however, is to connect Jesus not only with God, whose son he is more directly also, but with the whole of humanity.[37] This foreshadows one of the tasks of Luke–Acts, to address the role of Jews and Gentiles (i.e., all the other nations) in salvation.[38] However, from early in Luke–Acts, in words spoken over the newborn Jesus, it is emphasized that the salvation brought by Jesus will be not only for Israel, the people of interest in the infancy narratives themselves, but also for the Gentiles (Luke 2:31–32). John's domain, on the other hand, is confined to Israel, both in the prophecies about him and the reports of his mission as an adult. Whereas John is reported to be not only Jewish, but doubly descended from priestly families (Luke 1:5), and thus embedded in the heart of the Jewish temple cult, Jesus' genealogy is construed more broadly, giving him a link to the Gentiles as well as the Jews.

Not only does Jesus' story interrupt John's, but the two are connected in Luke's account. Elizabeth is Mary's cousin, and the annunciation to Mary occurs when

36. Luke's genealogy of Jesus is not placed in the infancy narrative, where one might expect, although conceptually it obviously relates to the unborn Jesus. Instead, it is recorded just after Jesus is baptized, once he and his baptizer John have grown to adulthood (Luke 3:23–28).

37. Brown, *Birth of the Messiah*, 90–91.

38. The adult Jesus occasionally helps individual Gentiles and even visits Gentile territory during his public ministry (Luke 7:1–10; 8:26–39), but it is in the second volume of Luke–Acts, which speaks of the time after Jesus' ascension, that the Gentiles really come to the fore. Much of the narrative of Acts turns on the eager acceptance of the good news by many Gentiles and the difficulty that the first Christian preachers (who are Jews themselves) have in convincing large numbers of Jews to believe. It should be noted that this is a schematic and simplified picture of the ancient Christian mission, doubtless affected by conflicts over Jewish-Gentile relations and the role of Jesus as the first century CE wore on.

Elizabeth is in her sixth month of pregnancy (Luke 1:26). The angel ends his speech to Mary by announcing that her cousin, previously thought barren, is expecting, and offers this as a further proof that "nothing is impossible with God" (Luke 1:37). This sets up an intersection of the two stories, as the younger woman hastens to visit the older one. Mary arrives and greets Elizabeth, and the story continues:

> And when Elizabeth heard Mary's greeting, the child in her womb leapt, and Elizabeth was filled with the Holy Spirit, and she proclaimed with a great cry and said, "Blessed [εὐλογημένη] are you among women, and blessed [εὐλογημένος] is the fruit of your womb. And how has this happened to me, that the mother of my Lord should come to me? For behold, when the sound of your greeting came to my ears, the child in my womb leapt for joy. And fortunate [μακαρία] is she who believed that there would be a fulfillment of what was spoken to her by the Lord." (Luke 1:41–45)

Now, it is quite common for a pregnant woman in her sixth month to feel the unborn moving inside her, and not unusual for her to cry out in surprise or pain when it happens. However, Elizabeth places a very specific interpretation on the sensation she experiences, regarding it as an intentional and joyful leap by the unborn John in response to Mary's greeting. Agency is imputed to the unborn John here, although it is his mother who interprets his action.

The narrative endorses Elizabeth's interpretation: not only does it also call John's movement a leap, but it prefaces Elizabeth's words with the statement that she was filled with the Holy Spirit. The Holy Spirit often functions in Luke–Acts to provide divine inspiration in speech or action; here, Elizabeth is now participating in the knowledge that has been given to others in visions and angelic visitations. Thus Elizabeth can safely be said to be speaking the truth, within the theological understanding of the gospel: Mary and the unborn Jesus are both blessed, and Mary's unborn is Elizabeth's "Lord." Moreover, John's leap can be read as an inspired act too, in keeping with Gabriel's prophecy that John would be filled with the Holy Spirit while still inside his mother (Luke 1:15). Although it is not made explicit whether John's delight at hearing Mary's greeting stems from his joy in Mary's presence or Jesus' presence or both, Elizabeth is attending to both Mary and Jesus, and the narrative is signaling a unity of John's and Elizabeth's thought at this point. Thus John should be understood as rejoicing in the coming of both Mary and the unborn Jesus.

A delicate negotiation of power relations takes place in this scene. It might first be thought that since Mary is the one who goes to the effort of visiting Elizabeth, Elizabeth is superior. However, Elizabeth undercuts this with her surprise that "the mother of [her] Lord" should come to her and by her exclamation about Mary's extreme blessedness. Similarly, John sets aside any possibility that he is superior to Jesus, even though he is older and the story began with him, by leaping with joy at the pregnant Mary's approach. Mary's visit thus reflects well on her character, suggesting her courtesy and generosity to an older relative whose pregnancy is further advanced, while providing a narrative opportunity for her greatness to be proclaimed and her unborn's lordship to be recognized. As for John, the emphasis on his joy highlights the lack of contention in his relationship with Jesus; he delights to recognize his Lord, who is destined to usher in the eschatological time of jubilee when all shall rejoice (cf. Luke 4:18–19; 7:18–23). The role of the Holy Spirit in the recognition of Jesus by John is also entirely characteristic of Luke's theology; the Spirit authorizes the joyful recognition of divine presence, both authoring and authenticating it, so that the pattern of the relationship is not only in accord with the Spirit but also Spirit-given, Spirit-prompted at its very origins.

The unborn Jesus is inactive during the scene, being the only one of the four characters not to engage in greeting. To plead his extreme youth at this juncture would miss the point; in fact, Luke says nothing at all about the life of Jesus in Mary's womb. Unlike most of the major characters in Luke 1, the unborn Jesus is not said to have the Holy Spirit fill him or come upon him; that will happen at his baptism (Luke 3:22; 4:1), which still needs to be prepared for by John. There are several Spirit-inspired prophets in the infancy narrative, and there might otherwise have been the risk of depicting the unborn Jesus as just another prophet like the others. Instead, all these prophets focus their attention on Jesus, whether indirectly via John or directly.

The Magnificat (Luke 1:46–55), which comes just after the speech of Elizabeth quoted above, has traveled through the ages as the song of Mary, and she is the speaker of it in most of the manuscripts, but a few witnesses in the textual transmission credit the passage to Elizabeth. The weight of the manuscript evidence implies that Mary should be regarded as the correct speaker,[39] but it cannot be gainsaid that some early Christians thought of Elizabeth as the one who uttered these words. In its themes of salvation-through-reversal and God's fidelity to the Abrahamic covenant, the Magnificat actually suits Elizabeth's situation rather better.[40] Elizabeth the righteous Israelite, once barren and now fertile, is very much like the newly fertile Hannah, whose song of salvific reversal in 1 Sam. 2:1–10 has long been recognized as an influence on the Magnificat. Hannah's earlier prayer to the Lord for a child, "if you will look upon the humiliation of your slave" (ἐὰν ἐπιβλέπων ἐπιβλέψῃς ἐπὶ τὴν ταπείνωσιν τῆς δούλης σου, 1 Sam. 1:11 LXX) recurs almost verbatim in the Magnificat's declaration that the Lord has indeed done this ("[the Lord] has looked upon the humiliation of his slave," ἐπέβλεψεν ἐπὶ τὴν ταπείνωσιν τῆς δούλης αὐτοῦ, Luke 1:48),[41] and the divine mercy spoken of in the Magnificat (Luke 1:50) is exemplified in Elizabeth's giving birth ("the Lord had magnified his mercy with her," Luke 1:58). Mary, by contrast, has no reason to regard her pregnancy as a response to her prayers or a personal gain in the short term, however much Jesus will bring salvation to the world. Collectively, these

39. That is, "correct" within the closest approximation to the original of Luke that is recoverable using text-critical methods.

40. On Elizabeth versus Mary as speaker of the Magnificat, see Brown, *Birth of the Messiah*, 334–36; Fitzmyer, *Gospel according to Luke (I–IX)*, 359.

41. Admittedly, this verse in the Magnificat can also be seen as referring back to Mary's self-description as "the slave of the Lord" (ἡ δούλη κυρίου, Luke 1:38).

observations suggest that the evangelist may have found the Magnificat transmitted as a speech of Elizabeth's within a source of traditions associated with John and his disciples, but may have placed it on Mary's lips to give Mary (and her son) greater voice and importance. (The manuscript evidence shows that later on, some early Christians restored the Magnificat to Elizabeth, whether because they possessed a tradition in which it was her speech or they recognized the narrative appropriateness of doing so.) Under the pressures of the gospel's treatment of Jesus, John, and their mothers, a text that would have befitted Elizabeth well was transformed by the evangelist into a text for Mary to utter.

This investigation has shown how Luke 1 reworks various traditions, both scriptural patterns (such as the Elijah-forerunner motif or God's granting of children to the barren) and originally separate infancy narratives and hymns about John and Jesus, and shapes them into a narrative that structures the relationship of Jesus and John even from the time when they were not yet born. Being filled with the Holy Spirit from his mother's womb, John is comprehensively gathered up and formed from the start into one who recognizes and prepares for Jesus. His powers of recognizing Jesus as his Lord are totally contiguous with his identity. With this foundation to the structure of their relationship, all John's teachings and activities become understood in Luke as part of the activity of this role. John has been there, involved, recognizing, from the very beginning. His leap of joy is an initiatory moment of inspiration and discovery—the first of many moments of recognition throughout the gospel, but culminating in the meal along the road to Emmaus, when the disciples know the risen Jesus at the breaking of the bread (Luke 24:31). Furthermore, just as John's leap prepares Elizabeth to recognize and greet Jesus, her Lord, so too the story of his leap of recognition further prepares the audience to understand who Jesus is, to have the perspective that Luke requires. Knowing more than most of the characters, the hearers are brought to understand more deeply not only who Jesus is but how his mission is related to the tradition before his birth. As an initiatory moment, John's leap equips them to receive the gospel text rightly. It is as though Luke 1 is the womb of the gospel, marked in several ways by the intimacy of encounter—Zechariah in the silence of the temple offering; Mary in direct encounter with Gabriel; Elizabeth and Mary in the shared months of their time together in Elizabeth's home. The audience is accordingly brought by the narrative into these intimate spaces, into the gestation, as it were, waiting for the birth. Lastly, within the intimacy of this space resound the hymns, implicitly inspired texts that are grounded in the mouths of the characters but also are resources for communal utterance. Their resonance within this space serves to constitute the audience as themselves inspired, or at least participating in the chain of transmission of inspired responses to the activity of God.

The *Protevangelium of James*

The *Prot. Jas.*, which is generally dated to the middle of the second century CE, draws upon the infancy narratives of Matthew and Luke as well as some other traditions.[42] Indeed, it is written for an audience that already knows some at least some of this material; for instance, the events around John's origin are referred to quite allusively (*Prot. Jas.* 10, 12), as if assumed to be familiar.[43] One purpose of the text is to resolve problems that arise when these accounts are harmonized. For example, having placed the infant John (from Luke) and Herod the Great (from Matthew) in the same narrative, it explains why John was not killed when Herod massacred the male infants in an unsuccessful attempt to kill Jesus (*Prot. Jas.* 22–24; cf. Matt. 2:13–18). The text also mollifies awkward aspects of the earlier stories. It makes Mary a descendant of David (*Prot. Jas.* 10), for instance, so that Jesus need not rely on his mother's husband for his Davidic ancestry.[44]

The *Prot. Jas.* starts the story a generation earlier than Matthew and Luke do, reaching back to Mary's own conception; thus one of the ancient titles of the work is the *Genesis of Mary, Revelation of James.* This points to a second purpose of the text, namely, to extol Mary as having been "undefiled" or "unstained" (ἀμίαντος) right from the start. The meaning of this undefilement is illustrated by the narrative as it unfolds. Mary is the child specially given by God to the long-childless Anna and Joachim, and her conception is announced by an angel (*Prot. Jas.* 1–5).[45] In gratitude, her mother offers her as a gift to the Lord, as Hannah offered her son, Samuel (*Prot. Jas.* 4–7; cf. 1 Sam. 1).[46] She grows up in holy, uncontaminated places (a bedroom-sanctuary and then the Jerusalem temple), eating food from an angel's hand (*Prot. Jas.* 6–8). She does not engage in illicit—or indeed any—sexual activity (*Prot. Jas.* 9, 15), and she remains a virgin even after the birth of Jesus (*Prot. Jas.* 19–20).[47] Only at one point in the narrative is there the possibility that Mary could herself be an agent of pollution, when she is twelve years old and presumably approaching menarche. She then ceases to reside in the temple, lest she pollute it as a menstruant, and goes to live under the protection of Joseph, here portrayed as

42. Concerning the text's use of early Christian sources and the Septuagint, see Hock, *Infancy Gospels of James and Thomas*, 21–25; H. R. Smid, *Protevangelium Jacobi: A Commentary*, Apocrypha Novi Testamenti 1 (Assen, Netherlands: van Gorcum, 1965), 9–12. In regard to noncanonical infancy traditions or sources shared by the *Prot. Jas.* and the *Ascension of Isaiah*, and the dating of such material, see George T. Zervos, "Seeking the Source of the Marian Myth: Have We Found the Missing Link?" in *Which Mary? The Marys of Early Christian Tradition*, ed. F. Stanley Jones, SBL Symposium Series 19 (Atlanta: Society of Biblical Literature, 2002), 107–20.

43. The scholarly literature has a standardized division of the *Prot. Jas.* into short chapters but not into verses within those chapters, so references are made here to chapters only.

44. Solving exegetical problems by retelling stories was a common practice in this period. For an extensive analysis, focusing on Jewish examples, see James L. Kugel, *Traditions of the Bible: A Guide to the Bible as It Was at the Start of the Common Era* (Cambridge: Harvard University Press, 1998).

45. Mary's extraordinariness is marked from the womb in further ways, according to some of the ancient textual tradition for the work. In some manuscripts, Anna becomes pregnant without the contribution of her husband, who has been absent for forty days; twice in *Prot. Jas.* 4, there is a textual controversy as to whether before Joachim's return Anna "is pregnant" or "will be pregnant." Furthermore, according to some manuscripts, Mary is born not in the ninth month of Anna's pregnancy but in an earlier month, probably the seventh (*Prot. Jas.* 5). Such speedy gestation, especially at seven months, indicated an unusual child; see Pieter W. van der Horst, "Sex, Birth, Purity, and Asceticism in the *Protevangelium Jacobi*," in *A Feminist Companion to Mariology*, ed. Amy-Jill Levine with Maria Mayo Robbins (Cleveland, Ohio: Pilgrim, 2005), 56–60.

46. The resemblance is very strong, since in Greek (the language of the *Prot. Jas.* and of the translated version of the scriptures being used by the author and the audience) Hannah's name is rendered as Anna.

47. See two works by Mary F. Foskett: "Virginity as Purity in the *Protevangelium of James*," in *A Feminist Companion to Mariology*, ed. Amy-Jill Levine with Maria Mayo Robbins (Cleveland, Ohio: Pilgrim, 2005), 67–76; and *A Virgin Conceived: Mary and Classical Representations of Virginity* (Bloomington: Indiana University Press, 2002), 141–64.

an elderly widower (*Prot. Jas.* 8–9).[48] After she is removed from this extremely holy place, the text takes care to emphasize her virginity and undefilement once more (*Prot. Jas.* 10), and it notes that Joseph stays away from her (*Prot. Jas.* 9). Mary is described as Joseph's wife on occasion, but the understanding with the priests seems to be that she should remain a virgin for the time being.[49] Some time later, Mary becomes pregnant, provoking the assumption for many that her virginity has been "defiled." However, the text demonstrates by repeated proofs and heavenly testimonies that she remains a virgin, not only during the pregnancy but even in the birth itself (*Prot. Jas.* 11–16, 19–20).

Being childless and having a child are ethically and emotionally fraught states in the *Prot. Jas.* They are often very public states too, opportunities for praise or scorn according to the parents' marital circumstances. While Anna and Joachim are still childless, they are faced not only with their own grief but with the ridicule of others and restrictions on their worship activities, since all in the community have learned from scriptural models that God will grant children to Israelites who are righteous.[50] Anna declares, "The Lord God has humiliated me greatly" (κύριος ὁ θεὸς ἐταπείνωσέν με σφόδρα, *Prot. Jas.* 2). Thus the would-be parents engage in practices of lamentation appropriate to the absence of divine blessing (Joachim fasts in the wilderness, and Anna wears mourning clothes and later sings a lament) in order to ask God to visit them and remove the curse of barrenness. Angels then appear to them, to announce that God has heard their prayer. Anna and Joachim interpret Anna's pregnancy as God's blessing, mercy, and forgiveness upon them. The ensuing months pass without narration, but the public shame of Anna and Joachim would seem to have ceased. In striking contrast to the preceding lamentation, upon Mary's birth Anna declares, "My soul is magnified today" (*Prot. Jas.* 5); this alludes to the Magnificat in Luke, Mary's joyful song of praise at the coming of her child (Luke 1:46–55). Mary's first birthday becomes an occasion for the

48. In its discussion of the young Mary's residence in the temple, as of several other matters pertaining to Judaism in this period, the *Prot. Jas.* projects a confident verisimilitude but describes some situations and customs that, in the opinion of most current scholarship, cannot possibly have occurred. Refutations and ameliorations of certain specific indications of non-Jewish origin have been offered. See Hock, *Infancy Gospels of James and Thomas*, 9–13; Smid, *Protevangelium Jacobi*, 20–22; Tim Horner, "Jewish Aspects of the *Protoevangelium of James*," *Journal of Early Christian Studies* 12 (2004): 313–335; Saul Lieberman, *Hellenism in Jewish Palestine*, 2nd ed., Texts and Studies of the Jewish Theological Seminary of America 18 (New York: Jewish Theological Seminary of America, 1962), 167–69. (We thank Gary Anderson for the Lieberman reference, which pertains to evidence that girls wove the temple veil; cf. *Prot. Jas.* 10.) However, it still seems unlikely that the work came from a (Christian) Jewish community.

49. Against Hock (*Infancy Gospels of James and Thomas*, 49, note to 9:7, and 59, note to 15:6), who sees a change of plan, from wife to ward, during the negotiation for Mary to come under the care of a widower of Israel (*Prot. Jas.* 8–9), the situation is more easily interpreted as a version of the two-stage marriage indicated by Matt. 1:18–25. Joseph's initial objection to looking after Mary, that he has sons and is old but Mary is young (*Prot. Jas.* 9), indicates embarrassment about marrying someone far younger, not about caring quasi-parentally for such a person. Later on, when the priests berate Joseph for apparently having had intercourse with Mary, their objection is not that she was supposed to remain a virgin under all circumstances, but that Joseph has been fraudulently secretive about their wedding rather than revealing it to the Israelites and seeking God's blessing on their offspring (*Prot. Jas.* 15)—that is, that Joseph and Mary have advanced to the second, full stage of their marriage without public declaration and ceremony.

50. Joachim and Anna notice the parallel with Abraham and Sarah themselves (*Prot. Jas.* 1). Mary's parents express their gratitude in the same way as Samuel's parents Hannah and Elkanah did, giving their child to God by bringing the child to live in the temple (*Prot. Jas.* 4–7; cf. 1 Sam. 1–2).

Israelite people to bless the child and praise God, and (as Anna proclaims in song to the Lord) to see that Anna is suckling a child.

Whereas the lack of a child brings shame upon Anna and Joachim, the converse holds for Mary: the existence of an unborn in the womb of a woman who is supposed to be a virgin causes great scandal. In a passage closely modeled on the Lukan annunciation scene (Luke 1:26–38), Mary is visited by an angel and willingly accepts the news that she will conceive "out of the [Lord's] word" and "from the Lord, the living God" (*Prot. Jas.* 11). Soon afterward, she is blessed by Elizabeth and the leaping unborn John, and hailed as "the mother of [Elizabeth's] Lord" (*Prot. Jas.* 12; cf. Luke 1:39–56). However, in this account, Mary is puzzled by their reaction, having forgotten the angel's revelations.[51] Her pregnancy advances, and she hides from public view, frightened.

Mary is wise to be frightened, for once her pregnancy becomes visible, proclaiming the existence of an unborn, everyone rushes to interpret this unborn as the fruit of improper sexual relations. Joseph is the first to discover it, on his return to the house from his work when she is in her sixth month. Assuming Mary's virginity has been defiled, he blames both himself for leaving her alone to be deceived and Mary for humiliating herself when she had such a holy upbringing; the previous heights of Mary's undefilement make her apparent fall seem even more extreme. Yet Mary's insistence that she does not "know" a man and is ignorant of the origin of what is in her womb makes Joseph frightened in his turn.

It is at this stage that Joseph first entertains the possibility of Mary's innocence, and it comes in tandem with the possibility that the unborn might be "angelic" (*Prot. Jas.* 14). An unborn resulting from illicit sexual activity has no intrinsic interest to him, it would seem, but an unborn of mysterious origins signals heavenly involvement. Unsure of what has happened, Joseph wants neither to hide possible sin nor to risk the death of innocent blood if the child is angelic, and so he decides to divorce Mary quietly. Joseph's dilemma is based on Matt. 1:18–25, and the adaptation of that text continues as Joseph is told in a dream by an angel that he should marry Mary and that the unborn is from the Holy Spirit and should be named Jesus, "for he will save his people from their sins" (*Prot. Jas.* 14; cf. Matt. 1:21).

Mary now has Joseph's protection, but her vulnerability as a visibly pregnant woman continues, for now her situation is seen by a visiting scribe and reported to all the temple officials (*Prot. Jas.* 15). Mary and Joseph, like Anna and Joachim before them, live in a community where sexual and reproductive issues have public import. The priests summon Joseph and Mary, interrogating them both under the assumption that they have improperly had sexual relations together, but the two declare their innocence. As with Joseph's initial reaction, the existence of the unborn is only of interest to the court as a signal of apparent sin by the mother and presumed father, and Mary's undefilement earlier in her life makes her apparent defilement now all the more shocking. Being sure of Mary and Joseph's sin and wanting to disclose it clearly to them, the priests make them drink "the Lord's

51. This surprising forgetfulness serves the text's harmonizing agenda, for it allows Joseph to receive his own dream-revelation, based on Matt. 1:20–23, without its content being preempted by Mary's explanation.

water of testing" (*Prot. Jas.* 16).[52] To the surprise of all the people, they survive the ordeal unscathed, and so they are released to go home rejoicing and praising God; the explicit mention of their joy at this turn further emphasizes the divine blessing involved with the child to be born. The priestly and popular response is slightly muted—they acknowledge that Mary and Joseph's sin has not been revealed by God rather than that it does not exist. However, for the intended audience of this text, the drink ordeal is a public and pseudo-objective indication of Mary's virginity, adding to the two angelic testimonies and the acclaim by Elizabeth and John. All these indications thus contribute also to the interpretation of the unborn within Mary, testifying to Jesus' extraordinary nature.

In the next part of the narrative, Mary and Joseph travel toward Bethlehem for the census. The intended audience, familiar as it already was with infancy traditions about Jesus, would have known that the birth of Jesus was imminent in the narrative. En route, the following episode occurs:

> And they neared the third mile, and Joseph turned and saw her [Mary] gloomy [στυγνήν]. And he said to himself, "Perhaps what is within her is agitating her stormily [χειμάζει αὐτήν]." And again Joseph turned and saw her laughing [γελῶσαν] and he said to her, "Mary, what's the matter with you, that I see your face sometimes laughing and sometimes gloomy?"
>
> And she said to him, "Joseph, [it's] because I see with my eyes two peoples [δύο λαοὺς], one weeping and mourning [κλαίοντα καὶ κοπτόμενον] and one rejoicing and exulting [χαίροντα καὶ ἀγαλλιῶντα]."
>
> And they came halfway, and Mary said to him, "Joseph, get me down from the donkey, because what is within me is pressing urgently upon me to come forth [ἐπείγει με προελθεῖν]." (*Prot. Jas.* 17)[53]

Once again, the visual appearance of a pregnant woman is subject to interpretation. Mary's gloomy face causes Joseph to think that the unborn is moving uncomfortably

52. This ordeal appears to be loosely based on Num. 5:11–31, a ritual for testing a wife for unfaithfulness. The existence of either form of the ritual in the Judaism of the period is unlikely.

53. Our translation of the Greek text from Hock, *Infancy Gospels of James and Thomas*, 62, which contains a limited critical edition based principally on Constantinus de Tischendorf, ed., *Evangelia Apocrypha*, 2nd ed. (Leipzig, Germany: Harmann Mendelssohn, 1876) and Émile de Strycker, ed., *La forme la plus ancienne du Protévangile de Jacques: Recherches sur le papyrus Bodmer 5 avec une édition critique du texte grec et une traduction annotée*, Subsidia Hagiographica 33 (Brussels, Belgium: Société des Bollandistes, 1961). Direct examination of the Tischendorf and de Strycker editions shows that there are many variants in the textual tradition here, mostly trivial and of no importance to the present investigation. The emotive and rejoicing/lamenting vocabulary often gets repositioned or reordered, although without major changes in the meaning. Foskett observes that the early textual witness Papyrus Bodmer 5 calls Mary Μαριάμμη, rather than the more usual Μαρία, twice in the passage quoted here, and that Tischendorf's edition uses Μαριάμ in these places. However, her suggestion that this pertains to an early Christian association of the name Μαριάμ(μη) with prophetic-visionary activity (more usually associated with Miriam/Mariam from Exodus and with Mary Magdalene) is problematized by the use of Μαριάμμη (in the accusative) in P. Bodmer 5 also at the end of *Prot. Jas.* 16 (when Mary and Joseph return home after the testing scene) and Μαριάμ in Tischendorf at the same place and quite often elsewhere. See Mary F. Foskett, "Miriam/Mariam/Maria: Literary Genealogy and the Genesis of Mary in the Protevangelium of James," in *Mariam, the Magdalen, and the Mother*, ed. Deirdre Good (Bloomington: Indiana University Press, 2005), 68–69.

within her. It is a reasonable theory that might fit any pregnant woman and any unborn, but it seems less likely when she laughs soon afterward, so he asks Mary to explain. A second theory, which might occur to the intended audience in its awareness that Jesus' birth would soon occur, is that she is in labor, experiencing intermittent contractions. This theory, although sometimes dismissed in the scholarly literature,[54] is not untenable, since Mary soon feels sensations that she interprets as her unborn's urgent desire to be born, and the child is indeed born not long after.[55]

Mary's explanation to Joseph says nothing about whether the unborn is causing sensations inside her, either directly (by movement) or indirectly (through labor pains). Instead, she speaks of a vision of two peoples. If this episode were occurring in the real world, it might easily be the case that Mary's pregnancy was utterly irrelevant to her vision, but here it is embedded within a highly constructed narrative in which the pregnant Mary's unborn is always relevant. Thus, whether or not she is experiencing labor pains while having this vision, it is quite proper to interpret the vision (and the possible intermittent pains) in terms of her unborn. Moreover, the vision is an allusion to the pregnancy of Rebekah with the twins Jacob and Esau, who "leap" (σκιρτάω, like the unborn John in Luke 1:41–44 and *Prot. Jas.* 12) in her womb (Gen. 25:21–26). When Rebekah, suffering from their leaping, asks an oracle of the Lord about this, she is told, "Two nations [δύο ἔθνη] are in your womb, and two peoples [δύο λαοί] will be made distinct from your belly; and people will prevail over people, and the older will serve the younger" (Gen. 25:23 LXX). Esau and his slightly younger twin Jacob are understood by Genesis as the respective progenitors of the closely related nations Edom and Israel, and Israel is considered by the scriptures to hold sway over Edom.

The interpretative context supplied by the oracle to Rebekah implies that Mary's unborn, even though he is a singleton rather than a pair of twins, will be in some sense the origin of two peoples, two distinct groups standing in different relation to God's blessing.[56] Whereas much of the text has portrayed the unborn Jesus as a descendant (of David, of Israel, and of God), here he is a progenitor. The image collapses two generations into one, placing the sparring of the two peoples not when the two are in the womb but when their progenitor is. Mary shifts Joseph's mundane locutions of "gloomy" and "laughing" to a higher theological register, declaring that one people shall lament and the other shall rejoice. Granted the prophetic character of her utterance, she is not foretelling that these peoples will themselves behave in the way she is describing, but proclaiming that their situations, as judged theologically from a certain highly perspectival early Christian angle, will be grievous and divinely favored, respectively.

54. Smid, *Protevangelium Jacobi*, 122, 124.

55. There may also be an intertext active at this point. In Gen. 35:16–20, Rachel suffers a difficult labor in giving birth to Benjamin and dies soon afterward. Her tomb was on the road to Bethlehem, in approximately the location of the cave near Bethlehem where *Prot. Jas.* 17–19 says Mary gave birth; Smid, *Protevangelium Jacobi*, 123–24. Having established an initial parallel, the intertext works by contrast; Mary's birth experience is so much less damaging to her body than Rachel's is that not only does Mary survive, but her virginity is not impaired (*Prot. Jas.* 19–20).

56. Whereas the oracle to Rebekah in Gen. 25:23 uses "nations" (ἔθνη) and "peoples" (λαοί) in semantic parallelism, *Prot. Jas.* does not adopt the terminology of "nations."

The identity of the two peoples in Mary's vision is not specified by the text and has been subject to debate. Since the *Prot. Jas.* calls Israel a "people" (λαός) several times, the people that is lamenting might possibly have been heard by early audiences as Israel (understood here as rejecting Jesus), and the people rejoicing as the Gentiles collectively (understood as welcoming the gift of salvation made available to them through Jesus).[57] The lack of ethnic specificity in the vision, however, and the fact that the *Prot. Jas.* is not a clearly anti-Jewish text, suggest another interpretation. The dichotomy between the two peoples is identified only as a contrast between lamentation and joy. Recalling that lamentation is the set of practices appropriate in response to the departure of God or of God's blessing,[58] we propose that the members of the lamenting people are those whom the text understands as bereft of God. The members of the other people are accordingly those who are in receipt of God's blessing and presence. The attachment of this dichotomy to any specific groups known to the audience of the *Prot. Jas.* remains elusive.[59]

It is important that the unborn Jesus is the progenitor of this dichotomy. That is, by having the two peoples already visible to Mary's prophetic eyes while Jesus is still in her womb, the *Prot. Jas.* indicates that in Jesus a dichotomy of the world is present, thus giving the division ontological status. Whether this dichotomy is enacted in the coming of Jesus or simply unveiled is not articulated; both notions are available in other Christian texts of the time.[60] The text does not emphasize "response to Jesus" as a source of the dichotomy. Rather, it suggests that because of Jesus there are two peoples, one from whom God's presence and blessing have departed and one with whom God's presence and blessing rest. Lamenting and rejoicing function here to delineate religious difference. By exploring this difference through imagining the unborn in utero, the *Prot. Jas.* is able to highlight the action of God in bringing it about through the divine decision to withdraw or to bestow blessing. The *Prot. Jas.* does not explore the reasons why God would leave a people bereft and in lamentation; reading this dichotomy against the scriptural texts of lamentation in the prophets and Psalms would suggest that covenantal disobedience, idolatry, and grievous sin would form the conceptual framework whereby one group was

57. The medieval texts *Pseudo-Matthew* and *Leabhar Breac*, which draw upon the *Prot. Jas.*, both amplify the vision with a Jews-and-Gentiles interpretation along these lines. For translations of the passages, see Elliott, *Synopsis*, 60–62. Such an interpretation is unsurprising in the context of Christian anti-Judaism in the Middle Ages.

58. Anderson, "Expression of Joy," 225–27.

59. Brief summaries of interpretations from the modern period are provided in Smid, *Protevangelium Jacobi*, 121–22; de Strycker, *La forme la plus ancienne du Protévangile de Jacques*, 145 n. 9; Hock, *Infancy Gospels of James and Thomas*, 63, note to 17:9. Scholars who interpret the vision along the lines of our suggestion here often take their cue from Luke 2:34 in some way or other to distinguish Christians and non-Christians (whether Christian Jews versus non-Christian Jews or Christians versus Jewish and Gentile non-Christians). The version of this interpretation offered by van Stempvoort (the Church versus "Jews/Gentiles") assigns the lamentation to the Church, which seems very pessimistic for the narrative context; P. A. van Stempvoort, "The Protevangelium Jacobi, the Sources of Its Theme and Style and Their Bearing on Its Date," in *Studia Evangelica*, Vol. 3, ed. F. L. Cross, Texte und Untersuchungen 88 (Berlin: Akademie-Verlag, 1964), 422.

60. For example, the *Epistle of Barnabas* asserts that Israel, "they," lost the covenant with God when Moses smashed the tablets of the Law (Exod. 32:19), whereas the making of the new tablets of the Law indicates the covenant of the beloved made with "us," the text's audience, through Jesus' death. Thus in *Barnabas* the sharp dichotomy between its audience and others is enacted by Jesus. In the Gospel of John, however, the dichotomy between two groups is revealed by Jesus' presence and varying responses to it (see, for example, John 8:12–59).

characterized as abandoned by God.[61] In other words, the *Prot. Jas.* is interpreting a world of religious difference through Mary's own interpretation of her vision.

The *Prot. Jas.* shapes all this primarily within a Jewish framework, informed by the scriptures of Israel. Within early Christian circles, the sharpest religious dichotomy explored was usually that between those (both Jews and non-Jews) who understood their relationship to God as mediated through Jesus and those (both Jews and non-Jews) who did not. Much of the history of early Christianity can be viewed in terms of the construction and negotiation of multiple religious boundaries, not only those between non-Christian Jews and Christian Gentiles.[62] The overall conceptual framework of the *Prot. Jas.* suggests a primarily Jewish referent for both peoples; that is, the people lamenting would refer in the first place to Jews who did not think of their relationship with God in terms of Jesus, and the people rejoicing would refer in the first place to those Jews who did incorporate Jesus into their religious life. We would stress, however, that this is simply the dichotomy constructed by the Jewish horizon of the text's narrative world. Thus, since it cannot be established that the *Prot. Jas.* derives from circles of Christians who considered themselves Jews, the intended audience may have interpreted the referents much more fluidly, as corresponding also to non-Jews who were or were not devoted to Jesus. What is clear is that the *Prot. Jas.* recognizes—or asserts—a situation of profound and grievous religious difference, delineating it by means of Mary's vision of the two peoples. It thus dates such conflict to the earliest possible moment, immediately before Jesus' birth, and bestows on the conflict a tragic inevitability.[63] In contrast to Luke's portrayal of Jesus' coming as good news for all, both Jews and Gentiles (Luke 2:29–32), in the *Prot. Jas.* the coming of Jesus is said to be bittersweet, a source of division, and Mary reacts in sympathy, weeping with those who lament and exulting with those who rejoice.

Conclusion

Although depictions of the unborn are rare in Christian literature of the first and second centuries CE, narrative attention to the presence of the unborn in utero allows a text and audience to explore questions central to their religious identity. In other words, the situation of the unborn becomes an important site onto which to project concerns about the origins and definition of a religious movement, as

61. It is important to note that such lamentation and castigation function in the scriptures of Israel not as statements of eternal rejection by God, but rather as prophetic calls to repentance, framed within the assurance of God's steadfast love (see, for example, Lam. 3:22–33). With regard to the relation between Israel and those in Christ, the apostle Paul argues for the constancy of God's covenant with Israel and for an eschatological incorporation of both groups into one; see Rom. 9–11. *Prot. Jas.* remains silent on these matters, but it is possible that the momentary imagining of two peoples in relation to a single unborn indicates an essential unity of the two and therefore their possible reintegration into one at some future time.

62. See especially Boyarin, *Border Lines*.

63. Whether or not this is a plausible reconstruction of how the vision might have been interpreted by its intended audience, it should be clearly noted that such a characterization of religious difference in response to Jesus and his followers is historically unfair, sociologically oversimplified, and theologically dangerous.

well as the relations of one religious group with another. The unborn children in the texts considered here are, in the first place, descendants, heirs of a lineage presented to define their character and its implications. They are also progenitors: in Mary's case, of an extraordinary son, but in the cases of John and Jesus, of distinct groups of followers. In both capacities, they become pivotal figures as these texts conceptualize the origins and innovations of what scholars today call early Christianity.

"Christian origins" is not only a question of modern scholarly inquiry; it is also a preoccupation of the producers and users of at least some of the ancient texts as they seek rhetorically both to ground their beginnings in the heritage of Israel and to make a claim for a religious innovation inaugurated by Jesus. By focusing briefly on a time *prior* to birth, a few texts of this period undertake such originary speculation in a proleptic fashion. That is, the delineation of the unborns and the imaginative description of their actions provide ways of anticipating later convictions and relationships, not simply foreshadowing later developments, but implanting them in the womb itself. By inviting audiences to share in the interpretation of the unborn, the texts draw their users into the intimate space of a mother's reading of the movements in her womb. At the same time, they also view the pregnancy from the outside, exploring the social and religious complexities raised by the unborn's presence. The interplay between the two allows the texts to speak of the implications of what has been initiated by divine action.

As the analysis of all three texts has shown, questions of lineage and legitimacy become important for establishing the identity of the unborn children both in continuity with generations past and as progenitors of distinct groups of religious followers. Furthermore, by imagining and problematizing the causes of extraordinary, divinely bestowed conception, the texts can examine the agency of God, active within and sanctioning the construction of particular religious identity. Stories of how a mother interprets the movements of an unborn in her womb, as were seen in the Gospel of Luke and the *Prot. Jas.*, also allow for envisioning the relations—irenically cooperative or grievously separated—between closely related religious groups.

A leap of joy or a cry of lament? By drawing upon the scriptures of Israel as well as the religious practices of joy and lamentation, the infancy stories of Matthew, Luke, and the *Prot. Jas.* all imagine the unborns as the heirs of a rich religious tradition, capable variously of recognizing, embodying, and receiving the presence of the divine. The stories undertake these acts of imagination, however, cognizant of religious difference and conflict. As they thus explore the world of the unborn, they think in terms not only of genealogy and progeny, but also of joy and sorrow, in order to negotiate their understanding of an identity that recognizes and receives the beneficent activity of God in Jesus.

WORKS CITED

Anderson, Gary A. "The Expression of Joy as a Halakhic Problem in Rabbinic Sources." *Jewish Quarterly Review* 80 (1990): 221–52.

———. *A Time to Mourn, A Time to Dance: The Expression of Grief and Joy in Israelite Religion*. University Park: Pennsylvania State University Press, 1991.

Bakke, O. M. *When Children Became People: The Birth of Childhood in Early Christianity.* Translated by Brian McNeil. Minneapolis: Fortress, 2005.
Blenkinsopp, Joseph. *Isaiah 1–39.* Anchor Bible 19. New York: Doubleday, 2000.
Bonz, Marianne Palmer. *The Past as Legacy: Luke-Acts and Ancient Epic.* Minneapolis: Fortress, 2000.
Bovon, François. *Luke 1: A Commentary on the Gospel of Luke 1:1–9:50.* Translated by Christine M. Thomas. Edited by Helmut Koester. Hermeneia. Minneapolis: Fortress, 2002.
Boyarin, Daniel. *Border Lines: The Partition of Judaeo-Christianity.* Philadelphia: University of Pennsylvania Press, 2004.
Brown, Raymond E. *The Birth of the Messiah: A Commentary on the Infancy Narratives in the Gospels of Matthew and Luke.* 2nd ed. Anchor Bible Reference Library. New York: Doubleday, 1993.
Buell, Denise Kimber. *Making Christians: Clement of Alexandria and the Rhetoric of Legitimacy.* Princeton, N.J.: Princeton University Press, 1999.
———. *Why This New Race? Ethnic Reasoning in Early Christianity.* New York: Columbia University Press, 2005.
Cohen, Shaye J. D. *The Beginnings of Jewishness: Boundaries, Varieties, Uncertainties.* Hellenistic Culture and Society 31. Berkeley: University of California Press, 1999.
Collins, John J. *The Scepter and the Star: The Messiahs of the Dead Sea Scrolls and Other Ancient Literature.* Anchor Bible Reference Library. New York: Doubleday, 1995.
Dapaah, Daniel S. *The Relationship between John the Baptist and Jesus of Nazareth: A Critical Study.* Lanham, Md.: University Press of America, 2005.
Davies, W. D., and Dale C. Allison. *A Critical and Exegetical Commentary on the Gospel according to Saint Matthew.* International Critical Commentary. Vol. 1. Edinburgh: T. & T. Clark, 1988.
Elliott, J. K. *A Synopsis of the Apocryphal Nativity and Infancy Narratives.* New Testament Tools and Studies 34. Leiden, Netherlands: Brill, 2006.
Fitzmyer, Joseph A. *The Gospel according to Luke (I–IX).* Anchor Bible 28. Garden City, N.Y.: Doubleday, 1981.
Flannery-Dailey, Frances. *Dreamers, Scribes, and Priests: Jewish Dreams in the Hellenistic and Roman Eras.* Supplements to the Journal for the Study of Judaism 90. Leiden, Netherlands: Brill, 2004.
Foskett, Mary F. "Miriam/Mariam/Maria: Literary Genealogy and the Genesis of Mary in the Protevangelium of James." In *Mariam, the Magdalen, and the Mother*, edited by Deirdre Good, 63–74. Bloomington: Indiana University Press, 2005.
———. *A Virgin Conceived: Mary and Classical Representations of Virginity.* Bloomington: Indiana University Press, 2002.
Harrington, Daniel J. *The Gospel of Matthew.* Sacra Pagina. Collegeville, Minn.: Liturgical Press, 1991.
Hock, Ronald F. *The Infancy Gospels of James and Thomas.* The Scholars Bible 2. Santa Rosa, Calif.: Polebridge, 1995.
Horner, Tim. "Jewish Aspects of the *Protoevangelium of James.*" *Journal of Early Christian Studies* 12 (2004): 313–35.
Isaac, Benjamin. *The Invention of Racism in Classical Antiquity.* Princeton, N.J.: Princeton University Press, 2004.
Johnson-DeBaufre, Melanie. *Jesus among Her Children: Q, Eschatology, and the Construction of Christian Origins.* Harvard Theological Studies 55. Cambridge: Harvard Theological Studies, 2005.
Kelly, J. N. D. *Early Christian Doctrines.* Rev. ed. New York: HarperSanFrancisco, 1978.

Koester, Helmut. *Ancient Christian Gospels: Their History and Development.* Harrisburg, Pa.: Trinity, 1990.
Kugel, James L. *Traditions of the Bible: A Guide to the Bible as it was at the Start of the Common Era.* Cambridge: Harvard University Press, 1998.
Levine, Amy-Jill. "Anti-Judaism and the Gospel of Matthew." In *Anti-Judaism and the Gospels*, edited by William R. Farmer, 9–36. Harrisburg, Pa.: Trinity, 1999.
Levine, Amy-Jill, with Maria Mayo Robbins, ed. *A Feminist Companion to Mariology.* Cleveland, Ohio: Pilgrim, 2005.
Liddell, Henry George, Robert Scott, and Henry Stuart Jones. *A Greek-English Lexicon.* 9th ed. with revised supplement. Oxford: Clarendon, 1996.
Lieberman, Saul. *Hellenism in Jewish Palestine.* 2nd ed. Texts and Studies of the Jewish Theological Seminary of America 18. New York: Jewish Theological Seminary of America, 1962.
Miller, Patricia Cox. *Dreams in Late Antiquity: Studies in the Imagination of a Culture.* Princeton, N.J.: Princeton University Press, 1994.
Nasrallah, Laura Salah. *"An Ecstasy of Folly": Prophecy and Authority in Early Christianity.* Harvard Theological Studies 52. Cambridge: Harvard Theological Studies, 2003.
Nestle-Aland. *Novum Testamentum Graece.* Edited by Eberhard Nestle and Erwin Nestle. Revised by Barbara Aland, Kurt Aland, et al. 27th ed. Stuttgart, Germany: Deutsche Bibelgesellschaft, 1993.
Rahlfs, Alfred, ed. *Septuaginta.* Stuttgart, Germany: Deutsche Bibelgesellschaft, 1979.
Saldarini, Anthony J. *Matthew's Christian-Jewish Community.* Chicago Studies in the History of Judaism. Chicago: University of Chicago Press, 1994.
Schneemelcher, Wilhelm, ed. *New Testament Apocrypha.* Translated by R. McL. Wilson. 2 vols. Rev. ed. Cambridge: James Clarke, 1991–92.
Segal, Alan F. *Rebecca's Children: Judaism and Christianity in the Roman World.* Cambridge: Harvard University Press, 1986.
Smid, H. R. *Protevangelium Jacobi: A Commentary.* Apocrypha Novi Testamenti 1. Assen, Netherlands: van Gorcum, 1965.
Stempvoort, P. A. van. "The Protevangelium Jacobi, the Sources of Its Theme and Style and Their Bearing on Its Date." In *Studia Evangelica*, Vol. 3, edited by F. L. Cross, 410–26. Texte und Untersuchungen 88. Berlin: Akademie-Verlag, 1964.
Stendahl, Krister. *The School of St. Matthew and Its Use of the Old Testament.* 2nd ed. Acta Seminarii Neotestamentici Upsaliensis 20. Lund, Sweden: Gleerup, 1968.
Strycker, Émile de, ed. *La forme la plus ancienne du Protévangile de Jacques: Recherches sur le papyrus Bodmer 5 avec une édition critique du texte grec et une traduction annotée.* Subsidia Hagiographica 33. Brussels, Belgium: Société des Bollandistes, 1961.
Tannehill, Robert C. *The Narrative Unity of Luke–Acts: A Literary Interpretation.* 2 vols. Vol. 1, Philadelphia: Fortress, 1986; Vol. 2, Minneapolis: Fortress, 1990.
Taylor, Joan E. *The Immerser: John the Baptist within Second Temple Judaism.* Studying the Historical Jesus. Grand Rapids, Mich.: Eerdmans, 1997.
Tischendorf, Constantinus de, ed. *Evangelia Apocrypha.* 2nd ed. Leipzig, Germany: Harmann Mendelssohn, 1876.
Wainwright, Elaine M. *Shall We Look for Another? A Feminist Rereading of the Matthean Jesus.* The Bible and Liberation. Maryknoll, N.Y.: Orbis, 1998.
White, Hayden. *Metahistory: The Historical Imagination in Nineteenth-Century Europe.* Baltimore: Johns Hopkins University Press, 1973.
Zervos, George T. "Seeking the Source of the Marian Myth: Have We Found the Missing Link?" In *Which Mary? The Marys of Early Christian Tradition*, edited by F. Stanley Jones, 107–120. SBL Symposium Series 19. Atlanta: Society of Biblical Literature, 2002.

"Famous" Fetuses in Rabbinic Narratives

Gwynn Kessler

God said to them, "Do you see that I want to give the Torah to your parents, and you are the guarantors for them, that they will fulfill it?"
They said to God, "Yes."
God said to them, "I am the Lord your God who brought you out?"
They said to God, "Yes."
"There will be no other gods before you?"
They said to God, "No."
God said to them, "You will not swear falsely by the name of the Lord your God?"
They said to God, "No."
And so it was that they answered God "yes" to all the yes questions and "no" to all the no questions.

This conversation—between God and the Israelite fetuses in their mothers' wombs—takes place, according to medieval traditions, at Sinai, immediately before God delivers the Torah to Israel. The text, cited here from the Midrash on the Ten Commandments (ca. tenth century CE), reconceives revelation at Sinai, imagining that, before God gives the Torah to Israel, God asks for guarantors that Israel will fulfill it. Israel, according to this tradition, first offers its fathers, Abraham, Isaac, and Jacob, but God rejects them as suitable guarantors because of their past misdeeds. Then Israel offers God its fetuses. The children of Israel bring their pregnant women, and God makes their bellies like glass—rendering the fetuses visible and presumably giving them sight—and then God proceeds to ask if *they* will fulfill the commandments. The fulfillment of the Torah and its commandments cannot depend on the past, even the glorious past embodied by Israel's patriarchs. Rather, the text continues, the very foundations of the Torah rest upon fetuses, who embody Israel's future. And yet, the fetuses not only embody Israel's future, serving as the proper guarantors for their parents at Sinai, but the text further suggests that the fetuses enter into their own covenantal relationship with God, acknowledging God as the God who brought them out of Egypt and promising to have no other gods. As God renders the women's bellies like glass, the text renders the fetuses active participants in Israel's covenantal relationship with God, thereby locating the very beginnings of "Jewishness"[1] in the womb.

This chapter demonstrates that rabbinic narrative sources, beginning in the third century CE and continuing into the Middle Ages, consistently use the fetus as a vehicle to articulate that which is central to the construction of rabbinic Jewishness. Although the medieval tradition cited above represents the culmination of rabbinic narratives about the fetus discussed here, the Hebrew Bible already sets forth the textual beginnings.

In the Hebrew Bible, fertility rests in the purview of God.[2] Numerous biblical verses demonstrate God's involvement in granting or withholding pregnancy. For example, Genesis 20:18 states, "For the Lord had fast closed up all the wombs of the house of Avimelech," and Genesis 29:31 states, "And when the Lord saw that Leah was hated, he opened her womb." According to Genesis 30:1–2, when Rachel desperately desires children, Jacob responds, "Am I in God's place, who has withheld from you the fruit of the womb?" God's involvement in procreation is reiterated later in the same chapter, "And God remembered Rachel, and God listened to her, and opened her womb" (Gen. 30:22). And Hosea 9:11 states, "As for Ephraim, their glory shall fly away like a bird, no birth, no pregnancy, no conception."[3] Furthermore, multiple passages from Isaiah and Jeremiah credit God with the creation or formation of Israel in the womb.[4] For example, Isaiah 44:1–2 states, "Yet now hear O Jacob my servant and Israel whom I have chosen: Thus says the Lord that made you and formed you from the womb."[5] Job credits God with his formation (Job 10:8–12 and 35:15), and in Psalm 139:13–16 the psalmist attributes his creation to God, proclaiming, "You have formed my insides; You knit me together in my mother's womb." Finally, biblical passages already indicate that some kind of relationship between God and Israel begins in the womb. Jeremiah 1:5 states, "Before I formed you in the womb I knew you, and before you came forth out of the womb

1. I use the term rabbinic Jewishness throughout this essay as short-hand for rabbinic constructions of Israel. In my full-length study on rabbinic narratives about fetuses—*Conceiving Israel* (Philadelphia: University of Pennsylvania Press, forthcoming)—I discuss the problem of applying the term "Jewishness" to rabbinic traditions.

2. See Mary Callaway, *Sing, O Barren One: A Study in Comparative Midrash*, SBL Dissertation Series 91 (Atlanta: Scholars Press, 1986); and Tikva Frymer-Kensky, *In the Wake of the Goddesses: Women, Culture, and Biblical Transformation of Pagan Myth* (New York: Free Press), 97–99. See also Ronald Simkins, *Creator and Creation: Nature in the Worldview of Ancient Israel* (Peabody, Mass.: Hendrickson, 1994), 82–120.

3. See also Gen. 21:1, Gen. 25:21, Gen. 49:25, Exod. 23:26, Judg. 13:3, I Sam. 1:5, and Ruth 4:13.

4. See Isa. 43:1, which uses both *yatzar* (form) and *bara* (create), and 43:7, which uses both of these and adds *asah* (made). In Isa. 44:2 and 44:24 and Jer. 1:5, the Hebrew root *yatsar* (to form) is used. Cf. Gen. 2:6. In Ps. 139:15 and Job 10:8–9 and 31:15, the Hebrew root *asah* (to make) is used. For a rabbinic discussion about possible differences between *yatzar* and *bara*, see *b.* Nid. 22b and *b. Sanh.* 39a.

5. See also Isa. 29:15–16, Isa. 45:9–11, and Jer. 18:3–6.

I made you holy, and I ordained you a prophet to the nations." Isaiah 49:1 provides the corollary, that Israel likewise locates the beginnings of God's relationship with it in the womb: "The Lord appointed me before I was born, He named me while I was in my mother's womb." Although these verses might be understood to refer only to Israel's prophets and God's knowledge of them in utero, Psalm 22 and 71 establish that Israel recognizes God already from the womb. Psalm 22:11 asserts, "From my mother's womb you have been my God," and Psalm 71:6 proclaims, "I depended on You while in the belly; in the womb of my mother you were my support."

Rabbinic sources extend the mutual recognition between God and Israel in the womb to all "Jewish" "fetuses." The process by which the fetus might be considered Jewish will be traced throughout this chapter, but the use of the term "fetus" requires some immediate comment. Although rabbinic traditions about the fetus remain consistent with biblical sources insofar as both implicate God in the process of coming-into-being and locate the beginnings of Israel's relationship with God in the womb, one obvious difference presents itself through language. The Hebrew Bible has no distinct word for embryo or fetus.[6] Rabbinic traditions, however, use the words *valad* and *ubar,* both of which are almost always qualified by the phrase "in its mother's womb" or something similar.[7] While not altogether identical with contemporary uses of the word "fetus,"[8] the Hebrew words *valad* and *ubar,* followed by the specific location "in its mother's womb," nevertheless bear certain similarities with this term, and I translate the phrase as fetus throughout this chapter.[9]

Beyond this discrepancy in language, the difference between biblical and rabbinic traditions about the fetus is one of degree, not of kind. Rabbinic traditions that theorize procreation elaborate upon God's role in the process of coming-into-being already set forth in biblical sources. Most notably, rabbinic traditions about procreation, in contrast to biblical sources but consistent with Greco-Roman writings on the topic, set forth varying, even conflicting, theories of procreation that explicitly mention the human procreative substances with which God works, be it male seed, or male seed and female seed or blood.

Rabbinic traditions about the fetus also elaborate on the nature of the relationship between God and Israel in the womb, developing the biblical notion of mutual

6. The phrase "fruit of the womb," which appears in Gen. 30:2, Deut. 7:13, Isa. 13:18, Hosea 9:16, and Ps. 127:3, refers to children, or progeny. Gen. 25:22 uses the Hebrew word *banim* (sons/children); Exod. 21:22 uses the Hebrew word *yeladehah* (her offspring/her child).

7. *Ubar* is used in reference to human and animal fetuses. *Valad* is used in reference to human fetuses and, when unaccompanied by the phrase "in its mother's womb," to human and animal offspring. Sometimes, primarily in later compilations, the Hebrew word *tinukot* is used in references to fetuses as well, e.g.: *Song of Songs Rab.* 7:6; *Deut. Rab.* 9:2; *Mid. Tanhuma Ki Tissa* 2, *Tazria* 1, 3, and *Mid. Tehilim* 8:4.

8. For some of the difficulties involved in using the term "fetus" for premodern sources, see Barbara Duden, "The Fetus on the Farther Shore: Toward a History of the Unborn," in *Fetal Subjects/Feminist Positions,* ed. Lynn M. Morgan and Meredith W. Michaels (Philadelphia: University of Pennsylvania Press, 1999). See also Barbara Duden, *Disembodying Women: Perspectives on Pregnancy and the Unborn,* trans. Lee Hanoicki (Cambridge: Harvard University Press, 1993).

9. When translating passages that have to do with fetal creation, I use the term "embryo," which covers, in contemporary medical usage, the first two months of gestation.

recognition between the two already in utero into a thoroughly rabbinic articulation of what the relationship between God and Israel entails from its very beginnings. When rabbinic sources imagine that God creates and cares for the fetus and that the fetus sings praises to God and wishes to study and pray; that Israelite fetuses are present and participating at the Song of the Sea and revelation of Torah; and that some fetuses are even born circumcised—these sources simultaneously construct, or mark, the fetus as Jewish *and* locate the very beginnings of Jewishness in the womb. In rabbinic traditions about the fetus, the rabbis project their own practices and beliefs into the womb to such an extent that the fetus becomes a unique vehicle for conceiving Jewishness itself.

"And the sons struggled together inside her": Articulating Self and Other in the Womb

And the sons struggled together inside her; and she said, If it be so, why am I thus? And she went to inquire of God. And God said to her, Two nations are in your womb, and two peoples shall be separated from your bowels; and the one people shall be stronger than the other people; and the elder shall serve the younger. And when her days to be delivered were fulfilled, behold, there were twins in her womb. And the first came out red, all over like a hairy garment; and they called his name Esau. And after that came his brother out, and his hand took hold on Esau's heel; and his name was called Jacob.

(Gen. 25:22–26)

Through the various midrashic readings of Jacob, Esau, and their prenatal struggle within Rebekah, the rabbis theorize Jewishness, non-Jewishness, and the hostile relationship inherent in these two constructions—from their very conception. In these traditions, the rabbis reflect upon Jewishness in relation to its "other," non-Jewishness. More precisely, the rabbis articulate Jewishness, as embodied by Jacob, *over* and *against* non-Jewishness as embodied by Esau.

The biblical verse, "And the sons struggled together inside her; and she said, If it be so, why am I thus? And she went to inquire of God," provides the textual opening for midrashic readings of Jacob's in utero Jewishness and Esau's prenatal non-Jewishness. God's response to Rebekah's own searching (*l'drosh*) for some explanation for her pain and anxiety during pregnancy further provides the rabbis with the perfect *midrashic* opportunity to search out—to theorize—rabbinic Jewishness *and* its other. God answers Rebekah, explaining, "Two nations are in your womb, and two peoples shall be separated from your bowels; and the one people shall be stronger than the other people; and the elder shall serve the younger."

Genesis Rabbah, a rabbinic compilation of Palestinian provenance redacted during the fifth century CE, offers a line-by-line expansion of the book of Genesis. *Genesis Rabbah* 63:6–8 sets forth multiple interpretations of Genesis 25:22–24, all of which, despite their differences, consistently construct Jacob and Esau as polar opposites in an antagonistic relationship.

The rabbis begin by considering what Jacob and Esau may be fighting about already in the womb. These rabbinic traditions attempt to fill in the biblical story, which only mentions that they are struggling but does not explain the nature of their struggle. *Genesis Rabbah* 63:6 states: "And the sons struggled together [*vayitrotzatzu*] within her. R. Yohanan and Reish Lakish [interpreted the word *vayitrotzatzu*]. R. Yohanan said, 'this one ran [*ratz*][10] to kill this one and this one ran to kill this one.' R. Shimeon b. Lakish said, 'this one permitted[11] the [forbidden] commands of this one, and this one permitted the [forbidden] commands of this one.'"[12] This passage provides two explanations of Jacob and Esau's struggle within Rebekah's womb. The first interpretation, attributed to R. Yohanan, suggests that Jacob and Esau already engage in mortal struggle as fetuses, as they each try to physically kill each other. In contrast, R. Shimeon b. Lakish imagines Jacob and Esau as waging a spiritual/cultural battle, not a physical one. R. Shimeon b. Lakish's interpretation constructs Jacob in the womb as a rabbinic Jew, who observes commandments, and it constructs Esau as a non-Jew, who follows his own laws.[13] Although this text does not specify how Jacob and Esau follow their respective commandments or even what these commandments are, *Lekah Tov,* a later midrashic compilation (ca. twelfth century CE), provides some examples: "This one permitted the commands of this one. How so? This one forbids [work on] shabbat and this one forbids [work on] Sunday; this one forbids [the eating of] pork and this one permits it."[14] Thus Jacob already observes shabbat and kashrut, while Esau does not.

Genesis Rabbah 63:6 continues, returning to the physical struggle between Jacob and Esau in Rebekah's womb: "R. Berekiah in the name of R. Levi, 'Do not say that [only after] Esau went forth from his mother's womb did he attack him [Jacob]. But [even] while he was in his mother's womb, his fist [*zoro*] was stretched out against him. As it is written, The wicked are estranged [*zoru*/make fists] from the womb [they go astray from the womb] (Ps. 58:4).'"[15] This tradition again imagines that Esau attacks Jacob while in the womb. R. Berekiah's statement moves beyond the assertion of Esau's otherness to proclaim his "wickedness," thus conflating difference with wickedness.

10. The Hebrew word *ratzatz,* meaning to squeeze or crush, is also being punned here.

11. Reish Lakish interprets *vayitrotzatzu* as *vayeter tzivav*. Reish Lakish's explanation is based on a *notarikon*—a rabbinic hermeneutic which divides a word into two or more words. See Strack and Stemberger, *Introduction to the Talmud and Midrash,* trans. Markus Bockmuehl (Minneapolis: Fortress Press, 1992), 30.

12. Jehuda Theodor and Hanoch Albeck, *Midrash Bereshit Rabba: Critical Edition with Notes and Commentary,* 3 vols., 2nd ed. (Jerusalem: Wahrmann, 1965), 682. Theodor, in his comments on *Genesis Rabbah* 63:6, writes: "That which is forbidden to Israel is permitted to the nations of the world[,] and their laws which are forbidden to them [the nations], are permitted to Israel."

13. Ascribing to the patriarchs contemporary rabbinic practices is a common trope in rabbinic literature. See A. Marmorstein, "Quelques problemes de l'ancienne apologetique juive," in *Revue des Etudes Juives* 68 (1914), 161: "The idea that the patriarchs observed the commandments of the Torah and studied the law is already found in tannaitic sources."

14. See Theodor's comments on *Genesis Rabbah* 63:6 in *Midrash Bereshit Rabba: Critical Edition,* 682. *Genesis Rabbah* 63:7, discussed below, asserts that Jacob was born circumcised. Perhaps one of the *mitzvot* alluded to here that Israel permits but Rome prohibits is circumcision. Cf. *Ruth Rab.* Proem 3, discussed in note 21 below.

15. Theodor and Albeck, *Midrash Bereshit Rabba: Critical Edition,* 682. The verse from Psalms is translated differently. *The Jerusalem Bible* states, "The wicked are estranged from the womb: they err from birth." The Jewish Publication Society *Tanakh* writes, "The wicked are defiant from birth; the liars go astray from the womb."

Finally, *Genesis Rabbah* 63:6 offers one more interpretation of Jacob and Esau's in utero struggle: "*And the sons struggled together within her.* The sons hastened within her. She passes by houses of idolatry and Esau kicks to go out. As it is written, *The wicked are estranged from the womb* (Ps. 58:4). She passes by synagogues and houses of study and Jacob kicks to go out. As it is written, *Before I formed you in the womb, I knew you* (Jer. 1:5)."[16] Again, revisiting the spiritual/cultural aspect of Jacob and Esau's struggle, this part of the text portrays Esau as a wicked idolater already in the womb, wishing to worship "strange" gods. In contrast, Jacob—as a fetus—already wishes to pray and study, like the ideal rabbinic Jew. Furthermore, this midrash asserts that not only does Jacob wish to pray and study—to know God—but God already knows Jacob, just as God knew Jeremiah in the womb.

Up to this point, *Genesis Rabbah* 63:6 explicitly constructs Jacob and Esau, as individuals, in opposition to each other. However, throughout rabbinic literature, Jacob and Esau often represent the collective bodies of Israel and Rome, respectively.[17] That the rabbis understand Jacob as Israel and Esau as Rome becomes apparent in *Genesis Rabbah* 63:7:

> *Two nations are in your womb* (Gen. 25:23). Two proud nations are in your womb. This one is proud in his world and this one is proud in his world. This one is proud in his kingdom and this one is proud in his kingdom. Two proud nations are in your womb: Hadrian of the nations [of the world] and Solomon of Israel. Two hated nations are in your womb: All the nations hate Esau and all the nations hate Israel. Those who hate your children[18] are in your womb, as it is written, *But Esau I hated* (Mal.1:3).

Here the midrash explicitly connects Esau with Rome and Jacob with Israel, as Rebekah not only carries forth Esau and Jacob, but their offspring: Hadrian and Solomon. The rabbis portray both nations as proud and hated by others. The last line, as rendered above, also alludes to the hatred that Rome has for Israel. However, commentators have suggested a variant reading, which states, "Those hated by your Creator are in your womb." This amendation has the advantage of being closer to the biblical proof text, which has God express God's hatred for Esau. Furthermore, Malachi 1:2 has God stating, "Yet I loved Jacob" and then

16. Theodor and Albeck, *Midrash Bereshit Rabba: Critical Edition*, 682–83.

17. See Gerson D. Cohen, "Esau as Symbol in Early Medieval Thought," *Studies in the Variety of Rabbinic Cultures* (Philadelphia: JPS, 1991), 243–71. Cohen points out, however, that Christian exegetes (re)interpret Jacob as the church, the true Israel. See also Sacha Stern, *Jewish Identity in Early Rabbinic Writings* (Leiden, Netherlands: Brill, 1994), 18–21; and Jacob Neusner, *From Enemy to Sibling: Rome and Israel in the First Century of Western Civilization*, Ben Zion Bokser Memorial Lecture, Queens College, New York, 1986.

18. Almost all manuscripts state children (*banaiah*) However, see R. Enoch Zundel b. Joseph of Billenstock in his *Etz Yoseph* and R. Jacob Moses Ashkenazi in his *Yede Moshe* and also Issachar Ber Ashkenazi in his *Matnoth Kehunah* to *Gen. Rab.* 63:6 where all of these exegetes amend the text to *baraiah*, Creator. This reading has the disadvantage of amending the printed text, but it has the advantage of fitting more closely with the biblical prooftext, where God is the "speaker." Theodor rejects this reading in *Midrash Bereshit Rabba: Critical Edition*, 685. Cf. *Song of Songs Rab.* 1:4 for another tradition which teaches that God hated Esau.

continues to point out that God hated Esau (Mal. 1:3). Thus the text simultaneously asserts God's love of Jacob/Israel and God's hatred of Esau/the nations already in the womb.[19]

Genesis Rabbah 63:7 then interprets the continuation of Genesis 25:23: "*Two peoples shall be separated from your bowels.* R. Berekiah said, 'From here we learn that he (Jacob) was born circumcised.'"[20] The difference between Jacob and Esau—Israel and the nations—depends not only on theological beliefs (monotheism or polytheism) or practices (observance of the commandments; worship through study and prayer or observance of other laws and "strange" worship) already evident in utero, but the biblical separation of which God speaks in Genesis 25:23 manifests itself as a sign in the flesh—a physical demarcation of bodily difference. Jacob, already in Rebekah's womb, embodies rabbinic (male) Jewishness; Esau, already in the womb, embodies otherness, for presumably he remains uncircumcised.[21]

Genesis Rabbah 63:8 proceeds to assert that Jacob's righteousness and Esau's wickedness are apparent at birth. Thus Jacob and Esau, already as fetuses, embody the separation of Israel and the nations both bodily and spiritually: "*And when her days to be delivered were fulfilled* [*vayiml'u*] *behold, there were twins in her womb* (Gen. 25:24). Later [the word for twins is written] full [*malei*] and here it is deficient. [Here it doesn't say], 'Behold there were twins [*tomim*] in her womb' but twins [*tomm*] is written. There [where it is written full it refers to] Peretz and Zerah, both of them righteous. Here [it refers to] Jacob and Esau, one righteous and the other wicked."[22] Again, the text constructs Jacob and Esau as opposites. As Jacob is circumcised, so too is he righteous, and as Esau is uncircumcised, so too he is wicked—already in the womb.[23] That these traditions on the whole refer not only to Jacob and Esau, but also to Israel and Rome, surfaces again in the final sections of *Genesis Rabbah* 63:8. Interpreting Genesis. 25:25, "And the first came out completely red," the text states: "Why did Esau come forth first? So that he would come forth and take his foul matter with him. R. Abahu said, 'Like a bath attendant who washes the bath house and afterwards bathes the king, so too why

19. Cf. Rom. 9:11–13: "Even before they had been born or had done anything good or bad (so that God's purpose of election might continue, not by works but by his call) she was told, 'The elder shall serve the younger.' As it is written, 'I have loved Jacob, but I have hated Esau.'" Cf. Origen, *On First Principles*, Book II, 9:5, "the child of Isaac and Rebecca who, while yet lying in the womb, supplants his brother and is said, before he is born, to be loved by God."

20. Theodor and Albeck, *Midrash Bereshit Rabba: Critical Edition*, 685. For the motif of those born circumcised, see I. Kalimi, "'He Was Born Circumcised': Some Midrashic Sources, Their Concept, Roots and Presumably Historical Context," *Zeitschrift für die Neutestamentliche Wissenschaft und die Kunde der Alteren Kirche* 93, 1–2 (2002): 1–12.

21. *Ruth Rab.* Proem 3, interprets "The way of man is crooked and strange" (Prov. 21:8) to refer to Esau: "*Man*, refers to the wicked Esau, as it is said, *And Esau was a man, a cunning hunter* (Gen. 25:27). *And strange* [*zar*]—because he estranged himself from circumcision and he estranged himself from *mitzvot*." *B. Sanh.* 59b apparently excludes Esau's descendants from the commandment of circumcision. *Pirkei Rabbi Eliezer*, chapter 29, however, claims that Isaac circumcised Jacob and Esau.

22. Theodor and Albeck, *Midrash Bereshit Rabba: Critical Edition*, 686. See, e.g., *b. Meg.* 6a and 11a and *b. Sanh.* 39b for more on Esau's wickedness. For rabbinic traditions that retain some ambiguity about Esau see Stern, *Jewish Identity*, 20–21. See also Carol Bakhos, "Figuring (Out) Esau: The Rabbis and Their Others," *Journal of Jewish Studies* 58:2 (2007): 250–62. And see Neusner, *From Enemy to Sibling*.

23. Cf. *b. Nid.* 30b, where the fetus must make an oath that it will be righteous. Contrast *b. Nid.* 16b, where God decrees the fate of embryos at (or before) conception—except for whether the person will be righteous or wicked.

did Esau come forth first? So that he would come forth and [take] his foulness with him.'"[24]

Presumably, no foulness accompanies Jacob's birth; he is apparently born pure. Furthermore, the text compares Jacob to a king, thus alluding to Israel's eventual triumph over Rome, which is explicitly invoked in the final text from *Genesis Rabbah* 63:8 discussed here: "*And after that his brother came forth* (Gen. 25:26). A [Roman] prefect asked one from the house of Silna,[25] who will seize [power] after us? He [the one from the house of Silna] brought a piece of paper and took a quill and wrote on it, *And after that his brother came forth, and his hand seized Esau's heel.* They said, 'See: old words from the mouth of this new elder.'"[26]

Although Rome rules over Israel at this moment, Israel will ultimately triumph. Israel grasps Rome's heel, as it were, just as Jacob held fast to Esau's heel. And eventually, Rome will serve Israel just as Esau serves Jacob.

According to *Genesis Rabbah* 63:6–8, before birth and at birth, the character—the essences—of Jacob and Esau are already established. The rabbinic interpretation of Esau as Rome and Jacob as Israel already applies to Jacob and Esau as fetuses in Rebekah's womb. These traditions portray Esau as a wicked, filthy, uncircumcised idolater, who physically injures his mother and tries to kill his brother. In contrast, these same traditions cast Jacob as the paradigmatic rabbinic Jew. As much as Esau epitomizes non-Jewishness, Jacob embodies rabbinic Jewishness: he observes the *mitzvot* (specifically *kashrut* and shabbat according to a later tradition); he is known by, and he knows, God; he wishes to study and pray; he is righteous, although he too tries to kill his brother; and he is circumcised.

The lack of ambiguity or nuance in these traditions about Jacob and Esau as fetuses overlooks or simply ignores the depth of ambiguity that shadows these figures in the biblical sources. Although the rabbinic interpretations in *Genesis Rabbah* 63:6–8 portray Jacob as beyond reproach, Genesis does not readily suggest such a characterization as a given. And the rabbis, in these passages, portray Esau as beyond salvation, again despite biblical evidence to the contrary. The rabbis neglect, in this context, to comment upon the poignant reconciliation between Jacob and Esau in the book of Genesis: "And he passed over before them, and bowed to the ground seven times, until he came near to his brother. And Esau ran to meet him, and embraced him, and fell on his neck, and kissed him; and they wept" (Gen. 33:3–4).

This rabbinic portrayal of Jacob and Esau as so diametrically opposed throughout *Genesis Rabbah* 63:6–8 suggests that these traditions have much to do with the construction of rabbinic Jewishness on a national level in the rabbis' own

24. Theodor and Albeck *Midrash Bereshit Rabba: Critical Edition,* 687–88. A reading of biblical texts for the inheritance of the firstborn, as far as the patriarchs and leaders of the Israelite people are concerned, would of course find that the firstborn is almost never the elected or anointed.

25. Theodor, *Midrash Bereshit Rabba: Critical Edition,* 692, notes that Siloni is a prominent Palestinian philanthropical family. Cf. *Lev. Rab.* 5:4.

26. Theodor and Albeck, *Midrash Bereshit Rabba: Critical Edition,* 692. See Cohen, "Esau as Symbol," 244, where he translates from the Apolcalypse of Ezra, "From him sprang Jacob and Esau, but Jacob's hand held the heel of Esau from the beginning. The heel of the first age is Esau; the hand of the second is Jacob." Cohen continues, "Latin and Arabic versions of the book render the answer even more pointedly: 'For Esau is the end of this world, and Jacob is the beginning of the one which follows.'"

political-cultural setting, when no such reconciliation seems imminent. In these traditions the rabbis do not merely playfully imagine the essences of the battling siblings Jacob and Esau, but they simultaneously, and in all seriousness, construct and essentialize both rabbinic Jewishness and its other. For the rabbis, the biblical figure of Jacob, who becomes/is *Israel* (Gen. 32), reflects their own group identity. And Esau, who becomes/is *Rome*, provides the mirror image from which to reflect all that appears anathema to them.

The rabbis do not appeal to Jacob and Esau's biblical reconciliation. Instead, they grasp hold, perpetuate, and almost eternalize—and they certainly *internalize*—their difference(s). The rabbis cling to the hope that once again, the older will serve the younger, and on the heels of Roman domination, Israel will once again prevail. The rabbis anachronistically portray Jacob as a rabbinic Jew while in his mother's womb—reading the rabbinic present into the biblical past—as they foretell the future of Israel's triumph and redemption through this foundational story of their past. Jacob becomes a rabbinic Jew—both the progenitor and product, the father and son, of the rabbis—as the rabbis make themselves the continuing line of Israel.[27]

Rabbinic traditions about Jacob and Esau as fetuses expand the biblical passage in Genesis 25 that briefly mentions their prenatal struggle. According to the midrashim, Jacob and Esau struggle over matters of survival and national identity, perhaps equating the intensity of both struggles. Rabbinic Jewishness, no less than physical survival, is a matter of life and death. God's pronouncement about the future of Rebekah and Isaac's twins in Genesis 25 provides the rabbis with the opportunity to theorize the difference between Jacob and Esau, and the nations they have engendered: Israel and Rome. Both nations, both peoples, struggle together in Rebekah's womb, because, according to these rabbinic traditions, Jewishness and non-Jewishness begin in the womb.

I have focused at some length on the traditions about Jacob and Esau set forth in *Genesis Rabbah* because these siblings are construed, already as fetuses, as paradigms for Israel and Rome, provocatively exemplifying—and internalizing—rabbinic cultural articulations of "otherness" and selfhood. Since Jacob and Esau symbolize Israel and Rome on a national level, prenatal Jacob and Esau are not, or at least not only, exceptional or extraordinary; they are paradigmatic. Indeed, this is already alluded to when the rabbis remake Jacob into a rabbinic Jew already in the womb, since he is Israel's namesake; Jacob *is* Israel. Jacob's in utero rabbinic Jewishness, therefore, not only designates Jacob as extraordinary but further suggests that all *Israel* as Jewish already in the womb.

"Before I formed you in the womb": Rabbinic Articulations of Jewishness in the Womb

In contrast to the traditions discussed above, where rabbinic Jewishness is theorized in relation to its other, rabbinic traditions about the fetus discussed in

27. In *Genesis Rabbah* 63:6–8, Jacob is likened to a king, sage, prophet, and symbol for the redemption of Israel.

the following section theorize rabbinic Jewishness by itself, from within. We have already seen that *Genesis Rabbah* 63:6 applied the verse from Jeremiah, "Before I formed you in the womb I knew you, and before you came forth out of the womb I made you holy" (1:5), to Jacob in Rebekah's womb. Since Jacob symbolizes Israel on a collective level, the application of this verse to Jacob in the womb suggests that God knows all Israelite fetuses, not just famous fetuses. Indeed, another rabbinic tradition uses Psalm 139, "Your eyes have seen my unformed shape" to demonstrate that God knows the fetus, "famous" or not, in its mother's womb.[28] This more general application further indicates that, according to rabbinic narrative traditions, God knows all Israel already as fetuses.

This section focuses on rabbinic traditions that imagine Israelite fetuses as a collective at the birth of the nation—singing after crossing the Red Sea and receiving Torah at Sinai—along with rabbinic traditions that imagine that all Israel already as fetuses praise God and receive God's Torah. Again I suggest that these traditions provide insights into the rabbinic construction of Jewishness itself. These sources not only describe how the rabbis conceived the fetus in its mother's womb, but they also demonstrate how the rabbis used the fetus to articulate that which they themselves saw as essential to, and perhaps even constitutive of, rabbinic Jewishness.

In contrast to the rabbinic traditions about Jacob and Esau examined in the previous section, which were all recorded in one section of *Genesis Rabbah,* this section more broadly surveys rabbinic narratives about the fetus from a variety of rabbinic compilations of different time periods (third through eighth centuries CE) and geographical locations (Palestine and Babylonia). Despite some methodological difficulties inherent in such a broad survey, a distinct advantage gained from such an investigation is that it demonstrates that rabbinic traditions about the fetus, like the fetus itself, develop over time.

Singing Fetuses

One of the most pervasive rabbinic traditions about the fetus recorded in both *tannaitic* (ca. third century CE) and *amoraic* sources (ca. fourth through sixth centuries CE) teaches that after Israel crosses the Red Sea, the fetuses join in singing their God's praises. The *Mekhilta of R. Ishmael,* the *Mekhilta of R. Shimeon bar Yohai,* the *Tosefta,* the *Yerushalmi,* and the *Bavli,* as well as later midrashic compilations, all record a version of this teaching.[29] At a moment of national birth, when Israel ceases to be just Jacob as an individual and becomes a collective people, the rabbis consistently assert that the fetuses in their mothers' wombs praised God. Citing just the end of a lengthy discussion, the *Mekhilta of R. Ishmael (d'Shira* 1) states:[30] "R. Meir says: 'Even the fetuses in their mothers' wombs opened their mouths and sang before God. As it

28. See *y. Nid.* 3:3;50d; *Lev. Rab.* 14:8.

29. *Mekhilta of R. Ishmael (d'Shira* 1). See also *t. Sot.* 6:4; *y. Sot.* 5:6 (20c); *b. Sot.* 30b; *Mid. Tanh.* (Warsaw) *b'Shalakh* 11; *Mid. Tehillim* 8:5 and 68:14. Cf. *b. Ber.* 50a and *b. Ket.* 7b for partial parallels.

30. H. Horovitz and I. A. Rabin, *Mekhilta D'Rabbi Ishmael* (Jerusalem: Wahrmann, 1970), 120–21; Jacob Lauterbach, *Mekhilta of Rabbi Ishmael: A Critical Edition on the Basis of MSS and Early Editions with an English Translation, Introduction and Notes,* Vol. 2 (Philadelphia: JPS, 1933–35), 11–12.

is said, *Bless God in the congregations, the Lord from the womb* [*m'makor*][31] *of Israel* (Ps. 68:27)." R. Meir interprets *m'makor Israel* as "from the womb of Israel" and so the fetuses, Israel from the womb, opened up in song to praise God after the crossing of the sea. These collective Israelite fetuses recognize God as the God who delivered them out of Egypt, and thus they praise God for their deliverance.[32]

Beyond this often-repeated tradition about the collective Israelite fetuses of the generation of the Exodus praising God as their deliverer, Palestinian *amoraic* sources also indicate that God delivers all individual fetuses, if not from Egypt, at least from the womb. Indeed, the crossing of the sea itself has been interpreted as nothing short of a miraculous birth story on a national level. Ilana Pardes characterizes the parting of the Red Sea as the preeminent wonder God performs for the Israelites, explaining that the passage "marks the nation's first breath—out in the open air—and serves as a distinct reminder of the miraculous character of birth. Where there was nothing, a living creature emerges all of a sudden." She continues, "It is an intensified miracle: a wonder on a great scale. The two enormous walls of water, the ultimate breaking of the waters, and the exciting appearance of dry land all seem to represent a gigantic birth, a birth that is analogous to the creation of the world."[33] Thus, God "births" the Israelites out of Egypt, and, in like fashion, as the following traditions suggest, God brings forth every fetus from the womb.

Leviticus Rabbah 14:2 likens the womb to a prison, in which God cares for the fetus and from which God releases and "brings forth" the fetus.[34] *Leviticus Rabbah* 14:4 interprets Job 38:8, "Who shut up the sea with doors, when it broke forth and came out of the womb," to describe the gestation and birth, or delivery, of the fetus from its mother's womb, suggesting that just as God let the sea issue out of the womb, God brings forth the fetus from the womb. Furthermore, just as the collective Israelite fetuses praise God after crossing the sea, so too every fetus praises God from the womb. *Leviticus Rabbah* 4:7 interprets Psalms 103 and 104, which mention the word soul (*nefesh*) five times:[35] "R. Yehoshua ben Levi said: 'Five times the word soul is written here. Five times stands for the five worlds that a person sees. *Bless the Lord, O my soul: and all that is within me* [*k'ravai*] (Ps. 103:1). [This is said] at the time that one dwells in its mother's womb."[36] Psalm 103:1 is interpreted as, Bless the Lord, O my soul, from within the womb, which is understood as the first world one sees. Thus the fetus praises God already in the womb. *Leviticus Rabbah* 4:7 does not specify for what the fetus praises God, but Psalms 103 and 104 provide ample statements affirming God as the creator of everything. Furthermore, Psalm

31. Here *m'makor* is midrashically understood as from the womb. Cf. *t. Shab.* 9:14; *Sifra Tazria* 3:6; *Lev. Rab.* 14:9; *b. Nid.* 17b, 18a, 22a, 41b.

32. According to the *Bavli* (*Sot.* 30b), the fetuses see the Shekhinah after God turns their mothers' bellies into glass.

33. Ilana Pardes, *The Biography of Ancient Israel: National Narratives in the Bible* (Berkeley: University of California Press, 2000), 27–28.

34. The fourteenth chapter of *Leviticus Rabbah* deals almost exclusively with the creation and care of the fetus.

35. *Lev. Rab.* 4:7 comments upon Lev. 4:2, "If a soul shall sin through ignorance." Cf. *b. Ber.* 10a, where a similar tradition is applied to David.

36. The word *k'ravai* suggests while inside his mother, as in Gen. 25:22, "And the sons struggled within her [*b'kirbah*]." See M. Margulies in *Midrash Wayyikra Rabbah: A Critical Edition Based on Manuscripts and Geniza Fragments with Variants and Notes,* 2 vols. (New York: JTSA, 1993), 94–95.

103:4 states, "[Bless the Lord, O my soul . . .] Who redeems your life from the pit, who encircles you with loving kindness and compassion." Although *Leviticus Rabbah* 4:7 does not explicitly state that the fetus utters this specific verse while in its mother's womb, the biblical context and proximity of these verses suggest that, once again, God redeems or delivers all Israel from the womb, just as God delivered the Israelites—even those in the womb—from Egypt.

Finally, if, as Pardes asserts, the passage of the Israelites through the sea represents a moment of national birth, which recalls Creation, the collective Israelite fetuses, along with Israel, not only praise God as deliverer, but also God as creator. Pardes writes, "Accordingly, God is defined as the 'maker' of the nation [*am zu kanita*], a term that otherwise is used only in the context of the creation (Exod. 15:16)."[37] Numerous rabbinic traditions about procreation attribute the creation of the embryo to God, as will be discussed below. Here I mention just one tradition, which in the midst of a description of the fetus in its mother's womb, applies Psalm 139:16, "Your eyes have seen my unformed shape," to the fetus (*y. Nid.* 3:3;50d; *Lev. Rab.* 14:8).[38] The overall context of Psalm 139:13–17 teaches that God has created the fetus, with Psalm 139:13 stating, "For you have made [*atah kanita*] my insides." Since Psalm 139 uses the second-person "you," the rabbinic attachment of this psalm to the fetus suggests that the fetus itself acknowledges God as its creator. It is as if the fetus recites this psalm in the womb.[39] Furthermore, Psalm 139:9–10 states, "If I take the wings of the morning, and dwell in the uttermost parts of the sea, even there shall your hand lead me, and your right hand shall hold me." According to these verses, every fetus, not only those of the generation of the Exodus, acknowledges God as both its deliverer in the sea, or womb, and as its creator.

The rabbinic traditions discussed above indicate that fetuses, be they the collective Israelite fetuses of the Exodus generation or the individual fetus as imagined by the rabbis in their own time, praise God as their creator and deliverer. The fetuses recognize God as the God who creates and brings Israel forth, from Egypt and the womb. These traditions emphasize God's roles as deliverer and creator of Israel, and because they are projected onto the fetus in its mother's womb, they highlight the importance, the centrality of the belief in God as the creator and deliverer of Israel for the construction of rabbinic Jewishness. This belief, apparently, exists while one is still a fetus, and thus, in some way, this belief is not only essential, but also innate, to rabbinic Jewishness.

Studying Fetuses

Revelation at Sinai follows the Exodus not only in Israelite history but, according to rabbinic traditions, also in fetal development. The medieval tradition cited at the opening of this chapter has it that the collective Israelite fetuses who sing to

37. Pardes, *Biography of Ancient Israel*, 28.

38. Cf. *t. Nid.* 4:10; *b. Nid.* 25a, which describe the fetus's creation similarly, but apply Job 10:10–12.

39. Although this rabbinic tradition does not explicitly teach that the fetus utters this psalm in the womb, it seems a plausible reading given that *Lev. Rab.* 4:7, discussed above, teaches that the fetus recites Ps. 103 in the womb. Furthermore, since Ps. 139:13 and Exod. 15:16 both refer to God as "maker," it seems worthwhile to connect the two passages.

God after crossing the sea also bear witness to, and even participate in, the giving of Torah at Mt. Sinai. As the following rabbinic traditions demonstrate, all fetuses, not only the collective Israelite fetuses of the generation of the Exodus, receive Torah already in the womb.

As seen above in *Genesis Rabbah* 63:6, Jacob, already in the womb, sought to enter synagogues and houses of study. According to a rabbinic tradition first recorded in the *Babylonian Talmud* (or *Bavli*, ca. sixth century CE), the fetus not only desires to study Torah but actually learns Torah in the womb, only to be slapped by an angel at the moment of birth, causing it to forget what was learned.[40] *Bavli Niddah* 30b, in the context of an extended discourse about the fetus attributed to R. Simlai,[41] states, "And they teach it [the fetus] all the Torah in its entirety."[42] In order to substantiate this claim, the text first cites Proverbs 4:4, applying it to the fetus, "He taught me also, and said to me, Let your heart hold fast to my words: keep my commandments and live." Presumably this is a fitting proof text for the fetus because it teaches that if the fetus keeps the commandments, the fetus will live, that is, be born, and/or it is fitting because the previous verses state, "Hear, *you children*, the instruction of a father. . . . For I give you good doctrine, do not forsake *my torah*" (Prov. 4:1–2). The *Bavli* then brings another proof text, "And scripture says, *[As I was in the days of my youth] when the teaching [sod] of God was upon my tent* (Job 29:4)." This verse is also applied to the fetus in its "tent" or dwelling, which is to say, in its mother's womb.[43] But the *Bavli* then pauses to consider why this second verse was cited, because presumably one proof text would be enough to prove that the fetus learns Torah. The text answers, "You might have said that a prophet was the one who stated it; Come and learn, *When the teaching of God was upon my tent* (Job 29:4)." This answer is somewhat ambiguous, because according to rabbinic traditions, both Solomon and Job were prophets.[44] In either case, the concern is that one might think that only Solomon or Job knew Torah in the womb.[45] Thus the *Bavli* repeats Job 29:4, asserting that each fetus learns Torah, not just Solomon or Job.[46] Finally, although the text does not explicitly mention who teaches the fetus Torah, both proof texts suggest that the fetus receives Torah from God.

The motif about the fetus learning Torah is unique to the *Bavli*; it does not appear in *tannaitic* or *amoraic* Palestinian compilations. However, post-talmudic sources record a similar, though slightly modified tradition. *Midrash Tanhuma (Tazria)* asserts that the fetus receives Torah: "So this fetus, before he comes forth from his mother's womb, the Holy Blessed One commands him, 'From this you

40. For discussion of the Platonic elements of this tradition, see E. E. Urbach, *The Sages: Their Concepts and Beliefs*, trans. Israel Abrahams (Cambridge: Harvard University Press, 1987), 246–48.

41. R. Simlai was a second-generation *amora* who was born in Babylonia but taught in Israel.

42. The Hebrew states, "And they teach him [*oto*, sing. masc.] all the *Torah* in its entirety." It is unclear, at this point, who precisely teaches the fetus Torah, as the text simply states "they." I discuss the gender of the fetus below.

43. The *Bavli* (*Nid.* 30b) previously applied Job 29:3, "When his candle shone upon my head," to the fetus. Cf. *Lev. Rab.* 14:2 and 31:8.

44. Solomon is referred to as a prophet on *b. Sot.* 48b and Job on *b. Bab. Bat.* 15b.

45. Alternatively, or additionally, the concern might be that neither Prov. 4:4 or Job 29:2–4 explicitly refer, in their biblical context, to the womb.

46. Cf. *Mid. Tanhuma Tazria* 1 (Warsaw). Job 10:10–12 is used to describe the formation of the embryo in *Genesis Rabbah* 14:5 and *Lev. Rab.* 14:9, and it is applied to the fetus in *t. Nid.* 4:10 and *b. Nid.* 25a.

shall eat and from this you shall not eat and this is unclean to you.' And when he accepts upon himself in his mother's womb all of the commandments that are in the Torah, after that he is born. As scripture states, *When a woman conceives and gives birth to a male* (Lev. 12:2)."[47] According to this tradition, God first teaches, or commands, the fetus the instructions of *kashrut*, echoing the language of Deuteronomy 14. Furthermore, the fetus is born only after he has accepted all of the commandments in the Torah, and in contrast to *Bavli Niddah* 30b, here the fetus apparently does not forget what he has learned upon birth. The fetus, in other words, is born only once he has been modeled after the rabbis themselves, or molded in their own image.

The medieval text cited at the beginning of this chapter, where the collective Israelite fetuses accept the Torah at Mt. Sinai on their parents' and their own behalf, builds upon the *Bavli's* and *Tanhuma's* traditions that individual fetuses learn (or receive) Torah. By making the fetuses not only the guarantors for their parents but also the direct recipients of Sinaitic revelation, the rabbis mark the relationship between God and the fetus as covenantal. Even though this tradition explicitly initiates the Israelite fetuses of the generation of the Exodus and revelation into the covenant, the text implicitly reaches its medieval audiences—and beyond—as an affirmation of both their own present and future. The previous generations cannot guarantee the Torah's fulfillment any more than the biblical patriarchs could. The foundations of the Torah still rest upon the fetuses, from generation to generation.

Furthermore, this medieval tradition refashions the covenantal relationship as a covenant of equals, as it were. God no longer commands the ten "commandments," and Israel no longer pleads to be removed from God's awesome speech acts (Exod. 20:16). Now God *asks* the fetuses if they will fulfill God's Torah, and the fetuses, Israel, must agree. Although the tannaitic tradition about the Israelite fetuses singing to God at the crossing of the Red Sea and the medieval tradition about the Israelite fetuses at Mt. Sinai are surely separated by a considerable chronological gap, the two traditions might be brought together, such that the covenantal relationship between God and the fetus—and thus God and Israel—becomes clear. According to the tannaitic tradition, the singing fetuses at the crossing of the sea would have sung, "Who is like you, God among the gods?" (Exod. 15:11) and in reciprocal fashion, at the end of the medieval tradition about the fetuses receiving God's Torah, God states, "Happy are you, Israel: Who is like you?" (Deut. 33:29).

47. *Mid. Tanh. Tazria* 2 (Buber); cf. *Midrash Tanh. Tazria* 1 (Warsaw). This midrash interprets Lev. 12:2 in light of Ps. 139:5, midrashically understood as "You have created me after and before." The text offers multiple interpretations of "after" and "before." In this section, the text imagines Adam saying, "*After* the Holy Blessed One created the beasts and living things, God created me?" Thus the text tries to understand why God created Adam after the beasts and other living creatures. The answer offered is that, presumably, God was busy commanding Adam, and so too all fetuses, on the laws concerning which living creatures they were permitted to eat and which were unclean. Furthermore, God instructs Adam and every fetus all the mitzvot in the Torah, and after that, they are born. Why Lev. 12:2 proves this lesson remains somewhat unclear. Perhaps this tradition is not directly connected to that verse, and it is stated here because the rabbis are interpreting Ps. 139:5 with its mention of "after and before." Perhaps Lev. 12:2 is being interpreted as, "When a woman conceives and [after] gives birth to a male." I have referred to the fetus as "he" because this tradition specifically comments on Lev. 12:2, which is concerned with the birth of a male child.

The rabbinic traditions set forth in this section demonstrate that Exodus and revelation, or the belief in a God who delivered Israel out of Egypt and then delivered the Torah to Israel, are, somewhat obviously, fundamental to the construction of rabbinic Jewishness. Less obvious, however, is the provocative result of the rabbinic projection of these collective—and timeless—events onto the fetus in its mother's womb: belief in a God who delivered Israel out of Egypt and gave the Torah to Israel is not only fundamental to rabbinic Jewishness, it is innate—inborn—in every Jew.[48]

In contrast to rabbinic traditions about Jacob and Esau discussed in the first section of this chapter, where Jewishness is articulated in opposition to non-Jewishness, the traditions just examined offer an internalized conception of Jewishness on its own terms. Jewishness is not defined by what it is not as much as by what it is. Here Jewishness is defined solely by the foundational affirmation of the covenantal relationship between God and Israel, which begins in the womb.

Conclusion: Conceiving Israel

Rabbinic narratives about the fetus, both those that theorize Jewishness in relation to its other and those that articulate Jewishness by itself, provide significant insight into the rabbinic construction of Jewishness. Taken together, these traditions set forth both quintessentially rabbinic Jewish practices and essential rabbinic Jewish beliefs. Rabbinic traditions about the fetus enhance contemporary scholarly endeavors to reconstruct rabbinic Jewishness because they celebrate the importance of both internal beliefs and external practices—even projecting them inside—to the construction of rabbinic Jewishness.

When rabbinic sources portray the fetus as righteous, circumcised, wishing to enter synagogues and houses of study, observing *mitzvot*, fasting on Yom Kippur,[49] and according to later traditions, studying Torah, cognizant of the laws of *kashrut*, accepting the Ten Commandments and even all the commandments in the Torah, the rabbis construct the fetus as Jewish. Part of what makes the fetus Jewish is its (imagined) performance of these Jewish practices, thus highlighting the importance of these practices for rabbinic Jewishness, even internalizing them. However, the (imagined) performance of these practices remains only part of what makes the fetus Jewish. The rabbis further construct the fetus as Jewish by projecting the covenantal relationship between God and Israel onto the fetus. The fetus ostensibly performs such Jewish practices because of, and to express, Israel's covenantal relationship with God.

48. When the rabbis imagine the collective Israelite fetuses singing after crossing the sea and accepting Torah at Sinai, there seems little reason to believe that this collective would not include female fetuses—had the rabbis asked themselves or been asked. Although the *Bavli* and *Tanhuma* traditions discussed above seem to take for granted that the fetus learning Torah is a male fetus, it is clear that, according to the book of Exodus, women sing to God at the sea (15:20–21); and although one might legitimately ask where women were at Sinai, when the rabbis do pose this question to themselves in later traditions, they answer that women were there, with their fetuses and sucklings. See *Ex. Rab.* 28:6 and *PRE* 40. Of course, women are there *because* of their fetuses and sucklings.

49. See *y. Yoma* 8:4;45a and *b. Yoma* 82b-83b.

Although the previous section of this chapter demonstrated the centrality of the Exodus from Egypt and revelation of Torah for the construction of rabbinic Jewishness, one further central belief of rabbinic Jewishness is repeatedly articulated in rabbinic narratives about the fetus: the belief in a God who created the world—and Israel—and who continues to do so. As mentioned in the beginning of this chapter, in the Hebrew Bible, God controls fertility; God grants pregnancy; God creates the embryo. Rabbinic traditions concur. Quite succinctly and unequivocally, *Genesis Rabbah* 73:4 asserts, "Three keys are in the hands of the Holy Blessed One: the key to the grave [resurrection], rain, and the womb."[50] Although this midrash comments upon Genesis 30:22, "And God remembered Rachel and opened her womb," the rabbis interpret this verse to teach that God opens all wombs. The rabbis have learned that God holds the key to all wombs directly from scripture. In fact, except for God's involvement in biblical pregnancies, the Bible lacks any explicit theory of precisely how pregnancy occurs. Of course, sexual intercourse is often—but not always—alluded to or mentioned, but the Hebrew Bible lacks any explicit mention of the substances involved in bringing about pregnancy. Rabbinic sources record varying theories of conception, with significant overlap—and certain divergence from—Greco-Roman theories. However, what is common to all rabbinic narratives that theorize procreation is God's involvement in the process. To cite just one example, *Leviticus Rabbah* 14:9 states: "The womb of the woman is always full of blood and from it [blood] goes forth to the source of her menstrual flow. And by the will of the Holy Blessed One, a drop of white falls into it [the womb] and immediately, the embryo is created. [This may be compared] to milk that was put in a bowl. If one puts a curdling agent in it, it coagulates and stands. And if not, it moves and shakes."[51] This tradition imagines that God causes the man's semen to enter the womb, where it interacts with the woman's blood, causing the creation of the embryo. Thus God is not only instrumental for the conception of famous biblical heroes, but God continues to create each embryo.

Furthermore, the creation of each embryo recalls the creation of the world—Creation itself. In a striking parallel, *Genesis Rabbah* 4:8 states:

> *And God called the firmament heaven/shamayim* (Gen. 1:8). . . . R. Yitzhak said, [*shamayim* means] to be laden with water. [This may be compared] to milk that was placed in a bowl. Before one drop of a curdling agent descends into it, it shakes. When one drop of a curdling agent descends into it, immediately it curdles and stands still. So [scripture says], *The pillars of heaven shake* (Job 26:11) but the curdling agent was placed in them, *And there was evening and morning the second day* (Gen. 1:8). This is supported by Rav's statement, "The works [of God] were liquid and became solid on the second day."[52]

50. Cf. *b. Tan.* 2a; *b. Sanh.* 113a; and *Deut. Rab.* 7:6. See also *b. Bekh.* 45a.

51. Margulies, *Midrash Wayyikra Rabbah: A Critical Edition*, 316–17.

52. Theodor and Albeck, *Midrash Bereshit Rabba: Critical Edition*, 31. Cf. *Genesis Rabbah* 4:2, "At the time that God said, *Let there be a firmament in the midst of the waters* (Gen. 1:6), a drop of the middle waters became solid and

Just as an embryo comes to be, so too, the heavens came to be. Both began as liquid, and both become solidified. The creation of an embryo recalls and repeats the creation of the cosmos. Both are created from a "drop," which once placed by the will of God into the cosmos or into the womb, acts as a curdling agent upon previously unsolidified matter. Rabbinic traditions about procreation are thus imbued with cosmic significance. A later rabbinic tradition makes this explicit: "The creation of the embryo is like the creation of the world because a person is a small world" (*Tanh. Pikudei* 3).[53] Rabbinic traditions bring together the macrocosm (cosmos) and the microcosm (embryo), and attribute the creation of both to God.

In addition to internalizing the rabbinic belief in a God who delivered Israel out of Egypt and gave the Torah to Israel, rabbinic narratives about the fetus internalize—and eternalize—Creation. The fetus not only serves as a unique vehicle for conceiving Jewishness, it also provides a bridge between the biblical and rabbinic "worlds."

The Jewishness the rabbis ascribe to the fetus reaches beyond exceptional biblical figures as the rabbis locate the very beginnings of Jewishness in the womb for all Israel, rendering all fetuses not only Jewish, but also extraordinary—like their biblical ancestors. The very distinction between "famous" fetuses and not-famous fetuses, between the collective Israelite fetuses of the past and fetuses of the present, collapses because every fetus is created by God, delivered by God, and given God's Torah.

WORKS CITED

Bakhos, Carol. "Figuring (Out) Esau: The Rabbis and Their Others." *Journal of Jewish Studies* 58, 2 (2007): 250–62.

Callaway, Mary. *Sing, O Barren One: A Study in Comparative Midrash*. SBL Dissertation Series 91. Atlanta: Scholars Press, 1986.

Cohen, Gerson D. "Esau as Symbol in Early Medieval Thought." Reprinted in *Studies in the Variety of Rabbinic Cultures*, 243–71. Philadelphia: JPS, 1991.

Duden, Barbara. *Disembodying Women: Perspectives on Pregnancy and the Unborn*. Translated by Lee Hanoicki. Cambridge: Harvard University Press, 1993.

———. "The Fetus on the Farther Shore: Toward a History of the Unborn." In *Fetal Subjects/Feminist Positions*. Edited by Lynn M. Morgan and Meredith W. Michaels. Philadelphia: University of Pennsylvania Press, 1999.

Frymer-Kensky, Tikva. *In the Wake of the Goddesses: Women, Culture, and Biblical Transformation of Pagan Myth*. New York: Free Press, 1992.

Horovitz, H., and I. A. Rabin. *Mekhilta D'Rabbi Ishmael*. Reprint. Jerusalem: Wahrmann, 1970.

Kalimi, Isaac. "'He Was Born Circumcised': Some Midrashic Sources, Their Concept, Roots and Presumably Historical Context." *Zeitschrift für die Neutestamentliche Wissenschaft und die Kunde der Alteren Kirche* 93, 1–2 (2002): 1–12.

---

the lower heavens and the water of the upper heavens were made. Rav said, the works of God were as liquid and on the second day they were made solid."

53. The context of this midrash is the construction of the *mishkan*, which is equated with the creation of the world and the creation of humanity. Just as the embryo develops from the navel, the world develops from the "founding-stone" just below the *mishkan*.

Lauterbach, Jacob. *Mekhilta of Rabbi Ishmael: A Critical Edition on the Basis of MSS and Early Editions with an English Translation, Introduction and Notes.* 3 vols. Philadelphia: JPS, 1933–35.
Mandelbaum, Bernard. *Pesikta de Rav Kahana: According to an Oxford Manuscript with Variants, Commentary and Introduction.* 2 vols. New York: JTSA, 1962.
Margulies, M. *Midrash Wayyikra Rabbah: A Critical Edition Based on Manuscripts and Geniza Fragments with Variants and Notes.* 2 vols. New York: JTSA, 1993.
Marmorstein, A. "Quelques problemes de l'ancienne apologetique juive." *Revue des Etudes Juives* 68 (1914): 161–73.
Morgan, Lynn M., and Meredith W. Michaels, eds. *Fetal Subjects/Feminist Positions.* Philadelphia: University of Pennsylvania Press, 1999.
Neusner, Jacob. *From Enemy to Sibling: Rome and Israel in the First Century of Western Civilization.* The Ben Zion Bokser Memorial Lecture, Queens College, New York, 1986.
Pardes, Ilana. *The Biography of Ancient Israel: National Narratives in the Bible.* Berkeley: University of California Press, 2000.
Simkins, Ronald. *Creator and Creation: Nature in the Worldview of Ancient Israel.* Peabody, Mass.: Hendrickson, 1994.
Stern, Sacha. *Jewish Identity in Early Rabbinic Writings.* Leiden, Netherlands: Brill, 1994.
Strack, H. L., and G. Stemberger. *Introduction to the Talmud and Midrash.* Translated by Markus Bockmuehl. Minneapolis: Fortress Press, 1992.
Theodor, Jehuda, and Hanoch Albeck. *Midrash Bereshit Rabba: Critical Edition with Notes and Commentary.* 3 vols. 2nd ed. Jerusalem: Wahrmann, 1965.
Urbach, E. E. *The Sages: Their Concepts and Beliefs.* Translated by Israel Abrahams. Cambridge: Harvard University Press, 1987.

A Prophet Emerging: Fetal Narratives in Islamic Literature

Daniel C. Peterson

The Qur'an regards ordinary human conception, gestation, and birth as miraculous signs of God. In what are traditionally considered the first two verses of the Qur'an revealed to the Prophet Muhammad, God is identified as the agent who forms the fetus: "Recite, in the name of your Lord, who created [*khalaqa*], created man from a clot of blood [*min 'alaqin*]."[1] Using a verb (*khalaqa*) that is frequently employed to describe God's action as creator of the universe, the Qur'an says that God creates humans "in stages" (*atwaran*).[2] "He creates you in the wombs of your mothers, creation after creation [*khalqan ba'da khalqin*]."[3]

However, in addition to echoing the original creation of the universe, the miraculous development of the fetus also foreshadows the resurrection of the body at the end of time.[4] The human body will be "created" again, when it is nothing but bones and dust.[5] "Were we exhausted by the first creation? Yet they are in doubt about a second creation!"[6] "Do they not see that God, who created the heavens and the earth, and was not wearied thereby, is able to bring the dead to life?"[7] When Muhammad's Meccan critics demand that he tell

1. Qur'an 96:1–2. All translations from the Qur'an are mine.
2. Qur'an 71:14.
3. Qur'an 39:6.
4. In addition to the other passages cited here, the creation of the fetus is very clearly used as a parallel to the resurrection at Qur'an 22:5–6; 36:77–82; 75:37–40; 86:5–8. See the treatment of Edvard Lehmann and Johan Pedersen, "Der Beweis für die Auferstehung im Koran," *Der Islam* 5 (1914): 54–61.
5. Qur'an 13:5; 17:49–51, 98–99; 32:10; 34:7; 36:77–82.
6. Qur'an 50:15.
7. Qur'an 46:33.

them who will bring them back after they are dead, he is instructed to answer them, "He who originated you the first time."[8]

The Qur'anic argument is remarkably similar to that advanced by St. Justin Martyr several centuries earlier, in his first *Apology*:

> We expect to receive again our own bodies, though they be dead and cast into the earth, for we maintain that with God nothing is impossible.
>
> And to any thoughtful person would anything appear more incredible, than, if we were not in the body, and some one were to say that it was possible that from a small drop of human seed bones and sinews and flesh be formed into a shape such as we see? . . . But as at first you would not have believed it possible that such persons could be produced from the small drop, and yet now you see them thus produced, so also judge ye that it is not impossible that the bodies of men, after they have been dissolved, and like seeds resolved into earth, should in God's appointed time rise again and put on incorruption.[9]

Little if anything in the Qur'an suggests that the conception, gestation, and birth of the Prophet Muhammad himself were any more miraculous than is the everyday taken-for-granted wonder of the human fetus. This is not surprising: when Muhammad was asked to produce a miracle, he responded that the Qur'an was his miracle.[10] (The Arabic word that is used to denote the verses of the Qur'an [*aya*; pl. *ayat*] also means "sign" or "miracle.") He is said to have denied the ability to perform miracles otherwise; his only supernatural achievement was the revelation, through him, of the holy book of Islam.[11]

Yet the Qur'an informs its audience that the Prophet Muhammad was sent *rahmatan li-al-'alamin*, "as a mercy to the worlds."[12] In that light, and in view of his absolutely central role both in formative Islamic history and in Islamic piety throughout the intervening centuries, it is also not surprising that, very early, legends of spectacular miracles began to accumulate around the biography of the Prophet, not excluding the time that elapsed between his conception and his birth.

8. Qur'an 17:51. The parallel between God's "creation" of the human fetus, his re-creation of the human body from bones and dust at the resurrection, and his original creation of the universe is rendered closer by the fact that, as I have argued elsewhere, the divine creation of the universe no more involves *creatio ex nihilo* than does the origination of the fetus. See D. C. Peterson, "Does the Qur'an Teach Creation *Ex Nihilo*?" in *By Study and Also by Faith: Essays in Honor of Hugh W. Nibley*, ed. J. M. Lundquist and S. D. Ricks (Salt Lake City, Utah: Deseret Book and the Foundation for Ancient Research and Mormon Studies, 1990), 1:584–610; and D. C. Peterson, "Creation," in *Encyclopaedia of the Qur'an*, ed. J. D. McAuliffe et al. (Leiden, Netherlands: Brill, 2001–2006), 1:472–480.

9. Justin Martyr, *The First Apology*, 1:18–19, as translated in Alexander Roberts and James Donaldson, *Ante-Nicene Fathers* (Peabody, Mass.: Hendrickson, 1995), 1:169.

10. Qur'an 17:90; compare 6:37.

11. Josef Horovitz, "Zur Muhammadlegende," *Der Islam* 5 (1914): 41–55; translated as "The Growth of the Mohammad Legend," *Moslem World* 10 (1920): 49–58. Also Adam Mez, "Geschichte der Wunder Muhammads," *Verhandlungen des. 2. Internationalen Kongresses für Allgemeine Religionsgeschichte* (Basel, Switzerland: Helbing und Lichtenhahn, 1905); Arthur Jeffrey, *Reader on Islam* (The Hague: Mouton, 1962), 309–30.

12. Qur'an 21:107.

The so-called *sira* ("biography") that was composed by Ibn Ishaq, who died in roughly 768 CE, and was then edited by Ibn Hisham (d. ca. 830) has served, on the whole, as the basis for all subsequent biographies of Muhammad. It is evident that miraculous stories had already attached themselves to the Prophet in great profusion by that very early period, between roughly a century and two centuries after his death in 632 CE.[13] The early twentieth-century British orientalist Sir William Muir informed the readers of his biography of the Prophet that he was "passing over, as fabulous and unworthy of credit, the marvelous incidents related of the gestation of the infant."[14] Our method in this essay will be strikingly different, for we have a different aim in mind. However problematic the materials we will be discussing may be for retrieving the Muhammad of history, they are extremely useful for obtaining a portrait of what has, at least in some circles and eras, passed as the Muhammad of faith—and, thus, they provide a window into the heart and soul of Islamic piety. Muhammad's great modern Western biographer, W. Montgomery Watt, has justly observed that

> There is . . . a large number of stories of what might be called a theological character. It is almost certain that they are not true in the realistic sense of the secular historian, for they purport to describe facts to which we might reasonably have expected some reference at later periods of Muhammad's life; but there is no such reference. Yet they certainly express something of the significance of Muhammad for believing Muslims, and in that sense are true for them and a fitting prologue to the life of their prophet. Perhaps they might also be regarded as expressing what anyone "with eyes to see" might have seen had he been there.[15]

The Antemortal Light of Muhammad

Many Muslims believe that Muhammad's coming was prophesied in various of the world's sacred books—including the prophecy in which Jesus promises his disciples that, following his death, they will be granted a "Comforter."[16] With regard to that particular text, Muslim apologists frequently contend that the Greek word *parakletos* ("paraclete," "comforter") should actually read *periklytos* ("famous," "renowned"). They then connect that term with the name *Muhammad* and its variant *Ahmad*, both of which come from a triconsonantal Arabic verbal root (*hmd*) that connotes fame and praise.

13. There are many modern biographies of Muhammad, a few of which are cited in the notes to this article. Perhaps not the worst among them is D. C. Peterson, *Muhammad: Prophet of God* (Grand Rapids, Mich.: Eerdmans, 2007).

14. William Muir, *The Life of Mohammed from Original Sources*, rev. ed. (Edinburgh: John Grant, 1912), 4.

15. W. M. Watt, *Muhammad at Mecca* (Oxford: Clarendon, 1953), 33–34. Watt then proceeds to quote at length, on pages 34–38, from the biography of Ibn Ishaq/Ibn Hisham, the familiar stories of the miraculous prosperity of the infant Muhammad's wet nurse, the shaman-like "splitting" of the young Muhammad's chest, and the youthful Muhammad's encounter with the Syrian monk Bahira.

16. John 14:16.

Common Muslim belief also has it that Muhammad actually lived before his birth. The medieval Turkish poet ʿAshiq Pasha, for example, referred to Muhammad's primordial existence, declaring that when "Adam was still dust and clay—Ahmad was a prophet then."[17]

Islamic tradition has not, however, been content merely to assert Muhammad's premortal existence. It has ornamented that bare doctrine with a profusion of rich detail in glorification of the Prophet. "One of the central themes (if not the central theme) of mystical prophetology [in Islam]," wrote the late Annemarie Schimmel, "is that of the Light of Muhammad, *nur Muhammad*."[18] The identification of the Prophet with light came naturally. Muhammad's poet Hassan b. Thabit said that, during the battle of Badr, the Prophet's face shone like the full moon (Arabic *badr*).[19] Muhammad is identified in the Qur'an as a *sirajun munirun*, "a shining lamp."[20] "O people of the Book," God is represented as saying, "our messenger has come to you to clarify to you much of what you used to conceal of the Book and to forgive much. A light has come to you from God, and a clear book."[21] Obviously, the "clear book" was the Qur'an, but many Muslims came very soon to believe that the "light" was Muhammad himself. Moreover, one of the most common epithets applied by believers to Muhammad is *nur al-huda* ("the light of guidance").[22]

But such notions were expanded to literally cosmic proportions in the centuries that followed his death. Already in the eighth century, the theologian Muqatil was interpreting the "lamp" in the Qur'an's famous "Light Verse" as referring to Muhammad: "God is the light of the heavens and the earth. The similitude of his light is like a niche in which is a lamp. The lamp is in a glass, and the glass is, as it were, a shining star kindled from a blessed tree, an olive tree neither eastern nor western, whose oil would almost shine out even if fire did not touch it. Light upon light. God leads to his light whom he will."[23]

Among the songs most frequently sung at Indo-Pakistani *qawwalis* (gatherings for religious music), is a Persian ghazal attributed to the medieval Indian poet and musician Amir Khusraw. The poem begins *Namidanam che manzil bud shabgahi ki man budam* ("I do not know which place it was, the nightly place in which I was") and then, after describing a nighttime event at which God himself served as the cupbearer, concludes by reporting that *Muhammad shamʿ-i mahfil bud* ("Muhammad was the candle there"). Commenting on the passage, Annemarie Schimmel remarks that "the Prophet Muhammad is the candle of the assembly, *shamʿ-i mahfil*, the light that illuminates the darkness of this world in which the

17. A. Schimmel, *And Muhammad Is His Messenger: The Veneration of the Prophet in Islamic Piety* (Chapel Hill: University of North Carolina Press, 1985), 101, citing Ananiasz Zajączkowski, *Poezje stroficzne ʿAsiq-pasa* (Warsaw, 1967), 8.

18. Ibid., 123.

19. Ibid., 124.

20. Qur'an 33:46.

21. Qur'an 5:15.

22. Schimmel, *And Muhammad Is His Messenger*, 124.

23. Qur'an 24:35. For Muqatil, see Schimmel, *And Muhammad Is His Messenger*, 124.

listeners are gathered, the radiant candle around which human hearts throng like spellbound moths."[24]

A prayer attributed to Muhammad that, as Schimmel puts it, "has belonged to the most precious treasures of the faithful for century after century," nicely illustrates the Prophet's connection with light: "O God, place light in my heart, and light in my soul, light upon my tongue, light in my eyes and light in my ears, place light at my right, light at my left, light behind me and light before me, light above me and light beneath me. Place light in my nerves, and light in my flesh, light in my blood, light in my hair and light in my skin! Give me light, increase my light, make me light!"[25]

The Iraqi Sufi Sahl al-Tustari (d. 896) taught that Muhammad, in the form of a column of light, was the first creation of God. "The very first thing that Allah Almighty ever created was my soul," says a statement attributed to Muhammad. And, elsewhere, he is supposed to have said that, "First of all things, the Lord created my mind."[26] Adam, in turn, was created from the crystallized light of Muhammad, which is the source for the light of all the prophets, as well as of this world itself, the world to come, and the heavenly kingdom.[27] Similar notions continue to be taught in Muslim circles even today: "Verily, before your Lord made any other thing, He created from His own Light the light of your Prophet, and that Light rested *haithu mashaAllah*, where Allah willed it to rest. And at that time there existed [n]aught else—not the Preserved Tablets, not the Pen, not Heaven nor Hell, not the Angelic Host, not the heavens nor the earth; there was no sun, no moon, no star, no jinn nor man nor angel—none was as yet created, only this Light."[28]

It is difficult in this context not to think of the *logos* theology in the first chapter of the Gospel of John: "In the beginning was the Logos, and the Logos was with God, and the Logos was God. This [Logos] was in the beginning with God. Everything came to be through him, and without him nothing came to be that came to be. In him was life, and the life was the light of human beings. And the light shone in the darkness, and the darkness did not comprehend it."[29]

One wonders whether rivalry with the Christians' very high Johannine Christology played a role in motivating the elaboration of the accounts of the light of Muhammad that we are discussing here. Moreover, when it is said that God "created from His own Light the light of [the] Prophet," one is forcefully reminded of such Christian texts as the fourth-century Nicene Creed, which holds, in part, that the Second Person of the classical Trinity was "born of the

24. Schimmel, *And Muhammad Is His Messenger*, 123–24.

25. C. E. Padwick, *Muslim Devotions* (London: SPCK, 1961), 212. Schimmel's characterization can be found in *And Muhammad Is His Messenger*, 124.

26. Both statements are cited at H. A. Adil, *Muhammad, The Messenger of Islam: His Life and Prophecy* (Washington, D.C.: Islamic Supreme Council of America, 2002), 29.

27. See G. Böwering, "The Prophet of Islam: The First and the Last Prophet," in *The Message of the Prophet* (Islamabad: Government of Pakistan, 1979), 48–60.

28. Adil, *Muhammad*, 1.

29. John 1:1–5 (my translation).

Father before all ages, light from light, true God from true God."[30] (One is also reminded of the emanation of the *Nous*, or Intellect, in Plotinian Neoplatonism.) Of course, whereas the creed insists that the Son was "born, not made," and that he was "true God," "consubstantial with the Father," Muslim tradition is forbidden by its rigorous monotheism and by the Qur'an's teaching that God "neither begets nor is he begotten" from abolishing the distinction between God and even his most exalted creation.[31] Muhammad remains a creature, not a divine son, though the accounts come remarkably close in some cases to treating him as a kind of deity.

In any event, Muhammad's status as the first of God's creations was and is extremely high: "As Muhammad was the Light, his station in the Lord's Presence was an exalted one. His inner truth is of the truth of all truths, and his name is the greatest name, it combines all divine names and attributes within itself. His spiritual reality is from the light of the divine essence itself. His mind is from the light of the names of divine essence. His heart is from the light of all the divine attributes combined. His self is from the light of the names of all divine actions."[32]

"Were it not for you," says God to Muhammad in one of the so-called *hadith qudsi*, "I would not have created the universe."[33] "It is for him," says a divine voice to a foreign ruler on the night of Muhammad's birth, "that all eighteen thousand worlds were created, that the whole universe was called into being."[34] Some say that the creation of the light of Muhammad occurred three hundred and sixty thousand years before the creation of the world; others say that only God knows how much time elapsed.[35]

> It is narrated that the Holy Prophet Muhammad asked the angel Jibra'il, "How long is it since you were created?" The angel answered, "Oh, Rasulullah [Messenger of God], I don't know the number of years, all I know is that every seventy thousand years a tremendous light shines forth from behind the Canopy of the Divine Throne; since the time of my creation this light has appeared twelve thousand times." "Do you know what this light is?" asked Muhammad. "No, I don't know," said the angel. "It is the light of my soul in the world of the spirit," replied the Holy Prophet. Consider then how immense a number it must be if 70,000 is multiplied by 12,000![36]

30. Translations mine. The relevant Greek and Latin texts are given in P. Schaff and D. S. Schaff, eds., *The Creeds of Christendom*, 6th ed., 3 vols. (Grand Rapids: Baker Book House, 1983), 2:57

31. See Qur'an 112:3.

32. Adil, *Muhammad*, 26. This book is a very convenient and accessible compendium of traditional pious Muslim narratives about Muhammad, already translated into English, so I have used it extensively in retelling the stories here.

33. H. A. Adil, *Muhammad*, 95. A *hadith qudsi* occupies something of a middle ground between the Qur'an, which represents the *ipsissima verba* of God himself, and the ordinary *hadith*, which, though authoritative, represents merely the (presumably inspired) judgment of Muhammad or one of his "companions." The *hadith qudsi* is regarded as containing God's own thoughts, but not necessarily in God's own language.

34. Adil, *Muhammad*, 29.

35. Ibid., 3, 8.

36. Ibid., 8.

God is also said to have created a tree from the light of Muhammad, "the pride of the world," that is called "the tree of certainty," and to have placed the light upon that tree in the form of a veil of white pearls. Subsequently, however, God turned his gaze upon that light, and, from shame, the light began to perspire under the gaze of the Lord. From the sweat of various parts of the light were then created the angels, the divine throne, and court, the tablets of the celestial Book and the pen by which divine decrees are inscribed within it, the sun, the moon, the stars, the prophets and the messengers, the holy martyrs, the learned men of religion, the righteous saints, the various worlds and what is contained within them, and even the lowest portions of hell.[37]

When it came time for Adam to be created, God sent the archangel Gabriel (*Jibril, Jibra'il*) to the spot of ground where Muhammad would someday be buried, to take from it a piece of clay that God then formed into something like a white pearl. When this was completed, it was placed upon Adam's forehead. Adam heard a sound like the rushing of waters coming from the pearl, and he inquired what caused it. He was told that it was the sound of praise for the future prophet Muhammad, and that the light pearl was to be passed down through a pure line of his posterity until the actual advent of the Prophet.[38] From that time until the end of his life, the luminous pearl of the light of Muhammad shone forth upon Adam's forehead, and it was constantly accompanied by the adoration of angels.[39]

Adam and his wife Eve were mindful of their responsibility to pass the light of Muhammad on through their posterity, and they always approached marital relations in the strictest condition of ritual purity. However, time and again, when Eve conceived a child, the light of Muhammad remained upon Adam's forehead. It was only when she conceived Seth that the light was transferred to her forehead, so that she knew that Muhammad's line had been commenced. And when Seth was born, she instantly recognized the light of Muhammad shining on her new baby's brow.

Seth, too, took upon himself the covenant to make certain that the light of Muhammad was passed only to pure and undefiled women. And this was the pattern thereafter. The light would shine from the forehead of the male heir until his wife conceived his successor. During her pregnancy, the light would shine forth from her forehead until the birth of her destined child.

Seth passed the light of Muhammad on to his son Enos, and eventually it reached Noah, who, in his turn, conveyed it to his son, Shem. Eventually, it reached Abraham, and was transferred from that patriarch to his eldest son, Ishmael, who was born to Abraham by the slave woman Hagar.[40] Ishmael passed it on to his

37. Ibid., 30, 31. The origin of the five canonical daily Muslim prayers is also connected with this stage of Muhammad's antemortal existence, although other accounts connect it with the miraculous *mi'raj* or ascension into heaven that is ascribed to him during his mortal life. For the latter, see Ibn Ishaq, *The Life of Muhammad*, trans. A. Guillaume (Oxford: Oxford University Press, 2002), 112–14.

38. Another account says that the light of Muhammad was always accompanied by a sound like the buzzing of bees, which represented its continual invocation of God. Adil, *Muhammad*, 52.

39. At this point, I'm drawing from Adil, *Muhammad*, 35–36, 41–45, 52, 55, 93.

40. Abraham's wife, Sarah, had hoped that she would be able to produce her husband's heir and was jealous when the honor went to Hagar instead. But Sarah was granted Isaac as a consolation.

second son, Kedar, who is typically thought of as the father of the northern Arabian tribes, and, with the passage of centuries, the light of Muhammad came to pre-Islamic Arabia in the generations just prior to the commencement of the final revelation, where, among others, it was transmitted by Mudar to Ilyas. Finally, it arrived to Muhammad's paternal grandfather, ʿAbd al-Mutallib. God favored him because of the light and, for his sake, sent rain upon the parched land around Mecca. Furthermore, also because of the light, everyone loved and respected him and sought to do him favors. It is said that ʿAbd al-Mutallib would go to the Kaʿba and pray fervently, imploring God to bless him and his people on account of the light of Muhammad that was on his forehead.

ʿAbd al-Mutallib transmitted the light of Muhammad on to his son, fittingly named ʿAbdullah ("servant/slave of God").[41] It is said that infidel scholars in Syria—presumably Christians—recognized that the father of the final prophet had been born by means of the mantle of the Prophet John (the Baptist), which they possessed. It was the robe in which John had been martyred, and it was still marked with his blood. In their scriptures, they had located a prophecy informing them that, whenever this long-dried blood moistened again, that would be the sign that the last of the prophets was born in Mecca. Every morning, they would carefully inspect the mantle, and, one morning, they found that the sign had been given.

With each passing day, as ʿAbdullah grew up, the light of Muhammad grew stronger in him, and his beauty and his virtue increased. He saw many visions signaling his important role as one in the chosen line, and divine voices addressed him frequently. Whenever he sat down beneath a dry, barren fig tree, the tree would immediately spring back to life, blossoming with leaves so that he was protected from the harsh Arabian sun. And whenever he rose to depart, the tree would instantly die and wither away again. He was protected from error, temptation, and sin by angelic interventions. Whenever he thought of entering the Kaʿba, which had been founded by Abraham but had since been polluted by idolatry, the idols within the structure would cry out to him, "Oh ʿAbdullah! Beware, do not come near us! The light of the Pride of the Worlds is in your safekeeping, it is the light of the Prophet of the last times, and through his hand all idolatry will be wiped out—he will destroy us and all our worshippers!"[42]

Finally, ʿAbdullah reached the age of twenty-five. He was in the prime of his manhood, and the light of Muhammad glowed upon his forehead as it had upon the foreheads of his fathers before him all the way back to Adam. Soon, word of ʿAbdullah's remarkable character and beauty reached the ears of a man by the name of Wahb, "the leading man of the Banu Zuhrah in age and eminence at that time," who lived in a town called Yathrib (later Medina) and had a daughter named Amina.[43] Wahb set out to Mecca to see this fabled youth. In the meantime, ʿAbdullah had set forth from Mecca to go hunting.

41. The stories relating to ʿAbdullah are conveniently summarized in Adil, *Muhammad*, 57–62.

42. Adil, *Muhammad*, 60. I have altered Adil's transliteration of ʿAbdullah's name to bring it into conformity with my own.

43. The characterization of Wahb's status comes from Al-Tabari, *The History of al-Tabari* [*Taʾrikh al-rusul waʾl-muluk*], Vol. 6, trans. W. Montgomery Watt and M. V. McDonald (Albany: State University of New York Press, 1988), 5–6.

Wahb saw 'Abdullah coming from afar. He was a handsome young man, mounted on a beautiful camel, but the most remarkable thing about him was the radiant light that shone from his brow. "This can be no other than 'Abdullah, the son of 'Abd al-Mutallib, whom I have come to see," said Wahb to himself, "for the light of Muhammad is shining on his brow." Wahb immediately realized that this young man was the predestined father of the last prophet, and he resolved to marry Amina to him.

That marriage, however, did not occur without some significant opposition. When the time for it had arrived, 'Abd al-Mutallib took 'Abdullah by the hand to lead him to his bride and his soon-to-be father-in-law.[44] As they passed by the Ka'ba, however, a woman of the Banu Asad was standing there. Looking at 'Abdullah, she asked him where he was going. He responded that he was going with his father. At that, she offered him a large number of camels if he would turn aside and sleep with her. But 'Abdullah reiterated that he was with his father, and added that he could not go against his father's wishes by leaving him. So the marriage to Amina took place, "she being the most excellent woman among the Quraysh in birth and position at that time," "the most excellent woman in Quraysh as regards genealogy and status."[45]

> It is alleged that 'Abdullah consummated his marriage immediately and his wife conceived the apostle of God. Then he left her presence and met the woman who had proposed to him. He asked her why she did not make the proposal that she made to him the day before; to which she replied that the light that was with him the day before had left him, and she no longer had need of him. She had heard from her brother Waraqa b. Naufal, who had been a Christian and studied the scriptures, that a prophet would arise among this people.[46]

Other sources provide slightly varying backgrounds for this story:

> My father Ishaq b. Yasar told me that he was told that 'Abdullah went in to a woman that he had beside Amina d. Wahb when he had been working in clay and the marks of the clay were still on him. She put him off when he made a suggestion to her because of the dirt that was on him. He then left her and washed and bathed himself, and as he made his way to Amina he passed her and she invited him to come to her. He refused and went to Amina who conceived Muhammad. When he passed the woman again he asked her if she wanted anything and she said "No! when you passed me there was a white blaze between your eyes and when I invited you you refused me and went to Amina and she conceived the apostle of God." So the apostle of God was the noblest of

44. These stories occur in Ibn Ishaq, *Life of Muhammad*, 68–69.
45. Ibid., 68; al-Tabari, *History*, 6:6.
46. Ibn Ishaq, *Life of Muhammad*, 68–69; compare al-Tabari, *History*, 6:6.

> his people in birth and the greatest in honour both on his father's and his mother's side. God bless and preserve him![47]

According to one version of the tale, Abdullah "had between his eyes something like the white blaze on a horse's forehead."[48] Yet another variant relates that, when 'Abd al-Muttalib was leading 'Abdullah to Amina, it was a female soothsayer from the tribe of Khath'am called Fatima bt. Murr, a convert to Judaism from the people of Tabalah, whom they passed on their way. She had herself read the scriptures, and she saw a light in his face. "Young man," she said, "would you like to lie with me now, and I will give you a hundred camels?" But 'Abdullah piously replied,

> As for unlawful relations, I would sooner die,
> And as for lawful marriage, there can be none, as
> I clearly recognize.
> So how can that be which you desire?[49]

Then he explained to her, as in the other versions, that he was with his father and could not leave him. But, after he had married Amina and stayed with her for three days, he left his wife and again passed by the Khath'ami woman. His function in the sacred story now apparently fulfilled—he would die soon thereafter, prior to Muhammad's birth—he felt a desire to accept her blunt earlier proposition. "Would you like what you wanted before?" he asked. "Young man," she replied, "I am not, by God, a woman of questionable morals. I saw a light in your face and wished it to be within me, but God willed that He should place it where He wished." She then asked him where he had been for the past three days, and, when he told her of his marriage, she recited a spontaneous poem (as Arabian soothsayers were wont to do):

> I saw a sign which shone
> and gleamed in the black rainclouds.
> I comprehended it as light which illuminated
> what was around it like a full moon.
> I hoped to have it as a source of pride which
> I might take back with me,
> but not everyone who strikes a flint produces fire.
> By God, no other Zuhri woman has plundered
> your person of that which Aminah has, and yet
> she is unaware of it. . . .
> When Aminah conceived that which she conceived
> from him, she conceived an incomparable glory.[50]

47. Ibn Ishaq, *Life of Muhammad*, 69; compare al-Tabari, *History*, 6:6.
48. Al-Tabari, *History*, 6:6.
49. Ibid.
50. The poem occurs at al-Tabari, *History*, 6:6–8.

Amina's Pregnancy

Unlike the experience of previous generations of couples in the prophetic line, 'Abdullah was successful in his very first attempt at passing on his sacred charge: "That very night the pure elements composing the light-filled body of Muhammad descended from Abdullah's loins and settled within Amina's womb, as a pearl will form in the shell of the sea. The scholars maintain that this event took place while their bodies were in a state of ritual purity."[51]

And if, as the Khath'ami woman is supposed to have said, Amina was unaware of her pregnancy and of its cosmic significance, traditional legends do not permit her to have remained in the dark for very long. When it was time for Muhammad's conception, God sent messengers out to all the inhabitants of the heavens and the earth to share the good news with them that, on this very night, the concealed light of Muhammad was finally to descend into his mother's womb.[52] The angelic hosts were commanded to anoint their dwellings with perfume and incense, and to prepare a joyful feast and celebration. During that same night, the animals of Mecca themselves were given the gift of speech and employed as messengers, and the wild beasts and the birds congratulated themselves on Muhammad's advent. In the meantime, the thrones of all the monarchs of the entire world were shaken and trembled, the idols fell upon their faces and were broken, and the roofs of many churches collapsed. The seers and the fortune-tellers were silenced and, frightened and concerned, called an assembly to counsel with one another as to what these things meant.

> They concluded that all these signs heralded the coming of the Prophet Muhammad, the long awaited prophet of the Arabs who that night was conceived in his mother's womb in the holy city of Mecca. Of this they informed their kings and potentates, and told them that they would be overcome and defeated, their sovereignty wrested from them and their code of law abolished. It was to be replaced by the divine law this messenger of light was to bring the world. They informed their kings that the revelation he would bring was to remain on earth until the last day of the world. It would supercede all previous revelations and invalidate them. Thereupon great fear and apprehension seized the hearts of the kings for the awesomeness of this divine envoy.[53]

"There was nothing unusual about Aminah's pregnancy or delivery," writes Muhammad's modern biographer Muhammad Husayn Haykal, speaking for conventional academic historians, both Muslim and non-Muslim.[54] Or, if there was, it was relatively minor and not at all clearly miraculous. "It is said," writes

51. Adil, *Muhammad*, 63.
52. Accounts of the night of Muhammad's conception are gathered at Adil, *Muhammad*, 63–64.
53. Ibid., 64–65.
54. M. H. Haykal, *The Life of Muhammad* (N.p.: North American Trust Publications, 1976), 47.

M. A. Salahi, "that Aminah, the Prophet's mother, had no great trouble with her pregnancy. Everything went right for her."[55] Even on this point, though, traditional sources go further, reporting that Amina never experienced any of the customary discomforts of pregnancy, nor even the pangs of childbirth. She felt none of the weight or pressure that pregnant women typically feel, and only actually knew that she was pregnant—apart, presumably, from the frequent angelic and prophetic declarations to that effect—because her menstrual periods had ceased.[56]

But pious traditional accounts go far beyond merely stating that Amina had an easy time with Muhammad. At the beginning of each month of her pregnancy, which commenced in the lunar month of Rajab, she heard a heavenly voice that seemed to come from below as well as from above her, which called out to her, saying, "Blessings upon you and tidings of joy! The felicitous advent of Abu-Qasim [Muhammad's *kunya* name] to the world has indeed drawn nigh!" In the beginning of her first month, Adam, the first man, visited her during her sleep to announce that she was pregnant "with the Crown of Creation, the Prince of the Worlds," and to pronounce a blessing upon the fetal prophet. She received similar, confirmatory, visits at the beginning of each successive month, from Seth, Idris,[57] Noah, Hud,[58] Abraham, Ishmael, Moses, and Jesus, each of whom likewise invoked blessings upon the unborn child. Heavenly angels, it is said, descended and surrounded Amina on all sides, so that she was protected from the malicious *jinn* or genies, and from the evil eye, and bore witness to her of the supreme role that her son was to play in the salvation-history of humankind.[59] And, while she was pregnant with Muhammad, Amina saw a light come forth from her by which she was able to see the castles of Busra, in distant Syria.[60]

In the sixth month of Amina's pregnancy, it is said that she dreamed of a person who commanded her to give her baby the name *Muhammad* and stressed to her the importance of providing the best possible care for her child. As one source tells it, "It is alleged in the popular stories (and only God knows the truth) that Amina d. Wahb, the mother of God's apostle, used to say when she was pregnant with God's apostle that a voice said to her, 'You are pregnant with the lord of this people and when he is born say, "I put him in the care of the One from the evil of every envier; then call him Muhammad."'"[61]

55. M. A. Salahi, *Muhammad: Man and Prophet: A Complete Study of the Life of the Prophet of Islam* (Shaftesbury, England: Element, 1995), 22.

56. Adil, *Muhammad*, 68–69.

57. Idris is commonly identified as the biblical Enoch (Gen. 5:18–24).

58. Hud is a prophet known to the Qur'an. The eleventh chapter of the Qur'an bears his name, and he is mentioned in such passages as 7:65–72; 11:50–60; 26:123–40; 46:21–25. His name, which may be cognate with the Arabic word equivalent of *Jew* or *Jewish* (*yahudi*), suggests that he might have been Hebrew. For a provocative look at Hud and certain other figures mentioned in the Qur'an, see W. J. Hamblin, "Pre-Islamic Arabian Prophets," in *Mormons and Muslims*, ed. S. J. Palmer (Provo, Utah: Religious Studies Center, Brigham Young University, 2002), 135–55.

59. Adil, *Muhammad*, 65, 69. These prophetic visits suggest a pregnancy that lasted the normal nine months. However, as Adil reports in *Muhammad* (68), there is some disagreement among Muslim authorities as to that point. Estimates range between six and nine.

60. Ibn Ishaq, *Life of Muhammad*, 72.

61. Ibid., 69.

To aid her in her responsibility, the angels gave her words for recitation over the infant that would ward off any evil or malice, and provided an amulet to be attached to the baby—"a page of silver" that she found at her head upon waking—with similar words of blessing inscribed upon it.[62] These words appear to have been effective even before the baby's birth, for all went better than well. "From my belly," Amina is supposed to have reported, "there always emerged a beautiful scent, and at night I would hear the voice of *dhikr and tasbih* (praise and invocation) coming from within. I heard angels' voices saying to me, 'Oh Amina, you who are pregnant with the most excellent creature in all the universe, surely you are most favored of womankind!'"[63]

But the blessings extended far beyond the baby himself. In the year of Muhammad's conception, the people of Mecca and environs had suffered greatly from drought, famine, and violent unrest among tribes. When Amina conceived, however, all of these afflictions suddenly ceased. God sent down rain, the land produced food again, and tensions ceased among the warring tribes. Because of all this, the people began to call that year "the year of the solving of difficulties." It was such a good year, in fact, that all of the women who were pregnant during it gave birth to boys.[64] Also in the year associated with Muhammad's birth, which is usually identified as 570 CE or thereabouts, according to very widespread Muslim tradition a foreign army was besieging Mecca. Suddenly, that army turned away. Since the aggressor army included an elephant, the chapter of the Qur'an in which that story is recalled is appropriately titled "The Elephant." In its entirety, the chapter reads as follows: "In the name of God, the Merciful, the Compassionate. Did you not see how your Lord dealt with the owners of the elephant? Did he not bring their plot to nothing? He sent against them the *ababil* birds, which pelted them with stones of baked clay [*sijjil*] and made them like corn stalks eaten [by cattle]."[65]

This event—other accounts add that the elephant prostrated itself toward the Meccan Ka'ba—is typically interpreted as a miracle portending the advent of the Prophet of Islam, and the images recur frequently in Muslim poetry as signs pointing to Muhammad's future role.[66]

Muhammad's Birth

"There was nothing unusual about the birth of Muhammad," writes M. A. Salahi. "The only thing worth mentioning is that his mother reported later that she had

62. Adil, *Muhammad*, 69–70. The practice of writing sacred texts upon sheets of metal is very ancient. The oldest known text of the Bible was found written on silver in Jerusalem. (The finds were reported by G. Barkay in "The Divine Name Found in Jerusalem," *Biblical Archaeology Review* 9, 2 [1983]: 14–19, and in his "Priestly Blessings on Silver Plates" [in Hebrew], *Cathedra* 52 [1989]: 46–59.) In one of the accounts, Amina is informed that although the baby's name is to be Muhammad, he is known in the Torah under the name *Ahmad*. This probably refers, again, to Muslim readings of John 14:16, and, thus, strictly speaking, to the Gospel (*injil*) rather than to the Torah (*tawra*). The command to name the baby Muhammad may also have been given to his grandfather, 'Abd al-Mutalib. See Maulana Muhammad 'Ali, *Muhammad the Prophet* (Lahore, Pakistan: Ahmadiyya Anjuman Isha'at Islam, 1984), 47.

63. Adil, *Muhammad*, 69. Compare the words of Gabriel's annunciation to Mary as given at Luke 1:28.

64. Ibid., 67.

65. Qur'an 105. See R. Paret, *Der Koran: Kommentar und Konkordanz*, 2nd ed. (Stuttgart, Germany: Verlag Kohlhammer, 1980), 522.

66. Schimmel, *And Muhammad Is His Messenger*, 265 n. 7.

an easy delivery."[67] "According to some writers," says the Anglo-Arab biographer Ghulam Malik, "Aminah was alone when she gave birth to Muhammad without feeling any pain of delivery."[68] But, again, much more is relayed in the stories by traditional piety.

When the moment approached for the delivery of the Prophet, the Meccan Ka'ba, long polluted by idol worship, suddenly split in two. A voice came from within the structure, saying,

> Oh men of Quraysh! This holy house has not come apart on account of the death of any, but rather because the time of birth has drawn nigh for the Light of this world, the Glory of the world to come, the shining Lamp of Paradise, Muhammad bin Abdullah to emerge from his mother's womb. He is to be a great prophet, he will cleanse this holy house of the abominations and idols that are polluting my precincts, and he will make me pure and pristine once more with the light of true faith; I will become the Qibla [the geographical focus of prayer] of his entire nation and the annual pilgrimage will be held on my grounds. Know that it is in honor of his long desire to advent that this edifice has cracked and split.[69]

Also on that night, all of the idols in the Ka'ba fell from their places and were broken into pieces—presumably for the second time, since the same story is told about the night on which the Prophet was conceived. A voice was heard, coming from some unseen place, announcing "Woe and perdition on Quraysh, for the glorious and trusted prophet has come in truth, embellished with adornments from the loftiest gardens of Paradise. Lat and Uzza and all other idols are now finished and done for, Iblis himself is imprisoned."[70] Indeed, on that night all of the idols in the entire world fell from their pedestals and were shattered to bits, and Satan's throne was overturned so that it hung upside down and the devil fell off from it. The fires of the Zoroastrians, which had been burning, continuously tended, for a thousand years, went out, and no trace of either fire or heat remained. The hearths became, in fact, as cold as ice, far colder than the fiercest winter. The Euphrates dried up at Sawa, in the land of Persia, and the river bed became as if no water had ever flowed there. Fourteen of the twenty-two palaces and domed mansions of the Khosroes of Persia collapsed, his throne tumbled over, and he himself was terrified by an ominous dream.[71]

Yet the tidings were not solely of destruction and doom. Also on the night of Muhammad's birth, God commanded the angels to open all of the gates of heaven

67. Salahi, *Muhammad*, 22.

68. G. Malik, *Muhammad: An Islamic Perspective* (Lanham, Md.: University Press of America, 1996), 3.

69. Adil, *Muhammad*, 83.

70. Al-Lat and al-'Uzza were two of the daughters ascribed by the pagans of Mecca to Allah. The Qur'an mocks the Meccans because although they valued male children far more than females, they ascribed only daughters to God (see Qur'an 53:19–22). *Iblis* is an Arabic corruption of the Greek *diabolos*, and denotes Satan, or the devil.

71. Adil, *Muhammad*, 87, 90–91.

and of Paradise widely, and, on the day that followed, the sun shone with unusual brilliance. "Greater was its light than on other days, and the whole world was gladdened."[72]

> Abdullah bin Salam reports: On the night the prophet was born, I was sitting together with a learned Jew. He raised his face to Heaven and spoke to me, "Ya Ibn Salam! This very night at Mecca the Arabian prophet Muhammad ibn Abdullah is to be born who will illuminate the world." I said to him, "What do these words of yours mean, how do you know such a thing?" He answered me, "I have been watching the skies and I see now such a light as has not been seen since the world began. That is how I come to know of this event."[73]

According to one account, the Prophet's grandfather, 'Abd al-Mutallib, was inside the Ka'ba when Amina gave birth—presumably uninjured when, as other sources relate, the building had split in half (his son, 'Abdullah, had already died by this time). Amina sent him word of the happy event, inviting him to come to where she was and see her newborn son, Muhammad. "I was at the time within the building of the Kaba," he is said to have related afterward. "There I witnessed how the walls of the building themselves began to shake and tremble with joy, calling out to each other: 'The Lord Almighty has bestowed great honor on us that we might see the coming of the prophet who will cleanse us of the filth of these idols!' I was amazed at hearing this, and I understood then that you must have given birth, and that these words heralded the importance of the child you had borne."[74]

As for Amina herself, she is said to have related that, at the time she was ready to give birth, there was nobody with her. Neither man nor woman attended her, because, for some reason, everybody had gone to the Ka'ba for the *tawaf* or ritual circumambulation of the building (the reason for 'Abd al-Mutallib's presence there). And yet she would not remain alone. First she heard a loud and terrifying noise. Then a white bird appeared, alighting on her breast, and all fear, pain, and anxiety departed. She was handed a cup of sweet white sherbet, which she drank and which filled her heart with peace, joy, and light. At this point, she saw a number of tall and astonishingly beautiful women approaching, "as tall and slender as cypress trees." They seated themselves around her in a circle. One of them then spoke, introducing herself as Eve, the wife of the prophet Adam, whereupon another identified herself as Sarah, the wife of the prophet Abraham. A third introduced herself as the piously believing wife of the pharaoh of Egypt who had opposed Moses, while a fourth told Amina that she was Mary, the mother of Jesus. The others were all introduced as some of the houris of Paradise. The entire delegation had come to escort the Prophet into his earthly life and to provide him with a suitable welcome. A white curtain was then lowered down from heaven so as to veil Amina from the envious and malicious gaze of the jinn, and a flock of birds

72. Ibid., 83.
73. Ibid., 84.
74. Ibid., 83.

surrounded her, going around and around her and her soon-to-be-born child in the same way that the Meccans were performing the *tawaf* of the Ka'ba at that very moment.[75] "The Lord Almighty then removed the veil from my eyes so that I beheld the whole world from east to west. Three flags I saw them bring down from Heaven: one they planted in the ground in the east, one in the west, and one right atop the Kaba. In the heavens that were open to my eyes I beheld men bearing bejeweled vessels of gold, and they assisted at the birth of the blessed child, and I suffered neither pain nor trouble."[76]

Muhammad was born circumcised, and his birth was accompanied by a very great light. His umbilical cord had been cut by divine ministrants, and he was wrapped in a piece of white silk. There was no need to wash him, as he was already washed and cleansed. He immediately bowed himself to the ground, touching it with his head, and, during his prostrations, he repeated the words "*Ummati, ummati*" ("my people, my people"). Moreover, lifting the forefinger of his right hand, he commenced to make supplications to God. Among the words that he uttered was a variant of the traditional Islamic profession of faith, as only Muhammad was in a position to say it: *Ashadu an la ilaha illa-llah wa inni rasulullah* (I testify that there is no god but God and that I am the messenger of God). Similar words ("there is no god but God; Muhammad is the messenger of God") were written upon his back.[77]

> The Kaba itself was inwardly hung with golden lamps from Paradise, and all creatures of the heavens and the earth, the youths and the maidens from Paradise, all created beings other than mankind rejoiced and gave each other the glad tidings. "Oh Muhammad," they wished, "may Allah make you happy and always pleased, for there is no creature born with greater honor than you, and none that is more excellent. Never have the angels celebrated the birth of any created being as they now celebrate your birth into this world!" Between Heaven and earth there were raised pillars of support, and all were made of precious stone, and not one of them was alike unto another.[78]

The birth of the Prophet was even announced in the seas, to all the fish that inhabited them. An enormous fish called "Zalmusa," many times larger than many mountains and plains together, with seventy heads and seventy tails, was so convulsed with joyous emotion at the advent of Muhammad that the seven seas were caused to heave with the same enthusiasm, so that all of the creatures of the deep were aware that the last prophet had finally arrived upon the earth.[79]

Shortly after his birth, the Prophet's mother saw a white cloud in the sky that moved rapidly toward her. She could hear sounds within it like those of horses. It

75. Ibid., 84–85.
76. Ibid.
77. Ibid., 85–86.
78. Ibid., 87–88.
79. Ibid., 88.

descended and enveloped the baby and carried him away, and a voice explained to her that Muhammad was being taken to see the entire world. "We shall encircle it," the voice said, "and dive into the depths of the ocean, so that all that lives in and under the earth may know of the advent of this noble being and shall have seen his face and learn of his arrival. Hereafter the world shall be filled with the light of faith; of unbelief and rebellion against the Lord Almighty nothing will remain."[80]

The baby's miraculous circumnavigation of the globe took only a few moments, and then the cloud returned, gently depositing the infant Muhammad, who was by then wrapped in a piece of green silk—green is, traditionally, the Prophet's color—and fragrantly scented, and whose face "was radiant as the moon on her fourteenth night." The baby was washed by angelic servants, and then an angel held Muhammad under one wing for a full hour, all the while whispering secrets and blessings into his ears.[81] Miraculous cures are also reported, as the angels fanned out over the globe after attending Muhammad's birth.[82]

Analysis

Unless one accepts these stories as literally true, they are manifestly partisan and tendentious. This is precisely what we should expect, since they were forged out of the ideological competition, first, between Islam and Arabian paganism, and then between Islam and the faiths (most notably Christianity and, for at least the first few centuries, Zoroastrianism) that it confronted on the broader world stage. The procession of pre-Islamic biblical prophets that came to praise and bless Amina's unborn baby each month, and the similar procession of women from Old and New Testament stories who came to be with Amina as she approached the birth—all of these worthies appearing in order of their historical sequence—pointedly represent Muhammad and Islam as the culmination of the biblical story. Nearly as graphically and, one suspects, just about as deliberately, as did the seventh-century placement of the Dome of the Rock, with its elaborate ornamentation of triumphalist passages from the Qur'an, on the Temple Mount in Jerusalem, they announce a hegemonic claim. Muhammad was to be seen as "the seal of the prophets" (*khatim al-nabi'in*).[83] Everything else was a prelude to his appearance.

The stories are, thus, political in the broadest sense. We are told repeatedly that the idols fell upon their faces and were broken to pieces, that the roofs of many Christian churches collapsed, and that the seers and fortune-tellers were

80. Ibid., 86–87. The cloud that takes the baby Muhammad briefly away parallels the cloud in which Jesus ascends into heaven, and in which he will return, according to the account given in Acts 1:9, as well as the "bright cloud" (*nephele photeine*) that accompanies the transfiguration of Christ as it is described in Matthew 17:5, Mark 9:7, and Luke 9:34–35. M. Barker, *Temple Theology: An Introduction* (London: SPCK, 2004), 32, derives the motif of the cloud of the ascension from the incense smoke that accompanied the entry of the Jewish high priest into the holy of holies of the temple at Jerusalem.

81. Adil, *Muhammad*, 86–87.

82. One such is recounted at Adil, *Muhammad*, 86–87.

83. Qur'an 33:40.

silenced by the advent of Muhammad. The point could scarcely have been made more clearly than in the accounts of the extinguishing of the Zoroastrians' long-tended sacred fires. And when the elderly Jew reports that he knows of the birth of Muhammad at Mecca because of a light that he has seen in the skies, it is impossible not to be reminded of an earlier story, in which "wise men from the East" saw the star in the sky that heralded the birth of Jesus—a story that this account is plainly intended to equal and, being more recent, to displace.[84]

But the stories are also political in the stricter sense, because Muhammad came not merely as a prophet but also, in the event, as a ruler and as the founder of a world-transforming empire. Thus, there is an unmistakable political manifesto contained in accounts that represent the thrones of all the monarchs of the entire world shaken and trembling at the advent of the final prophet, most of the palaces of the ruler of Sassanid Persia—with the Byzantines, one of the two great powers of Muhammad's world—collapsing, and the economically vital Euphrates River drying up.

Significantly, the fetal Muhammad is never represented as speaking or acting. Indeed, the manner in which he is depicted is entirely devoid of individual human personality. He is, rather, a symbol of Islam's claim to be the final and definitive revelation from God and of its parallel claim to universal political sovereignty. In that sense, it is fitting that, when Amina was near to giving birth, divinely sent birds were, in effect, performing the ritual circumambulation or *tawaf* around Muhammad that the pagan Meccans were, at the very same time, performing around the not yet purified Ka'ba. The exaltedness of Muhammad's status in traditional piety could hardly be more clearly expressed than it is in that image.

A Possible Sequel

When he died rather suddenly in 632, Muhammad had no living son, and only one surviving daughter. Moreover, he had left no clear instructions for succession in the leadership of the Islamic community. Shi'ite tradition insists that he had designated his cousin and son-in-law, 'Ali, and there may be truth in this.[85] Nonetheless, it is unlikely that such sincerely faithful and devoted disciples as Abu Bakr and 'Umar, the first two Sunni caliphs, would have ignored Muhammad's wishes on this matter if those wishes had been unmistakably evident. Significantly, the surviving daughter, Fatima, who was married to 'Ali and who herself died shortly after the Prophet, came to be known as al-Zahra': "Luminous," or

84. Matt. 2:1–12.

85. I find the stories of Muhammad's investment of 'Ali as his successor at the pond of Ghadir Khum, in the last year of the Prophet's life, plausible, but not decisively so. 'Ali did eventually reign, for about five years, as the fourth of the four "orthodox caliphs" in the Sunni line. But he had not succeeded Muhammad immediately, his posterity did not succeed him, and his relatively brief and delayed reign was far from enough to satisfy the *shi'at* 'Ali, or "faction of 'Ali," from which the anglicized term *Shi'ite* derives.

"the Radiant." "The legendary figure of this ailing woman," writes Annemarie Schimmel,

> was soon adorned with miracles, especially in the Shia tradition: her birth was surrounded by light; she was absolutely pure and had no menstruation, and her sons were born through her left thigh. Thus she was honored with the title batul, "virgin," and later she assumed also the position of a true Mater Dolorosa after the [martyr's] death of her younger son Husain. That she was called as well Umm abiha, "her father's mother," gave rise to high-soaring speculations about her cosmic role in God's Heilsgeschichte. . . . Weeping for Husain opens the gates of Paradise, and Fatima, like Mary the mother of Jesus, will intercede for those who shed tears for her son.[86]

Thus, the "Muhammadan light" may have been transmitted through Fatima into one or more of the lines of the Shiʿite imams that sprang from her union with ʿAli—including, but not limited to, the so-called Fatimids who ruled Egypt during the tenth and eleventh centuries. But that is another story, and a very long one.

WORKS CITED

Adil, H. A. *Muhammad, The Messenger of Islam: His Life and Prophecy*. Washington, D.C.: Islamic Supreme Council of America, 2002.

Barkay, G. "The Divine Name Found in Jerusalem." *Biblical Archaeology Review* 9, 2 (1983): 14–19.

———. "Priestly Blessings on Silver Plates" (in Hebrew), *Cathedra* 52 (1989): 46–59.

Barker, M. *Temple Theology: An Introduction*. London: SPCK, 2004.

Böwering, G. "The Prophet of Islam: The First and the Last Prophet." In *The Message of the Prophet,* 48–60. Islamabad: Government of Pakistan, 1979.

Hamblin, W. J. "Pre-Islamic Arabian Prophets." In *Mormons and Muslims,* edited by S. J. Palmer, 135–55. Provo, Utah: Religious Studies Center, Brigham Young University, 2002.

Haykal, M. H. *The Life of Muhammad*. N.p.: North American Trust Publications, 1976.

Horovitz, J. "Zur Muhammadlegende." *Der Islam* 5 (1914): 41–55.

Ibn Ishaq. *The Life of Muhammad*. Translated by A. Guillaume. Oxford: Oxford University Press, 2002.

Jeffrey, A. *Reader on Islam*. The Hague: Mouton, 1962.

Justin Martyr. "The First Apology." In *Ante-Nicene Fathers*, Vol. 1. Translated by A. Roberts and J. Donaldson. Peabody, Mass.: Hendrickson, 1995.

Lehmann, E., and J. Pedersen. "Der Beweis für die Auferstehung im Koran." *Der Islam* 5 (1914): 54–61.

Malik, G. *Muhammad: An Islamic Perspective*. Lanham, Md.: University Press of America, 1996.

Mez, A. "Geschichte der Wunder Muhammads." *Verhandlungen des. 2. Internationalen Kongresses für Allgemeine Religionsgeschichte*. Basel, Switzerland: Helbing und Lichtenhahn, 1905.

86. Schimmel, *And Muhammad Is His Messenger*, 18, 20.

Muhammad ʻAli, M. *Muhammad the Prophet*. Lahore, Pakistan: Ahmadiyya Anjuman Ishaʻat Islam, 1984.

Muir, W. *The Life of Mohammed from Original Sources*. Rev. ed. Edinburgh: John Grant, 1912.

Padwick, C. E. *Muslim Devotions*. London: SPCK, 1961.

Paret, R. *Der Koran: Kommentar und Konkordanz*. 2nd ed. Stuttgart, Germany: Verlag Kohlhammer, 1980.

Peterson, D. C. "Creation." In *Encyclopaedia of the Qur'an*. Vol. 1. Edited by J. D. McAuliffe et al., 472–480. Leiden, Netherlands: Brill, 2001–2006.

———. "Does the Qur'an Teach Creation *Ex Nihilo*?" In *By Study and Also by Faith: Essays in Honor of Hugh W. Nibley*. Vol. 1. Edited by J. M. Lundquist and S. D. Ricks. Salt Lake City, Utah: Deseret Book and the Foundation for Ancient Research and Mormon Studies, 1990.

———. *Muhammad: Prophet of God*. Grand Rapids, Mich.: Eerdmans, 2007.

Salahi, M. A. *Muhammad: Man and Prophet: A Complete Study of the Life of the Prophet of Islam*. Shaftesbury, England: Element, 1995.

Schaff P., and D. S. Schaff, eds. *The Creeds of Christendom*. 6th ed. 3 vols. Grand Rapids, Mich.: Baker Book House, 1983.

Schimmel, A. *And Muhammad Is His Messenger: The Veneration of the Prophet in Islamic Piety*. Chapel Hill: University of North Carolina Press, 1985.

Al-Tabari. *The History of al-Tabari* [*Ta'rikh al-rusul wa'l-muluk*]. Vol. 6. Translated by W. Montgomery Watt and M.V. McDonald. Albany: State University of New York Press, 1988.

Watt, W. M. *Muhammad at Mecca*. Oxford: Clarendon, 1953.

The Colossal Fetuses of La Venta and Mesoamerica's Earliest Creation Story

Carolyn E. Tate

About three thousand years ago, preliterate peoples across southern Mexico, the Olmec, carved stone sculptures of human fetuses (see fig. 1). These are the earliest accurate images of the fetus yet recognized in any artistic tradition.[1] The sculptures showed the fetuses as alive, standing on deeply flexed legs, their arms in a variety of positions. As this chapter will demonstrate, the ancient Olmec recognized the fetus as a liminal being, with great potential for rapid transformation and growth but with a tenuous, and sacred, grasp of life.

As one can imagine, these fetus sculptures pose a formidable interpretive challenge. Ordinarily, to explore the significance of an ancient art object that had a religious function, art historians consult scriptural texts, records of ritual practice, or documents relating to the commission of a work. If such texts are lacking, we turn to the spatial context of the object, considering its relationships with associated materials, sculptures, iconography, and ritual spaces. In the case of the fetus sculptures, although the Olmec manipulated a relatively consistent system of incised

I gratefully acknowledge Dumbarton Oaks, Washington, D.C., and the Harvard Center for the Study of World Religions for generous research support. Many thanks to Vanessa R. Sasson and Jane Marie Law for inviting me to participate in the American Academy of Religions Eastern Regional meeting in Montreal and for their gracious good cheer and insightful editing during this project. I truly appreciate the knowledge, ideas, and support (although they do not necessarily agree with me) that the following individuals have shared with me over the years: Jennifer Ahlfeldt, Joe Arredondo, Gordon Bendersky, Davíd Carrasco, Flora Clancy, Constance Cortez, Sam Edgerton, the late Stuart Gentling, Terry Grieder, Cecelia Klein, Allan Maca, Jeff Quilter, Kent Reilly, Richard Townsend, Steve Wernke, and most, Rick Dingus. Special thanks are due to the students who have participated in my Mesoamerican Creation Stories courses, especially Megan Grann and Maggie Hilburn, and to Corey Escoto for his drawings.

1. Carolyn E. Tate and Gordon Bendersky, "Olmec Sculptures of the Human Fetus," *Perspectives in Biology and Medicine* 42, 3 (1999).

FIGURE 1. Olmec sculptures of the human fetus, about 900 BCE. Left: Agnathic fetus effigy from Guerrero, collection National Museum of Anthropology, Mexico. Center: Fetus effigy with hand to ear, Gulf Coast of Mexico, height 18 centimeters, collection National Museum of Anthropology, Mexico. Right: Fetus effigy from Guatemala, height 25 centimeters, collection Smithsonian Institution Museum of the American Indian. Drawings by C. Tate.

symbols during this era (Mesoamerica's Formative Period, 1400–400 BCE),[2] none of their societies used a linguistically complete writing system, so we cannot turn to written texts to reveal why so many fetus sculptures were made or how they expressed their makers' religious beliefs. And unfortunately, most of the sixty known fetus sculptures were looted from the significant arrays in which they were placed. Thus, their syntagmatic relationships to other message-bearing objects have been lost. However, a few of the sculptures do have an archaeological context. Five fetus sculptures (three of them are more than six feet high) have

2. The term "Mesoamerica" refers to the high culture area of Mexico and Central America. Major civilizations of Mesoamerica include the pre-literate Olmec (1400–400 BCE), the literate Maya (200–1521), and several civilizations that produced pictorial manuscripts with informational and religious content, including the Mixtec (750–1521) and Aztec (1200–1521). The sixteenth-century European invasions of Mesoamerican societies triggered the destruction of hundreds of ancient texts; only sixteen pre-Hispanic manuscripts survived. Fortunately, many Mesoamerican cultures conveyed through art their complex conceptualizations of society, as well as how they conceived of their rulers, their spiritual beliefs, and their world. Much of the art of earlier civilizations was already buried by natural processes of growth and decay when the Europeans arrived. Although the Europeans attempted to destroy what they could of the ritual objects that were in use by indigenous people in the sixteenth century, some survived and are still being unearthed today. Pre-Hispanic traditions survive in many locations, though they have inevitably been altered by changing social pressures.

been scientifically excavated from the extraordinary ancient ritual site/civic center called La Venta in the state of Tabasco, near the Gulf of Mexico.

Between about 900 and 400 BCE, its inhabitants erected more than a hundred monumental stone sculptures and deliberately buried in significant arrays more than seventeen hundred stone figurines, highly polished celts, and jade images of such things as clam shells and stingray spines. After the Olmec abandoned the area around 400 BCE, a few Mesoamericans continued to visit La Venta, but it gradually disappeared under the tropical vegetation. Not until 1925 was La Venta rediscovered by modern investigators.

Numerous individuals have excavated bits of the site and published their findings, but there is no comprehensive documentation of the contexts in which the sculptures were abandoned. Because monumental sculpture in ancient Mesoamerica functioned as public expressions of political and religious paradigms, if one can establish the spatial relationships of the sculptures, one can explore how (and whether) they formed meaningful visual texts. Combing through archaeological reports to plot locations of monuments at the site has been my task as an art historian endeavoring to think about the sculptures of fetuses. What I have discovered reveals radically new insights about both La Venta and the role of fetuses in Olmec religious thought.

My simulated reconstruction of the monumental sculptures as they appeared in the ritual center leads me to propose that many of La Venta's sculptures, including the fetuses, were placed in six sets. Each set consisted of three, four, or five similar objects, but each set was completely different from the others.[3] The sets extended about a mile and a half along a central axis marked by green and red stone columns. The composition of the sets includes all the elements essential for a visual narrative, including a beginning and end, characters, setting, action, and such storytelling devices as pacing, reiteration, and foreshadowing. I suggest that La Venta's fetuses formed the first set, or station, in a processional visual narrative. This tale of cosmogony and the origins of humans was probably narrated or enacted on certain occasions, possibly over several days or more. This may have been the earliest attempt to create a permanent record of or visible parameters for a creation-and-origins narrative in Mesoamerica.

This chapter introduces its topic by providing a brief reprise of previously published evidence that a group of Olmec sculptures represented fetuses. Next, it leads readers through new material: the narrative stations within La Venta's sacred gendered landscape. As La Venta's narrative unfolds, its elements are compared with

3. Previously, scholars have recognized a few of the sculptural sets at La Venta. Several have written about my Set (or Station) 3, including Rebecca B. González Lauck, "Acerca de Piramides de Tierra y Seres Sobrenaturales: Observaciones Preliminares en Torno al Edificio C-1. La Venta, Tabasco," *Arqueología* 17 (1997); Karl Taube, "The Olmec Maize God: The Face of Corn in Formative Mesoamerica," *RES* 29/30 (1996). Monuments around my Stations 2 and 3 have been discussed by David C. Grove, "Public Monuments and Sacred Mountains: Observations on Three Formative Period Landscapes," in *Social Patterns in Pre-Classic Mesoamerica*, ed. David C. Grove and Rosemary A. Joyce (Washington, D.C.: Dumbarton Oaks, 1999); F. Kent Reilly III, "Mountains of Creation and Underworld Portals: The Ritual Function of Olmec Architecture at La Venta, Tabasco," in *Mesoamerican Architecture as a Cultural Symbol*, ed. Jeff Karl Kowalski (Oxford: Oxford University Press, 1999). However, no one has published an integrated view of all monuments.

creation-related myth and art from the later Maya, Mixe, and Aztec civilizations.[4] Of these, the twentieth-century Mixe are especially interesting as they are probably descendants of the Gulf Coast Olmec. These iconographic, contextual, and analogical interpretive strategies reveal patterns of symbols that allow us to make a preliminary interpretation of the La Venta colossal fetuses as self-sacrificial ballplayers who regenerated time and nature.

Identifying the Fetus and the Embryo in Olmec Sculpture

While making a comprehensive study of Olmec objects in collections around the world, I located about sixty small stone sculptures that were anthropomorphic and had huge heads and infantile features. Some had been identified by various authors as dwarfs, infants, dancers, and servants of a rain god. However, no one had methodically examined the sculptures as a group, considering the consistent features and the range of variations. To explore possible identifications, I consulted medical texts on dwarfism and also on human gestation. It was immediately apparent to me that the proportions of these the figures were those of a late-term fetus. More specifically, the sculptures exhibited a head-to-body ratio of approximately 1:4, had short limbs, deeply flexed legs, no hair, and infantile facial features. I realized that any conclusive identification was beyond my expertise, so I collaborated with physician Gordon Bendersky of Philadelphia, who had an interest in the Olmec. He showed photos of about thirty sculptures to a group of neonatologists and other specialists. They concurred that the sculptures were very accurate images of human fetuses, and they could even specify the week of gestation portrayed by the sculptures. Subsequently, Dr. Bendersky and I published an article in *Perspectives in Biology and Medicine* and the *New York Times* reported on it.[5] As a result of the publications, we received dozens of letters from medical specialists around the world, all of which agreed that the sculptures indeed represent fetuses. Shortly afterward, I visited La Venta and saw for the first time three very eroded colossal sandstone blocks, first discovered in 1941. They were so huge that they could not be moved when they were discovered. The visible surfaces had seemed uncarved. But archaeologist Rebecca González had recently managed to move them and had exposed previously unseen sides.[6] To my amazement, their large heads, deeply

4. By comparing the Olmec material with later myths, I do not assume that Olmec ritual and belief were identical to those of the Aztec or Maya. My method examines *clusters of symbols* that might confirm or repudiate the idea that La Venta's sets of monuments formed a creation narrative. The later cultures, without doubt, developed more complex rituals that responded to increased social differentiation, political demands, more sophisticated knowledge of astronomy and other technologies, and differing strategies for coping with environmental issues and population pressures. I propose that La Venta's narrative is quite different from the later ones in many respects, especially in view of the prominence of the fetus and embryo. The later creation stories seem to have differentially adapted creation tales told with local variations throughout Formative Mesoamerica and codified at La Venta around 800–600 BCE.

5. Tate and Bendersky, "Olmec Sculptures"; Ralph Blumenthal, "Ancient Art of Mexico May Depict the Unborn," *New York Times*, June 12, 1999.

6. Rebecca B. González Lauck, "Proyecto Arqueológico La Venta," *Arqueología* 4 (1988).

flexed knees, poses, and gestures were identical to several of the small sculptures of human fetuses holding their heads.

Since then, I've found that Olmec sculptors also made images of the human embryo, and in fact these were much more numerous than those of the fetus.[7] Most images depicted the embryo at the end of the first trimester of gestation when it has lidless eyes, nascent leg buds, webbed fingers, and a swollen upper lip that has just formed (see fig. 2). This identification eluded modern scholars for several reasons. First, most Olmec specialists focus on issues of political and economic development. Despite the presence of hundreds of life-size ceramic babies in the archaeological record, it did not occur to scholars that the Olmec might have been interested in—or able to study—human gestation.

Furthermore, public discussion of miscarriages, fetuses, and embryos rarely occurred in Euro-American society until rather recently.[8] Now, thanks to various developments over the past half-century—Lennart Nilsson's 1965 *Life* magazine publication, "The Drama of Life before Birth" and its spectacular photographs; ultrasound studies of the fetus; and the debates about contraception, abortion, and fetal rights—contemporary society has learned a great deal about human gestation.[9] We know that scientists call the stage of gestation from conception to approximately day 18 the "pre-embryonic period," which terminates with a spherical organism called the zygote. About day 20 the zygote elongates, and the embryonic period begins. Arms begin as buds that appear about day 26, and leg buds appear about six days later. By about day 57, embryos measure slightly more than one and a quarter inches (about 32 mm) from the top of the head to the rump; fingers and toes are visible; the nose, puffy upper lip, and mouth have formed; and eyelids have begun to cover the almond-shaped eye. It is at about this stage, from four to six weeks of gestation, that many human embryos are lost through spontaneous miscarriages—today this occurs in about 22 percent of pregnancies in the United States and England. Women who experience painful contractions and abnormal bleeding are alerted to look for an unusual discharge (beyond that of menstruation) as first trimester miscarriages occur. After the human survives the rapid transformation and growth of the embryonic stage, it looks more recognizably human, and we call it a fetus.[10] The fetal stage continues until birth at about week 38 (day 266). Once the embryo successfully achieves the fetal stage, the incidence of miscarriage and stillbirth is much lower, but is not uncommon.

We can reasonably assume that in the ancient world at least as many pregnancies (22 percent) spontaneously aborted as embryos, so Formative Period Mesoamericans would have had regular access to visible forms of life expelled from the womb in sacs of bloody tissue attached to a long cord. Pre-Olmec images show that by 1400 BCE in Mesoamerica, women studied the embryo when it spontaneously

7. Carolyn E. Tate, "Olmec Knowledge of the Human Body and Gestation," in *The Encyclopaedia of the History of Science, Technology, and Medicine in Non-Western Cultures*, ed. Helaine Selin (Dordrecht, Netherlands: Kluwer Academic Publishers, 2008), 11, 1203–12.

8. Barbara Duden, "The Fetus as an Object of Our Time," *RES: Anthropology and Aesthetics* 25 (1994).

9. Lennart Nilsson, "The Drama of Life before Birth," *Life*, April 30, 1965.

10. Marjorie England, *Life before Birth*, 2nd ed. (London: Mosby-Wolfe, 1996).

a.

b.

c.

FIGURE 2. Olmec sculptures of the human embryo, about 900 BCE: (a) jade fetus of about ten weeks standing in jade canoe incised with embryo images on prows from Cerro de las Mesas, Veracruz, collection National Museum of Anthropology, Mexico; (b) jade embryo figurine, private collection; (c) stone embryo sprouting maize from fontanel, in form of axe, collection Denver Art Museum. Drawings by Corey Escoto. Used with permission.

aborted, as well as the fetuses that were lost. The earliest known sculpture of a pre-birth human was made in highland Oaxaca, Mexico, about 1400 BCE. It consists of a ceramic figurine of a female with a cavity between the legs. When the piece was excavated, a tiny fetus with crossed arms filled this cavity.[11] By 1200 BCE in the highland Basin of Mexico (the location of modern Mexico City, approximately three hundred miles away from Oaxaca), a stylized embryo face with its characteristic almond eyes and puffy upper lip decorated ceramic vessels. The idea of portraying the embryo seems to have spread to other developing societies. About five hundred miles from Oaxaca, also by 1200 BCE, an early form of the embryo image appeared on a columnar, phallic-shaped monument at the Gulf Coast Olmec site of San Lorenzo (Monument 41).

Formative Period Mesoamericans apparently had a sophisticated grasp of the process of gestation, even as it coincided with astronomical cycles. Human gestation occurs, on average, over 266 days; nine lunations transpire in about 261 days. The most ancient calendrical count in Mesoamerica was a 260-day cycle composed of thirteen numbers and twenty named days. Among some later Mesoamerican groups, the day of birth in this cycle (e.g., 8 Deer) became the name given to the person. Wherever it was used, the 260-day count was a divinatory tool. Each number and day name was linked to a series of metaphoric concepts that, when combined, provided unique portents for each of the 260 days. It is well known that among later Mesoamerican cultures, the commensuration of calendrical cycles with each other and with natural cycles was a standard practice of calendar specialists. And numerous authors[12] have argued that this 260-day calendar arose primarily because of observations of human gestation. What has been elusive is the origins of these practices and of the 260-day count itself. Now that it is clear that embryos and fetuses were common subjects of sculpture in several major cultural areas by 1200 BCE, at least we know that a significant part of the conceptual framework for the divinatory calendar—the knowledge of gestational processes—existed by that early time.

Metaphorically, Mesoamericans considered embryos to be the seeds of human life. The human embryo became one of the principal symbols in Olmec religion, represented visually as both naturalistic figurines and conventionalized forms. By 900 BCE, the human embryo symbol was often conflated with maize imagery, creating a seminal human-maize being. The Olmec devised numerous ways to create a visual conflation of maize symbols with the embryo image (see fig. 3). Often they showed initial germination of the seed by means of a single maize sprout emerging from the embryo's fontanel. Another frequent symbolic device was the "maize seed headband," or four maize seeds flanking a central element on a headband worn by the embryo. Alternatively, they incised maize seeds onto the face. Many large stone axes were given the features of the embryo and the axe itself was similar in shape to a maize seed. Clearly, Olmec religion focused on states of potential life, or a

11. Joyce Marcus, *Women's Ritual in Formative Oaxaca: Figurine-Making, Divination, Death, and the Ancestors*, ed. Kent V. Flannery and Joyce Marcus, *Memoirs of the Museum of Anthropology, 33, University of Michigan* (Ann Arbor: Museum of Anthropology, University of Michigan, 1998).

12. See, for example, Helen Neuenswander, "Vestiges of Early Time Concepts in a Contemporary Maya (Cubulco Achi) Community: Implications for Epigraphy," *Estudios de Cultura Maya* (13) 1981: 125–63.

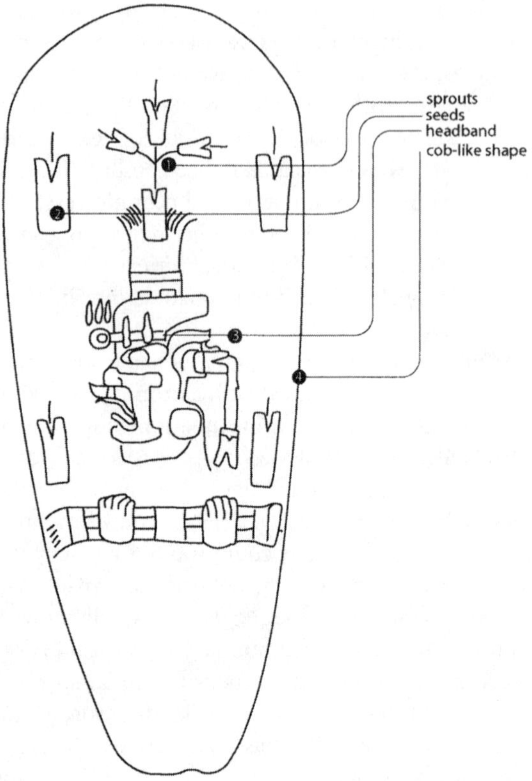

FIGURE 3. Olmec celt incised with head of embryo and maize symbols. Drawing by Corey Escoto. Used with permission.

pervasive life force, which it described as a co-identity between the embryonic states of humans and maize.[13] The notion of the human seed applied to the fetus as well, as we shall see.

The La Venta Fetuses and a Visual Narrative of Creation

In the lowlands along the southern Gulf of Mexico (see fig. 4), the maize plant was introduced by about 5100 BCE, but its use as a staple food remained marginal

13. The co-identity between humans and maize seems to have been preceded by a conceptual equivalence between humans and other plants. Evidence for this was excavated at El Manatí, the spring-shrine site near San Lorenzo. At some time between 1200 and 1000 BCE, pilgrims (there was no local population) deposited at least twenty anthropomorphic wooden sculptures that consisted only of the upper half of the body. These were wrapped with fiber mats, as were actual human burials throughout much of later Mesoamerican culture. Adjacent to the bundled sculptures were bundled plant materials: leaves, whole plants, and reeds, wrapped just as carefully as the wooden humans. See Ponciano Ortiz and María del Carmen Rodríguez, "The Sacred Hill of El Manatí: A Preliminary Discussion of the Site's Ritual Paraphernalia," in *Olmec Art and Archaeology in Mesoamerica*, ed. John E. Clark and Mary E. Pye (Washington, D.C.: National Gallery of Art, 2000).

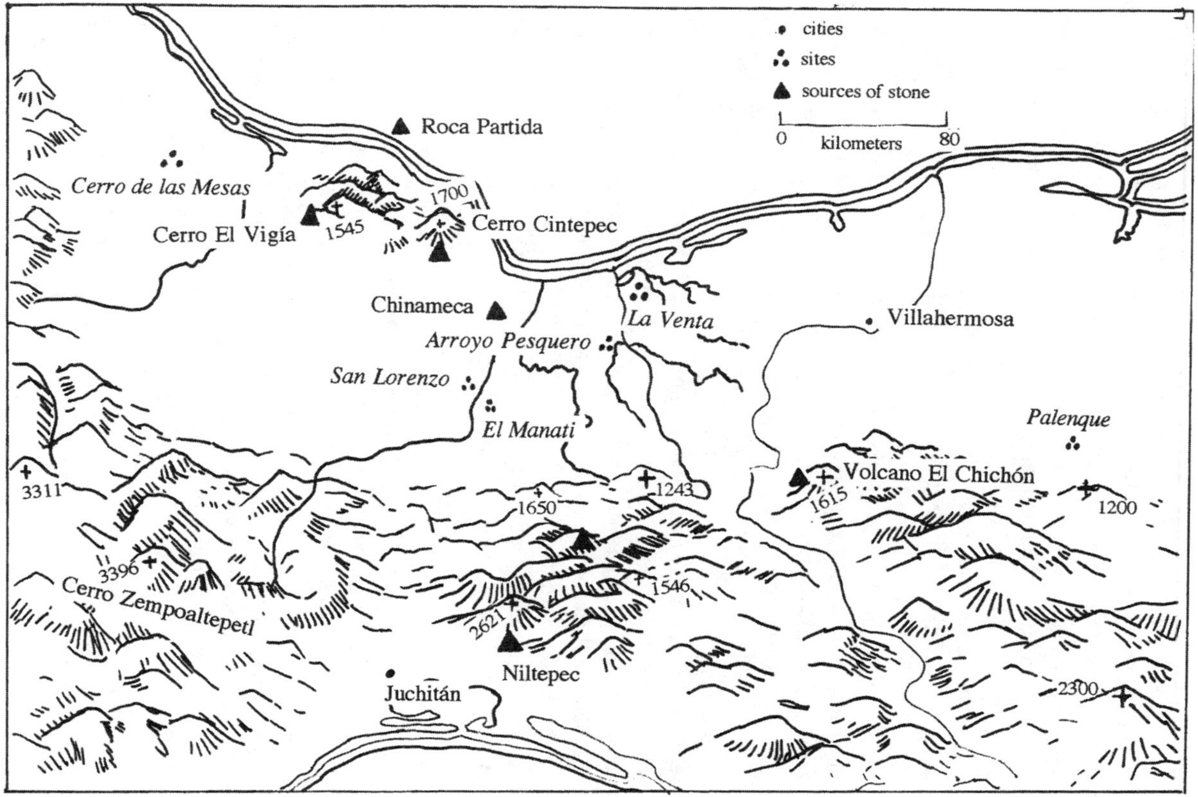

FIGURE 4. Map of the Gulf Coast Olmec region around La Venta. Drawing by C. Tate.

until about 800 BCE. An early example of the ritual use of the landscape during this period, is the site of El Manatí. Between 1600 and 1200 BCE, in a freshwater spring adjacent to a hill, humans cached (deliberately buried) finely polished jade celts from hundreds of miles away, along with rubber balls and wooden busts of human figures. Near El Manatí was the first urban center of Mesoamerica, San Lorenzo, which flourished between 1250 and 900 BCE. At this site, on a plateau, regional inhabitants carved huge boulders of basalt into the forms of colossal heads, thrones, and other monuments. By about 900 BCE, the breeding of maize had resulted in a cob about two and a half inches long, and people began to use it as a staple food.[14] During the regional transition to maize as a staple crop, the La Ventans began to build their ritual center to serve as a microcosm of the mountains and seas of the known world, which for them was the Isthmus of Tehuantepec in southern Mexico.[15] In their efforts to describe the role of humans within the regional environment and the cosmos, La Venta's inhabitants and visitors drew upon at least five hundred years of regional developments in empirical knowledge, subsistence and ritual technologies, and political systems. Not only was La Venta constructed to emulate the regional topography, it also contained sculptures and mounds that explicitly represented male and female genitalia, claims that are developed below. The fetus monuments were situated within this sexually charged, sacred landscape.

The site's largest feature was an earthen mound built as an effigy of the inhabitants' sacred mountain, which was seventy miles to the south. The line between the actual mountain peak and the artificial earthen mound ran 8 degrees west of north and became the central axis of the site's architecture (see fig. 5). Along this axis, just north of the hundred-foot-high mound, the La Ventans used green stone blocks to create huge effigies of lakes[16] that honored the goddess of childbirth and fishing who gave the fetus its vital soul.[17] They also made a mosaic of greenstone blocks in a pattern that signified a female supernatural flowering earth surface with a stylized four-directional body, cleft head, and fringed diamond skirt.

My recent reconstruction of the locations of monuments reveals that the La Ventans marked the central axis with five green and red stone columns soaring up to eighteen feet high. The northernmost column was incised with the stylized face and hand of the human seed or embryo. Three similarly carved columns have been excavated at the earlier site, San Lorenzo. The one most recently discovered, Monument San Lorenzo 103, shows a stylized infant or (more likely) an embryo by means of low relief that wraps around the "front" and "sides" of the figurelike column.

14. Kevin O. Pope, Mary E. D. Pohl, and John G. Jones et al., "Origin and Environmental Setting of Ancient Agriculture in the Lowlands of Mesoamerica," *Science* 292, 5520 (2001); William F. Rust and Barbara Leyden, "Evidence of Maize Use at Early and Middle Preclassic La Venta Olmec Sites," in *Corn and Culture in the Prehistoric New World*, ed. S. Johannessen and C. A. Hastorf (Boulder, Colo.: Westview Press, 1994).

15. Carolyn E. Tate, "Patrons of Shamanic Power: La Venta's Supernatural Entities in Light of Mixe Beliefs," *Ancient Mesoamerica* 20, 2 (1999).

16. F. Kent Reilly III, "Enclosed Ritual Spaces and the Watery Underworld in Formative Period Architecture: New Observations on the Function of La Venta Complex A," in *Seventh Palenque Round Table, 1989*, ed. Merle Greene Robertson and Virginia M. Fields (San Francisco: Pre-Columbian Art Research Institute, 1994).

17. Tate, "Patrons of Shamanic Power."

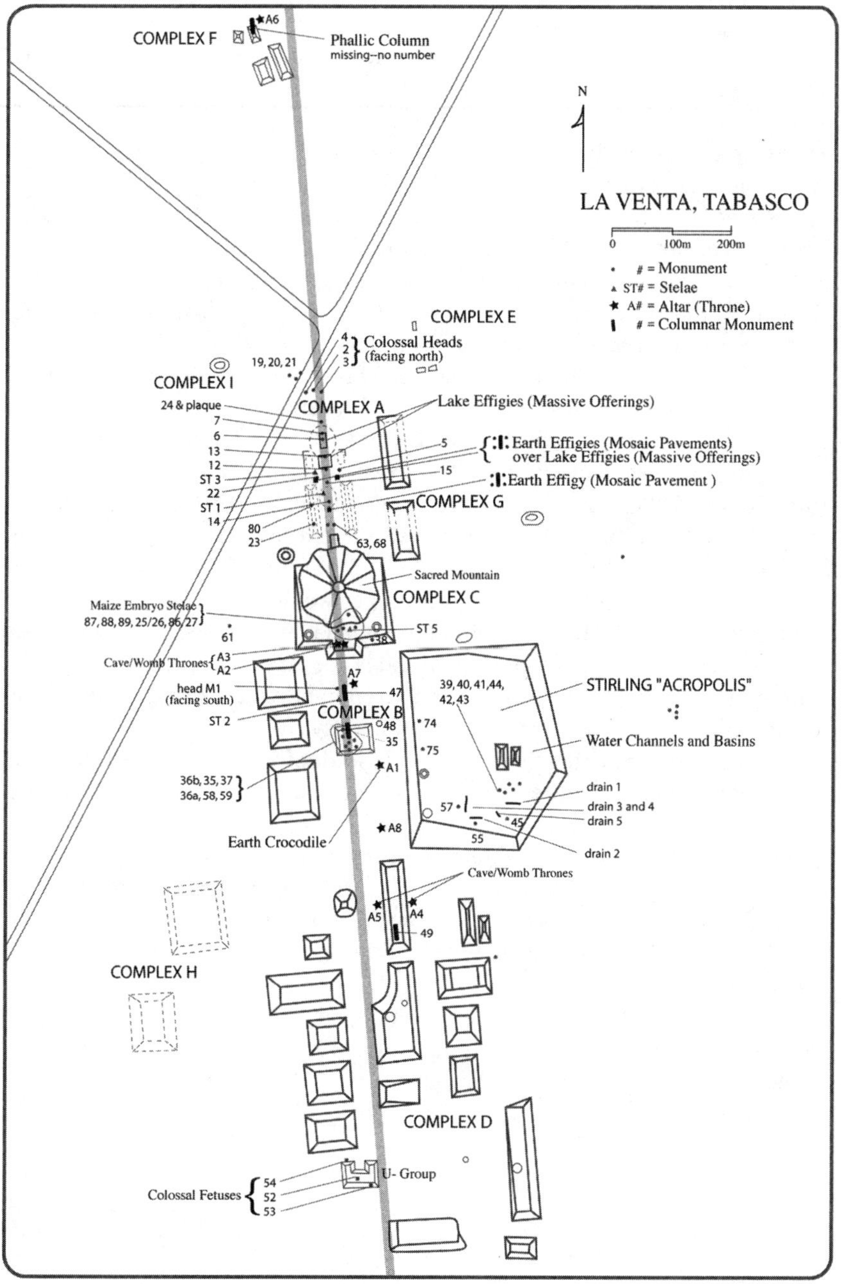

FIGURE 5. Plan of La Venta's mounds and monuments. Drawing by Corey Escoto. Used with permission.

The "back" is nearly plain, with the exception of a constricted area and a bulge on the top right and left, such that the whole resembles a phallus.[18] At La Venta, the surviving fragment of the northernmost column measures about seven feet. It rose above the flat northern plain on a "steeply conical" mound about twenty feet high.[19] These freestanding columns (which supported nothing) seem to be primal symbols of fertilization. Like the *coa* (the Nahuatl term for a digging or planting stick), they pierce the earth so that insemination can occur. Such a stick was likely in use by 1700 BCE in Oaxaca and perhaps along the Gulf Coast as well.

It is clear that Mesoamerican peoples viewed aspects of their world in what might be called an isomorphic parallelism—if things have a similar shape or function, then they form a category in which things share a related meaning. This kind of logic suggests that the columns metaphorically represented male sexual organs penetrating the earth surface. Isomorphically, they also represented lightning and rain penetrating the earth to initiate seasonal cycles of seed germination and fruiting.

The notion that a long stone object such as a column, celt, knife, or axe might metaphorically represent the phallus and its fertilizing function was common among later Mesoamerican cultures. An Aztec creation tale, recorded by Gerónimo Mendieta, Francisco Clavigero, and others between the late 1500s and late 1700s, illustrated this concept. It concerns a female celestial being called Citlalinicue or Stars-Her-Skirt, the womb of the sky and mother of all stars. At the beginning of creation, a flint knife fell from her womb and penetrated a cave in the surface of the earth. This was none other than Chicomoztoc, the seven-lobed cave considered to be the ancestral womb and home of the Aztecs (see fig. 6). Once fertilized by the knife, the cave bore the sixteen hundred (or innumerable) gods. These gods lacked beings to provide devotion, services, and food, so Citlalinicue sent them a message advising them to seek the seeds of the human race in the form of bones of the people of a previous creation. To obtain these ancient seed-bones from the underworld, the gods elected one named Xolotl. After a struggle with the Lord of the Underworld, Xolotl obtained the bones but in the process, he dropped and shattered them. When he returned to the surface of the earth, he and the other gods fertilized the bone-seeds with their own blood. The seed-bones then became a male human child and a female human child, progenitors of the human race, created to serve the gods.[20]

Similar to the Aztec tale in concept, although distinct in details, is the opening of the sixteenth-century Quiché Maya creation story, the *Popol Vuh*. The Quiché referred to the "womb of the sky" that was present but empty at the era of creation,

18. Ann Cyphers, *Escultura Olmeca de San Lorenzo Tenochtitlán* (Mexico City: Universidad Nacional Autónoma de México, Instituto de Investigaciones Antropológicas, 2004), 173–75. Cyphers refers to the "front" image as an infant. Because its face has been mutilated, she thinks it might represent a specific individual. I disagree with this; however, the issue of portraiture is beyond the scope of this chapter. In a previous article, Cyphers did describe this sculpture as "phallic" in form. See Ann Cyphers, "San Lorenzo," *Arqueología Mexicana* 4, 19 (1996), 64.

19. Philip Drucker, "La Venta, Tabasco: A Study of Olmec Ceramics and Art," *Bulletin* 153 (Smithsonian Institution Bureau of American Ethnology, 1952); Matthew W. Stirling, "Stone Monuments of Southern Mexico," *Bulletin* 138 (Smithsonian Institution Bureau of American Ethnology, 1943).

20. Burr C. Brundage, *The Fifth Sun: Aztec Gods, Aztec World* (Austin: University of Texas Press, 1979), 35–37.

FIGURE 6. The "seven caves of origin," Chicomoztoc, from the Aztec Historia Tolteca Chichimeca (16th century). Drawing by Corey Escoto. Used with permission.

above a motionless sea.[21] The creation of the world occurred when a council of gods or potencies formed the intention of creating earth and accomplished it through the spoken word. This seems to have taken the form of several long flashes of lightning that united sky and water, causing "germination and creation" of plants, life, and humanity.[22] Such unions between elements of sky and earth are similar to the hierogamies found in ancient myths of creation and procreation found in many North American societies, as well as in the Old World.[23] However, few other cultures have chosen to monumentalize procreation, gestation, and birth to the extent that the La Ventans did.

To populate their landscape of insemination and generation, La Ventans placed more than 120 monuments on its surface and buried within it hundreds of precious stone sculptures. Among these sculptures, six sets of identical monuments apparently illustrated a creation narrative.[24] Since this is the first publication to identify the sculptural sets and discuss them as a continuous narrative, the story will be very tentative, consisting more of units of discourse than actual narrative. At this early stage of scholarship, it is not even possible to state definitively whether a fixed order of narrative existed and, if so, from which end of the site it began. Also, it will be necessary to make several detours from the basic story to suggest some new interpretations of Olmec iconography that affect our understanding of the fetus sculptures. Nevertheless, I hope this initial study will suffice to create a context for the fetus sculptures and will allow us to glimpse their role in a creation story sketched through art.

Narrative Station 1: Fetuses in a Womb

The story told by La Venta's narrative stations (see fig. 7) probably began in the south, at the entrance through which travelers from the rest of Mesoamerica would have arrived.[25] The southernmost feature was a low U-shaped mound.[26] It was unique in Mesoamerica at that time, although Andean peoples had already built similar U-shaped mounds prior to 1000 BCE. According to archaeologist Bill Isbell, the Andean U-groups symbolized the vagina as a passage into the uterus as well

21. Allen J. Christenson, *Popol Vuh: The Sacred Book of the Maya*, 2 vols. (Winchester, England: O Books, 2003), I:145–47.

22. Ibid., 70 n. 62.

23. Marta Weigle, *Creation and Procreation: Feminist Reflections on Mythologies of Cosmogony and Parturition* (Philadelphia: University of Pennsylvania Press, 1989). Weigle compiled a diverse body of literature on themes of creation to demonstrate the androcentric bias this topic had received and to offer a broader conception of the varieties of cosmogonic myths. In many such stories from around the world, cosmogony involved acts such as accretion, secretion (such as vomit, sweat, parthenogenesis), sacrifice, division, diving into primordial earth or sea, emergence, battle, and the like. The La Venta story contains many of these elements and deserves a more thorough comparative treatment than can be accomplished here.

24. Other clusters of dissimilar monuments recorded political histories of rulers. However, because this volume focuses on fetuses, I shall disregard the political histories and discuss only the narrative stations.

25. Rebecca B. González Lauck, "La Venta: An Olmec Capital," in *Olmec Art of Ancient Mexico*, ed. Elizabeth P. Benson and Beatríz de la Fuente (Washington, D.C.: National Gallery of Art, 1996), 80; Matthew W. Stirling, "Great Stone Faces of the Mexican Jungle," *National Geographic* 77 (1940).

26. M. Judith Gallegos Gómora, "Excavaciones en La Estructura D-7 En La Venta, Tabasco," *Arqueología* 4 (1990).

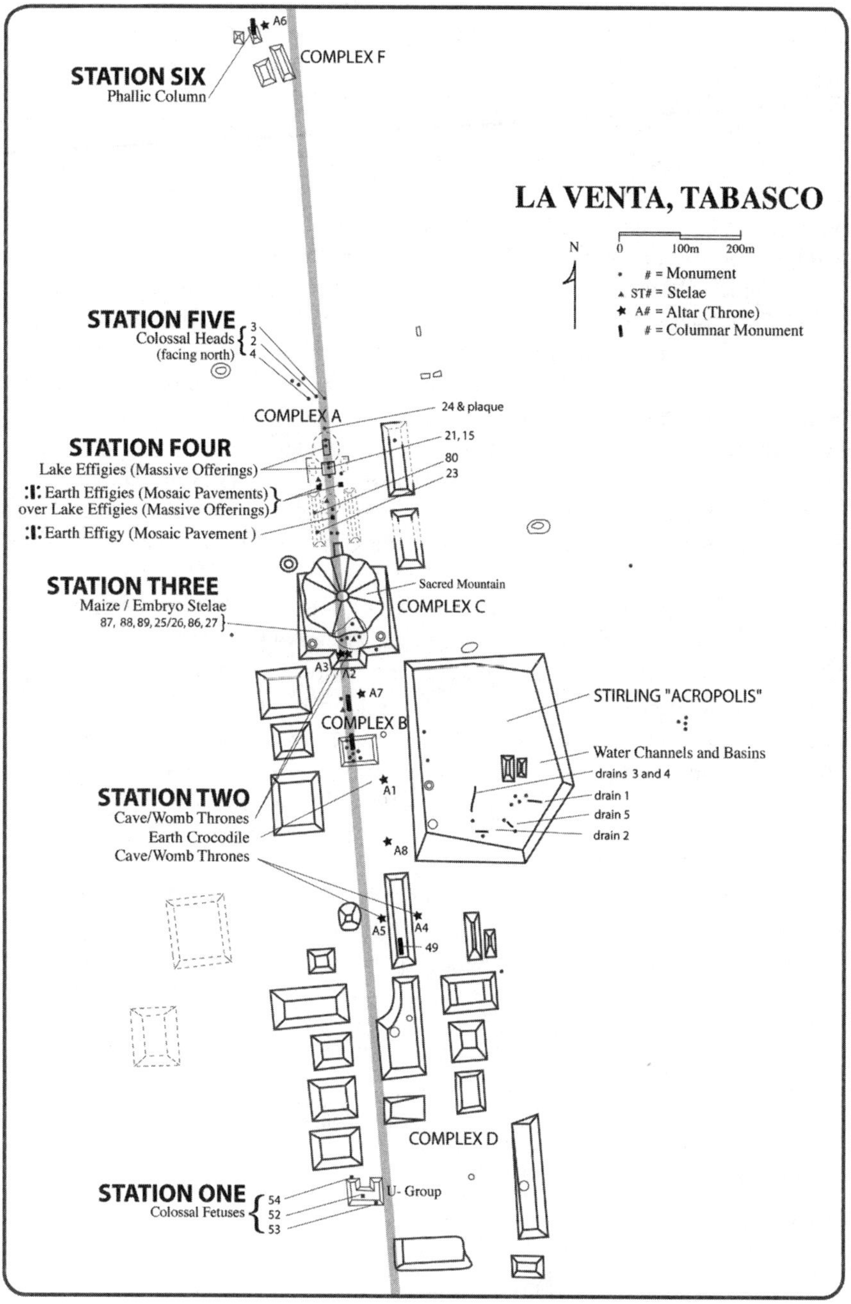

FIGURE 7. Plan of La Venta's narrative stations. Drawing by Corey Escoto. Used with permission.

as into another cosmic level. They were associated with cosmogonic origins and were loci where humans could contact other realms to acquire spiritual power.[27] The gestational significance of the U-shaped construction was well known in the Americas. At the great highland Mexican city Teotihuacan (200 BCE–750 CE), the pyramid of the Sun was built over a cave whose form was modified to resemble a vaginal passage with lobed womblike chambers.[28] A mural in the Tepantitla apartment complex at that city shows an almost stratigraphic view of an Earth Goddess in the form of a mountain, at the center of which is a large U-shaped womb. Numerous images of flesh-lined U-shaped openings in sky and earth forms that symbolize wombs appear in pictorial manuscripts of the Mixtec, Mixteca-Puebla, and Aztec. For example, in sixteenth-century Mexico, an Aztec creator couple, shown in the Codex Borbonicus, divined in a U-shaped sacred enclosure that represented a cave and womb releasing the waters of birth (see fig. 8).[29] The grandmother cast seeds, and the grandfather held a sacrificial implement and brazier. Similarly, the three-temple groups of the Maya, such as the Cross Group at Palenque (dedicated 690 CE), formed a U-shaped arrangement around a central plaza. At the Cross Group, the texts refer to the innermost temples (U-shaped enclosures) as *pib-na,* "oven" or "womb," and indicate that they were the birthplace of the local deities.[30] Based on these parallels, I suggest that the La Venta U-shaped platform symbolized the earth's vulva, vagina, or womb.

On this symbolic womb stood the largest sculptures at the site, the three sandstone fetuses mentioned above (see fig. 9). The choice of sandstone for these sculptures was significant. Few Olmec figural monuments were made of sandstone, only two from San Lorenzo and these three fetuses. Most monuments were carved of basalt, an igneous stone, or some metamorphic rocks, especially green schist and gray gneiss. Both the igneous and metamorphic stones were "cooked" or subjected to high heat and pressure. A widespread metaphor for gestation is "cooking"[31] so I suggest that making the fetuses of sedimentary sandstone indicated their "uncooked" state.

More than six feet high, the colossal fetuses stood upright on flexed legs, as if they were alive. Their hands grasped their helmeted heads.[32] The tight-fitting helmet appeared on only these fetus sculptures, the four colossal heads, and a high-relief

27. William Isbell, "Cosmological Order Expressed in Prehistoric Ceremonial Centers," *Actes de XLII International Congress of Americanists, Paris* 4 (1977).

28. Doris Heyden, "Caves, Gods, and Myths: World-View and Planning in Teotihuacan," in *Mesoamerican Sites and World Views,* ed. Elizabeth P. Benson (Washington, D.C.: Dumbarton Oaks, 1981), 4.

29. Susan Milbrath, "Birth Images in Mixteca-Puebla Art," in *The Role of Gender in Pre-Columbian Art and Architecture,* ed. Virginia E. Miller (Lanham, Md.: University Press of America, 1988), 153–78.

30. Stephen Houston, "Symbolic Sweatbaths of the Maya: Architectural Meaning in the Cross Group at Palenque, Mexico," *Latin American Antiquity* 7, 2 (1996): 132–51.

31. John Monaghan, "Dedication: Ritual or Production?" in *The Sowing and the Dawning: Termination, Dedication, and Transformation in the Archaeological and Ethnographic Record of Mesoamerica,* ed. Shirley Boteler Mock (Albuquerque: University of New Mexico Press, 1998), 49.

32. Despite the concurrence of medical specialists with my identification of these figures as fetuses, some members of the Mesoamerican archaeological community continue to resist the idea, referring to these and other fetus figures as infants or dwarfs. However, their proportions indicate that they are not infants, and they cannot be dwarfs because one of the limitations on the movements of achondroplastic dwarfs is that they are unable to raise their arms as these figures do.

FIGURE 8. Aztec creator couple in a U-shaped (celestial womb) enclosure. From the Codex Borbonicus (16th century). Drawing by Corey Escoto. Used with permission.

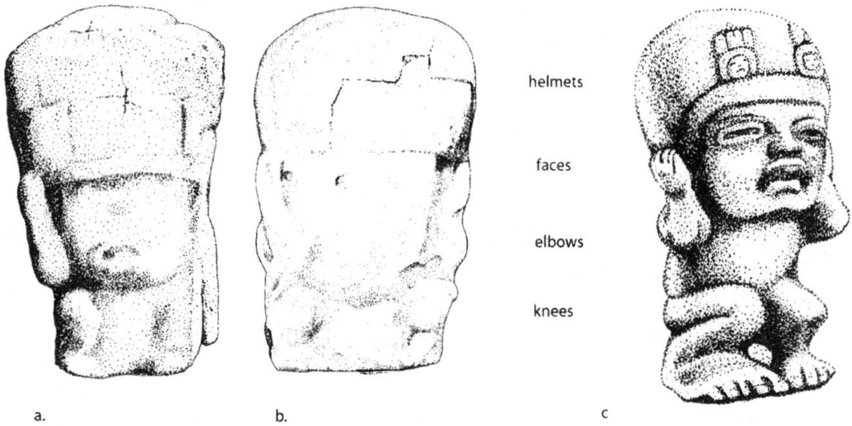

FIGURE 9. Station 1. La Venta's colossal fetuses and a small fetus sculpture in the Metropolitan Museum of Art: (a) La Venta Monument 54, height 375 centimeters, drawing by Corey Escoto, used with permission; (b) La Venta Monument 52, height 200 centimeters, drawing by Corey Escoto, used with permission; (c) figure holding head, height 26 centimeters, collection Metropolitan Museum of Art, drawing by C. Tate.

sculpture of a female, possibly a goddess. Several scholars have considered the colossal heads as representations of decapitated heads and have suggested that this particular headgear associated the heads, which likely represented rulers, with the ballgame.[33] Headgear in Mesoamerica usually contained symbols that identified the wearer by name. The symbols on the helmets of the basalt colossal heads are still visible, but those on the sandstone fetuses are severely eroded. Nevertheless, the similar headgear indicates that the two sets of monuments were conceptually related, perhaps in terms of activity (ballplaying and/or decapitation) or possibly, specific identity.

In Mesoamerica, the ballgame was a metaphor for creation, death, and rebirth on social, agricultural, and cosmic levels. Scholars describe it as a symbolic battle between opposing cosmic forces, such as sky and earth, sun and moon, darkness and light.[34] I suggest that these dueling opposites were metaphors for sexual intercourse as well, with the intention of generating life. To consider what the Olmec might have intended by portraying the fetuses as ballplayers, we must examine some later references to decapitated ballplayers.

Several eighth-century Maya monuments referred to decapitations during primordial ballgames and their role in creation. As art historian Linda Schele and archaeologist David Freidel have shown, the hieroglyphic text of a carved Maya stair (Yaxchilan Structure 33 Step VII) tells of three decapitations of young maize-humans that had occurred in the distant past in a sacred ball court. Each sacrificial victim was referred to as a bundled skull or seed. Scribes continued the story by linking the ancient decapitations to a living king's ballgame.[35] Interestingly, two small infantile beings accompany the king in this scene, and they wear helmets much like those on the La Venta fetuses. In this Classic Period Maya story, the decapitated head (or skull-bone) of a ballplaying hero of an earlier era became the seed for the next generation. This use of bones of a previous group of humans as seeds for new life parallels the Post-Classic era Aztec Citlalinicue tale discussed above.

The fullest surviving text that explained the link between the ballgame and creation is the Maya *Popol Vuh*, an alphabetic text written in sixteenth-century Guatemala.[36] The story featured several sets of twin brothers, some of whom were Hero Twins. The first generation of twins, One Hunahpu and Seven Hunahpu,

33. For colossal heads and the ballgame, see Douglas E. Bradley, "Gender, Power, and Fertility in the Olmec Ritual Ballgame," in *The Sport of Life and Death: The Mesoamerican Ballgame*, ed. E. Michael Whittington (Charlotte, N.C.: Mint Museum, 2001), 33; Susan Gillespie, "Ballgames and Boundaries," in *The Mesoamerican Ballgame*, ed. Vernon L. Scarborough and David R. Wilcox (Tucson: University of Arizona Press, 1991); and Christopher L. Moser, "Human Decapitation in Ancient Mesoamerica," *Studies in Pre-Columbian Art and Archaeology* 11 (Washington, D.C.: Dumbarton Oaks, Trustees for Harvard University, 1973).

34. Marvin Cohodas, "The Symbolism and Ritual Function of the Middle Classic Ballgame in Mesoamerica," *American Indian Quarterly* 2, 2 (1975), Esther Pasztory, "Artistic Traditions of the Middle Classic Period," in *Middle Classic Mesoamerica: A.D. 400–700*, ed. Esther Pasztory (New York: Columbia University Press, 1978).

35. Linda Schele and David A. Friedel, "The Courts of Creation: Ballcourts, Ballgames, and Portals to the Maya Otherworld," in *The Mesoamerican Ballgame*, ed. Vernon L. Scarborough and David R. Wilcox (Tucson: University of Arizona Press, 1991). The authors report that several Maya ball courts were called Ox Ahal Em, or "thrice-made descents," possibly a reference to the previous primordial eras mentioned in the *Popol Vuh*.

36. Several translations of the *Popol Vuh* from Quiché Mayan into English exist. The two most recent are Christenson, *Popol Vuh: The Sacred Book of the Maya,* and Dennis Tedlock, *Popol Vuh: The Mayan Book of the Dawn of Life* (New York: Simon and Schuster, 1996). The plot as I describe it is similar in both, but each translation pursues different tropes.

were somewhat indolent. They amused themselves with ballplaying and were summoned to the underworld for a match. Once they descended through the Western Ballcourt to the underworld, they failed the many tests[37] put to them by the Lords of Xibalba (the underworld), whom I call the Lords of Anti-Life. In fact, they did not even think to bring their own ball to the underworld match and were sacrificed before they could play ball. Before their burial, one twin, One Hunahpu, was decapitated. His head was placed in a tree, where the skull became a calabash fruit. The fruit/skull spit into the hand of a princess of the underworld, impregnating her, and she rose to the earth surface and bore another set of Hero Twins.[38]

The younger Hero Twins, despite ill treatment as children, took their ballplaying seriously. When called to contest the Lords of the Underworld, Hunahpu and Xbalanque determined to avenge and resurrect their fathers. They brought with them the ball their fathers had left behind in their home. After entering the underworld through a ball court, they outsmarted the lords in many trials, in ballgame matches, and they even survived decapitation. During one trial, the twins were locked inside Bat House for the night. To escape the screeching bats, they hid inside their blowguns for hours. Finally, Hunahpu decided it must be dawn, so he peeped out the blowgun. A lightning-swift bat snatched off his head. The Lords of Anti-Life placed the head on top of the ball court until the next day, when it would be used as a ball in the game. Meanwhile, his twin, Xbalanque, arranged to fashion a large squash into the form of his brother's head and placed it on Hunahpu's still-living torso. During the game, when Hunahpu's real head was kicked out of bounds, Xbalanque yanked the squash head off Hunahpu's torso, sent it bouncing into the ball court, then (with the aid of a rabbit) grabbed the real head and replaced it on his brother's body. Both twins battled the Lords of Anti-Life on the court until Xbalanque struck the squash, causing it to burst and its seeds to be strewn over the court. The lords were shocked, asking what the squash was and where it came from. The text specifies that this was the moment of the lords' defeat.[39]

I propose that by scattering seeds in the underworld and by bringing his own ball, Xbalanque introduced life into the realm of Anti-Life. It was this fecundation, not merely surviving decapitation and winning the game, which defeated the Lords of Xibalba. Although they were victorious, the twins' task of fertilization and insemination was not finished. They voluntarily entered a fiery pit oven (like a womb) in a valiant act of self-sacrifice. They had previously connived to have the lords remove their bones from the oven, grind them, and scatter them into a river. Five days later, they resurrected as catfish-humans who worked as dancers and entertainers. The rebirth of the twins from a river as fish is similar to the belief of the modern Mixe in the female supernormal power Higiny, who rules rivers, fishing, and midwifery, and brings the spirit of the child to its mother's womb.[40] The twins

37. One of the tests given to both sets of twins in the underworld was to keep their cigars lit all night without burning them up. This seems like an obvious isomorphic reference to sexual prowess to me!

38. D. Tedlock, *Popol Vuh*, 91–104.

39. Ibid., 104–30; Christenson, *Popol Vuh* I:176 and II:135.

40. Frank J. Lipp, *The Mixe of Oaxaca: Religion, Ritual and Healing* (Austin: University of Texas Press, 1991), 32–33.

entered the fiery earth womb, their ground bones were scattered like seeds into the river, where they were transformed and revitalized, finally emerging from the female river as fish-humans with godlike abilities. As a result of their self-sacrifice, Hunahpu and Xbalanque gained complete control over life and death—they could decapitate or burn things and bring them back, including themselves.[41]

In Euro-American thought, decapitation is ordinarily considered a decisive termination of life, but in Mesoamerica, it had other meanings. As Schele and Freidel explained, the death and rebirth of the younger Heroes of the *Popol Vuh* following their ballgame was a metaphor for the cycle of the maize plant: mature tasseling, withering, decapitating or beheading the seed ears, burning the fields, planting the seed, fertilizing with rain, and sprouting again. Decapitation of the maize ear, like burning the field and planting, is a part of the life cycle of maize in which humans intervene, so it is a human cultural construction. When applied to humans, decapitation destroyed the wholeness of the body. However, because animating cosmic forces lodged in the head, decapitation did not produce a lifeless head, but, as archaeologist Susan Gillespie has written, one that can "jump, roll, and fly." She pointed out that whereas in Mesoamerican thought the primordial cosmos was a unity and the original human body was whole, decapitation is the "introduction of a disjunction—the division of the body into its parts."[42] This segmentation produced periodicity and created cyclical movement, which manifested in agricultural and celestial cycles. The essential element of the ballgame was to keep the ball in constant motion, to make it like the sun and planets. The ballgame and its bouncing ball represented astronomical cycles as well as, I suggest, the rhythmic, life-promoting activity of sexual intercourse.

The Hero Twins story in the *Popol Vuh* was replete with fecundating tropes. The ball, made of rubber from the sap of a tree, was metaphorically an agent of insemination and fertilization, likened to human seminal fluid and blood. The earliest known rubber balls were found at the earliest levels (1600 BCE) of the Olmec ritual site El Manatí. Pilgrims laid a layer of sandstone (uncooked!) blocks into a spring. On this floor they deposited nine rubber balls (possibly referring to the nine lunations of gestation) along with expertly wrought jade celts. This enacted an insemination of the sacred female waters with rubber (representing male seminal fluid) and the phallic metamorphic stone celts. Producing the axes and balls required great effort, self-control, and intention. In a later phase (1200–1000 BCE), the insemination complex included wooden anthropomorphic busts, plants material and seeds, jade axes arrayed in flower-like patterns, rubber balls, and bones of infants.[43] By this time, the concept of what constituted fecundating materials had expanded. By 300 CE, the Maya linked rubber to blood, and used tied balls to substitute for human sacrifices. Of course, self-sacrifice of blood was most potent when drawn from the penis and scattered like seeds onto strips of fiber that would be burned. Similarly, rubber was also ritually spattered onto

41. Christenson, *Popol Vuh*, 160–84; D. Tedlock, *Popol Vuh*, 105–42.
42. Gillespie, "Ballgames and Boundaries," 326, 333.
43. Ortiz and Rodríguez, "The Sacred Hill of El Manatí."

bark paper and burned.[44] Thus a conceptual link between rubber, semen, seed, and blood seems to have existed among the Maya. That skulls could produce fertilizing liquid was clearly an element of Aztec thought around 1400. A Nahuatl word for semen, *omicetl*, means "coagulated bone substance."[45] A much later parallel to the El Manatí spring offering was recently excavated in the Aztec ball court of Tenochtitlan. Ball court Offering 4 included a flint knife (for penetration of the earth/womb), a small rubber ball (signifying spurting semen), and objects of shell (from female fecund waters) including a flower (like the jade axe arrangement of El Manatí—the desired life form), hands (for scattering blood, casting seed, or catching semen), and bones (like the infant bones, a metaphor for seed and semen).[46] Thus the ball, from the earliest times, functioned on a symbolic level as a visible metaphor for fertilizing, life-giving fluids that fly, spurt, bounce when stimulated (and drip and sag when not). This isomorphic-equivalence set included semen, blood, rubber, and seeds. In the *Popol Vuh*'s ballgames, bouncing rubber balls, ball-skulls and seed-filled squashes within the underworld courts were metaphors for darting semen in the womb.

The younger Maya Hero Twins took their own ball/seed to the underworld. By bouncing the balls in the underworld court, the twins intended to avenge their fathers, to defeat the Lords of the Underworld, and possibly to vindicate their ill treatment as children by becoming heroes. At first, they seem not to have intended to regenerate the world. Yet this was a result of their sport. Similarly, a person may engage in copulation for reasons other than to produce offspring, yet a pregnancy may result.

However, self-sacrifice, and the self-control it requires, was the essential catalyst for regeneration. In the Maya *Popol Vuh*, the first Hero Twins did not really intend to sacrifice themselves, but managed one act of insemination (humorously, spitting from the "wrong end"). For the second twins, after the squash seeds were scattered and they were able to regenerate Hunahpu, they realized their power, and their intention broadened. With deliberate and cunning intention, they sacrificed themselves by entering a fiery womb, fully aware of their power to regenerate. They ultimately rose to dwell in the womb of the sky as sun and moon, at approximately the same time that the creator couple found the seeds of maize at Split Mountain, ground them with primordial water, and formed the first humans.[47]

We can reconsider La Venta's fetus-ballplayers within a constellation of contexts and draw some inferences about their significance. They emerged from a U-shaped womb-vagina as ballplayers. Their big round heads with helmets were isomorphic symbols of rubber balls, which contained their skulls and referred to fecundating semen and seed. They raised their arms deliberately to grasp their

44. Andrea J. Stone, "Spirals, Ropes, and Feathers: The Iconography of Rubber Balls in Mesoamerican Art," *Ancient Mesoamerica* 13 (2002).

45. Alfredo López-Austin, *The Human Body and Ideology: Concepts of the Ancient Nahuas*, trans. Thelma Ortiz de Montellano and Bernard Ortiz de Montellano (Salt Lake City: University of Utah Press, 1980), 176.

46. E. Michael Whittington, "Catalogue," in *The Sport of Life and Death: The Mesoamerican Ballgame*, ed. E. Michael Whittington (Charlotte, N.C.: Mint Museum; New York: Thames and Hudson, 2001), 248.

47. Christenson, *Popol Vuh*, I:191.

heads, either to remove them as a self-sacrifice or to replace them and restart life with full power over seasons, celestial movements, life and death.

It is possible that the La Ventans deliberately connected the helmeted fetuses to the Colossal Heads and that both represented local rulers. It was common for Classic Period (250–900) Maya rulers to describe themselves as ballplayers, both in pictorial imagery and hieroglyphic texts. Rulers who played the cosmic ballgame claimed powers of regeneration for themselves and their communities.[48] Clearly, when played in civic-ceremonial courts like the one at La Venta, the ballgame had an important political-ritual component as well as a religious or conceptual one. A brief examination of the remaining sculptural stations in La Venta's visual narrative will reveal further subtleties in the significance of the fetuses.

Narrative Station 2: Rituals at Sacred Caves of the Four Directions

Proceeding northward, the next narrative station is composed of five basalt thrones,[49] two in the south, two in the north, and one in the center. These form a quincunx, which in Mesoamerica refers to four sacred intercardinal directions (points at which the sun enters and emerges from the earth's surface) and a central axis.

The central of the five thrones represented a crocodilian creature (see fig. 10a). This crocodile portrayed a female earth-surface supernatural who sustained an earlier creation. Both the Maya and Aztec retained the concept that the primordial earth took the form of a female crocodile who inhabited the primal waters. For example, among the Aztecs, the crocodile could refer to Tlaltecutli, Earth Goddess.[50] In some tales, twin heroes slew her, causing trees and grasses, flowers, rivers, and mountains to spring forth from her dismembered body.[51]

Sculpted into the "front" of the four other La Venta thrones were large U-shaped niches that scholars agree referred to caves and wombs. The thrones probably supported rulers, and their caves represented loci of mythical origins. Generally speaking, caves are, in Mesoamerican cognition, the most dangerously powerful places—sources of rain, seeds, and other aspects of life force. The northwest and southeast thrones (Altars 3 and 4) showed adult shamans seated in the cave-wombs (see fig. 10b). Symbols on the thrones continued the generative themes, and included ancestors, flowering umbilical cords, and pots of fertilizing rain.[52]

48. For another dimension of the game as institutionalized boundary conflicts and competition among farmers, to promote solidarity for long-term survival, see Schele and Freidel, "Courts of Creation," 308–10.

49. For Olmec altars as thrones, see David C. Grove, "Olmec Altars and Myths," *Archaeology* 26, 2 (1973); David C. Grove, "The Olmec Paintings of Oxtotitlan Cave, Guerrero," *Studies in Pre-Columbian Art and Archaeology* 6 (1970).

50. For Tlaltecutli, see Brundage, *Fifth Sun*, 31; Henry B. Nicholson, "Religion in Pre-Hispanic Central Mexico," in *Handbook of Middle American Indians*, Vol. 10, ed. Gordon F. Eckholm and Ignacio Bernal (Austin: University of Texas Press, 1971), 400.

51. At La Venta, the other crocodile was on a sarcophagus. It emitted flowers, suggesting the rebirth of the person symbolically buried within.

52. Julia Guernsey Kappelman and F. Kent Reilly III, "Paths to Heaven, Ropes to Earth: Birds, Jaguars, and Cosmic Cords in Formative Period Mesoamerica," *Ancient America* 2 and 3 (2001): 46. These authors describe Throne 4 as combining avian and jaguarian imagery to create "a potent statement of supernatural contact" between sky and

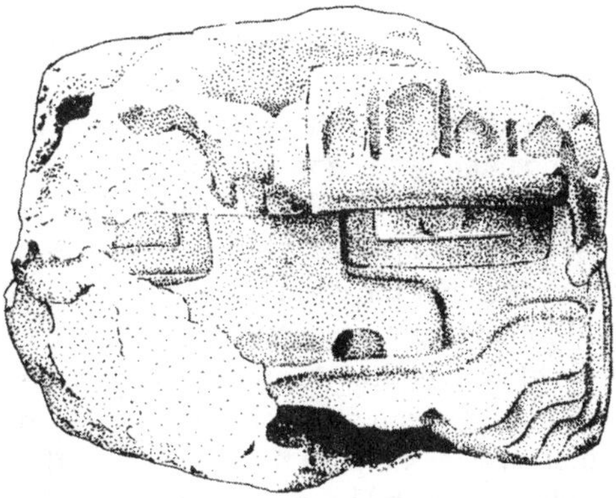

a.

b.

c.

FIGURE 10. Station 2. Three of the five thrones of La Venta: (a) Altar 1, the crocodile or earth of a previous creation, drawing by Corey Escoto, used with permission; (b) Altar 4, the southeast throne, showing a shaman in a cave-womb-sweatbath surrounded by a flowering umbilicus, drawing by C. Tate; (c) Altar 5, the southwest throne, showing an adult in a cave-womb-sweatbath holding an infant. Four other infants, some with embryo-like cleft heads, are on the sides, also held by adults. Drawing by Corey Escoto, used with permission.

The thrones emulated the form of the sweatbath, a place of childbirth in Mesoamerica as well as a place for creation as fire mingled with its complementary fluid, water. In the Aztec culture, individuals were proscribed from entering a sweatbath without a companion of the opposite sex. The womblike sweatbath was not to be used for sexual activity; I suspect that maintaining a complementary balance of sexes in the most powerful sacred places was seen as necessary for promoting a similar balance throughout the cosmos and ultimately for ritually enacting the essential juxtaposition of generative forces.

On the northeast and southwest thrones (Altars 2 and 5) (see fig. 10c) a male adult sat within the cave-womb cavity, holding an infant.[53] Although these may have portrayed humans emerging from a cave-womb, they have more often been interpreted as depictions of child sacrifice. Many skeletons of fetuses, neonates, and children have been found, beginning in the earliest Olmec times at El Manatí, later cached under stone thrones and altars and in pyramids. Some bones showed evidence of cutting and scraping, suggesting murder or cannibalism. However, authors have tended to ignore the high incidence of miscarriage and infant death.[54] If these scenes refer to sacrifice, it is unclear whether the La Ventans would have ritually deposited infants who died naturally, seeing them as self-sacrifices, or whether adults offered their most precious fruit to the earth as the Aztec did later.[55] This question cannot be resolved based on the current archaeological data. In any case, the infants on the La Venta thrones seem to have functioned multivalently. One can consider them within a range of possibilities: as ritual sacrifices by adults of infants, whose potent little bones would fecundate the earth's fiery cave-womb; as sacrifices to a rain god;[56] or as the emergence of new life from the cave, as in the story of Citlalinicue.[57] The quincunxial arrangement of the cave-womb thrones

underworld cosmic realms. The jaguar on the upper edge held a flowering cord in its mouth, a symbol of a flowering cosmic umbilicus (40) or the flowery menstrual flow of the primordial earth female; see Barbara Tedlock, *The Woman in the Shaman's Body* (New York: Bantam Dell, 2005). The four flowers have also been seen as pots of rain emanating from a cave. The emerging adult held a thick umbilicus that led to figures on the sides, probably his ancestors, and wore an eagle headdress, suggested by Grove, "Olmec Altars and Myths," that some think identified him as a shaman (see F. Kent Reilly III, "Visions to Another World: Art, Shamanism, and Political Power in Middle Formative Mesoamerica," Ph.D. diss., University of Texas, 1994). The scene suggests that this shaman inherited power from his ancestors, sought it in generative caves, and manipulated it to bring rain to fertilize the earth, causing human-maize to sprout and flower.

53. On Throne 5, the adult wore an embryo-maize diadem, referring to regeneration from seed.

54. For infant mortality and miscarriage at Teotihuacan, see Rebecca Storey, *Life and Death in Teotihuacan: A Modern Paleodemographic Synthesis* (Tuscaloosa: University of Alabama Press, 1992).

55. For the significance of Aztec child sacrifice, see Philip P. Arnold, "Eating Landscape: Human Sacrifice and Sustenance in Aztec Mexico," in *To Change Place: Aztec Ceremonial Landscapes*, ed. Davíd Carrasco (Boulder: University of Colorado Press, 1991).

56. For an interpretation of La Venta infants as sacrifices to the rain god, see Peter David Joralemon, "A Study of Olmec Iconography," *Studies in Pre-Columbian Art and Archaeology* 7 (Washington, D.C.: Dumbarton Oaks, Trustees for Harvard University, 1971).

57. Supporting the idea of the La Venta caves as places of birth for culture heroes is a modern Mixe story of the birth of their culture hero, Kondoy. He was born near a cave in "Hill of the Woman." People used to go there to offer their mature cob of maize to the female earth spirit. The next day, they would return to find the cob of maize seeds transformed into two eggs. People collected the eggs and took them home to eat. One day a couple went to the cave and saw that the two eggs were in a well. The woman asked her husband to cut a pole so she could fish them out. He cut the pole and she successfully extracted the eggs. Three days later they cracked open. From one came Kondoy, the culture hero, and from the other, his brother, a huge snake. This myth is recorded in Walter S. Miller, *Cuentos*

could refer to specific caves in the four sacred directions, to the ordering of the cognitive space on the earth surface, and might have served as loci for shamanic ritual as well.[58]

Although I think it is premature to attempt a narration of La Venta's sculptural creation and origins story, I can imagine several tentative explanations for the sequence of fetuses and infants plus caves. If the narrative is one of human origins, like parts 3 and 4 of the *Popol Vuh*, then the fetuses may represent the elder ballplayers who failed the tests but, when decapitated, formed seed for the next generation. The infants on the thrones may refer to a second generation of Heroes who emerged victorious from the underworld after self-sacrifice. Alternatively, this sequence might be part of a cosmogonic tale of previous eras like the Aztec *Legend of the Suns*, which described four attempts to make proper humans, or the *Popol Vuh*, which told of three. Looking back from about 700–400 BCE, the La Ventans could have conceptualized the rise and fall of cultures contemporary with El Manati (1600–1250 BCE) and later San Lorenzo (1250–900 BCE) as two previous eras or ages in which mythic heroes established templates for ritualized action on the earth.

Narrative Station 3: The Dawning of Human-Maize

The northern two thrones stood on the edge of a platform from which rose La Venta's Great Mound, the largest in Mesoamerica at that time. It was a human-made Mountain of Sustenance in which seeds were stored.[59] Both Maya and Aztec creation stories feature a Mountain of Sustenance that hid the seeds of human food, especially maize. At the very foot of the Mound was Station 3, a series of six stelae.[60] Four of these depicted sprouting human-maize seeds, one for each of the four cardinal directions (see fig. 11). These represented the creation of the first humans, who were made of maize.

On each stela was the face of a human embryo wearing a headband of four maize seeds. The three horizontal bands that wrapped each embryo probably referred to the triple sacs that enclosed the embryo in the womb. The undulating upper edges of the stelae resemble the mountain from which the triple sprouts of the maize seed appeared. These three sprouts typify the germination of a maize seed. The Olmec frequently gave an embryo symbol the shape of a stone axe, which is similar to that of a maize seed. As archaeologist James Porter observed, axes and

---

Mixes, Biblioteca de Folklore Indígena (Mexico D. F.: Instituto Nacional Indigenista, 1956, 105–109).Today the Mixe frequently employ eggs in ceremonies performed for Holy Mother Earth. They are usually placed inside grass wreaths that represent the uterus, see Lipp, *The Mixe of Oaxaca*. Clearly the eggs of today substitute for the Olmec embryo symbol. This story includes embryos in the form of eggs, and, like the *Popol Vuh* tale, involves fish, maize, and sacred water in the generation of the Hero Twins.

58. For examples of the ritual use of caves in Mesoamerica, see James E. Brady and Keith M. Prufer, eds., *In the Maw of the Earth Monster: Mesoamerican Ritual Cave Use* (Austin: University of Texas Press, 2005).

59. Reilly, "Mountains of Creation."

60. González Lauck, "Acerca de Piramides de Tierra y Seres Sobrenaturales: Observaciones Preliminares en Torno al Edificio C-1. La Venta, Tabasco."

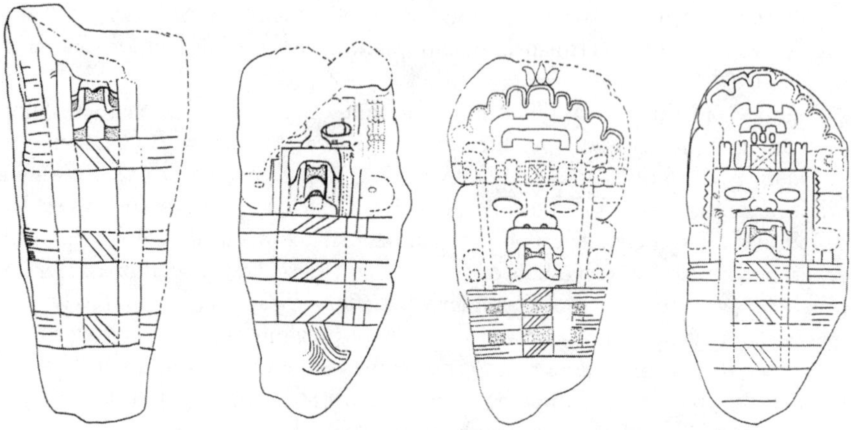

FIGURE 11. Station 3. La Venta's Human Embryo/Maize stelae. From left to right as they stood in front of Mound C: Monuments 89, 88, 25/26, and 27. Heights range from 203 centimeters to 497 centimeters. Drawing by C. Tate.

celts (such as those from El Manatí) were related to the form of these particular stelae.[61]

The four embryo-maize seed stelae may have referred to the first four androgynous ancestors. In the case of the Maya, only after the sacrifices of the two sets of Maya Hero Twins did the creator grandparents form, from ground maize seeds obtained from a mountain, four androgynous ancestors of the present race of humans. In the case of the Olmec, the four embryo stelae represented the first human-maize beings as embryos bundled in the womb. Embryos inherently appear androgynous, since until week 9 (when the embryo becomes a fetus), the "external genitalia of the two sexes are similar in appearance."[62] In most Mesoamerican societies, gender was not a fixed identity assigned to an individual but varied according to age and other factors.[63] This notion may have stemmed from Formative Period observations of the embryo.

To recapitulate, at the foot of ancient La Venta's Mountain, the site's center, human embryos as maize seed, still bundled in three uterine sacs, sprouted from the sacred earth-womb. To use Maya words, human-maize had been sown and was now dawning. I suggest they were the offspring of the stone phalluses and the U-shaped womb, regenerated through two sacrifices. Probably these were the androgynous ancestors or seeds of the human race. Now that the humans were

61. James Porter, "Celtiform Stelae: A New Olmec Sculpture Type and Its Implications for Epigraphers," in *Beyond Indigenous Voices: Laila/Alila 11th International Symposium on Latin American Indian Literatures (1994)*, ed. Mary H. Preuss (Lancaster, Calif.: Labyrinthos Press, 1996).

62. England, *Life before Birth*, 160.

63. For variation in gender according to age, see Rosemary Joyce, *Gender and Power in Prehispanic Mesoamerica* (Austin: University of Texas Press, 2000); Carolyn E. Tate, "Cuerpo, Cosmos, Y Género," *Arqueología Mexicana* 11, 65 (2004).

born, they had to fulfill their function by revering the Female Earth and Waters from which they sprang.

Narrative Station 4: The Goddesses, Sources of Life

To the north of the Great Mound lay two successive enclosed courtyards. The southernmost was defined by long, low parallel mounds and is likely to have been a ball court.[64] Kent Reilly sees this zone as a vertical model of the Olmec cosmos.[65] Among the many sculptures once situated here, most relevant to this discussion are stylized effigies of female generative beings and the only "scientifically" excavated fetus figurine. The low boundary platforms (Mounds A-4 and A-5) may have supported a series of sculptures. One life-size statue of an adult human, seated cross-legged, was found on one of the low mounds, and I suspect that the nine other life-size adult statues (not archaeologically documented) also sat in the cross-legged posture of spiritual authority on these two mounds. The sculptures, probably of local heroes or ballplayers, presided over a Mosaic Pavement of green serpentine stone placed exactly at the center of the court, and on the central axis of the site. The Mosaic Pavement took the shape of an earth design (a north-south bar and four apertures at the intercardinal points) with a skirt of fringed diamonds, which represented vegetation.[66] These La Venta Mosaic Pavements were the earliest visual example of the metaphor of the sacred Mother Earth and her flowery skirt.[67]

Over the northernmost edge of this Holy Mother Earth Pavement, a mound (A-3) was constructed during a late phase of the site, precisely on the central axis of La Venta. On top of it was a bathtub-shaped monument containing a deep relief carving of a female wearing a helmet (like those worn by the fetuses and decapitated heads) and a fringed skirt, and contained within an earthband frame. This perhaps represented an anthropomorphic version of Holy Mother Earth herself. Within this small mound was an interesting cache germane to our discussion of fetuses.[68] A few feet from the Mosaic Pavement was a bed of cinnabar or ground red mercury ore that held the symbolic burial of a child. Adjacent to it, four stone figurines formed a little row along the south-north axis (Offering 1943-m). Progressing from south to north, the first was a human embryo figurine, the next portrayed a human fetus, then a small female child, and last an older girl (see fig. 12). An adult-size burial[69] containing the figurine of an adult female

64. John A. Graham and Robert F. Heizer, "Possible Ball Court at La Venta, Mexico," *Nature* 232, 27 (August 1971).

65. Reilly, "Mountains of Creation."

66. For the southern end of the Mosaic Pavement design as vegetation, see Reilly, "Enclosed Ritual Spaces."

67. For the Mosaic Pavements as representative of a Mesoamerican female earth supernatural, see Carolyn E. Tate, "Holy Mother Earth and Her Flowery Skirt: The Role of the Female Earth Surface in Maya Political and Ritual Performance," in *Ancient Maya Gender Identity and Relations*, ed. Lowell S. Gustafson and Amelia M. Trevelyan (Westport, Conn.: Bergin and Garvey, 2002).

68. For a description of the material excavated in this mound, see Drucker, "La Venta, Tabasco," 73, 159.

69. Few actual burials containing traces of human remains, or any evidence that bodies were ever deposited, have been found at La Venta. The child's and adult's "burials" in this mound (A-3) contained regalia laid out as if the earspools and necklaces adorned a human figure, but in such pristine placement that it is clear that no human body occupied the "tomb." This phenomenon has been dubbed a "pseudo-burial."

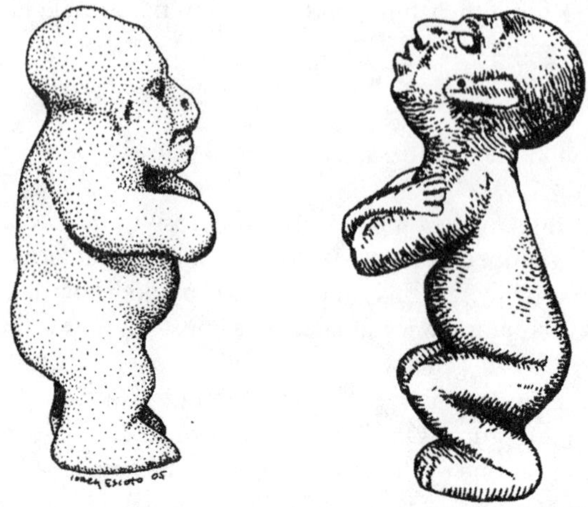

FIGURE 12. Station 4a. Two of the four figurines in a cache adjacent to a child's grave in the ball court. Left: an embryo, drawing by Corey Escoto, used with permision; right: a fetus, drawing by C. Tate.

was a few feet to the north.[70] Just as at the southern end of the site, where fetus sculptures preceded the infants in caves, in this series of cached figurines we see the theme of progressive development from fetus to child to adult proceeding from south to north.[71]

Just beyond Mound A-3 was the northernmost courtyard, a U-shaped enclosure with its opening to the south. The U-shaped boundary was formed of natural basalt columns that penetrated the earth. At the open southeast and southwest

70. For a cogent study of gendered human forms in Olmec art, see Billie Follensbee, "Sex and Gender in Olmec Art and Archaeology," Ph.D. diss., University of Maryland, 2000.

71. The other excavated fetus figurine is the well-known jade "crying baby" found at Cerro de las Mesas by Miguel Covarrubias, reported in Matthew W. Stirling and Marian Stirling, "Finding Jewels of Jade in the Mexican Swamp," *National Geographic* 82 (1942). It was found on top of a tiny canoe carved of the same bright green jade, with incised embryo faces on both prows. In the same deposit, there were many objects from later cultures—the fetus and canoe seem to have been antiques or heirlooms—and one jade skull. According to Philip Drucker, who described the excavated materials, the fetus (he called it a dwarf) sculpture fit snugly into the canoe's cavity; see P. Drucker, "The Cerro de Las Mesas Offering of Jade and Other Materials," *Anthropological Papers of the Bureau of American Ethnology* 44 (Washington, D.C.: 1955): 31.

Mayanists will note that that the legend of the so-called Maize God (who I think is an archetypal human-maize being) includes the transportation of the Maize Being in a canoe across the sky, his/her adornment with jade jewels, and sometimes, his/her emergence from a skull which functions as a seed within the turtle-shell earth.

The transportation of an Olmec fetus in an embryo-decorated canoe also seems to be an antecedent to the Mixe belief that Higiny, "goddess" of lakes, rivers, childbirth, and midwifery, whose calendar name is One Fontanelle, transports the spirit of the fetus to its mother's womb, see Lipp, *The Mixe of Oaxaca*). And the skull also included in the cache seems to represent the skull as the seed for new life, as we found in the later example of the Maya Elder Hero Twin, Hun Hunahpu, as well as in the Aztec god Xolotl's retrieval of the bones of people of an earlier age from the underworld as the raw material for a new race of humans.

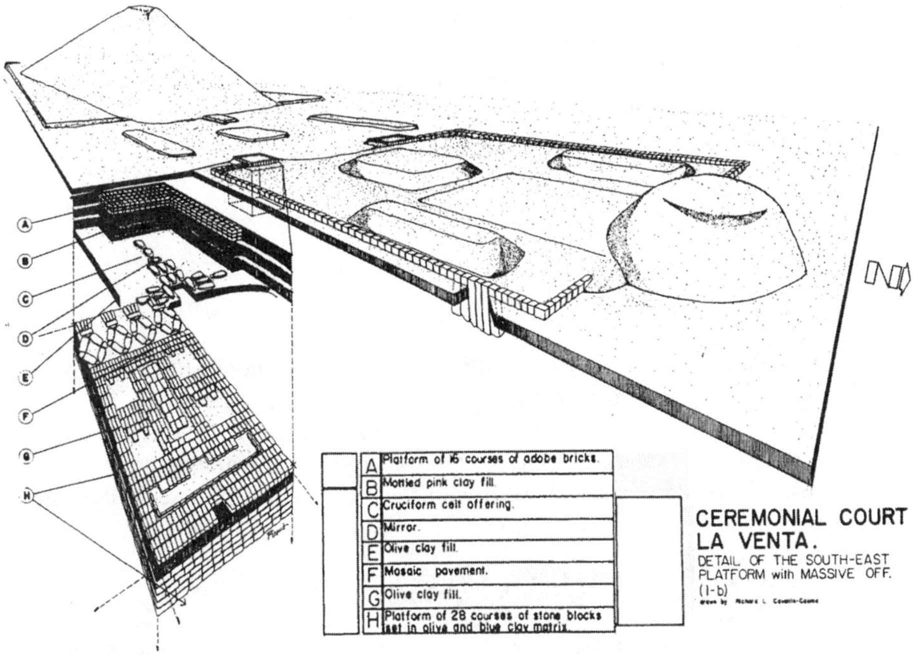

FIGURE 13. Station 4b. A cutaway drawing of one of the Massive Offerings and Mosaic Pavements (or Lake and Earth goddess effigies) in the northern U/womb court. Drawing by Richard Cavallin-Cosma. Used with permission.

corners of the courtyard were platforms that covered the buried stone effigies of the generative Lake and Earth goddesses, traditionally called, respectively, the Massive Offerings and Mosaic Pavements (see fig. 13). These deposits of green stone (the goddess effigies) were in pits about twenty feet square and equally deep. The goddess effigies, deeply buried in many layers of carefully sorted, brightly colored local clays, were probably the most sacred part of the site. They were enormous and represented equally vast quantities of effort to carry thousands of tons of green stone across the mountains from more than a hundred miles away. Many caches of buried greenstone figurines and celts impregnated both courts and two more embryo-maize stelae (Monuments 15 and 22), one gray and one green stone, sprouted from the platforms above the buried Lake and Earth goddess effigies.

If religious specialists existed among the Olmec, access to this courtyard was likely restricted to them.[72] I think the mosaics were giant altars to Mother Earth to which people from near and far journeyed to perform their most important ceremonies. If this courtyard was part of the processional creation narrative as

72. Reilly, "Mountains of Creation."

well, those who participated in the procession may have gathered outside the court boundaries. The narrative at this station probably involved local heroes, including important female healers or leaders, who had contacted the Holy Mothers of Earth and Waters to gain guidance, to heal, or to revitalize creation. And there were probably ceremonies that involved the ancestors whose effects were buried within the mounds.

Narrative Stations 5 and 6: The Decapitated Heads and the Phallic Column

About five hundred feet beyond the basalt-column northern enclosure, three colossal heads formed the northernmost set of similar sculptures (see fig. 14a). The heads depicted mature individuals with furrowed brows. Many investigators consider these to represent the rulers of Olmec La Venta. Apparently these rulers, like those of the Maya, were charged with the ultimate test of descent into the

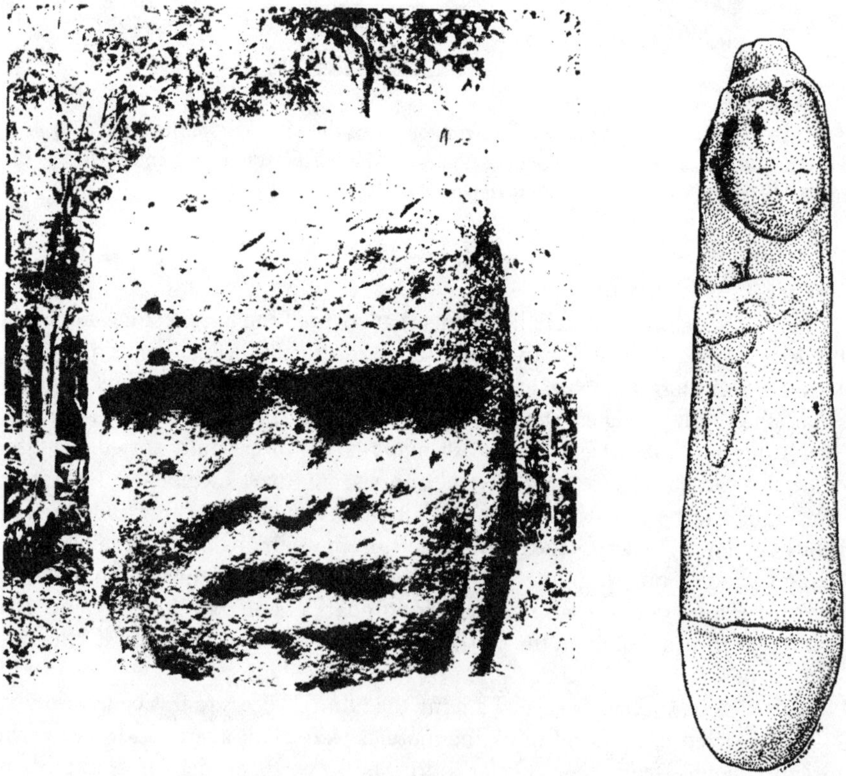

FIGURE 14. Station 5. One of the three colossal heads situated north of the enclosed court and the northern phallic column. Left: Monument 3, height 198 centimeters, author photo. Right: green schist column from the northern edge of La Venta, height 236 centimeters, drawing by Corey Escoto, used with permission.

underworld to contest the power of death, for, like the colossal fetuses, they wore the tight-fitting helmets of ballplayers. The fetuses' gestures indicated they would offer the sacrifice of their own heads to create seeds. That promise seems to have come to fruition here in the form of their mature heads, which rested on the sacred earth. The three decapitated heads, like the head of the elder twin in the *Popol Vuh*, were like plump fruits, seeded squashes, or giant rubber balls that would produce the seeds of the next generation of human-maize.

The heads gazed northward toward the northern phallic green schist column, which stood high atop a twenty-foot earthen pedestal (see fig. 14b). Traces of a face and hand suggest that a rudimentary embryo face was at the top of the column. At the foot of the earthen pedestal was found a cave-niche throne, or earth womb, which was left unfinished, in a rough state. Apparently this cave was intended to catch the seed from the phallic column, beginning the cycle of gestation that would produce the fetuses on the womb platform more than a mile to the south.[73]

Conclusions and Questions

The concepts conveyed by the imagery of La Venta's sculptural groups (or narrative stations) were precursors to the themes of creation tales in later Mesoamerican cultures. They included features of a sacred, vital landscape such as caves, waters, and mountains of sustenance. La Venta's sculpture provided visual antecedents in the form of phallic columns and U-shaped enclosures to acts from later stories such as the penetration of earth with flint knives. One also sees the prominence of the ballgame—at La Venta in the form of the helmeted fetuses and heads as well as the ball court—and a probable focus on decapitation associated with the ballgame, as in later Mesoamerican traditions of creation. These and other parallels strongly suggest that the several groups of similar sculptures at La Venta indeed formed stations along a ritual processional way created for the narration of a creation story.

Yet this initial recognition of an ancient creation narrative in visual form, and my attempt to imagine its themes, pose many more questions than they answer. Did the La Ventans erect five, six, seven, or more narrative stations? Were there officially sanctioned narrators, and if so, were they part of a religious institution? So much of La Venta's story existed in earlier places—the ballgame, the concept of cave as womb, the recognition of the embryo and fetus and knowledge of embryogenesis, infant sacrifice or ritual burial of infants who died naturally, the domestication of maize and its conceptual co-identity with humans, and more. What were the mechanisms by which so many disparate, preexisting elements of culture were forged into a coherent narrative? What was the story, really? Were several previous creations entailed? How did politics and religions interweave in the creation of the narrative and in the patronage of the site and its sculpture? Who organized the labor required to conceptualize this vast microcosm of cosmic processes and

73. In the 1990s, a large monument depicting a vulva was excavated at La Venta by Rebecca González. I have seen no publication of it, and I wonder if it was adjacent to one of the columns.

physical space? Was the creation landscape a giant altar for ritual events staged by pilgrims from all over Mesoamerica?

Although we will never know precisely La Venta's creation myth or the poetic terms used to express it, we can discern its major elements. There probably was never a canonical version; each time a narrator enlivened with words the sculptures along the processional way, the emphases, names, purposes, and beliefs shifted. Nevertheless, each set of sculptures provided parameters within which narrators expressed a sophisticated conceptualization of creation and regeneration. The columns and U-group, the caves with their infants and male visitors, and the stone celts that impregnated earth and lake female effigies manifested the coupling of male and female cosmic elements to generate life. The La Venta creation story used the ballgame, its inseminating ball, and the decapitation of heroes as metaphors for an animate cycle involving death, seed formation, fertilization of the female by enhancing the womb and earth with offerings, insemination, gestation, and birth, all leading to the flowering of humans and maize. Human life cycles reflected the cyclical, seasonal routines of agriculture. Nourishing these cycles required the self-control of deliberate self-sacrifice or disciplined action. At La Venta, humans expended colossal efforts to convey in material form ("art") these concepts that became fundamental to Mesoamerican thought.

The human fetuses played an essential role in this drama—apparently as primordial ballplaying heroes who died, but whose heads became seeds and regenerated the processes of life. I suspect that the Olmec considered an in utero death of the fetus (or miscarriage of the pregnancy) to be a self-sacrificial act that led to transformation of the life force and ultimately to the birth of another life. The Olmec made many more images of fetuses than have been discussed here. For some reason, however, the use of the fetus and embryo as symbols of potential life force became less obvious in later societies. The concept was given form as small abstract figures with crossed legs and arms, dredged in red cinnabar and placed in Late Pre-Classic Maya cache vessels, in Mixtec peñate sculptures, and even in seedlike figures in the Aztec Templo Mayor caches. But the Olmec, the first Mesoamerican civilization to codify their empirical observations of the human, agricultural, seasonal, and astronomical cycles, expressed human embryogenesis most explicitly.

WORKS CITED

Arnold, Philip P. "Eating Landscape: Human Sacrifice and Sustenance in Aztec Mexico." In *To Change Place: Aztec Ceremonial Landscapes*, edited by Davíd Carrasco, 219–31. Boulder: University of Colorado Press, 1991.

Bassie-Sweet, Karen. *From the Mouth of the Dark Cave: Commemorative Sculpture of the Late Classic Maya*. Norman: University of Oklahoma Press, 1991.

Bellas, Monica L. "The Body in the Mixtec Codices: Birth, Purification, Transformation, and Death." Ph.D. diss., University of California, 1997.

Blumenthal, Ralph. "Ancient Art of Mexico May Depict the Unborn." *New York Times*, June 12, 1999, B7–B9.

Bradley, Douglas E. "Gender, Power, and Fertility in the Olmec Ritual Ballgame." In *The Sport of Life and Death: The Mesoamerican Ballgame*, edited by E. Michael Whittington, 32–39. Charlotte, N.C.: Mint Museum and New York: Thames and Hudson, 2001.

Brady, James. "The Sexual Connotation of Caves in Mesoamerican Ideology." *Mexicon* 10, 3 (1988): 51.

Brady, James E., and Keith M. Prufer, eds. *In the Maw of the Earth Monster: Mesoamerican Ritual Cave Use*. Austin: University of Texas Press, 2005.

Brundage, Burr C. *The Fifth Sun: Aztec Gods, Aztec World*. Austin: University of Texas Press, 1979.

Christenson, Allen J. *Popol Vuh: The Sacred Book of the Maya*. 2 vols. Winchester, England: O Books, 2003.

Cohodas, Marvin. "The Symbolism and Ritual Function of the Middle Classic Ballgame in Mesoamerica." *American Indian Quarterly* 2, 2 (1975): 99–130.

Cyphers, Ann. "El Contexto Social de Monumentos en San Lorenzo." In *Población, Subsistencia y Medio Ambiente en San Lorenzo Tenochtitlán*, edited by Ann Cyphers, 163–93. Mexico City: Universidad Nacional Autónoma de México, 1997.

———. *Escultura Olmeca de San Lorenzo Tenochtitlán*. Mexico City: Universidad Nacional Autónoma de México, Instituto de Investigaciones Antropológicas, 2004.

———. "San Lorenzo," *Arqueología Mexicana* 4, 19 (1996): 64.

Drucker, Philip. "The Cerro de Las Mesas Offering of Jade and Other Materials." *Anthropological Papers of the Bureau of American Ethnology* 44, Washington, D.C. (1955): 25–68.

———. "La Venta, Tabasco: A Study of Olmec Ceramics and Art." *Bulletin* 153, Smithsonian Institution Bureau of American Ethnology, Washington, D.C. (1952).

Duden, Barbara. "The Fetus as an Object of Our Time." *RES: Anthropology and Aesthetics* 25 (1994): 132–35.

England, Marjorie. *Life before Birth*. 2nd ed. London: Mosby-Wolfe, 1996.

Fash, William L. "Altar and Associated Features." In *Ancient Chalcatzingo*, edited by David C. Grove, 82–94. Austin: University of Texas Press, 1987.

Follensbee, Billie. "Sex and Gender in Olmec Art and Archaeology." Ph.D. diss., University of Maryland, 2000.

Freidel, David A., Linda Schele, and Joy Parker. *Maya Cosmos: Three Thousand Years on the Shaman's Path*. New York: William Morrow, 1993.

Gallegos Gómora, M. Judith. "Excavaciones en la Estructura D-7 en La Venta, Tabasco." *Arqueología* 4 (1990): 17–24.

Gillespie, Susan. "Ballgames and Boundaries." In *The Mesoamerican Ballgame*, edited by Vernon L. Scarborough and David R. Wilcox, 317–45. Tucson: University of Arizona Press, 1991.

González Lauck, Rebecca B. "Acerca de Piramides de Tierra y Seres Sobrenaturales: Observaciones Preliminares en Torno al Edificio C-1. La Venta, Tabasco." *Arqueología* 17 (1997): 79–98.

———. "Proyecto Arqueológico La Venta." *Arqueología* 4 (1988): 121–65.

———. "La Venta: An Olmec Capital." In *Olmec Art of Ancient Mexico*, edited by Elizabeth P. Benson and Beatríz de la Fuente, 73–82. Washington D.C.: National Gallery of Art, 1996.

Graham, John A., and Robert F. Heizer. "Possible Ball Court at La Venta, Mexico." *Nature* 232, 27 (August 1971): 650.

Grove, David C. "Olmec Altars and Myths." *Archaeology* 26, 2 (1973): 129–35.

———. "The Olmec Paintings of Oxtotitlan Cave, Guerrero." *Studies in Pre-Columbian Art and Archaeology* 6. Washington D.C.: Dumbarton Oaks, Trustees for Harvard University, 1970.

———. "Public Monuments and Sacred Mountains: Observations on Three Formative Period Landscapes." In *Social Patterns in Pre-Classic Mesoamerica*, edited by David C. Grove and Rosemary A. Joyce, 255–300. Washington, D.C.: Dumbarton Oaks, 1999.

Guernsey Kappelman, Julia, and F. Kent Reilly III. "Paths to Heaven, Ropes to Earth: Birds, Jaguars, and Cosmic Cords in Formative Period Mesoamerica." *Ancient America* 2 and 3 (2001): 33–52.

Heyden, Doris. "Caves, Gods, and Myths: World-View and Planning in Teotihuacan." In *Mesoamerican Sites and World Views*, edited by Elizabeth P. Benson, 1–40. Washington D.C.: Dumbarton Oaks, 1981.

Houston, Stephen. "Symbolic Sweatbaths of the Maya: Architectural Meaning in the Cross Group at Palenque, Mexico." *Latin American Antiquity* 7, 2 (1996): 132–51.

Isbell, William. "Cosmological Order Expressed in Prehistoric Ceremonial Centers." *Actes de XLII International Congress of Americanists, Paris* 4 (1977): 269–97.

Joralemon, Peter David. "A Study of Olmec Iconography." *Studies in Pre-Columbian Art and Archaeology* 7. Washington, D.C.: Dumbarton Oaks, Trustees for Harvard University, 1971.

Joyce, Rosemary. *Gender and Power in Prehispanic Mesoamerica*. Austin: University of Texas Press, 2000.

Lipp, Frank J. *The Mixe of Oaxaca: Religion, Ritual, and Healing*. Austin: University of Texas Press, 1991.

López-Austin, Alfredo. *The Human Body and Ideology: Concepts of the Ancient Nahuas*. Translated by Thelma Ortiz de Montellano and Bernard Ortiz de Montellano. Salt Lake City: University of Utah Press, 1980.

López Luján, Leonardo. *The Offerings of the Templo Mayor of Tenochtitlan*. Boulder: University of Colorado Press, 1994.

MacLeod, Barbara, and Dennis E. Puleston. "Pathways into Darkness: The Search for the Road to Xibalba." In *Tercera Mesa Redonda De Palenque, 1978*, edited by Merle Greene Robertson and Donnan C. Jeffers, 71–78. Monterey, Calif.: Pre-Columbian Art Research Center, 1978.

MacNeish, Richard S. "Tehuacan's Accomplishments." In *Archaeology, Supplement 1, Handbook of Middle American Indians*, edited by Jeremy A. Sabloff and Victoria R. Bricker, 31–47. Austin: University of Texas Press, 1981.

Marcus, Joyce. "Archaeology and Religion: A Comparison of the Zapotec and Maya." *World Archaeology* 10, 2 (1978): 172–91.

———. "Women's Ritual in Formative Oaxaca: Figurine-Making, Divination, Death, and the Ancestors." Edited by Kent V. Flannery and Joyce Marcus. *Memoirs of the Museum of Anthropology, University of Michigan, 33*. Ann Arbor: Museum of Anthropology, University of Michigan, 1998.

Milbrath, Susan. "Birth Images in Mixteca-Puebla Art." In *The Role of Gender in Pre-Columbian Art and Architecture*, edited by Virginia E. Miller (Lanham, Md.: University Press of America, 1988), 153–78.

Miller, Walter S. *Cuentos Mixes, Biblioteca De Folklore Indígena*. Mexico City: Instituto Nacional Indigenista, 1956.

Monaghan, John. "Dedication: Ritual or Production?" In *The Sowing and the Dawning: Termination, Dedication, and Transformation in the Archaeological and Ethnographic Record of Mesoamerica*, edited by Shirley Boteler Mock, 47–52. Albuquerque: University of New Mexico Press, 1998.

Moser, Christopher L. "Human Decapitation in Ancient Mesoamerica." *Studies in Pre-Columbian Art and Archaeology 11*. Washington, D.C.: Dumbarton Oaks, Trustees for Harvard University, 1973.

Neuenswander, Helen. "Vestiges of Early Time Concepts in a Contemporary Maya (Cubulco Achi) Community: Implications for Epigraphy." *Estudios de Cultura Maya* 13 (1981): 125–63.

Nicholson, Henry B. "A Fragment of an Aztec Relief Carving of the Earth Monster." *Journal de la Société des Américanistes* 56 (1967): 81–94.

———. "Religion in Pre-Hispanic Central Mexico." In *Handbook of Middle American Indians*, Volume 10, edited by Gordon F. Eckholm and Ignacio Bernal, 395–445. Austin: University of Texas Press, 1971.

Nilsson, Lennart. "The Drama of Life before Birth." *Life*, April 30, 1965, 62–69.

Ortiz, Ponciano, and María del Carmen Rodríguez. "The Sacred Hill of El Manatí: A Preliminary Discussion of the Site's Ritual Paraphernalia." In *Olmec Art and Archaeology in Mesoamerica*, edited by John E. Clark and Mary E. Pye, 75–94. Washington, D.C.: National Gallery of Art, 2000.

Pasztory, Esther. "Artistic Traditions of the Middle Classic Period." In *Middle Classic Mesoamerica: A.D. 400–700*, edited by Esther Pasztory, 108–42. New York: Columbia University Press, 1978.

Pope, Kevin O., Mary E. D. Pohl, John G. Jones, et al. "Origin and Environmental Setting of Ancient Agriculture in the Lowlands of Mesoamerica." *Science* 292, 5520 (2001): 1370–73.

Porter, James. "Celtiform Stelae: A New Olmec Sculpture Type and Its Implications for Epigraphers." In *Beyond Indigenous Voices: Laila/Alila 11th International Symposium on Latin American Indian Literatures (1994)*, edited by Mary H. Preuss. Lancaster, Calif.: Labyrinthos Press, 1996.

Reilly, F. Kent, III. "Art, Ritual, and Rulership in the Olmec World." In *The Olmec World: Ritual and Rulership*, edited by Jill Guthrie and Elizabeth Benson, 27–46. Princeton, N.J.: Princeton University Art Museum, 1995.

———. "Enclosed Ritual Spaces and the Watery Underworld in Formative Period Architecture: New Observations on the Function of La Venta Complex A." In *Seventh Palenque Round Table, 1989*, edited by Merle Greene Robertson and Virginia M. Fields, 125–36. San Francisco: Pre-Columbian Art Research Institute, 1994.

———. "Mountains of Creation and Underworld Portals: The Ritual Function of Olmec Architecture at La Venta, Tabasco." In *Mesoamerican Architecture as a Cultural Symbol*, edited by Jeff Karl Kowalski, 14–39. Oxford: Oxford University Press, 1999.

———. "Visions to Another World: Art, Shamanism, and Political Power in Middle Formative Mesoamerica." Ph.D. diss., University of Texas, 1994.

Rust, William F., and Barbara Leyden. "Evidence of Maize Use at Early and Middle Preclassic La Venta Olmec Sites." In *Corn and Culture in the Prehistoric New World*, edited by S. Johannessen and C. A. Hastorf, 181–201. Boulder, Colo.: Westview Press, 1994.

Schele, Linda, and David A. Friedel. "The Courts of Creation: Ballcourts, Ballgames, and Portals to the Maya Otherworld." In *The Mesoamerican Ballgame*, edited by Vernon L. Scarborough and David R Wilcox., 289–316. Tucson: University of Arizona Press, 1991.

Scott, John F. "Dressed to Kill: Stone Regalia of the Mesoamerican Ballgame." In *The Sport of Life and Death: The Mesoamerican Ballgame*, edited by E. Michael Whittington, 50–63. Charlotte, N.C.: Mint Museum; and New York: Thames and Hudson, 2001.

Stirling, Matthew W. "Great Stone Faces of the Mexican Jungle." *National Geographic* 77 (1940): 309–34.

———. "Stone Monuments of Southern Mexico." *Bulletin* 138, Smithsonian Institution Bureau of American Ethnology, Washington, D.C. (1943).

Stirling, Matthew W., and Marian Stirling. "Finding Jewels of Jade in the Mexican Swamp." *National Geographic* 82 (1942): 535–51.

Stone, Andrea J. "Spirals, Ropes, and Feathers: The Iconography of Rubber Balls in Mesoamerican Art." *Ancient Mesoamerica* 13 (2002): 21–39.

Storey, Rebecca. *Life and Death in Teotihuacan: A Modern Paleodemographic Synthesis.* Tuscaloosa: University of Alabama Press, 1992.

Sullivan, Thelma. "Tlazolteotl-Ixcuina: The Great Spinner and Weaver." In *The Art and Iconography of Late Post-Classic Central Mexico*, edited by Elizabeth Boone, 7–36. Washington, D.C.: Dumbarton Oaks, 1982.

Tate, Carolyn E. "Cuerpo, Cosmos, y Género." *Arqueología Mexicana* 11, 65 (2004): 36–41.

———. "Holy Mother Earth and Her Flowery Skirt: The Role of the Female Earth Surface in Maya Political and Ritual Performance." In *Ancient Maya Gender Identity and Relations*, edited by Lowell S. Gustafson and Amelia M. Trevelyan, 281–318. Westport, Conn.: Bergin and Garvey, 2002.

———. "Olmec Knowledge of the Human Body and Gestation." In *The Encyclopaedia of the History of Science, Technology, and Medicine in Non-Western Cultures*, edited by Helaine Selin, 11, 1203–12. Dordrecht, Netherlands: Kluwer Academic Publishers, 2008.

———. "Patrons of Shamanic Power: La Venta's Supernatural Entities in Light of Mixe Beliefs." *Ancient Mesoamerica* 20, 2 (1999): 169–88.

Tate, Carolyn E., and Gordon Bendersky. "Olmec Sculptures of the Human Fetus." *Perspectives in Biology and Medicine* 42, 3 (1999): 303–32.

Taube, Karl. "The Olmec Maize God: The Face of Corn in Formative Mesoamerica." *RES* 29/30 (1996): 39–81.

Tedlock, Barbara. *The Woman in the Shaman's Body*. New York: Bantam Dell, 2005.

Tedlock, Dennis. *Popol Vuh: The Mayan Book of the Dawn of Life*. New York: Simon and Schuster, 1996.

Weigle, Marta. *Creation and Procreation: Feminist Reflections on Mythologies of Cosmogony and Parturition*. Philadelphia: University of Pennsylvania Press, 1989.

Whittington, E. Michael. "Catalogue." In *The Sport of Life and Death: The Mesoamerican Ballgame*, edited by E. Michael Whittington. Charlotte, N.C.: Mint Museum; and New York: Thames and Hudson, 2001.

Out of Place: Fetal References in Japanese Mythology and Cultural Memory

Jane Marie Law

Recent scholarship on the fetus as understood in Japanese religious thought and practice has centered on the widespread practice of individuals requesting priests at Buddhist temples and in some cases shrines to perform appeasement rituals for their aborted or miscarried fetuses. This practice is known in Japanese as *mizuko kuyō*, literally, "appeasement rites for the water child." The excellent work of the American scholar William LaFleur in his book *Liquid Life: Abortion and Buddhism in Japan* revealed the complex cultural history of ideologies about reproduction and the fetus, beginning during the Edo period, and drawn upon in contemporary, Buddhist, Shinto, and New Age practices of *mizuko kuyō*, all lucrative ritual practices generating income for religious centers.[1] Although very sensitive to the political and ideological uses of *mizuko kuyō*, LaFleur in the end argues that the act of performing rituals of separation and farewell for an aborted fetus has a healing effect for the women and couples who commission and consume these ritual services. In spite of the obvious controversies surrounding abortion, LaFleur notes there will always be circumstances in which abortion is a chosen option (legal or not), and he argues that it should be legal. The arguments of what he calls "fecundist religions" that one's purpose is to be fruitful and multiply put us on a collision course with the limited resources of the natural world. Therefore, LaFleur argues, abortion will always be a necessary option in Japan and similar developed countries. He contends that perhaps there is something other cultures, such as our own, can learn from this ritual process so

1. William LaFleur, *Liquid Life: Abortion and Buddhism in Japan* (Princeton, N.J.: Princeton University Press, 1992).

prominent in Japan, a religious way with dealing with the emotions and spiritual issues raised by the practice of abortion.

In 1997 there appeared another major work by a Western scholar that dealt with the practice of *mizuko kuyō*, Helen Hardacre's *Marketing the Menacing Fetus in Japan.*[2] Hardacre's analysis, however, focused not on the healing effects of these rituals, but on the misogynistic commodification of this practice and the manipulation of the fear of retribution of an aborted fetus to market this ritual in Buddhist, Shinto, and New Age contexts. Hardacre notes that with the widespread availability and dissemination of sonographic images of the fetus in the womb as part of the standard pregnancy experience (as discussed in Sally Han's chapter in this volume), there had also emerged a more visually cogent notion of fetal personhood. This idea of fetal personhood in Japan has been transformed into a notion of fetal agency, in which the aborted fetus has the ability to haunt and torment those who brought it into being and "sent it back," to use the Japanese understanding of abortion. The first writer to present a strongly feminist view of the practice of *mizuko kuyō*, Hardacre sharply criticized the abuse of and intrusion into women's reproductive issues for profit within religious institutions offering these rituals.

Since these two major works first appeared, a large number of articles and monographs by Japanese and Western scholars have provided careful ethnographic detail and analysis of this ongoing and evolving practice, leading one scholar to remark that *mizuko kuyō* should be regarded as a new religion in its own right, existing trans-traditionally, that is to say in religious contexts no longer confined to Buddhism, apart from its particular traditional ritual offerings as a Buddhist kuyô, or rite of appeasement.

In a book designed to explore a broader range of references to the fetus as symbol, a mention of this vast scholarship is in order. However, one of the objectives of this volume was to present those materials not dominated and produced by the abortion discourses. To a certain extent, it can be said that the fetus in the abortion debates is not operating symbolically but as a medical and political subject, as a rhetorical subject to drive one side or the other of the debates concerning fetal personhood and a woman's right to choose. For this reason, here I will refer the reader to the scholarship of these two seminal and in many ways contrasting studies on the aborted fetus in Japan.

Here, the task is different and more modest: to provide a look at three references to fetal imagery in Japanese mythology and cultural memory where the fetal reference clearly works as symbol. Though historically dispersed (two that find literary expression in the Japanese chronicles from the early eighth century, and one from the postwar era), these three examples provide a map for locating a certain kind of fetal imagination: the fetus that is unusual, out of place, or somehow violated. I will show that these examples offer a typology of sorts for imagination of the fetus. The fetus that garners attention is the fetus that does not turn out right, somehow does not follow the norms of reproduction, or explodes an essential counter-memory dominating collective memory of the past. While minor

2. Helen Hardacre, *Marketing the Menacing Fetus in Japan* (Berkeley: University of California Press, 1997).

examples, each of those modes of imagination informs a number of larger visions of fetal life in Japan.

Ancient Cases: *Kojiki* and *Nihongi* Examples

Kojiki, "Chronicle of Ancient Matters," is a document purporting to be a seamless history, produced in 712 to provide a coherent narrative for imperial rule and to "correct" existing accounts of genealogies of the imperial family. Its complier, Oho no Yasumaro, was enlisted to create the seamless document by Emperor Temmu (reigned 673–86), and yet the final document did not appear until after his reign. It opens with mythologies of the creation of the world and mythic events of animals and deities, then moves into a chronology of the imperial line. The text becomes the first in a series designed to weave a single narrative to support the sacrality of the Japanese body politic and the continuity of the imperial line. There are two cases from this text that merit our attention for this discussion of the fetus in Japanese religious history. They are both mirrored in a text that appeared eight years after *Kojiki*, namely the *Nihongi*. I present them in the order in which they occur in the classical texts.

The Leech Child: Born of Transgression, Not Reckoned as One of Their Children

One of the questions raised by this volume concerns the status of fetal tissue that does not become an infant. Miscarriages, stillbirths, aborted fetuses—these not-quite- or not-yet-human but not-just-ordinary-tissue subjects occupy a problematic place in the continuum of the imagination of the fetus. Medical abortion or infanticide focuses attention on a woman's agency to terminate a pregnancy. But what of a spontaneous abortion: a miscarriage?[3] How is this reckoned in the imagination, and what other ideological purposes can it serve? Early (pre-eighth-century) Japanese mythological collections reflect a possible way of imagining the miscarried fetus, the failed attempt at procreation. Cast onto the acts of earth-creating deities, we see that even deities have miscarriages, which they subsequently seek to abandon. In chapter 4 of the *Kojiki*, the following myth is recounted. I summarize it here for readability.[4]

Izanagi (the male earth-creating deity) and Izanami (the female earth-creating deity) descended from the heavens to an island they had created known as Self

3. Confusion can result when medical terminology and popular usage come into conflict. "Spontaneous abortion" is the medical term for miscarriage. In this article, in an effort to defer to the vernacular and head off confusion, I will use the nonmedical term "miscarriage."

4. The excellent translation of this difficult text by Donald Philippi preserves nuances of linguistic reconstruction in the spelling of names and lists all names in their long and archaic versions. Thus, nonspecialist readers are often alienated by the text. For this reason, following the lead of many Japan scholars writing for wider audiences, I am paraphrasing the text.

Curdling Island, Onogoro-jima.[5] On this island, they erected a pillar and a palace. The male deity asked the female deity, "How is your body formed?" to which she replied, "My body, formed though it be formed, has one place which is formed insufficiently." Izanagi responded, "My body, formed though it be formed, has one place which is formed to excess. Therefore I would like to take that place in my body which is formed to excess and insert it into that place in your body which is formed insufficiently, and thus give birth to the land. How would that be?" He then suggested that the two of them should walk in opposite directions around the heavenly pillar, meet, and have sexual relations. As they met, the woman spoke first, and said, "How good a lad!" to which Izanagi replied, "How good a maiden!" Izanagi, the male, then chastised his spouse for having spoken first, saying, "It is not proper that the woman speak first." However, they went ahead and had conjugal relations, and the result of this improper union was a Leech, called in the text "The Leech-child, Hiruko." The text tells us that they placed this child in a boat of reeds and floated it away, and this is the last we hear of it in the *Kojiki*.[6]

Eight years after the completion of *Kojiki*, an expanded version of the mythology of the Japanese imperial line known as *Nihongi* (or alternately *Nihonshoki*) is created, the compilation of which was finished in 720.[7] This text provides a richer reading than the singular narrative of *Kojiki*, by providing variants of the myths that were redacted into *Kojiki*. The *Nihongi* recounts this narrative with a slightly different twist:

The deities repeat their foreplay exchange of discussing their body parts, and again the goddess Izanami speaks first, with the deity Izanagi protesting that it is improper for a woman to speak first. They then repeat the exercise, and the text narrates what happens: "Now when the time of birth arrived, first of all the island of Ahaji[8] was reckoned as the placenta, and their minds took no pleasure in it." The text's insistence that an island is a placenta invites a literal mapping of other products of primal creation onto actual physiological substances. This segment of the text then recounts the creation of a number of islands.

A bit further, we get an expanded version of the "female speaks first and messes everything up" motif. In this case, the woman speaks first. The couple proceeds to copulate, the woman gives birth to a leech, which "they straightaway place in a reed boat and set adrift." Then, after birthing the island of Awaji, they return again to heaven and make a report. The heavenly gods report to them that "it is by reason of the woman's having spoken first; ye had best return thither again."[9] In other words, the gender hierarchy created by this failed creation attempt is sanctioned by the heavenly deities.

5. In some accounts in *Nihongi*, Onogoro-jima is regarded as a placenta. W. G. Aston, trans., *Nihongi: Chronicles of Japan from the Earliest Times to A.D. 697* (London: George Allen and Unwin, 1956). The section of this text recounting this creation myth can be found on pp. 11–17.

6. Donald Philippi, trans., *Kojiki: Record of Ancient Matters* (Tokyo: University of Tokyo Press, 1968), bk. 1, chap. 4, 50–51.

7. Aston, *Nihongi*, 11–17.

8. Commonly understood in Japanese culture and mythology to be the island of Awaji in the Inland Sea of Japan.

9. Aston, *Nihongi*, 15.

For the purposes of this discussion, I would like to suggest that the physiological reading of this myth invites an identification of a leech with a miscarried fetus. As Carolyn Tate has shown in her chapter of this volume, the early Olmec most likely studied miscarried and stillborn fetuses to get an idea of fetal development, which then found visual representation in their sculptural traditions. I would suggest that the similarity between a leech and a miscarried fetus is striking enough that it is no accident that a text that mentions a placenta (a requisite product of a pregnancy impossible to ignore) also provides the leech as a symbol for a miscarried fetus. The text suggests in a sense that this product is a child of sorts, just not a very pleasant one (for few people like leeches). Identified and named, it is set adrift.[10] The text makes no mention of any ritual process of grieving, seen in other deaths in the *Kojiki* and *Nihongi* narratives (such as when Izanami herself later dies after giving birth to fire). The deities simply put the Leech Child in a reed boat and then move on with their real work of creating the Japanese archipelago. Their failure is cast on the waves.[11]

This text offers an explanation for failed creation attempts, miscarriages if you will: they are transgressions of gender roles. In other words, a miscarriage points to a nascent theodicy: gender hierarchies need to be observed, or otherwise monstrosities are born. This mythical theme is certainly in the early texts of *Kojiki* and *Nihongi*, dating the concern with gender and linking gender roles to success in procreation to at least as early as these texts were redacted. But what I find most interesting about this abandoned failed creation is what popular tradition does with it almost eight hundred years later.

According to tradition dating from the late fifteenth century, the problematic deity Ebisu is understood as being the adult of the Leech Child.[12] Why is this interesting for a study of the imagination of the continuum of fetal beings, including miscarriages?

The founding mythic narrative (*engi*) from a subsidiary shrine of the dominant shrine for the worship of the deity Ebisu, Nishinomiya Ebisu Jinja (which, though badly damaged by the Kobe earthquake, still stands), indicates the shrine was started in the sixteenth century when a fisherman by the name of Hyakudayû (actually a mythical being from another ritual cycle in Japan, but beyond the scope of this discussion) found a small child floating on the waves of the sea. When the child turned to the fisherman and spoke, the child identified itself as the "Leech Child of Long Ago." This child deity requests that the fisherman take him ashore and build a worship hall in his honor, since this Leech Child is the

10. Further evidence to suggest that the Leech Child was regarded as a primordial miscarriage can be found in the fact that prior to the advent of *mizuko kuyō* rites, women often made offerings to the Leech Child/Ebisu worship halls for safe childbirth. Further, Leech Child shrines may have served as places to make offerings in the case of a miscarriage, connecting the miscarriage of Izanagi and Izanami with human miscarriage.

11. It could be argued that the very act of putting the Leech Child in a boat on the waves represented a kind of funerary practice in its own rite, though I know of no scholar who has so argued.

12. For example, the original version of Aston's translation includes a plate, probably dating from mid Tokugawa, clearly labeled "Hiruko" (Leech Child) but which is iconographically identical to the deity Ebisu. This was a common *o-fuda* (shrine placard) for Ebisu shrines, conflating these two figures. It served to tie Ebisu, a deity not recognized in *Kojiki* or *Nihongi*, into the grander narratives, but it also had a certain mythological logic.

neglected deity of the Kojiki and Nihongi myth cycles and has never been properly worshipped.[13]

This identification of Ebisu as the adult Leech Child is a standard feature of Ebisu worship, and is a central feature of Ebisu ritual at the Nishinomiya Shrine. Furthermore, since the Nishinomiya Shrine served as the head shrine for Ebisu subshrines throughout central Japan from the fifteenth century on, this pattern of identification is replicated everywhere there is an Ebisu shrine. This deity can be simultaneously worshipped as both child and adult, and small shrines dedicated to both separately can be found within the same shrine precincts.

The Leech Child–Ebisu continuum has a number of common mythic themes: both deities have an ugliness so intense that it is dangerous to gaze upon them, both have the ability to inflict curses (including earthquakes, epidemics, crop disasters, pestilence, and typhoons) on those who do not give proper respect through ritual performances addressed to them,[14] and both are clearly identified by the markers of liminality, deformity, amorphousness, and sexual ambiguity. In other words, the Leech Child–Ebisu deity complex represents the dangerous, the marginal, the undifferentiated, and all things that go bump in the night.

Ebisu worship becomes one of the most common forms of ritual appeasement among itinerant spirit appeasers during the Tokugawa period (1603–1868). The ritual specialists who conducted these rites appeasing this potentially dangerous deity centered on Nishinomiya and later on the island of Awaji (the very same placenta from the *Kojiki* narratives). They used small body substitute puppets in their shamanic rites and had a great influence on the development of more sophisticated forms of Japanese theater, including what is regarded as the classical puppet theater, Bunraku. What does the original ritual impulse of these ritual specialists say to our discussion about imagining the fetus in Japanese popular imagination?

First of all, the identification of the Leech Child with Ebisu—a deity known to bestow blessings but only when treated well, and more often regarded as a deity capable of inflicting curses (*tatari*) on people—suggests that to handle one's failed creation attempts (pregnancy) inadequately subjects one to the risk of retribution. In a sense, the Leech Child becomes the prototype for all other ignored and abandoned, ritually uncelebrated failed creations, including miscarriages. The actions of the earth-creating deities Izanagi and Izanami of setting their failure adrift on the waves and abandoning it with no ritual actions to speak of suggests that while at the time of the compilation of the *Kojiki* and *Nihongi* this may have seemed reasonable, the later mythological imagination recognized in this an ignorance of the emotional difficulty of the experience of a miscarriage. Miscarriages, when recognized as such and not subsumed into a late menstrual cycle, can stir emotionally charged feelings in the woman and in her partner. The physical encounter with miscarried tissue can be alarming. If this is an embryo, why is it dead? If it is not

13. I discuss this identification at length in my book *Puppets of Nostalgia: The Life, Death and Rebirth of the Awaji Ningyō Jōruri Tradition* (Princeton, N.J.: Princeton University Press, 1997), chap. 3, "A Crippled Deity, A Priest, A Puppet," pp. 89–136.

14. Here, we see a strong parallel to the fear of *tatari* (retribution or vengeful spite) that an unattended aborted fetus can elicit.

a fetus, promising life, what is it? If it was never alive, what ritual obligations do I have to this tissue? It is the job of myth to find a symbolic location for the fabric of the human life cycle, and yet miscarriage is often excluded from this myth-making process. The ritual identification of the Leech Child with the deity who demands ritual attention in exchange for protection from his malevolent tendencies suggests an awareness that amorphous, unformed "almost fetal" tissues demand ritual attention, too. They may be ugly, like leeches, they may be out of place, appearing in the world too unformed to merit identification as a human or funerary practices, but they occupy a place in the imagination nonetheless. The later traditional appropriation of the Leech Child myth into the Ebisu saga suggests that one abandons their memory at one's own peril.

The Emperor in the Womb: Emperor Ōjin's Long Gestation

Our next example also comes from the *Kojiki*. Again, we find an expanded discussion in *Nihongi*. The text, a composite of many different sources, includes at a pivotal juncture a complex narrative describing the vague participation of a fetus in the womb in affairs of state by his ability to stay put. The fetus, not just anybody, becomes the emperor widely regarded as the first stable leader of the line, Emperor Ōjin. Ōjin later becomes identified as the deity Hachiman, protector of the imperial line and understood to be an avatar of Amida in some cases. So, that the fetal life of this personage should be mentioned merits our attention. What kind of fetus was Ōjin?

In book 2, chapters 92 through 95 of *Kojiki*, the fuller story is narrated. The chapter preceding this narrative (chap. 91), an out-of-place assertion referring to characters not yet introduced, makes one point very clear: a fetus, to be born in subsequent chapters, ruled from the womb, and to prove it, he had a growth on his arm. So we are alerted: the fetus about to be born is no ordinary fetus. The narrative then begins in a more user-friendly version in chapter 92. I renarrate it here, to allow non-Japan specialists to follow the story line.

The Empress Okinaga Tarashi Hime no Mikoto[15] (also commonly referred to as Empress Jingū) often summoned deities. Her husband, the Emperor Chūai, as his forces were about to attack the land of Kumaso, sat in the palace playing the koto (or cither, understood to be a musical instrument used to aid a spirit medium in summoning spirits and deities). He was accompanied by his oracle interpreter,[16] Takeno Uchi Sukune, and the empress. Both awaited the emperor's trance as he sat playing his musical instrument.

But it was the empress who became possessed, and, serving as spirit medium for a deity, she told the emperor of a shining land to the west, covered in gold

15. This name is used interchangeably with the given name of this figure, Jingū. It has been suggested that the name Okinaga Tarashi Hime was a generic category used to demarcate a shamaness. Given that shamanic rule was an early form of governance in Japan, it is not surprising that in this mythical account of an emerging ruling line, we will see many references to the activities of female shamans.

16. The Japanese term is sanipa, meaning, literally, "interpreter of the words of deities." See Philippi, *Kojiki*, 257 n. 4.

and silver and dazzling treasures, awaiting delivery to the emperor if he would but go and conquer it. The emperor replied to her that to the west was nothing but water, and he sent her away (which amounted to a rejection of the deity she was divining at the time). He stopped playing his koto, clearly not having gotten the oracle he was hoping for. The deity, enraged, and still being channeled by his wife, rebuked him: "You are not to rule this kingdom! Go straight in one direction!"[17] This statement amounted to a death sentence. (We have a similar turn of phrase, with a slightly warmer destination.) Stunned, his attendant urged him to keep playing, but shortly, the sound of the koto stopped, and he was found dead.

Everyone was terrified, and, as was the custom in early Japanese funerary practices, the body of the emperor was moved to a mortuary palace. A search was carried out for the cause of this death (the usual suspects: "skinning alive, skinning backwards, breaking down the ridges, covering up ditches, defecation, incest, and sexual relations with horses, cows, chickens and dogs,"[18] references to the pollutions inflicted upon the sun goddess Amaterasu by her brother, Susanō, earlier within the same mythology).

Again, the oracle decoder came into the palace, and again the deity, through the spirit mediumship of Empress Jingū, repeated its instructions about conquering the bejeweled land, adding a new layer: "This land is the land to be ruled by the child who is inside your womb."[19]

The oracle decoder asked the deity to state its identity, and it was revealed that the deity was none other than the sun goddess, Amaterasu, the Heavenly Shining One, born of the purification of the eye of her father, the earth-creating deity Izanagi no O-Mikoto. Also present in the oracle were three other deities, the three deities of Sumino-e, sea deities who granted protection for sea travel. They said, "Enshrine our spirit at the top of the ship . . . and cross over!"[20] All subsequent references to Empress Jingū always insist on her being pregnant at the time she crossed over on her conquest, an important fact as we shall see.

Empress Jingū, accompanied by her husband's oracle interpreter, crossed over and was met by the king of the country, who readily surrendered and offered to become the empress's stable groom. The lands of Shiragi and Kudara then came under the rule of the Japanese imperial line, according to this myth.

During her three-year-long conquest, the empress once was about to go into labor and tied stones onto her skirt to prevent it. (*Nihongi* narrates that she received a magical stone that would delay labor.)

The delayed birth of Emperor Ōjin becomes an important matter of state and is again revisited in the fourteenth century as a matter to be spelled out. The author Kitabatake Chikafusa, in an attempt to rhetorically stabilize any doubts about the divinity of the Japanese imperial line, wrote in 1339 (to be finally finished in 1343)

17. Ibid., 258.
18. Ibid., 259–60.
19. Ibid., 260.
20. Ibid., 263.

his well-known text *Jinnō Shōtōki* (The Chronicle of Gods and Sovereigns).[21] In this text, he writes the following about the pregnancy of Empress Jingū and the delayed birth of Emperor Ōjin:

> Thus directed by the kami [deities], Jingū set forth to attack and subjugate Silla, Paekche and Koguryō. . . . On the way, a god of the sea appeared and took her under his protection, enabling Jingū to pacify Korea at her will. . . . While at sea, Empress Jingū obtained a sacred stone [*nyoi no tama*] and by this means was able to delay the birth of her son, the future Emperor Ōjin, until her return to Kyushu. . . . While the empress was still in Kyushu, Ōjin's older brother by a different mother . . . had rebelled and sought to block the return of her party to the capital region. Placing Ōjin in the care of O-omi Takeuchi, who took him to Minato in Kii Province, the empress went directly to Naniwa and soon quelled the rebellion. Ōjin, now an adult, was made crown prince . . . and from this time on the Koreans rendered annual tribute and we, in return, sent officers over to protect their country. As a result of relations with Korea, Japan flourished exceedingly.[22]

This mythic narrative in both its eighth-century version and again in its fourteenth-century recasting provides a somewhat garbled account of a delayed birth. On the surface, the facts of the case are pretty suspicious to any reasonable mortal. The emperor dies suddenly; his wife and the emperor's counselor, both present at his death (which was ascribed to his not having confirmed the wishes of his wife's oracle vision), set out together to conquer a foreign land. They succeed, and upon the woman's return three years later she gives birth, having been accompanied on her travels the entire time by the counselor of her dead husband. She wants her son to assume the role of monarch. The missing piece in this record is to fill in those three years. She needs to prove that her son is the child of a man who died three years ago. That the birth was delayed by three years puts it in the category of mythical, but the reasons are not much different from when mere mortals manipulate birth records, marriage records, and dates of conception: there is never any doubt about who the mother is, but establishing paternity can be a trickier business. In the case of Empress Jingū, a lot rides on her being able to claim that the child who is born *after* she returns from her conquest of Korea (and the narratives all agree that this conquest was successful and necessary for Japan's success) was in fact the child of Emperor Chūai, *who had died three years* before her return to Japan. So the text has to work out some important affairs of state by paying attention to this fetus: It has a special mark on its arm, indicating that it had ruled from the womb (thus legitimating Jingū's right to have conquered a foreign land in the

21. This text has been translated, with an excellent introduction, by H. Paul Varley: *The Chronicle of Gods and Sovereigns: Jinnō Shōtōki of Kitabatake Chikafusa* (New York: Columbia University Press, 1980).

22. Ibid., 102.

name of the imperial line); the fetus is kept in the womb by magical stones offered by the same sea deities who are enabling the conquest of this land; the fetus is born at a time when Emperor Chūai's son by another mother is attempting to assume the role of emperor. Myth here works to provide supernatural cover for an oddly timed pregnancy and birth.

This child, Ōjin, becomes the figure who stabilizes the Japanese imperial line in this mythical account. That he behaved himself as a fetus and stayed in the womb for three years is seen as proof that he is indeed the rightful heir to the imperial line. On the surface, he behaved very well as a fetus. He could have been out of place. But that he waited to be born is seen as proof of the very fact the myth needs to ascertain: his imperial paternity.

The early Japanese mythical narratives of *Kojiki* and *Nihongi* show no interest in the fetal life of the other characters. What happens in between conception and birth is of no consequence, suggesting that there is not only a lack of fetocentric discourse; there is an utter lack of interest in fetal life altogether apart from an interest in the unusual, out-of-place fetus: the miscarried fetus, or the fetus who can be regarded as the antithesis of a miscarriage—the fetus who waits for the most politically convenient moment to be born. As it is said, "normal things are normal, rare things are rare." It is the rare that attracts attention as symbol.

Hierarchies of Innocence: The Nanjing Massacre and the Violated Fetus in Japanese Postwar Cultural Memory

For the final example, I turn to a disturbing vision of the fetus in postwar Japan. It is, I argue, the fetus most out of place, and its dislocation becomes the very basis for utterly banning it from consciousness. Its very existence challenges the postwar counter-memory of Japanese war responsibility. An undeniable victim, this fetus, which may have been thousands of fetuses (and we shall never know for sure) just does not go away from popular imagination. Attempts to banish this fetus just seem to bring it back.

On August 15, 2004, I attended commemorations of Japan's surrender in World War II at the Yasukuni Shrine in Tokyo. The shrine, created in 1869 by the Emperor Meiji, originally enshrined the dead from the Boshin War (a civil war that lasted from 1868 to 1869 in which samurai loyal to the imperial line fought those loyal to the shogunate). The establishment of the shrine, then, can be regarded as an attempt to ritually locate national unity following a civil war. In 1879, its name was changed to Yasukuni (peaceful nation) Shrine, and it became a national shrine for accepting the souls of war dead killed in other battles. During World War II, weekly ceremonies were held in which the names of war dead (limited to those who died in battle, a way of focusing national attention on one category of the dead and ignoring civilian casualties) were read over national radio, and a horse-drawn white palanquin bore the written names of the dead for enshrinement at Yasukuni. Currently, the shrine's "Book of Souls" includes 2,466,532, with the largest majority by far being those killed in World War II. This number includes 27,863 aboriginal Taiwanese who were forced to fight on the side of the Japanese and 21,181 Koreans whose willing participation in the war is also a matter of contention. The shrine is highly controversial both for these reasons and for the inclusion in the Book of Souls of the names of 1,068 convicted war criminals. Among the latter are 12 Class A (crimes against peace) war criminals (which includes Hideki Tōjō, Itagaki Seishiro, Heitarō Kimura, Kenji Doihara, Iwane Matsui, Akira Muto, and Koki Hirota, all of whom were hanged after the International Military Tribunal for the Far East concluded in November 1948). Visits to the shrine by prime ministers of Japan anger Asian leaders whose populations were victims of Japanese aggression. Each year, this controversy heats up around the date of the anniversary and is manipulated by radical right-wing groups in Japan to mobilize voters.

The shrine has become a center for historical revisionism about Japanese atrocities during the war. The shrine's museum, Yūshūkan, offers a version of events explaining Japanese involvement in China and Asia that is boldly revisionist. The shrine's narrative claims that Japan's involvement in World War II and previous incursions in Asia were necessitated by the prevalence of Western colonialism in Asia. Japan, as the only military power in Asia capable of taking on a Western power, had to act as the big brother and protect its neighbors. Further, the shrine singles out the Nanjing Massacre for denial and quotes the only dissenting judge on the Military Tribunals of the Far East, Judge Radhabinod Pal, who indicated that he did not see any evidence that the Nanjing Massacre ever occurred. At Yasukuni, this judge, who served as an anti-Western and anticolonialist voice of dissent on most opinions of the court, is given a shrine all his own, alongside the shrines dedicated to mothers who raised children alone, horses who gave their lives on the battlefields of the war, and dogs who served and died in battle. So, regardless of the shrine's history as a symbol of national unity following the Meiji Restoration and its role in the nation during the war as a focal point of national, collective grieving, it is now known as a center of hard-line radical right-wing activity and historical revisionism that openly celebrates Japan's military past. One T-shirt often seen at the shrine sports an imperial flag and urges the Japanese people to "be proud of being of the Yamato race—next time, we win!!"

On August 15 each year, Yasukuni assumes a festival atmosphere. People clearly too young to have been alive during World War II parade around the grounds in military uniforms of the Japanese Imperial Army's air force, army, and navy. Small groups congregate singing war songs, and ragtag military groups of mixed ages (but almost all less than fifty) march in formation. Young women dress in nurse uniforms from the war era, and they stand alongside young men dressed as soldiers, singing and laughing. Small military camps are set up and serve food to those dressed in uniform.

In the center of the main procession, a huge tent is set up, and speeches by prominent right-wing government officials and revisionist "scholars" are broadcast throughout the shrine precincts.

Meanwhile, a steady stream of elderly people, many holding photographs of dead relatives (all depicted as young men in uniform) make a solemn procession to the worship hall of the shrine to pay respects to their war dead who are enshrined at Yasukuni. Often, they ignore the festivities, the police, and the Soviet-style communist worker music blaring from a communist truck outside the shrine precincts.

They ignore the foreign media, the Japanese religion scholars from abroad (and we are legion), and the onlookers. They head to the main worship hall, say a prayer, and leave.

At noon, the moment of the surrender proclamation by the emperor on August 15, 1945, a bell sounds, and all (except the communists outside and the camera bugs inside) observe a moment of silence.

August 15, 2005 was not the first time I had visited Yasukuni on the commemoration of the day or surrender. But this particular year, the sixtieth anniversary, was important because the performative dimension of a revised cultural memory was more pronounced—more costumes, more singing groups, and, in one case, a pronounced and unusual spectacle: a middle-age man dressed in an army uniform recounting *in the first person* the "alleged" atrocities of the Japanese army in the city of Nanjing from December of 1937 until early February of 1938, in which up to three hundred thousand Chinese men, women, and children were slaughtered.[23]

The performance was animated, watched almost entirely by elderly people holding parasols on this hot day. His "act" consisted of repeated denials of any wrongdoing by the Japanese in Nanjing. He reiterated charges in great detail: burning people alive locked in sheds and houses, rape, throwing children into flames or wells, sword killing contests. As he listed each of the charges brought against the Japanese army for atrocities in Nanjing, he ended his sentences with the refutation, "I did not do that." Or "I would never do that." Sometimes he posed this as a question to a small and entranced crowd of onlookers, "Do you believe your fathers and brothers would do such a thing?"

I stood and listened to him for about twenty minutes, and it appeared that he had a routine he went through that lasted about three or four minutes. But central to his narrative were two alarming and graphic images he kept repeating: the dismemberment of women's bodies by cutting off their breasts, and the image of a fetus cut from the belly of a pregnant woman and held up on a sword. In fact, this latter particular refutation, delivered each time with a sort of wave of his arm, hand held as if grasping a sword, as if to enact the process of dismembering a pregnant woman, seemed to be repeated each time a new member of the audience walked up. These two images he described in some detail, always ending with the pronouncements (which varied): "I did not cut these fetuses out of their mother's bodies" (referring to himself using the first-person male pronoun "boku") or "I would not have done such a thing." He would then ask, "Would your father or brother have cut a fetus (or baby; he used both terms) out of a pregnant woman's (mother's) body?" Unlike the other pronouncements, which were left vague, these pronouncements always mentioned the act of cutting open a pregnant body. It was clear he relished the shock value of his refutation. He did not want a single member of his small and shifting audience to get away without having this one well-known allegation (widely established as fact by those familiar with the atrocities) refuted. Most people could not listen to him for long and left as soon as it was clear he was repeating himself. Many of the people seemed visibly upset, and it was clear that

23. As is to be expected, Japanese and Chinese estimates of those killed in the massacre vary greatly.

the pronouncement offered no relief but rather called up a horrifying image of atrocity.

Finally, a woman who appeared to be about eighty-five years old walked up to him, took a look at his flag, and demanded that he stop acting as if he had been at Nanjing. As she started to argue, he walked away to set up his small performance space out of her range.

In large part, scholars and political analysts observing the dramas at Yasukuni Shrine on this given day regard the costuming and small performances as a kind of nationalist display. It would also be possible at some (generous) level to regard them as a kind of historical reenactment, a social hobby akin to Civil War reenactments in the United States. But with this shrine, there is no doubt that the performances and costume play at Yasukuni are in the service of historical revisionism. In this particular case, something else was being performed. This middle-age man who claimed to have been at Nanjing was hitting on what might be called the most horrifying image of brutality and atrocity: a fetus ripped from its mother's body by a sword.[24] What place, then, does this single image hold in Japanese postwar cultural memory?

This is arguably the most disturbing image in this volume. The claim that pregnant women's bodies were violated by soldiers using swords is present in all eyewitness accounts, and it was central in the Military Tribunals of the Far East immediately following the war. This single act was often pointed to as evidence that the Japanese had acted as barbarians. It became the single image that needed to be overcome, but overcoming it required imagining it, and this was just too difficult. The task became, then, to either ignore it, develop a counter-memory, or attempt to revise it.

Details of this this six-week-long massacre of the population of a major Asian city entered domestic media over time. Selected (but still violent) events entered Japanese consciousness through the Japanese war propaganda almost as soon as it happened (ostensibly to display Japanese military prowess). Because of the rampant brutality of the Nanjing Massacre, to a large extent popular Japanese response was initially shock, even denial, and later a complex process of subtle revisionisms. Yoshida Takashi, in his article titled "A Battle over History: The Nanjing Massacre in Japan"[25] argues that controversies surrounding the various ways that a revisionist project concerning the Nanjing massacre get worked out dominated the edges of Japanese political discourse from the 1970s through the 1990s. The reality is just so terrifying that cultural memory almost begs that one deny the past.

Honda Katsuichi, a Japanese journalist who in 1971 traveled to China and collected first hand accounts from people living in Nanjing, published his interviews under the title *Chūgoku no Tabi* (Travels to China). He published an additional

24. The use of rape to terrorize a population during war is commonplace but often underreported, and only recently has it been recognized as a war crime. See Anne Llewellyn Barstow, ed., *War's Dirty Secret: Rape, Prostitution, and Other Crimes against Women* (Cleveland, Ohio: Pilgrim, 2000).

25. In *The Nanjing Massacre in History and Historiography,* ed. Joshua A. Fogel and Charles S. Maier (Berkeley: University of California Press, 2000), 70–132.

book in 1987, based on additional interviews.[26] In his first work, which has now been translated into English under the title *The Nanjing Massacre: A Japanese Journalist Confronts Japan's National Shame,* he narrates a number of witness accounts provided to him by Chinese people still living in Nanjing in the late 1970s. A number of them describe violations of pregnant women, regarded as a subcategory of rape in the book. Here is one straightforward sentence from an eyewitness account: "They cut open the belly of the pregnant woman and gouged out the fetus."[27] Let us allow that one sentence to stand for all the occasions where this violation happened.

Here, I am interested in how the process of postwar cultural memory in Japan works to find a place for this most disturbing image. This image, along with the accounts of sword killing contests, shocked not only Japanese people, but all paying attention to the Military Tribunals for the Far East. I do not contest that these atrocities occurred, but in this discussion, what is at stake is not historicity but location in memory of that which begs forgetting by virtue of its sheer horror.

Why, besides its shock value, does the man at Yasukuni Shrine select this one image as the centerpiece of his refutation of the atrocities at Nanjing (a task that incidentally is center stage at the shrine, i.e., refuting the Nanjing massacre)?

I would like to suggest, tentatively, that this image makes a good candidate for a refutation precisely because it so haunts postwar Japanese cultural memory, because it utterly explodes the careful counter-memory that was produced to allow for a shifting of blame away from Japanese *culture* and onto a freak government and military. Narratives about victims ("victimology") were and continue to be a core component of postwar reflections on the war.[28] Locating innocence within Japan was an important project for postwar Japanese nation building. To be innocent is to be freed from moral responsibility for the war. Recent *anime* films such as Isao Takahata's 1988 masterpiece *Grave of the Fireflies* focus on Japanese children as the victims of war, and discussions of the atomic blasts often focus on women and children as "innocent victims" subliminally contrasted with "guilty victims." Reiko Tachibana's work on counter-memory has suggested that crafting narratives that allow for people from aggressor nations to regard themselves primarily as victims becomes a matter of national importance. Without such counter-memories, the process of nation rebuilding cannot go on, even if the narratives, while acknowledging the war and ostensibly appearing to claim it, amount to a subtle form of revisionism.[29]

The fetus assumes a high position in a hierarchy of innocent victims. The postwar Japanese counter-memory, which allows for the rebuilding of Japan in the

26. Daqing Yang, "The Challenges of the Nanjing Massacre: Reflections on Historical Inquiry," in ibid., 140.

27. Honda Katsuichi, *The Nanjing Massacre: A Japanese Journalist Confronts Japan's National Shame*, trans. Karen Sandness, ed. Frank Gibney (Armonk, N.Y.: M. E. Sharpe, 1999), 64. Though a number of other references to the violation of pregnant women occur in this text, and throughout the literature on the Nanjing Massacre, I have chosen to use only this one straightforward image.

28. See Carol Gluck's article, "The Past in the Present," in *Postwar Japan as History*, ed. Andrew Gordon (Berkeley: University of California Press, 1993), 64–98.

29. Reiko Tachibana, *Narrative as Counter-Memory: A Half Century of Postwar Writings in Germany and Japan* (Albany: State University of New York Press, 1998).

postwar era freed from its fascist and brutal militaristic past, posits the existence of an innocent Japan that existed simultaneously with a fascist Japan. Yet the horrors of Nanjing, though committed by soldiers, force everyone to examine the roots of violence in their own culture close to home.

In a sense, the fetus in the womb is the ultimate victim with no agency in the face of war. The case of a violated fetus from Nanjing presents a problematic subject: not only is the victim identified with the "other," enforcing the image of Japanese aggression, but this victim has trumped all other victims in the hierarchy of innocence. The violated fetus assumes this highest place when a cultural memory tries to grapple with wartime memory.

I would not argue that the image of this atrocity in Nanjing has been the centerpiece of the postwar revisionists' project. It would appear that at some level, the agents of the revisionist project recognize in this one symbolic image of violation a sympathetic victim too powerful to ignore. But I would contend that the selection of this image is designed to bring the most relief to a guilty national conscience. If you can erase the reality of that most sympathetic of victims, you have come a long ways toward revising an image of the Japanese military that flies in the face of the claims made at Yasukuni and is advanced by the Japanese far right that Japan entered the war to protect the rest of Asia from Western colonialism, as a caring big brother capable through military might of taking on these Western giants. Unlike these other references in Japan, the violated fetus of a non-Japanese woman is at once foreign, anonymous, collective, and utterly without agency.

Surprisingly, if what I witnessed at Yasukuni was any indication, the attempts to relieve that guilty conscience only brought the subject into sharper view and further traumatized the people listening. I saw small groups of people recoil as the performer pronounced "his" innocence at having violated a pregnant woman and her fetus. It is a victim one would prefer not to think about, and consequently, it is always there, haunting the national body politic.

WORKS CITED

Aston, W. G., trans. *Nihongi: Chronicles of Japan from the Earliest Times to A.D. 697.* London: George Allen and Unwin, 1956.

Barstow, Anne Llewellyn, ed., *War's Dirty Secret: Rape, Prostitution and Other Crimes against Women.* Cleveland, Ohio: Pilgrim, 2000.

Fogel, Joshua A., and Charles S. Maier, eds. *The Nanjing Massacre in History and Historiography.* Berkeley: University of California Press, 2000.

Gluck, Carol. "The Past in the Present." In *Postwar Japan as History,* edited by Andrew Gordon, 64–98. Berkeley: University of California Press, 1993.

Hardacre, Helen. *Marketing the Menacing Fetus in Japan.* Berkeley: University of California Press, 1997.

Honda Katsuichi, *The Nanjing Massacre: A Japanese Journalist Confronts Japan's National Shame.* Translated by Karen Sandness. Edited by Frank Gibney. Armonk, N.Y.: M. E. Sharpe, 1999.

LaFleur, William. *Liquid Life: Abortion and Buddhism in Japan.* Princeton, N.J.: Princeton University Press, 1992.

Law, Jane Marie. *Puppets of Nostalgia: The Life, Death, and Rebirth of the Awaji Ningyō Jōruri Tradition.* Princeton, N.J.: Princeton University Press, 1997.

Philippi, Donald, trans. *Kojiki: Record of Ancient Matters.* Tokyo: University of Tokyo Press, 1968.

Tachibana, Reiko. *Narrative as Counter-Memory: A Half Century of Postwar Writings in Germany and Japan.* Albany: State University of New York Press, 1998.

Varley, H. Paul, trans. *The Chronicle of Gods and Sovereigns: Jinnō Shōtōki of Kitabatake Chikafusa.* Introduction by H. Paul Varley. New York: Columbia University Press, 1980.

Yang, Daqing. "The Challenges of the Nanjing Massacre: Reflections on Historical Inquiry." In *The Nanjing Massacre in History and Historiography,* edited by Joshua A. Fogel and Charles S. Maier, 133–68. Berkeley: University of California Press, 2000.

Yoshida Takashi. "A Battle over History: The Nanjing Massacre in Japan." In *The Nanjing Massacre in History and Historiography,* edited by Joshua A. Fogel and Charles S. Maier, 70–132. Berkeley: University of California Press, 2000.

Seeing Like a Family: Fetal Ultrasound Images and Imaginings of Kin

Sallie Han

At four months into her pregnancy, Josie already was carrying "baby pictures" and showing them to family members, friends, coworkers at the real estate office where she worked, and an anthropologist who happened to ask.[1] "I wouldn't be a good mommy if I didn't," she exclaimed as she pulled out from her wallet a pair of grainy, white-on-black images, which already were showing a little wear. They had been taken a few weeks earlier at a ten-week ultrasound scan, which her obstetrician had performed as a "quick look" for the heartbeat to confirm that she was pregnant.[2] Josie had told me excitedly that she had some "cute" pictures to show me. However, when she handed me the thin, curling slips of paper, what I saw were black-and-white blurs that bore no resemblance to a baby. Here were the proofs of life to which Josie already had attached so much importance and meaning.

Josie's story illustrates the ways in which American middle-class women and men have embraced the ultrasound scan, or sonogram, as a routine practice of prenatal medical care and as a ritual practice of American kinship and family. It also illuminates the broader context in which it emerges. Across cultures and societies, and throughout their histories, the confirmation of a pregnancy might come only with the birth of a living child, whose condition as a human being had not been

I received funding for this research from the Alfred P. Sloan Foundation through the Center for the Ethnography of Everyday Life at the University of Michigan, and the Rackham School of Graduate Studies and the Department of Anthropology at the University of Michigan.

1. My deepest gratitude belongs to the women and men who shared their experiences of expectancy with me. All names were changed to protect the identity and respect the privacy of the expectant parents and birth professionals involved in my study.

2. I interviewed Josie during preliminary fieldwork that I conducted for this study in the summer of 2000.

assumed as given. As anthropologists have documented, status as a human being or, more specifically, as a cultural and social person, is not necessarily established at birth, but becomes constituted and recognized through rituals and rites of passage. However, in contemporary American culture and society, personhood is assumed at birth, and assigned even long before birth, as the coming into being of a person has come to be defined as a matter of medicine, science, and technology.

This chapter considers the relationship between fetal imagining and fetal imaging. The womb and especially its contents long have been mysteries of human experience and the subjects of imaginative (and magical) speculation, as the chapters in this volume vividly illustrate. The importance and meaning attached to fetal ultrasound imaging in the United States today can be understood in terms of this tradition of fascination with the fetus. From the perspective of Josie and other American middle-class women and men, sonograms replace imaginings of the fetus with "real" images. They are "real" as ostensibly objective observations of the fetus, which in turn becomes "real" itself *because* of the apparent realness of the image. The significant difference between fetal imagining and fetal imaging lies with the assumption—identified most strongly with modern Western thinking—that while imagining involves creativity and interpretation, imaging does not. One sees simply what is. In fact, fetal ultrasound imaging belies such a conceit. Today, sonograms seem self-evident as images because improvements in technology now produce sharper, more detailed, clearer images bearing closer resemblance to photography than radiography (X-rays). However, fetal ultrasound images remain subject to multiple interpretations, including the "expert" reading of the obstetrician who examines the images to make medical diagnoses, and the loving gaze of expectant parents in whose eyes the black-and-white blurs become baby pictures. As a result, sonograms call to attention seeing as a cultural and social practice of imagination.

This chapter draws from anthropological research on the childbearing experiences of contemporary American middle-class women. As a cultural anthropologist interested in experiences of kinship and reproduction in the United States, I engaged in a study with pregnant women in and around Ann Arbor, Michigan, from June to August 2000 and from October 2002 to January 2004. I conducted formal and informal interviews with pregnant women, their partners, and other family members, as well as with sonographers, doctors, midwives, and other birth professionals. I also engaged in participant observation in a variety of settings, including prenatal visits, baby showers, and childbirth education classes, in addition to ultrasound scans.

It was through such engagement in the everyday lives of pregnant women—sitting in their living rooms and admiring an expectant mother's baby book or viewing the video taken at a recent ultrasound scan—that I began to see what they saw. For women like Josie, the practice of fetal ultrasound imaging replaced uncertainties and imaginings with "concrete" images of the fetus. However, I also came to see that far from being replaced, imaginings of kin contribute to the apprehension of so-called concrete images of the fetus. When Josie referred to her "baby pictures" and described them as "cute," the cuteness lay in the eye of the beholder.

Pregnant women in my study did not simply see. When they regarded fetal ultrasound images, they were seeing like a family.

The Ritual of Seeing

Aside from the pregnancy test, fetal ultrasound imaging is one of the more widely used prenatal diagnostic technologies in the United States today. There is a range of "medical" reasons for performing scans. Most American women have at least one scan performed during their pregnancies, typically at around twenty weeks to evaluate the condition of both the fetus and the organs that support the pregnancy, such as the placenta and cervix. A scan might be performed as early as several weeks into the first trimester to detect a fetal heartbeat, confirming that a pregnancy is "viable." The ultrasound scan also is used as a screening for serious developmental problems caused by genetic anomalies, such as Down syndrome.

However, reliance upon ultrasound scans to make certain kinds of diagnoses is not without controversy. Overall, studies show that the routine use of ultrasound scans has not necessarily improved the health and well-being of mothers and newborns (maternal and infant outcomes).[3] With the development of evermore sophisticated technologies, there are expectations that the scan can be used to detect and diagnose a wider range of conditions, but evidence suggests that these expectations are outpacing the technologies themselves.[4] A number of medical researchers and practitioners now caution that there is an overuse of fetal ultrasound imaging in the United States today.[5]

Although the medical value of routine sonograms has been called into question, their importance and meaning as rituals remain undiminished for the expectant parents who anticipate their ultrasound scans with anxiety and eagerness. For Kerri, a woman in my study whose reproductive history had included a miscarriage, a diagnosis of infertility, and two rounds of in vitro fertilization (both unsuccessful), the ultrasound scan represented one of the "hoops" or "tests" that she had to pass as a pregnant woman: "It felt like there were so many hoops that we had to jump through in the first trimester. . . . At any point, your joy could be shattered." Fetal ultrasound imaging represents an important rite in the passage from woman to pregnant woman to mother.

In the United States, "fetuses" emerged first in public imagination, then in private experience. Feminist scholar Rosalind Pollack Petchesky first called attention to the "power of visual culture" and the significance of seeing, imaging, and

3. Linn Getz and Anne L. Kirkengen, "Ultrasound Screening in Pregnancy: Advancing Technology, Soft Markers for Fetal Chromosomal Aberrations, and Unacknowledged Ethical Dilemmas," *Social Science and Medicine* 56, 10 (2003): 2045–57.

4. Ibid., 2045.

5. This is to say nothing of the uses of fetal ultrasound imaging in other societies, notably as a tool of prenatal sex selection. Barbara Miller describes an increase in sex-selective abortion in Asian societies where sons are preferred. See B. Miller, "Female-Selective Abortion in Asia: Patterns, Policies, and Debates," *American Anthropologist* 103, 4 (2004): 1083–95. Nikky-Guninder Kaur Singh considers the particular case of female feticide among Sikhs in India in her chapter in this volume.

visual media in the public construction of fetuses as "persons."[6] However, Meredith Michaels and Lynn Morgan observed more recently that "fetuses have spilled out from the borders of the bitter abortion debate and become a regular, almost unremarkable feature of the public landscape. They have come to occupy a significant place in the private imaginary of women who are or wish to be pregnant."[7]

Until recently, relatively little attention had been paid to the social relations in which fetal images materialized and mattered privately. However, this is a dimension of human experience that now is being exploited. In February 2005, almost twenty years after Petchesky published her essay, the *New York Times* reported that church groups, including the Southern Baptist Convention and Focus on the Family, have been installing ultrasound equipment and training technicians to operate it in the "pregnancy crisis" clinics that they sponsor—for the purpose of persuading women, individually, not to have abortions. Journalist Neela Banerjee described this development as "a sign of how the opponents of abortion are dividing their efforts—seeking to chip away at abortion through legislation but also waging a battle for women's hearts."[8] In this context, it seems an important and meaningful endeavor for scholars to consider fetal ultrasound imaging in terms of women's hearts and their private imaginary. In the private experiences of expectant parents, fetuses matter and materialize as particular "persons." Ultrasound images represent pictures not of "a baby," but of "my baby."

Ideas and practices of kinship and conventions of family photography appear to influence the experience of fetal ultrasound imaging in the United States today. Cultural theorist Marianne Hirsch describes the significance of family photography as "integrally tied to the ideology of the modern family": "The family photo both displays the cohesion of the family and is an instrument of its togetherness; it both chronicles family rituals and constitutes a prime objective of those rituals."[9] In the case of fetal ultrasound imaging, the technology might be new, but its use is consistent with older, established rituals of imaging and imagining kinship. Expectant parents in my study experienced the ultrasound scan as baby pictures, home movies, and family videos. Indeed, the sonographers (and occasionally, doctors and midwives) who performed the scans also recognized their significance in terms of familial ritual. They also participated in and contributed to the construction of the sonogram as a kind of "Kodak moment."[10]

Anthropologist Mary Bouquet calls family a "photographic condition" and contends that "family photography was and remains deeply involved in constituting kinship through the coherent looking images it produces, which are

6. Rosalind P. Petchesky, "Fetal Images: The Power of Visual Culture in the Politics of Reproduction," *Feminist Studies* 13, 2 (1987): 264.

7. Meredith Michaels and Lynn Morgan, "Introduction: The Fetal Imperative," in *Fetal Subjects, Feminist Positions*, ed. L. Morgan and M. Michaels (Philadelphia: University of Pennsylvania Press, 1999), 2.

8. Neela Banerjee, "Church Groups Turn to Sonogram to Turn Women from Abortions," *New York Times*, Feb. 2, 2005, section A.

9. Marianne Hirsch, *Family Frames: Photography, Narrative, and Postmemory* (Cambridge: Harvard University Press, 1997), 7.

10. Sallie Han, "The Baby in the Body: Pregnancy Practices as Kin and Person Making Experience in the Contemporary United States," Ph.D. diss., University of Michigan, 2006.

simultaneously material artifacts that occupy space and demand classification."[11] Family photography might be less an illustration of kinship "in fact" than of imaginings of kin. The analysis that Bouquet proposes includes an examination of "production (such as pose, camera angle, portraiture conventions) and consumption (what is in the eye of the beholder: interpretation, decoding)."[12] Although fetal ultrasound imaging is not photography—indeed, the differences between the technologies is significant—its examination in terms of family photography illuminates the practices and ideas that enter into the production and consumption not only of fetal ultrasound "baby pictures" but also of the "baby" itself.

Fetal ultrasound images come to matter because of the imaginings of kin that influence the cultural and social practices of producing and consuming such images. The production of fetal ultrasound images involves what Bouquet calls "portraiture conventions" that shape the content and composition of the images themselves. There are conventions that concern the consumption of fetal ultrasound images. Ultrasound scans can be seen as practices that mediate social relations between persons—literally, the "media events" of families who gather together to view "baby pictures" and videotapes. Significantly, fetal ultrasound images also become consumed as material objects. Not only was it important to view the fetal ultrasound images, but expectant parents in my study also attached meaning to the "fact" of a slip of paper or a videotape that they could keep. Being able to touch pictures and tapes makes material and concrete the imaged and imagined "person."

Although I have used the terms "production" and "consumption" as if they were mutually exclusive, the cultural and social practice of fetal ultrasound imaging demonstrates the ways in which consumption might be considered production by other means. Pregnant women are simultaneously producers and consumers of fetal ultrasound images. Not only do they, in their own bodies, generate and gestate the bodies that are imaged, but through the activities of looking and seeing, they also apprehend fetuses and babies. They produce and consume family and kinship.

Looking Like a Baby

During conversations that were focused on the viewing of ultrasound pictures, it seemed that almost as a rule, someone would comment on how "real" or "human" or "just like a baby" the fetal ultrasound images appeared, even to the untrained eye. In this section, I briefly discuss the content or composition of the images that expectant parents take home as baby pictures. I suggest that the expected child becomes a composite of the views of the heart and other vital organs that are required for prenatal diagnosis, the images of the girl or boy "parts," and the pictures of the hands,

11. Mary Bouquet, "The Family Photographic Condition," *Visual Anthropology Review* 16, 1 (1999): 9.

12. Mary Bouquet, "Making Kinship, with an Old Reproductive Technology," in *Relative Values: Reconfiguring Kinship Studies*, ed. S. Franklin and S. McKinnon (Durham: Duke University Press, 2001), 87.

feet, and face of the "baby." "Cuteness" is constructed through particular kinds of "poses," which are drawn from the conventions of family photography, contributing to the sentimentalization of fetuses as "babies."

Just as there are conventional uses to which ultrasound pictures are put—in photograph albums as keepsakes or on a Web site that can be viewed by family and friends—there also are conventions regarding the content or composition of fetal ultrasound images. Some conventions are based on what is required of the ultrasound scan as a prenatal diagnostic test. During my fieldwork observations with Joan, a sonographer, I noted that she prioritized capturing certain "views" for the doctor. At the twenty-week scan, these included images of the heart, which Joan labeled "4CH" to indicate that all four chambers were developed, as well as of the brain, kidneys, and spine. Views of the long bones of the arms and legs were used to take measurements as irregularities in their growth are used as indirect or "soft" markers of other anomalies, such as Down syndrome. During my first prenatal visit, a "picture" was taken on a smaller machine that could be wheeled in and out of the exam rooms. Because the nurse-midwife had been unable to detect a heartbeat using a Doppler device, she had asked an obstetrician who was a colleague to perform an ultrasound scan on me. The purpose of the scan was both to confirm the viability of the pregnancy and to establish a due date. Using the date of my last menstrual period, it was calculated that I was about twelve weeks pregnant. However, based on the measurements taken during this early ultrasound scan, the obstetrician and midwife estimated that I was closer to ten weeks pregnant. As a result, my due date was recalculated to be almost twelve days later than originally thought.

The picture itself is an image of the dark rectangular screen on which the ultrasound scan was viewed. The location, time, and date appear in white at the top of the image and screen. (In other images, the name of the pregnant woman also appears at the top.) Inside the dark rectangle is a wedge that is gray and white in color. The wedge itself is the area that the transducer, or ultrasound device, actually images. The picture taken at my first prenatal visit shows a dark bean-shaped area that is my uterus and, inside it, a smaller, white bean that is the fetus at about ten weeks. Other women in my study had similar pictures taken at early ultrasound scans. Elizabeth showed me pictures from nine weeks, then eleven weeks, of what she called her "bean baby."

Other conventions are particular to the ultrasound scan, notably the images that are used both to determine and display the sex or "gender" of the expected child. Sybil, a grandmother-to-be, had watched a video of the ultrasound scan that had been performed on her daughter-in-law, Heather. Although Sybil said that she initially did not want to learn if the expected child was a girl or a boy, she laughed as she recalled seeing the "little penis," which the sonographer had circled on the monitor. At Sharon's twenty-week scan, the sonographer indicated the male genitalia with an arrow. In other pictures that I saw, the sonographer had composed the image so that the genitalia were roughly centered, then labeled them "boy parts" or "girl parts," or simply "boy" or "girl." Although expectant parents generally assumed that it was "easier" to see a boy than a girl, reasoning that "seeing something" (i.e., the presence of a penis) meant a boy, and not seeing it (the absence of one) a girl, I also heard from sonographers that this was not necessarily the case. They described "girl parts" as resembling a "tulip" or the outline of a "hamburger," adding that these images sometimes were easier to distinguish than a male "stem." In other words, sonographers were seeing "something" also to determine if the expected child was a girl.

If the content or composition of fetal ultrasound images is shaped in part by their uses in diagnosing problems and in determining the sex of the expected child, it also is shaped in part by conventions borrowed from photography, specifically that of children. In particular, there is a focus on such "parts" as feet and hands as well as the face in artistic photography of children, especially babies, and in family photography that is inspired by it. These images are familiar to American middle-class women and men, appearing as they do on TV commercials and in magazine advertisements, such as those decorating the reception office at the clinic where Joan, the sonographer, works. On the Internet, ultrasound pictures and videos can be viewed on Web sites that allow expectant parents to the track week-by-week development. Various Web sites also feature "photo albums" where expectant parents can post their "baby pictures," and even ultrasound "contests."

There is a focus on the feet and hands of a child or baby not only in photography, but also in other documentary forms. At the hospital where several women in my study delivered their babies, and where my daughter also was born, each mother received a keepsake card, decorated with drawings of ducklings, on which to record the baby's name, birth date, sex, weight, length, and hair color, with a space below where a nurse placed the baby's footprints. Baby books provide spaces for handprints as well. Besides the bronzing of baby booties, or first shoes, parents today can purchase kits to create casts of baby hands and feet, including one called My Little Hand In Yours, which provides materials to create a cast of baby's hand intertwined with a parent's.

Linda Layne, in her studies on pregnancy loss, suggests the importance both of handprints and footprints and of replicas and renderings of hands and feet because they symbolize both the humanness and the particularity of a child. Layne observes that images of hands and feet recall humanness more generally—"bipedalism and an opposable thumb being distinctive characteristics of the species."[13] In addition, handprints and footprints, "formed by a direct, physical connection with the baby," represent a particular baby: "Since the Victorian era and the discovery of the uniqueness of fingerprints, these prints have come to represent not only generic humanness but the idea of the unique individuality of each person."[14] Layne quotes Celeste Condit, who notes the use of such images in antiabortion campaigns. In particular, fetal feet, because they are "very close to baby feet in shape," become used as symbols of personhood: "Our visual logic 'recognizes' such feet as 'small human feet' and we synecdochically expand the unseen picture to see

13. Linda Layne, "'He Was a Real Baby with Baby Things': A Material Culture Analysis of Personhood, Parenthood, and Pregnancy Loss," *Journal of Material Culture* 5, 3 (2000): 333.

14. Ibid.

a full 'small human.'"[15] Layne observes the importance of replicas and renderings of feet and hands in the making of memorials for lost children, and suggests: "In the case of pregnancy loss, footprints seem to have an additional meaning (one that privileges them over handprints) in that they can evoke the sense that someone was here and now is gone. Like someone walking in the sand, the footprint is a fragile trace that a person passed this way."[16]

Like feet and hands, faces also symbolize general humanness and the particularity of a person. Despite the fact that ultrasound scans do not provide the most distinct or discernible images—it was often commented that the pictures of faces resembled "aliens"—expectant parents, grandparents, and other family members and friends sometimes scrutinized the "baby pictures" for evidence of Daddy's eyes, Mommy's nose, Grandpa's chin, and other such inheritances. When I asked expectant parents in my study what they most anticipated about the birth, I often heard the answer "seeing the baby's face." While pregnant women took home pictures of feet and hands and girl and boy "parts," these were in addition to other pictures of the expected child's face. Two of the pictures that I received at my own twenty-week scan resembled others that I saw during my research. In figure 1, the "baby" is shown in profile, with eyes, nose, and mouth just discernible. In figure 2, the "baby" appears to be lying horizontally, with its head tilted so that there is a three-quarters view of the face. The lower (right) arm is barely visible, but appears to be crossed over the chest, with the hand possibly around the mouth. The upper (left) arm is held slightly away from the face and chest, and the fingers on the hand are visible—as if the baby were waving. In fact, in a similar picture that I saw from another woman's twenty-week scan, the sonographer had typed the words "Hi Dad" across the top of the image. Such a combination of face and hands usually was considered especially "cute." During ultrasound scans, images of the expected child's hands moving across the screen, especially near the face, often drew coos from the sonographer and expectant parents or grandparents.

Coming full circle, the conventions of fetal ultrasound imaging also seem to have been integrated into photography. Anne Geddes, the photographer who is well known for her images of babies dressed as cabbages and bumblebees, opens her 2002 book, *Pure*, with a series of cloudy, grayscale images. They stand in stark contrast to the warm, clear images featured in the rest of the collection. One image depicts legs bent at the knees, and another a child in profile, with a hand covering the face. Prefacing a book that contains photographs first of pregnant and then of postpartum women as well as newborns, these images suggest fetal ultrasound images. However, each of these images is accompanied by a caption on the opposite page, which identifies the child in the photograph by name and age ("Poppy, 4 weeks" and "Brooke, 3 weeks"). Comparing the ultrasound picture in figure 3 with the Anne Geddes photograph illustrates the shared iconography of baby legs and feet found in fetal ultrasound imaging and in photography.

15. Celeste Condit, *Decoding Abortion Rhetoric* (Urbana: University of Illinois Press, 1990), 68–69, quoted in Layne, "'He Was a Real Baby,'" 334.

16. Ibid.

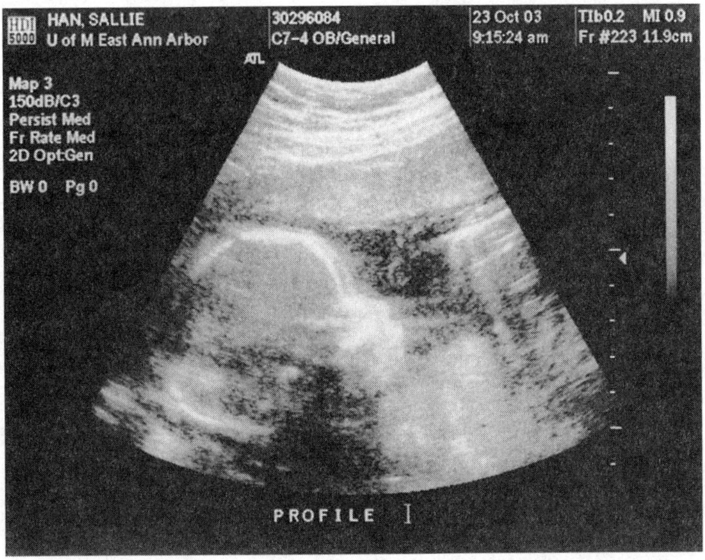

FIGURE 1. Taken at the author's twenty-week scan in October 2003, this image is composed as a portrait, specifically a facial profile. It was given to the author as a "baby picture."

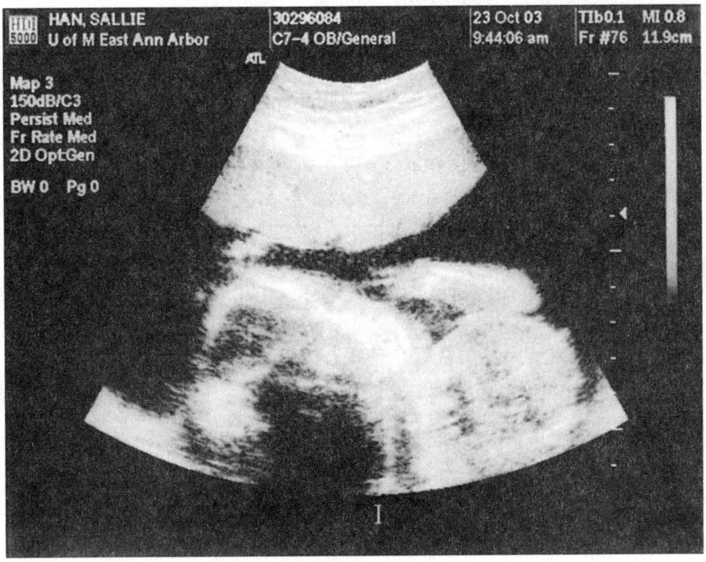

FIGURE 2. This ultrasound "baby picture," taken at the author's twenty-week scan in October 2003, shows the face and the arm apparently "waving" at the viewer.

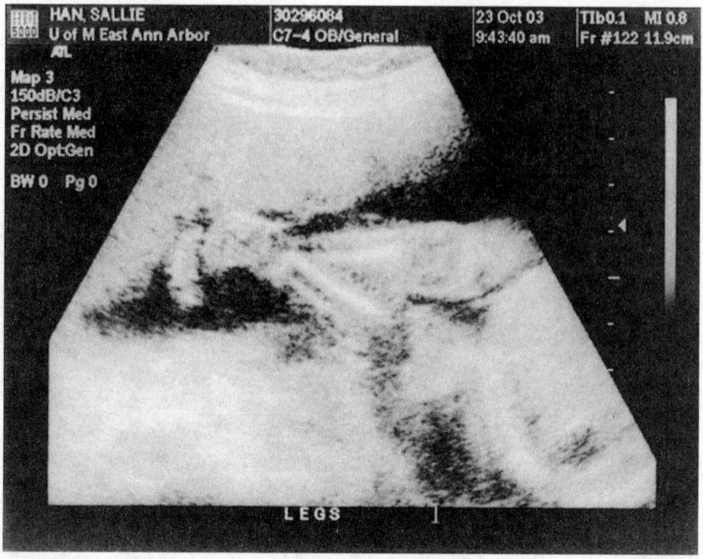

FIGURE 3. This ultrasound "baby picture," taken at the author's twenty-week scan in October 2003, shows the legs crossed at the ankles. An image like this is not used to make medical evaluations.

The Social Life of Fetal Ultrasound Images

Women and men in my study commented upon the "entertainment" value of various pregnancy experiences, especially the ultrasound scan. Joan, the sonographer, described part of her work as "giving a tour" or "putting on a show." Several pregnant women described their scans to me in terms of movies and TV. Indeed, the ultrasound scan especially resembles the experience of cinema as a practice that is both routine and ritual. "We're lying there, and there's the monitor, and the lights go down, and then all of a sudden—I mean, it was a wonderful experience," Josie recalled of her ten-week ultrasound scan.[17] She also later likened her twenty-week scan, to which her husband, her parents, and her parents-in-law had accompanied her, to watching a movie together. Though the scan is performed in a medical setting, expectant parents seemed to experience it in the familiar terms of a media event.

In fact, the ultrasound scan can become further emptied of medical value as it becomes removed from the medical setting. Heather and Megan were given videotapes that recorded fetal movements at their twenty-week scans. Heather later viewed the tape with her mother-in-law. Megan showed her video during a potluck

17. This was despite having to tolerate the discomfort of having the transducer inserted into her vagina and maneuvered internally. Early in the pregnancy, scans are not uncommonly performed vaginally because views of the uterus might be blocked by the pubic bone.

that her mother organized expressly to allow extended family to "see the baby." Up to now, fetal ultrasound imaging has been available primarily only at hospitals and medical offices, and health insurance companies have covered (and continue to cover) most of the cost of the scans as a standard practice of prenatal care. Now, at least some women seem to be willing to pay a few hundred dollars out of their own pockets for scans at "ultrasound boutiques" that recently have been opening for business in cities and even suburban malls across the United States.[18] In their advertisements, the businesses make no claims regarding fetal ultrasound imaging as medical technology. Instead, bearing such names as Baby Pictures and A Peek in the Pod, the boutiques emphasize that the ultrasound images that they produce are for "entertainment purposes" and "keepsakes."[19] In 2005, entertainment magazines reported that actor Tom Cruise had bought an ultrasound machine for his fiancée, who was pregnant with their child. As Janelle Taylor observes, the ultrasound scan has become a consumer good, which is involved also in the construction of still another object for consumption—the fetus or baby itself.[20]

Megan's videotape became a precious keepsake. Though it seems an unlikely "proxy" for the boy that she was expecting, the tape also contained images of the baby moving. In this way, the tape itself was connected immediately and intimately with the expected child. As the French scholar Roland Barthes observed in his essays on photography, *Camera Lucida*:

> The photograph is literally an emanation of the referent. From a real body, which was there, proceed radiations which ultimately touch me, who am here; the duration of the transmission is insignificant; the photograph of the missing being, as Sontag says, will touch me like the delayed rays of a star. A sort of umbilical cord links the body of the photographed thing to my gaze: light, though impalpable, is here a carnal medium, a skin I share with anyone who has been photographed.[21]

Here, Barthes applies the physics of photography to an exploration of its poetics. Significantly, he uses the metaphor of the umbilical cord to describe the connection, not only between these aspects of photography, but also between the body that is gazing and the body that is photographed. By describing photography in terms of an umbilical cord—which is iconic of the connection between mother and child—Barthes suggests that the processes involved in photography (such as taking a picture or having one's own picture taken, seeing a picture or showing a picture) are themselves a kind of kin making. He also emphasizes that photography

18. A 2004 article in the *New York Times* ("Fetal Photos: Keepsake or Health Risk?") reported on a new trend in "high-resolution, artistic photography of fetuses." Reporter Marc Santora described a New York City ultrasound boutique called A Peek in the Pod, where pregnant women can receive prints, a CD-ROM, and DVD of an ultrasound scan for $295.

19. For example, Baby Pictures, a Seattle-area company, pitched its services in a June 2001 magazine advertisement: "Our exclusive in utero videography allows you to put the customary ultrasound photography into timeless motion."

20. Janelle Taylor, "Of Sonograms and Baby Prams: Prenatal Diagnosis, Pregnancy, and Consumption," *Feminist Studies* 26, 2 (2000): 391–418.

21. Roland Barthes, *Camera Lucida* (New York: Hill and Wang, 1980), 80–81.

is an embodied experience. The umbilical cord or connection that he describes is light, or the radiations literally emanating from matter (bodies included). From this perspective, Megan's video not only is a precious keepsake or proxy of the baby, but also contains emanations of the expected child.

Fetal ultrasound imaging itself is significant as a material practice, producing such objects as "baby pictures" and videos. A practice such as carrying pictures in one's wallet is recognized socially as appropriate and not unusual behavior for mothers. By carrying "baby pictures" in her wallet, Josie became a card-carrying member of the "good mommy" club—even months before her child was born. Each time she opened her wallet to show and tell her "baby pictures," she performed her new role. Also, the fact that the images were taken as part of the medical care Josie has sought to manage and monitor her pregnancy serves as further demonstration of her standing as a "good mommy."

Other women in my study displayed their pictures in frames and photograph albums. One expectant couple posted their pictures on their Web site. Another father later included them in the introduction to the digital "slide show" that he had created from photographs taken before and after his child's birth. After hearing about parents incorporating their ultrasound pictures in their birth announcements, my husband and I designed our 2003 Christmas card around a picture that we had received at the twenty-week scan. It was as much a way of sharing the news that we were expecting as it was sending annual holiday greetings to friends from out of town and less frequently in touch. In fact, all of these ways of sharing and circulating ultrasound pictures were continued as ways of sharing and circulating birth announcements and later, baby pictures.

The circulation of ultrasound pictures is an important material practice, even when it involves clicking through the (virtual) pages of a Web site, where the pictures might be posted. The sharing of pictures is met with the writing of cards and e-mails expressing congratulations, the buying or making of gifts either for the child or the parents, and even the arranging of visits from family members and friends who are interested in delivering their well wishes in person. These practices all illustrate the ways in which pregnancy and parenthood significantly involve consumption. Fetal ultrasound imaging is a ritual, symbol, and consumer good of pregnancy and parenthood in the United States today. Not surprisingly, dramatizations of ultrasound scans are depicted in television commercials for Honda minivans, and still images from the scans are featured, in place of more traditional baby pictures, in magazine advertisements for Huggies diapers.

As material objects, the ultrasound pictures that I saw had been printed on ultrasound printer paper, which resembles thermographic fax paper in look and texture. At the scan, the pictures emerged from the printer in a long strip, like receipts from a cash register. Although they are prized as precious keepsakes, in fact the "baby pictures" are printed on relatively inexpensive paper that is not intended for preservation, serving as a reminder as to why paper collectibles are called ephemera. Nevertheless, the fact of the pictures provides tangible proof of the existence of an anticipated family member who can be imaged and not only imagined. Ultrasound pictures are important as objects that demonstrate the materiality of the expected child. Megan's "baby pictures" make concrete her expectations of a particular child and the new kinds of kin ties that will be formed with and around him or her. For example, as a gift for the grandmother-to-be, Megan had pasted a photograph of her mother's face alongside a "picture" from her ultrasound scan inside a storybook titled *Picture Me with My Grandma*. The book is designed to be personalized, so that the photographs pasted on the last page can be viewed through cutouts on each page. Megan's "baby" and mother appear as the faces of the little boy and grandmother whose story is told in the book. Though the gift was meaningful in the ways that the publishers of the book no doubt intended, both Megan and her mother also acknowledged that it was humorous in other ways. The grandmother in the book wears long, flowered dresses, ruffled aprons, and her gray hair in curls. She is a stereotype of a traditional, old-fashioned grandmother. In contrast, Megan's mother wore stylish, professional clothing and her blonde hair in a straight and simple style. Also, the black-and-white picture that Megan pasted into the book next to the color photograph of her mother's smiling face was a blurry profile of the expected child's head. The effect was, to quote one of Megan's cousins, "freaky."

A scrapbook enthusiast, Megan also collected various items, which she pasted into the baby book that she had started shortly after taking a pregnancy test. These items included fact sheets about prenatal care and fetal development that she had received during her visits with her doctor, cards and notes of congratulations, and narratives that Megan handwrote, describing the members of the expected child's family, including parents and grandparents. When she learned that she was expecting a boy, she began to decorate the pages of the scrapbook with designs cut from blue paper as well as colorful stickers of teddy bears, balls, trains, and trucks—toys that are associated stereotypically with boys. Megan also had designed the card on which the sonographer had written the sex of the expected child. This she pasted into the scrapbook opposite the pictures that she received at the ultrasound scan. In sum, Megan's scrapbook is a document of her pregnancy, recording prenatal visits with the doctor, the ultrasound scan, the family "screening," her baby shower, and finally the birth and first days at home. At the same time, then, it also is a record of the family life of which she and her expected child are a part. Keeping the scrapbook does not only "preserve" such experience, it also shapes them. In some cases, this entails a literal shaping of images. Megan carefully selects which photographs to use, then crops them in various shapes. Some of her scrapbook tools cut circles, whereas others crop photographs in the shapes of hearts and stars. The effect is not only to decorate the pages of the scrapbook, but also to highlight the faces of particular family members. Although often taken for granted as mere keepsakes, objects such as Megan's scrapbook and the ultrasound pictures pasted into it perform important cultural work in the making of kin and persons.

Seeing as an Embodied Experience

The importance and meaning that women like Megan attached to fetal ultrasound images suggests the relationship between imagining and imaging. Imaging the fetus involves creativity and interpretation. It is itself an assertion of imagination.

This contradicts modern Western thinking about what seeing is, in particular the assumption that it is purely visual perception.

Feminist scholars also have tended to focus on the power of visual culture. In her study of American middle-class couples, Margarete Sandelowski suggests that the ultrasound scan has become "a new kind of spectator sport for men."[22] She observes that "men were often fascinated by the fetal image and, at times, even more intrigued with the technological feat that made that image possible than with the image itself."[23] Like other feminist scholars, she characterizes men's increased involvement in reproduction as exacting a price from women's reproductive integrity. Sandelowski suggests: "This imaging technique serves to make the positions of expectant fathers and sonographers as knowers of the fetus more equal to that of the pregnant woman because her knowing is made less exclusive and singular and more dependent on technology. Fetal ultrasonography places a greater value on experience at a distance—on surrogate or voyeuristic, as opposed to direct bodily experience of the fetus. The dissociative mind's eye prevails over the connective body's eye."[24] Though it is recognized that fetal ultrasound imaging can contribute to the meaningful participation of a male partner in a woman's pregnancy, the consequences include alienating the pregnant woman from the "baby" in her body and discrediting and displacing her authoritative knowledge of her pregnancy.

In fact, the experiences of women and men in my study suggest the need to reconsider the significance of seeing—that is, ocularcentrism, or the privileging of seeing above other senses. The importance and meaning that expectant mothers attached in particular to being able to "connect" the feelings inside their bodies with images and imaginings of the expected child that produced such pangs and pokes might serve as a reminder that seeing itself is a kind of somatic experience. Expectant fathers also described the importance of seeing the baby in terms of becoming *closer* to the experience of pregnancy. As Constance Classen notes, the "fact" of the five senses of physical perception is a cultural and historical invention that lately "has been shattered by sensory scientists. Touch has been broken down into a multitude of specialized senses including kinesthesia—the sense of movement—perception of temperature and perception of pain."[25]

When a pregnant woman sees her baby during an ultrasound scan, she is not a disembodied eye. As Josie described her ten-week scan, she recalled: "I was holding my breath for some reason, I don't know why. We saw the screen, and my husband was next to me here." She indicated her shoulder. "He's looking over me because the screen is right here." She extended her arm. "I have this really deep belly laugh, and the baby was like *boi-oi-oing*. I was like, 'Oh, my God!'" Similarly, reconsidering seeing as an embodied experience becomes especially important in terms of understanding the involvement of expectant fathers. Liz, another

22. Margarete Sandelowsi, "Separate, but Less Unequal: Fetal Ultrasonography and the Transformation of Expectant Mother/Fatherhood," *Gender and Society* 8, 2 (1994): 235.

23. Ibid.

24. Ibid., 239.

25. Constance Classen, *Worlds of Sense: Exploring the Senses in History and across Cultures* (New York: Routledge, 1993), 5.

pregnant woman I knew, told me in an e-mail that her husband literally "jumped out of his seat" when he caught his first glimpse of the expected child's face on the screen. I also have heard about husbands fainting or "nearly fainting" from the excitement of seeing the "baby." Such reactions are dramatic, but not incomprehensible as ritualistic responses—for example, men's fainting is one of the behaviors that commonly have been described in practices of "couvade."[26] Indeed, these stories also draw attention to the impact that fetal ultrasound imaging has had on men as well as women as somatic experiences.

In short, this chapter suggests the significance of considering fetal ultrasound imaging in terms of cultural and social ideas and practices of kinship. In the United States today, fetal ultrasound imaging has emerged as an important and meaningful technology of fetal imagining and family making. It calls attention to the ways in which being a family involves seeing and being seen as a family. However, fetal ultrasound images also call into question the nature and culture of visual perception as not restricted to "simply" seeing. Instead, seeing itself involves a broader and bodily experience of imagination, perception, and creation.

WORKS CITED

Banerjee, Neela. "Church Groups Turn to Sonogram to Turn Women from Abortions." *New York Times*, Feb. 2, 2005.

Barthes, Roland. *Camera Lucida: Reflections on Photography*. New York: Hill and Wang, 1980.

Bouquet, Mary. "The Family Photographic Condition." *Visual Anthropology Review* 16, 1 (1999): 2–19.

———. "Making Kinship, with an Old Reproductive Technology." In *Relative Values: Reconfiguring Kinship Studies*, edited by Sarah Franklin and Susan McKinnon, 85–115. Durham, N.C.: Duke University Press, 2001.

Classen, Constance. *Worlds of Sense: Exploring the Senses in History and across Cultures*. New York: Routledge, 1993.

Condit, Celeste. *Decoding Abortion Rhetoric*. Urbana: University of Illinois Press, 1990.

Getz, Linn, and Anne Luise Kirkengen. "Ultrasound Screening in Pregnancy: Advancing Technology, Soft Markers for Fetal Chromosomal Aberrations, and Unacknowledged Ethical Dilemmas." *Social Science and Medicine* 56, 10 (2003): 2045–57.

Hirsch, Marianne. *Family Frames: Photography, Narrative, and Postmemory*. Cambridge: Harvard University Press, 1997.

Layne, Linda. "'He Was a Real Baby with Baby Things': A Material Culture Analysis of Personhood, Parenthood, and Pregnancy Loss." *Journal of Material Culture* 5, 3 (2000): 321–45.

Michaels, Meredith, and Lynn Morgan. "Introduction: The Fetal Imperative." In *Fetal Subjects, Feminist Positions*, edited by Lynn Morgan and Meredith Michaels, 1–9. Philadelphia: University of Pennsylvania Press, 1999.

Miller, Barbara. "Female-Selective Abortion in Asia: Patterns, Policies, and Debates." *American Anthropologist* 103, 4 (2001): 1083–95.

26. For a recent discussion of the couvade, see L. Rival, "Androgynous Parents and Guest Children: The Huaorani Couvade," *Journal of the Royal Anthropological Institute*, n.s., 4 (1998): 619–42. For a classic discussion of the couvade, see Peter Riviere, "The Couvade: A Problem Reborn," *Man*, n.s., 9, 3 (1974): 423–35.

Petchesky, Rosalind Pollack. "Fetal Images: The Power of Visual Culture in the Politics of Reproduction." *Feminist Studies* 13, 2 (1987): 263–92.

Rival, Laura. "Androgynous Parents and Guest Children: The Huaorani Couvade." *Journal of the Royal Anthropological Institute,* new series, 4 (1998): 619–42.

Riviere, Peter. "The Couvade: A Problem Reborn." *Man,* new series, 9, 3 (1974): 423–35.

Sandelowski, Margarete. "Separate, but Less Unequal: Fetal Ultrasonography and the Transformation of Expectant Mother/Fatherhood." *Gender and Society* 8, 2 (1994): 230–45.

Santora, Marc. "Fetal Photos: Keepsake or Health Risk?" *New York Times*, May 17, 2004.

Taylor, Janelle. "Of Sonograms and Baby Prams: Prenatal Diagnosis, Pregnancy, and Consumption." *Feminist Studies* 26, 2 (2000): 391–418.

Index

Page numbers in *italics* refer to figures and tables.